Book of Catechisms
Reference Edition

D1446126

Geneva Press
Louisville, Kentucky

Book design by Sharon Adams

First edition
Published by Geneva Press
Louisville, Kentucky

This book is printed on acid-free paper that meets the American National Standards Institute Z39.48 standard. ∞

PRINTED IN THE UNITED STATES OF AMERICA

01 02 03 04 05 06 07 08 09 10 — 10 9 8 7 6 5 4 3 2 1

Library of Congress Cataloging-in-Publication Data

A catalog record for this book is available from the Library of Congress.
ISBN 0-664-50153-2

CONTENTS

FOREWORD FROM THE PUBLISHER

Geneva Press is proud to publish this volume, *Book of Catechisms: Reference Edition,* as a service to the Presbyterian Church (U.S.A.). This volume brings together the texts of the three catechisms that are a part of our *Book of Confessions* with the three new catechisms approved for study by the 210th General Assembly (1998) of the PC(USA). This volume contains six catechisms:

Belonging to God: A First Catechism
The Study Catechism: Confirmation Version
The Study Catechism: Full Version
The Heidelberg Catechism
The Westminster Standards: The Shorter Catechism
The Westminster Standards: The Larger Catechism

A brief introduction precedes each catechism, highlighting its history and emphases. Another useful and unique feature of this book is the Parallel Index, which cross-references the major teachings of the Westminster Larger Catechism, The Study Catechism: Full Version, and the Heidelberg Catechism.

We hope that this volume will be a useful and much-used addition to the libraries of seminary students, ministers, church officers, Christian educators, and laypersons. And we hope that you will be stimulated to seek out more information about the history and theology of catechisms in the Presbyterian Church. Most of all, we hope that the *Book of Catechisms: Reference Edition* will bring all who explore the catechisms, confessions, and creeds of the Presbyterian Church to a deeper understanding of the Christian faith.

INTRODUCTION

Catechism. The word conjures up images of glum children memorizing abstract answers to long lists of impersonal questions. Catechisms seem hopelessly outdated, representing a teaching methodology more compatible with McGuffey's Readers than the Internet, more at home in rows of bolted-down desks than in the brightly carpeted learning centers of contemporary churches.

Presbyterians may wonder why their church approved three new catechisms in 1998—including one for children, one for adults, and a version of the adult catechism for youth. Presbyterians may also wonder why these new catechisms have been brought together with three centuries-old catechisms in a *Book of Catechisms.* Why are "Belonging to God: A First Catechism," "The Study Catechism: Confirmation Version," and "The Study Catechism: Full Version"—all approved by the Presbyterian Church (U.S.A.) in 1998—included in this volume with the Heidelberg Catechism from sixteenth-century Germany and the Westminster "Shorter" and "Larger" Catechisms from seventeenth-century England?

To confuse matters further, the old catechisms are part of the *Book of Confessions* of the PC(USA) while the recent catechisms are not. Why are confessional and nonconfessional documents mixed together in one volume, a *Book of Catechisms*? And why do the contemporary catechisms have less "authority" than the old ones?

Catechism is related to *catechesis,* the ongoing process of instruction that is central to the formation of faith and faithfulness in the lives of believers. Faith formation, even in its formal educational component, is far broader than formal written catechisms, of course. Yet catechisms have a part to play in the church's continuous conversation about the meaning of Christian faith as well as in its task of handing the faith on from one generation to the next. Catechisms provide summaries of the *church's* teaching rather than the insights or opinions of individuals. They embody the Christian community's collective wisdom about central beliefs to be shared within the church and imparted to the church's children and youth.

The church's catechisms have never been intended for rote memorization. Rather, the purpose of catechisms has been to provide inquirers, church members, and their children with ready access to the church's teaching on important matters of Christian faith and faithfulness. The reasons for the development of catechisms in the sixteenth century remain valid today. First, catechisms ensure that all baptized members of the church are given the opportunity to understand and confess the faith for themselves. Second, catechisms equip church members to live out "the priesthood of all believers" as the whole church shapes its life with scriptural and theological integrity. Finally, catechisms provide persons with a foundation that enables them to exercise freedom of conscience within Christian faith.

INTRODUCTION

The collection of catechisms in this *Book of Catechisms* indicates that no catechism embodies *the* truth, and that no catechism is intended as a test of orthodoxy. Instead, the collection of catechisms points to the church's broad consensus about foundational matters. Note that catechisms are usually shaped by the Apostles' Creed, the Lord's Prayer, and the Ten Commandments. That order—faith, prayer, law—is itself revealing. The truth of the gospel elicits our response of praise and faithfulness.

The *Book of Catechisms* provides families as well as church groups with the basis for lively discussion about Christian faith and Christian living. Reading through similar questions from different catechisms can broaden understanding of otherwise vague affirmations. For instance, both the seventeenth-century "Westminster Larger Catechism" and the 1998 "Study Catechism" deal with the sixth commandment, "Thou shalt not kill," and the eighth commandment, "Thou shalt not steal." Exploring the answers from these catechisms will reveal that both are strikingly relevant and both are wonderfully suggestive.

The *Book of Catechisms: Reference Edition* is a rich resource in basic Christianity for church groups, families, and individuals. This collection of catechisms is not "the final answer," but rather the beginning of discussing, learning, and professing the church's faith.

Joseph D. Small
Coordinator for Theology and Worship
Presbyterian Church (U.S.A.)

Belonging to God: A First Catechism

In 1998 the 210th General Assembly of the Presbyterian Church (U.S.A.) approved two new catechisms for use by the church as teaching tools. The first of these is Belonging to God: A First Catechism, written for third- and fourth-graders. The catechism begins with a brief prologue, then follows the biblical narrative through creation, the Fall, God's election of a covenant people, Jesus Christ and the church, and the Lord's Prayer. Scripture stories and verses are woven together with each of the questions and answers of the catechism.

BELONGING TO GOD:
A FIRST CATECHISM

Question 1. Who are you?

I am a child of God.

> *Gal. 4:6–7*   And because you are children, God has sent the Spirit of his Son into our hearts, crying, "Abba! Father!" So you are no longer a slave but a child, and if a child then also an heir, through God.

> *1 John 3:1*   See what love the Father has given us, that we should be called children of God. . . .

> *John 1:12*   But to all who received him, who believed in his name, he gave power to become children of God.

> *Rom. 8:15–17*   When we cry, "Abba! Father!" it is that very Spirit bearing witness with our spirit that we are children of God, and if children, then heirs. . . .

> *Gal. 3:25–27*   But now that faith has come, we are no longer subject to a disciplinarian, for in Christ Jesus you are all children of God through faith. As many of you as were baptized into Christ have clothed yourselves with Christ.

Question 2. What does it mean to be a child of God?

That I belong to God, who loves me.

> *Matt. 18:14*   So it is not the will of your Father in heaven that one of these little ones should be lost.

> *Matt. 19:14*   Let the little children come to me, and do not stop them; for it is to such as these that the kingdom of heaven belongs.

> *1 Cor. 3:23*   . . . and you belong to Christ, and Christ belongs to God.

> *2 Cor. 10:7*   If you are confident that you belong to Christ, remind yourself of this, that just as you belong to Christ, so also do we.

Gal. 3:28–29 There is no longer Jew or Greek, there is no longer slave or free, there is no longer male and female; for all of you are one in Christ Jesus. And if you belong to Christ, then you are Abraham's offspring, heirs according to the promise.

Question 3. What makes you a child of God?

Grace—God's free gift of love that I do not deserve and cannot earn.

Eph. 2:8–10 For by grace you have been saved through faith, and this is not your own doing; it is the gift of God—not the result of works, so that no one may boast. For we are what he has made us, created in Christ Jesus for good works. . . .

Gal. 4:4–5 But when the fullness of time had come, God sent his Son, born of a woman, born under the law, in order to redeem those who were under the law, so that we might receive adoption as children.

Heb. 4:16 Let us therefore approach the throne of grace with boldness, so that we may receive mercy and find grace to help in time of need.

Eph. 1:7–9 In him we have redemption through his blood, the forgiveness of our trespasses, according to the riches of his grace that he lavished on us. With all wisdom and insight he has made known to us the mystery of his will, according to his good pleasure that he set forth in Christ . . .

1 Cor. 4:7 What do you have that you did not receive? And if you received it, why do you boast as if it were not a gift?

Question 4. Don't you have to be good for God to love you?

No. God loves me in spite of all I do wrong.

John 8:10–11 Jesus straightened up and said to her, "Woman, where are they? Has no one condemned you?" She said, "No one, sir." And Jesus said, "Neither do I condemn you. Go your way, and from now on do not sin again."

Luke 15:21–24 Then the son said to him, "Father, I have sinned against heaven and before you; I am no longer worthy to be called your son." But the father said to his slaves, "Quickly, bring out a robe—the best one—and put it on him; put a ring on his finger and sandals on his feet. And get the fatted calf and kill it, and let us eat and celebrate; for this son of mine was dead and is alive again; he was lost and is found!" And they began to celebrate.

Rom. 5:8 But God proves his love for us in that while we still were sinners Christ died for us.

1 John 4:10 In this is love, not that we loved God but that he loved us and sent his Son to be the atoning sacrifice for our sins.

Question 5. How do you thank God for this gift of love?

I promise to love and trust God with all my heart.

Matt. 22:37 He said to him, "You shall love the Lord your God with all your heart, and with all your soul, and with all your mind."

Deut. 6:4–6 Hear, O Israel: The LORD is our God, the LORD alone. You shall love the LORD your God with all your heart, and with all your soul, and with all your might. Keep these words that I am commanding you today in your heart.

Ps. 9:1   I will give thanks to the LORD with my whole heart; I will tell of all your wonderful deeds.

Jer. 24:7   I will give them a heart to know that I am the LORD; and they shall be my people and I will be their God, for they shall return to me with their whole heart.

Question 6. How do you love God?

By worshiping God, by loving others, and by respecting what God has created.

John 4:24   God is spirit, and those who worship him must worship in spirit and truth.

Deut. 10:20   You shall fear the LORD your God; him alone you shall worship; to him you shall hold fast, and by his name you shall swear.

Ps. 95:6   O come, let us worship and bow down, let us kneel before the LORD, our Maker!

Luke 10:36–37   "Which of these three, do you think, was a neighbor to the man who fell into the hands of the robbers?" He said, "The one who showed him mercy." Jesus said to him, "Go and do likewise."

Matt. 25:40   Truly I tell you, just as you did it to one of the least of these who are members of my family, you did it to me.

1 John 4:19–21   We love because he first loved us. Those who say, "I love God," and hate their brothers or sisters, are liars; for those who do not love a brother or sister whom they have seen, cannot love God whom they have not seen. The commandment we have from him is this: those who love God must love their brothers and sisters also.

Gen. 1:28   God blessed them, and God said to them, "Be fruitful and multiply, and fill the earth and subdue it; and have dominion over the fish of the sea and over the birds of the air and over every living thing that moves upon the earth."

Gen. 2:15   The LORD God took the man and put him in the garden of Eden to till it and keep it.

Prov. 14:31   Those who oppress the poor insult their Maker, but those who are kind to the needy honor him.

Question 7. What did God create?

God created all that is, seen and unseen.

Gen. 1:1, 31   In the beginning when God created the heavens and the earth. . . . God saw everything that he had made, and indeed, it was very good.

Acts 4:24   When they heard it, they raised their voices together to God and said, "Sovereign Lord, who made the heaven and the earth, the sea, and everything in them . . ."

Ps. 8:3–4   When I look at your heavens, the work of your fingers, the moon and the stars that you have established; what are human beings that you are mindful of them, mortals that you care for them?

Ps. 19:1   The heavens are telling the glory of God; and the firmament proclaims his handiwork.

Question 8. What is special about human beings?

God made us, male and female, in the image of God.

Gen. 1:26–27   Then God said, "Let us make humankind in our image, according to our likeness; and let them have dominion over the fish of the sea, and over the birds of the air, and over the cattle, and over all the wild animals of the earth, and over every creeping thing that creeps upon the earth." So God created humankind in his image, in the image of God he created them; male and female he created them.

Col. 1:15   He is the image of the invisible God, the firstborn of all creation. . . .

2 Cor. 4:4   In their case the god of this world has blinded the minds of the unbelievers, to keep them from seeing the light of the gospel of the glory of Christ, who is the image of God.

Question 9. What does it mean that we are made in God's image?

It means we are made to reflect God's goodness, wisdom, and love.

Matt. 5:14–16   You are the light of the world. A city built on a hill cannot be hid. No one after lighting a lamp puts it under the bushel basket, but on the lampstand, and it gives light to all in the house. In the same way, let your light shine before others, so that they may see your good works and give glory to your Father in heaven.

2 Cor. 4:5–6   For we do not proclaim ourselves; we proclaim Jesus Christ as Lord and ourselves as your slaves for Jesus' sake. For it is the God who said, "Let light shine out of darkness," who has shone in our hearts to give the light of the knowledge of the glory of God in the face of Jesus Christ.

Question 10. Why, then, do we human beings often act in destructive and hateful ways?

Because we have turned away from God and fallen into sin.

Gen. 3:8   They heard the sound of the LORD God walking in the garden at the time of the evening breeze, and the man and his wife hid themselves from the presence of the LORD God among the trees of the garden.

Gen. 4:8   Cain rose up against his brother Abel, and killed him.

Rom. 1:18   For the wrath of God is revealed from heaven against all ungodliness and wickedness of those who by their wickedness suppress the truth.

Rom. 7:19–20   For I do not do the good I want, but the evil I do not want is what I do. Now if I do what I do not want, it is no longer I that do it, but sin that dwells within me.

Isa. 53:6   All we like sheep have gone astray; we have all turned to our own way. . . .

Question 11. What is sin?

Sin is closing our hearts to God and disobeying God's law.

4

Gen. 3:23–24   Therefore the LORD God sent him forth from the garden of Eden, to till the ground from which he was taken. He drove out the man; and at the east of the garden of Eden he placed the cherubim, and a sword flaming and turning to guard the way to the tree of life.

Matt. 15:19   For out of the heart come evil intentions, murder, adultery, fornication, theft, false witness, slander.

1 John 3:4   Everyone who commits sin is guilty of lawlessness; sin is lawlessness.

Gal. 3:10   For all who rely on the works of the law are under a curse; for it is written, "Cursed is everyone who does not observe and obey all the things written in the book of the law."

Rom. 1:22–25   Claiming to be wise, they became fools; and they exchanged the glory of the immortal God for images resembling a mortal human being or birds or four-footed animals or reptiles. Therefore God gave them up in the lusts of their hearts to impurity, to the degrading of their bodies among themselves, because they exchanged the truth about God for a lie and worshiped and served the creature rather than the Creator, who is blessed forever!

Isa. 59:1–2   See, the LORD's hand is not too short to save, nor his ear too dull to hear. Rather, your iniquities have been barriers between you and your God, and your sins have hidden his face from you so that he does not hear.

Question 12. What are the results of sin?

Our relationship with God is broken. All our relations with others are confused.

Rom. 6:23   For the wages of sin is death, but the free gift of God is eternal life in Christ Jesus our Lord.

Gen. 3:16–19   To the woman he said, "I will greatly increase your pangs in childbearing; in pain you shall bring forth children, yet your desire shall be for your husband, and he shall rule over you." And to the man he said, . . . "Cursed is the ground because of you; in toil you shall eat of it all the days of your life; thorns and thistles it shall bring forth for you; and you shall eat the plants of the field. By the sweat of your face you shall eat bread until you return to the ground, for out of it you were taken. . . ."

Eph. 2:1–3   You were dead through the trespasses and sins in which you once lived, following the course of this world, following the ruler of the power of the air, the spirit that is now at work among those who are disobedient. All of us once lived among them in the passions of our flesh, following the desires of flesh and senses, and we were by nature children of wrath, like everyone else.

1 Kings 18:18   I have not troubled Israel; but you have, and your father's house, because you have forsaken the commandments of the LORD and followed the Baals.

Question 13. How does God deal with us as sinners?

God hates our sin but never stops loving us.

Luke 19:5–7   When Jesus came to the place, he looked up and said to him, "Zacchaeus, hurry and come down; for I must stay at your house today." So he hurried down and was happy to welcome him. All who saw it began to grumble and said, "He has gone to be the guest of one who is a sinner."

2 Cor. 5:17–19, 21   So if anyone is in Christ, there is a new creation: everything old has passed away; see, everything has become new! All this is from God, who reconciled us to himself through Christ, and has given us the ministry of reconciliation; that is, in Christ God was reconciling the world to himself, not counting their trespasses against them, and entrusting the message of reconciliation to us. . . . For our sake he made him to be sin who knew no sin, so that in him we might become the righteousness of God.

Ps. 103:2–5   Bless the LORD, O my soul, and do not forget all his benefits— who forgives all your iniquity, who heals all your diseases, who redeems your life from the Pit, who crowns you with steadfast love and mercy, who satisfies you with good as long as you live so that your youth is renewed like the eagle's.

Ps. 107:10–16   Some sat in darkness and in gloom, prisoners in misery and in irons, for they had rebelled against the words of God, and spurned the counsel of the Most High. Their hearts were bowed down with hard labor; they fell down, with no one to help. Then they cried to the LORD in their trouble, and he saved them from their distress; he brought them out of darkness and gloom, and broke their bonds asunder. Let them thank the LORD for his steadfast love, for his wonderful works to humankind. For he shatters the doors of bronze, and cuts in two the bars of iron.

Question 14. What did God do to help us?

God chose the people of Israel to make a new beginning. They received God's covenant and prepared the way for Jesus to come as our Savior.

Gen. 12:1–3   Now the LORD said to Abram, "Go from your country and your kindred and your father's house to the land that I will show you. I will make of you a great nation, and I will bless you, and make your name great, so that you will be a blessing. I will bless those who bless you, and the one who curses you I will curse; and in you all the families of the earth shall be blessed."

Ex. 15:13   In your steadfast love you led the people whom you redeemed; you guided them by your strength to your holy abode.

Isa. 11:1–2, 3   A shoot shall come out from the stump of Jesse, and a branch shall grow out of his roots. The spirit of the LORD shall rest on him. . . . His delight shall be in the fear of the LORD.

Jer. 31:31   The days are surely coming, says the LORD, when I will make a new covenant with the house of Israel and the house of Judah.

Rom. 9:4–5   They are Israelites, and to them belong the adoption, the glory, the covenants, the giving of the law, the worship, and the promises; to them belong the patriarchs, and from them, according to the flesh, comes the Messiah, who is over all, God blessed forever. Amen.

Question 15. What is the covenant?

The covenant is an everlasting agreement between God and Israel.

Gen. 9:12–13   This is the sign of the covenant that I make between me and you and every living creature that is with you, for all future generations: I have set my bow in the clouds, and it shall be a sign of the covenant between me and the earth.

Rom. 11:29   For the gifts and the calling of God are irrevocable.

Gen. 15:18   On that day the LORD made a covenant with Abram, saying, "To your descendants I give this land. . . ."

Gen. 17:4   As for me, this is my covenant with you: You shall be the ancestor of a multitude of nations.

Ps. 89:3–4   You said, "I have made a covenant with my chosen one, I have sworn to my servant David: I will establish your descendants forever, and build your throne for all generations."

Heb. 8:10   This is the covenant that I will make with the house of Israel after those days, says the Lord: I will put my laws in their minds, and write them on their hearts, and I will be their God, and they shall be my people.

Question 16. What is in this agreement?

When God called Abraham and Sarah, God promised to bless their family, which was later called Israel. Through the people of Israel, God vowed to bless all the peoples of the earth. God promised to be Israel's God, and they promised to be God's people. God vowed to love Israel and to be their hope forever, and Israel vowed to worship and serve only God.

Gen. 12:1–3   Now the LORD said to Abram, "Go from your country and your kindred and your father's house to the land that I will show you. I will make of you a great nation, and I will bless you, and make your name great, so that you will be a blessing. I will bless those who bless you, and the one who curses you I will curse; and in you all the families of the earth shall be blessed."

Gen. 17:1–7   When Abram was ninety-nine years old, the LORD appeared to Abram, and said to him, "I am God Almighty; walk before me, and be blameless. And I will make my covenant between me and you, and will make you exceedingly numerous." Then Abram fell on his face; and God said to him, "As for me, this is my covenant with you: You shall be the ancestor of a multitude of nations. No longer shall your name be Abram, but your name shall be Abraham; for I have made you the ancestor of a multitude of nations. I will make you exceedingly fruitful; and I will make nations of you, and kings shall come from you. I will establish my covenant between me and you, and your offspring after you throughout their generations, for an everlasting covenant, to be God to you and to your offspring after you."

Ex. 6:6–7   I am the LORD, and I will free you from the burdens of the Egyptians and deliver you from slavery to them. I will redeem you with an outstretched arm and with mighty acts of judgment. I will take you as my people, and I will be your God.

Ex. 24:3   Moses came and told the people all the words of the LORD and all the ordinances; and all the people answered with one voice, and said, "All the words that the LORD has spoken we will do."

Jer. 7:23   But this command I gave them, "Obey my voice, and I will be your God, and you shall be my people; and walk only in the way that I command you, so that it may be well with you."

7

Gal. 3:14 . . . in order that in Christ Jesus the blessing of Abraham might come to the Gentiles, so that we might receive the promise of the Spirit through faith.

1 Peter 2:9–10 But you are a chosen race, a royal priesthood, a holy nation, God's own people, in order that you may proclaim the mighty acts of him who called you out of darkness into his marvelous light. Once you were not a people, but now you are God's people; once you had not received mercy, but now you have received mercy.

Question 17. How did God keep this covenant?

God led Israel out of slavery in Egypt, gave them the Ten Commandments through Moses, and brought them into the land that God had promised.

Ex. 15:13 In your steadfast love you led the people whom you redeemed; you guided them by your strength to your holy abode.

Josh. 1:1–3 After the death of Moses the servant of the LORD, the LORD spoke to Joshua son of Nun, Moses' assistant, saying, "My servant Moses is dead. Now proceed to cross the Jordan, you and all this people, into the land that I am giving to them, to the Israelites. Every place that the sole of your foot will tread upon I have given to you, as I promised to Moses."

Heb. 11:29–30 By faith the people passed through the Red Sea as if it were dry land, but when the Egyptians attempted to do so they were drowned. By faith the walls of Jericho fell after they had been encircled for seven days.

Question 18. What are the Ten Commandments?

The Ten Commandments are the law of God. When God gave them to Moses, God said, I am the Lord your God who brought you out of the land of Egypt, out of the house of slavery:

(1) You shall have no other gods before me.
(2) You shall not make for yourself an idol.
(3) You shall not make wrongful use of the name of the Lord your God.
(4) Remember the Sabbath day and keep it holy.
(5) Honor your father and your mother.
(6) You shall not murder.
(7) You shall not commit adultery.
(8) You shall not steal.
(9) You shall not bear false witness against your neighbor.
(10) You shall not covet what is your neighbor's.

Ex. 20:1–17 Then God spoke all these words: I am the LORD your God, who brought you out of the land of Egypt, out of the house of slavery; you shall have no other gods before me. You shall not make for yourself an idol, whether in the form of anything that is in heaven above, or that is on the earth beneath, or that is in the water under the earth. You shall not bow down to them or worship them; for I the LORD your God am a jealous God, punishing children for the iniquity of parents, to the third and the fourth generation of those who reject me, but showing steadfast love to the thousandth generation of those who love me and keep my commandments. You shall not make wrongful use of the name of the LORD your God, for the LORD will not acquit anyone who misuses his name. Remember the sabbath day, and keep it holy. Six days you shall labor and do all your work. But the seventh day is a sabbath to the LORD your God; you shall not do any work—you, your son or your daughter, your male or female slave, your livestock, or the alien resident in your towns. For in six days the LORD made heaven and earth, the sea, and all that is in them, but rested the seventh day; therefore the LORD blessed the sabbath day and consecrated it. Honor your father and your mother, so that your days may be long in the land that the LORD your God is giving you. You shall not murder. You shall not commit adultery. You shall not steal. You shall not bear false witness against your neighbor. You shall not covet your neighbor's house; you shall not covet your neighbor's wife, or male or female slave, or ox, or donkey, or anything that belongs to your neighbor.

Question 19. What is the main point of these commandments?

You shall love the Lord your God with all your heart, mind, and strength; and you shall love your neighbor as yourself.

Mark 12:29–31   Jesus answered, "The first is, 'Hear, O Israel: the Lord our God, the Lord is one; you shall love the Lord your God with all your heart, and with all your soul, and with all your mind, and with all your strength.' The second is this, 'You shall love your neighbor as yourself.' "

Deut. 6:4–5   Hear, O Israel: The LORD is our God, the LORD alone. You shall love the LORD your God with all your heart, and with all your soul, and with all your might.

John 15:12   This is my commandment, that you love one another as I have loved you.

Question 20. Did the people keep their covenant with God?

Though some remained faithful, the people too often worshiped other gods and did not love each other as God commanded. They showed us how much we all disobey God's law.

Ex. 32:1   When the people saw that Moses delayed to come down from the mountain, the people gathered around Aaron, and said to him, "Come, make gods for us, who shall go before us; as for this Moses, the man who brought us up out of the land of Egypt, we do not know what has become of him."

1 John 5:21   Little children, keep yourselves from idols.

Deut. 29:25–27   They will conclude, "It is because they abandoned the covenant of the LORD, the God of their ancestors, which he made with them when he brought them out of the land of Egypt. They turned and served other gods, worshiping them, gods whom they had not known and whom he had not allotted to them; so the anger of the LORD was kindled against that land, bringing on it every curse written in this book."

Question 21. What did God do to bring them back to the covenant?

Although God judged the people when they sinned, God still loved them and remained faithful to them. God sent them prophets to speak God's word. God gave them priests to make sacrifices for their sins. God called kings to protect the needy and guarantee justice. At last God promised to send the Messiah.

1 Sam. 3:19–20   As Samuel grew up, the LORD was with him and let none of his words fall to the ground. And all Israel from Dan to Beer-sheba knew that Samuel was a trustworthy prophet of the LORD.

Ex. 28:1   Then bring near to you your brother Aaron, and his sons with him, from among the Israelites, to serve me as priests.

1 Sam. 16:13   Then Samuel took the horn of oil, and anointed him in the presence of his brothers; and the spirit of the LORD came mightily upon David from that day forward.

Jer. 23:5   The days are surely coming, says the LORD, when I will raise up for David a righteous Branch, and he shall reign as king and deal wisely, and shall execute justice and righteousness in the land.

Isa. 9:6   For a child has been born for us, a son given to us; authority rests upon his shoulders; and he is named Wonderful Counselor, Mighty God, Everlasting Father, Prince of Peace.

Acts 3:18, 22   In this way God fulfilled what he had foretold through all the prophets, that his Messiah would suffer. . . . Moses said, "The Lord your God will raise up for you from your own people a prophet like me."

Heb. 4:14–16   Since, then, we have a great high priest who has passed through the heavens, Jesus, the Son of God, let us hold fast to our confession. For we do not have a high priest who is unable to sympathize with our weaknesses, but we have one who in every respect has been tested as we are, yet without sin. Let us therefore approach the throne of grace with boldness, so that we may receive mercy and find grace to help in time of need.

John 18:33–37   Then Pilate entered the headquarters again, summoned Jesus, and asked him, "Are you the King of the Jews?" Jesus answered, "Do you ask this on your own, or did others tell you about me?" Pilate replied, "I am not a Jew, am I? Your own nation and the chief priests have handed you over to me. What have you done?" Jesus answered, "My kingdom is not from this world. If my kingdom were from this world, my followers would be fighting to keep me from being handed over to the Jews. But as it is, my kingdom is not from here." Pilate asked him, "So you are a king?" Jesus answered, "You say that I am a king. For this I was born, and for this I came into the world, to testify to the truth. Everyone who belongs to the truth listens to my voice."

Question 22. Who was sent to be the Messiah?

God sent Jesus to be the Messiah. Messiah means "anointed one." The New Testament word for Messiah is Christ. Jesus is called the Christ, because God anointed him to be the Savior who would rescue us from sin and death.

Luke 2:26   It had been revealed to him by the Holy Spirit that he would not see death before he had seen the Lord's Messiah.

Luke 3:22   The Holy Spirit descended upon him in bodily form like a dove. And a voice came from heaven, "You are my Son, the Beloved; with you I am well pleased."

Luke 2:10–11   Do not be afraid; for see—I am bringing you good news of great joy for all the people: to you is born this day in the city of David a Savior, who is the Messiah, the Lord.

Phil. 3:20   But our citizenship is in heaven, and it is from there that we are expecting a Savior, the Lord Jesus Christ.

Luke 4:18   The Spirit of the Lord is upon me, because he has anointed me to bring good news to the poor.

Question 23. How did God keep the promise to Abraham by sending Jesus?

By sending Jesus, God opened up the covenant with Abraham to the whole world. God welcomed all who have faith in Jesus into the blessings of the covenant.

Gal. 3:6–7   Just as Abraham "believed God, and it was reckoned to him as righteousness," so, you see, those who believe are the descendants of Abraham.

John 8:56   Your ancestor Abraham rejoiced that he would see my day; he saw it and was glad.

Matt. 1:1   An account of the genealogy of Jesus the Messiah, the son of David, the son of Abraham.

Question 24. Was Jesus just another human being?

No. Although he was truly human, he was also God with us. As someone who was truly human, he could share all our sorrows. Yet because he was truly God, he could save us from all our sins.

Matt. 1:22–23   All this took place to fulfill what had been spoken by the Lord through the prophet: "Look, the virgin shall conceive and bear a son, and they shall name him Emmanuel," which means, "God is with us."

John 1:1, 14   In the beginning was the Word, and the Word was with God, and the Word was God. . . . And the Word became flesh and lived among us. . . .

Matt. 26:38–39   Then he said to them, "I am deeply grieved, even to death; remain here, and stay awake with me." And going a little farther, he threw himself on the ground and prayed, "My Father, if it is possible, let this cup pass from me; yet not what I want but what you want."

John 14:11   Believe me that I am in the Father and the Father is in me; but if you do not, then believe me because of the works themselves.

Col. 1:15, 19–20   He is the image of the invisible God, the firstborn of all creation. . . . For in him all the fullness of God was pleased to dwell, and through him God was pleased to reconcile to himself all things, whether on earth or in heaven, by making peace through the blood of his cross.

Question 25. What was Jesus like?

When Jesus spoke, he spoke with God's authority. When he acted, he acted with God's power. The people were amazed. He was also gentle and loving. He cared for us in all our needs as a shepherd cares for the sheep.

Mark 1:27   They were all amazed, and they kept on asking one another, "What is this? A new teaching—with authority! He commands even the unclean spirits, and they obey him."

11

Mark 4:41 And they were filled with great awe and said to one another, "Who then is this, that even the wind and the sea obey him?"

Luke 15:6 And when he comes home, he calls together his friends and neighbors, saying to them, "Rejoice with me, for I have found my sheep that was lost."

Matt. 11:28–30 Come to me, all you that are weary and are carrying heavy burdens, and I will give you rest. Take my yoke upon you, and learn from me; for I am gentle and humble in heart, and you will find rest for your souls. For my yoke is easy, and my burden is light.

Question 26. What did he do during his life on earth?

He called disciples to follow him. He fed the hungry, healed the sick, blessed children, befriended outcasts, required people to repent, and forgave their sins. He taught people not to fear, but to trust always in God. He preached the good news of God's love and gave everyone hope for new life.

Luke 5:9–11 For he and all who were with him were amazed at the catch of fish that they had taken; and so also were James and John, sons of Zebedee, who were partners with Simon. Then Jesus said to Simon, "Do not be afraid; from now on you will be catching people." When they had brought their boats to shore, they left everything and followed him.

Mark 6:41–42 Taking the five loaves and the two fish, he looked up to heaven, and blessed and broke the loaves, and gave them to his disciples to set before the people; and he divided the two fish among them all. And all ate and were filled.

Luke 5:13 Then Jesus stretched out his hand, touched him, and said, "I do choose. Be made clean." Immediately the leprosy left him.

Luke 5:20 When he saw their faith, he said, "Friend, your sins are forgiven you."

John 14:6 Jesus said to him, "I am the way, and the truth, and the life. No one comes to the Father except through me."

Matt. 6:25–26 Therefore I tell you, do not worry about your life, what you will eat or what you will drink, or about your body, what you will wear. Is not life more than food, and the body more than clothing? Look at the birds of the air; they neither sow nor reap nor gather into barns, and yet your heavenly Father feeds them. Are you not of more value than they?

Question 27. How did Jesus Christ prove to be our Savior?

He sacrificed his life for us by dying on the cross. He showed his victory over death by rising from the dead. He removed our guilt and gave us new, unending life with God.

2 Cor. 5:19 In Christ God was reconciling the world to himself, not counting their trespasses against them, and entrusting the message of reconciliation to us.

Isa. 53:5 But he was wounded for our transgressions, crushed for our iniquities; upon him was the punishment that made us whole, and by his bruises we are healed.

Rom. 4:24–25 It will be reckoned to us who believe in him who raised Jesus our Lord from the dead, who was handed over to death for our trespasses and was raised for our justification.

Question 28. How do we know that Jesus is Lord?

After he died and was raised from the dead, he appeared to his disciples, both women and men. He revealed himself to them as our living Lord and Savior. Through the Bible, he continues to reveal himself to us today.

John 21:12–14 Jesus said to them, "Come and have breakfast." Now none of the disciples dared to ask him, "Who are you?" because they knew it was the Lord. Jesus came and took the bread and gave it to them, and did the same with the fish. This was now the third time that Jesus appeared to the disciples after he was raised from the dead.

Luke 24:38–39 He said to them, "Why are you frightened, and why do doubts arise in your hearts? Look at my hands and my feet; see that it is I myself. Touch me and see; for a ghost does not have flesh and bones as you see that I have."

1 Cor. 15:3–4 For I handed on to you as of first importance what I in turn had received: that Christ died for our sins in accordance with the scriptures, and that he was buried, and that he was raised on the third day in accordance with the scriptures.

John 20:15–18 Jesus said to her, "Woman, why are you weeping? Whom are you looking for?" Supposing him to be the gardener, she said to him, "Sir, if you have carried him away, tell me where you have laid him, and I will take him away." Jesus said to her, "Mary!" She turned and said to him in Hebrew, "Rabbouni!" (which means Teacher). Jesus said to her, "Do not hold on to me, because I have not yet ascended to the Father. But go to my brothers and say to them, 'I am ascending to my Father and your Father, to my God and your God.' " Mary Magdalene went and announced to the disciples, "I have seen the Lord"; and she told them that he had said these things to her.

Luke 24:44–49 Then he said to them, "These are my words that I spoke to you while I was still with you—that everything written about me in the law of Moses, the prophets, and the psalms must be fulfilled." Then he opened their minds to understand the scriptures, and he said to them, "Thus it is written, that the Messiah is to suffer and to rise from the dead on the third day, and that repentance and forgiveness of sins is to be proclaimed in his name to all nations, beginning from Jerusalem. You are witnesses of these things. And see, I am sending upon you what my Father promised; so stay here in the city until you have been clothed with power from on high."

1 Cor. 15:5–8, 11 He appeared to Cephas, then to the twelve. Then he appeared to more than five hundred brothers and sisters at one time, most of whom are still alive, though some have died. Then he appeared to James, then to all the apostles. Last of all, as to one untimely born, he appeared also to me. . . . Whether then it was I or they, so we proclaim and so you have come to believe.

Question 29. What does it mean that Jesus ascended into heaven?

After his work on earth was done, he returned to heaven to prepare a place for us and to rule with God in love. He will come again in glory and remains with us now through the gift of the Holy Spirit.

Acts 1:6–11 So when they had come together, they asked him, "Lord, is this the time when you will restore the kingdom to Israel?" He replied, "It is not for you to know the times or periods that the Father has set by his own authority. But you will receive power when the Holy Spirit has come upon you; and you will be my witnesses in Jerusalem, in all Judea and Samaria, and to the ends of the earth." When he had said this, as they were watching, he was lifted up, and a cloud took him out of their sight. While he was going and they were gazing up toward heaven, suddenly two men in white robes stood by them. They said, "Men of Galilee, why do you stand looking up toward heaven? This Jesus, who has been taken up from you into heaven, will come in the same way as you saw him go into heaven."

Luke 24:50–53 Then he led them out as far as Bethany, and, lifting up his hands, he blessed them. While he was blessing them, he withdrew from them and was carried up into heaven. And they worshiped him, and returned to Jerusalem with great joy; and they were continually in the temple blessing God.

John 14:3 And if I go and prepare a place for you, I will come again and will take you to myself, so that where I am, there you may be also.

John 14:16, 26 And I will ask the Father, and he will give you another Advocate, to be with you forever. . . . But the Advocate, the Holy Spirit, whom the Father will send in my name, will teach you everything, and remind you of all that I have said to you.

Question 30. When was the Holy Spirit given to the first Christians?

On the day of Pentecost.

Acts 2:1–4 When the day of Pentecost had come, they were all together in one place. And suddenly from heaven there came a sound like the rush of a violent wind, and it filled the entire house where they were sitting. Divided tongues, as of fire, appeared among them, and a tongue rested on each of them. All of them were filled with the Holy Spirit and began to speak in other languages, as the Spirit gave them ability.

Question 31. What happened on the day of Pentecost?

When the first Christians met together in Jerusalem, the Holy Spirit came upon them like a mighty wind. They all began to speak in different languages. A crowd gathered in astonishment. Peter preached to them the gospel.

Acts 2:1–4 When the day of Pentecost had come, they were all together in one place. And suddenly from heaven there came a sound like the rush of a violent wind, and it filled the entire house where they were sitting. Divided tongues, as of fire, appeared among them, and a tongue rested on each of them. All of them were filled with the Holy Spirit and began to speak in other languages, as the Spirit gave them ability.

Acts 2:22–24   You that are Israelites, listen to what I have to say: Jesus of Nazareth, a man attested to you by God with deeds of power, wonders, and signs that God did through him among you, as you yourselves know—this man, handed over to you according to the definite plan and foreknowledge of God, you crucified and killed by the hands of those outside the law. But God raised him up, having freed him from death, because it was impossible for him to be held in its power.

Question 32. What is the gospel?

The gospel is the good news about Jesus. It promises us the forgiveness of our sins and eternal life because of him. Forgiveness and eternal life with God are what we mean by salvation.

Rom. 1:16   For I am not ashamed of the gospel; it is the power of God for salvation to everyone who has faith, to the Jew first and also to the Greek.

John 3:15   . . . that whoever believes in him may have eternal life.

Acts 2:38   Peter said to them, "Repent, and be baptized every one of you in the name of Jesus Christ so that your sins may be forgiven; and you will receive the gift of the Holy Spirit."

Rom. 6:23   For the wages of sin is death, but the free gift of God is eternal life in Christ Jesus our Lord.

Question 33. What were the results of Pentecost?

The Holy Spirit filled the first Christians with joy by revealing what Jesus had done for us. The Spirit inspired them to understand and proclaim the gospel, and to live a new life together in thanksgiving to God.

Acts 4:31–35   When they had prayed, the place in which they were gathered together was shaken; and they were all filled with the Holy Spirit and spoke the word of God with boldness. Now the whole group of those who believed were of one heart and soul, and no one claimed private ownership of any possessions, but everything they owned was held in common. With great power the apostles gave their testimony to the resurrection of the Lord Jesus, and great grace was upon them all. There was not a needy person among them, for as many as owned lands or houses sold them and brought the proceeds of what was sold. They laid it at the apostles' feet, and it was distributed to each as any had need.

Question 34. How do these results continue today?

The Holy Spirit also moves us to understand and believe the gospel, gives us strength and wisdom to live by it, and unites us into a new community called the church.

Acts 9:17–19   "Brother Saul, the Lord Jesus, who appeared to you on your way here, has sent me so that you may regain your sight and be filled with the Holy Spirit." And immediately something like scales fell from his eyes, and his sight was restored. Then he got up and was baptized, and after taking some food, he regained his strength.

Rom. 8:11   If the Spirit of him who raised Jesus from the dead dwells in you, he who raised Christ from the dead will give life to your mortal bodies also through his Spirit that dwells in you.

Eph. 4:4–6 There is one body and one Spirit, just as you were called to the one hope of your calling, one Lord, one faith, one baptism, one God and Father of all, who is above all and through all and in all.

Question 35. What is the church?

We are the church: the people who believe the good news about Jesus, who are baptized, and who share in the Lord's Supper. Through these means of grace, the Spirit renews us so that we may serve God in love.

Acts 2:38–47 Peter said to them, "Repent, and be baptized every one of you in the name of Jesus Christ so that your sins may be forgiven; and you will receive the gift of the Holy Spirit. For the promise is for you, for your children, and for all who are far away, everyone whom the Lord our God calls to him." And he testified with many other arguments and exhorted them, saying, "Save yourselves from this corrupt generation." So those who welcomed his message were baptized, and that day about three thousand persons were added. They devoted themselves to the apostles' teaching and fellowship, to the breaking of bread and the prayers. Awe came upon everyone, because many wonders and signs were being done by the apostles. All who believed were together and had all things in common; they would sell their possessions and goods and distribute the proceeds to all, as any had need. Day by day, as they spent much time together in the temple, they broke bread at home and ate their food with glad and generous hearts, praising God and having the goodwill of all the people. And day by day the Lord added to their number those who were being saved.

1 Cor. 12:4–7, 12–13 Now there are varieties of gifts, but the same Spirit; and there are varieties of services, but the same Lord; and there are varieties of activities, but it is the same God who activates all of them in everyone. To each is given the manifestation of the Spirit for the common good. . . . For just as the body is one and has many members, and all the members of the body, though many, are one body, so it is with Christ. For in the one Spirit we were all baptized into one body—Jews or Greeks, slaves or free—and we were all made to drink of one Spirit.

Eph. 3:14–19 For this reason I bow my knees before the Father, from whom every family in heaven and on earth takes its name. I pray that, according to the riches of his glory, he may grant that you may be strengthened in your inner being with power through his Spirit, and that Christ may dwell in your hearts through faith, as you are being rooted and grounded in love. I pray that you may have the power to comprehend, with all the saints, what is the breadth and length and height and depth, and to know the love of Christ that surpasses knowledge, so that you may be filled with all the fullness of God.

Question 36. What comfort does the good news give you?

That I belong to my faithful Savior Jesus Christ, who died and rose again for my sake, so that nothing will ever separate me from God's love.

Rom. 8:31–32 If God is for us, who is against us? He who did not withhold his own Son, but gave him up for all of us, will he not with him also give us everything else?

Rom. 8:38–39 For I am convinced that neither death, nor life, nor angels, nor rulers, nor things present, nor things to come, nor powers, nor height, nor depth, nor anything else in all creation, will be able to separate us from the love of God in Christ Jesus our Lord.

Question 37. How do we know this good news?

Through reading the Bible and hearing it taught and preached. The Holy Spirit inspired those who wrote the Bible and helps us rely on its promises today.

2 Tim. 3:16 All scripture is inspired by God and is useful for teaching, for reproof, for correction, and for training in righteousness.

Eph. 6:17 Take the helmet of salvation, and the sword of the Spirit, which is the word of God.

John 14:26 But . . . the Holy Spirit . . . will teach you everything, and remind you of all that I have said to you.

2 Peter 1:20–21 First of all you must understand this, that no prophecy of scripture is a matter of one's own interpretation, because no prophecy ever came by human will, but men and women moved by the Holy Spirit spoke from God.

Question 38. What else does the Holy Spirit do for the church?

The Spirit gathers us to worship God, builds us up in faith, hope, and love, and sends us into the world to proclaim the gospel and to work for justice and peace.

Rom. 8:15–16 When we cry, "Abba! Father!" it is that very Spirit bearing witness with our spirit that we are children of God. . . .

Acts 1:8 But you will receive power when the Holy Spirit has come upon you; and you will be my witnesses in Jerusalem, in all Judea and Samaria, and to the ends of the earth.

John 15:26–27 When the Advocate comes, whom I will send to you from the Father, the Spirit of truth who comes from the Father, he will testify on my behalf. You also are to testify because you have been with me from the beginning.

Question 39. Why do Christians gather for worship on the first day of the week?

Because it is the day when God raised our Lord Jesus from the dead. When we gather weekly on that day, the Spirit makes our hearts glad with the memory of our Lord's resurrection.

Matt. 28:1–10 After the sabbath, as the first day of the week was dawning, Mary Magdalene and the other Mary went to see the tomb. And suddenly there was a great earthquake; for an angel of the Lord, descending from heaven, came and rolled back the stone and sat on it. His appearance was like lightning, and his clothing white as snow. For fear of him the guards shook and became like dead men. But the angel said to the women, "Do not be afraid; I know that you are looking for Jesus who was crucified. He is not here; for he has been raised, as he said. Come, see the place where he lay. Then go quickly and tell his disciples, 'He has been raised from the dead, and indeed he is going ahead of you to Galilee; there you will see him.' This is my message for you." So they left the tomb quickly with fear and great joy, and ran to tell his disciples. Suddenly Jesus met them and said, "Greetings!" And they came to him, took hold of his feet, and worshiped him. Then Jesus said to them, "Do not be afraid; go and tell my brothers to go to Galilee; there they will see me."

Luke 24:1–2 But on the first day of the week, at early dawn, they came to the tomb, taking the spices that they had prepared. They found the stone rolled away from the tomb.

Acts 20:7 On the first day of the week, when we met to break bread, Paul was holding a discussion with them; since he intended to leave the next day, he continued speaking until midnight.

Question 40. What do we do in Christian worship?

We adore and praise God. We pray, sing hymns, and listen to readings from the Bible. We also give offerings to God for the work of the church, and commit ourselves to serve God and our neighbors. Above all, we hear the preaching of the gospel and celebrate the sacraments.

Acts 2:43–47 Awe came upon everyone, because many wonders and signs were being done by the apostles. All who believed were together and had all things in common; they would sell their possessions and goods and distribute the proceeds to all, as any had need. Day by day, as they spent much time together in the temple, they broke bread at home and ate their food with glad and generous hearts, praising God and having the goodwill of all the people. And day by day the Lord added to their number those who were being saved.

Eph. 5:19–20 [Be filled with the Spirit,] as you sing psalms and hymns and spiritual songs among yourselves, singing and making melody to the Lord in your hearts, giving thanks to God the Father at all times and for everything in the name of our Lord Jesus Christ.

1 Cor. 16:2 On the first day of every week, each of you is to put aside and save whatever extra you earn, so that collections need not be taken when I come.

Ps. 92:1–4 It is good to give thanks to the LORD, to sing praises to your name, O Most High; to declare your steadfast love in the morning, and your faithfulness by night, to the music of the lute and the harp, to the melody of the lyre. For you, O LORD, have made me glad by your work; at the works of your hands I sing for joy.

Question 41. What is a sacrament?

A sacrament is a special act of Christian worship which uses visible signs to present God's grace for us in Jesus Christ. We believe that two sacraments were given by Jesus: baptism and the Lord's Supper.

Mark 1:9–11 In those days Jesus came from Nazareth of Galilee and was baptized by John in the Jordan. And just as he was coming up out of the water, he saw the heavens torn apart and the Spirit descending like a dove on him. And a voice came from heaven, "You are my Son, the Beloved; with you I am well pleased."

Mark 14:22–25 While they were eating, he took a loaf of bread, and after blessing it he broke it, gave it to them, and said, "Take; this is my body." Then he took a cup, and after giving thanks he gave it to them, and all of them drank from it. He said to them, "This is my blood of the covenant, which is poured out for many. Truly I tell you, I will never again drink of the fruit of the vine until that day when I drink it new in the kingdom of God."

Question 42. What is baptism?

Through baptism I am adopted and welcomed into God's family. In the water of baptism I share in the dying and rising of Jesus, who washes away my sins. I am made one with him and with all who are joined to him in the church.

> *Rom. 6:3–4* Do you not know that all of us who have been baptized into Christ Jesus were baptized into his death? Therefore we have been buried with him by baptism into death, so that, just as Christ was raised from the dead by the glory of the Father, so we too might walk in newness of life.

> *Gal. 3:27–28* As many of you as were baptized into Christ have clothed yourselves with Christ. There is no longer Jew or Greek, there is no longer slave or free, there is no longer male and female; for all of you are one in Christ Jesus.

> *1 Cor. 12:12–13* For just as the body is one and has many members, and all the members of the body, though many, are one body, so it is with Christ. For in the one Spirit we were all baptized into one body—Jews or Greeks, slaves or free—and we were all made to drink of one Spirit.

> *1 Cor. 6:11* But you were washed, you were sanctified, you were justified in the name of the Lord Jesus Christ and in the Spirit of our God.

> *Acts 2:39* For the promise is for you, for your children, and for all who are far away, everyone whom the Lord our God calls to him.

> *Eph. 4:4–6* There is one body and one Spirit, just as you were called to the one hope of your calling, one Lord, one faith, one baptism, one God and Father of all, who is above all and through all and in all.

Question 43. Why are you baptized in the name of the Father, and of the Son, and of the Holy Spirit?

Because of the command Jesus gave to his disciples. After he was raised from the dead, he appeared to them, saying: "Go . . . and make disciples of all nations, baptizing them in the name of the Father and of the Son and of the Holy Spirit" (Matt. 28:19).

> *Matt. 28:16–20* Now the eleven disciples went to Galilee, to the mountain to which Jesus had directed them. When they saw him, they worshiped him; but some doubted. And Jesus came and said to them, "All authority in heaven and on earth has been given to me. Go therefore and make disciples of all nations, baptizing them in the name of the Father and of the Son and of the Holy Spirit, and teaching them to obey everything that I have commanded you. And remember, I am with you always, to the end of the age."

> *1 Peter 1:2* [To those] who have been chosen and destined by God the Father and sanctified by the Spirit to be obedient to Jesus Christ and to be sprinkled with his blood: May grace and peace be yours in abundance.

1 Cor. 12:4–6 Now there are varieties of gifts, but the same Spirit; and there are varieties of services, but the same Lord; and there are varieties of activities, but it is the same God who activates all of them in everyone.

Question 44. What is the meaning of this name?

It is the name of the Holy Trinity. The Father is God, the Son is God, and the Holy Spirit is God. And yet they are not three gods, but one God in three persons. We worship God in this mystery.

2 Cor. 13:13 The grace of the Lord Jesus Christ, the love of God, and the communion of the Holy Spirit be with all of you.

Rom. 8:11 If the Spirit of him who raised Jesus from the dead dwells in you, he who raised Christ from the dead will give life to your mortal bodies also through his Spirit that dwells in you.

John 1:1–4 In the beginning was the Word, and the Word was with God, and the Word was God. He was in the beginning with God. All things came into being through him, and without him not one thing came into being. What has come into being in him was life, and the life was the light of all people.

Question 45. What is the Lord's Supper?

In the Lord's Supper I am fed at the table of God's family. Through the bread that I eat and the cup that I drink, the Lord offers me his body and blood. He renews my faith and gives me the gift of eternal life. As I remember that he died for all, and therefore also for me, I feed on him in my heart by faith with thanksgiving.

1 Cor. 11:23–26 For I received from the Lord what I also handed on to you, that the Lord Jesus on the night when he was betrayed took a loaf of bread, and when he had given thanks, he broke it and said, "This is my body that is for you. Do this in remembrance of me." In the same way he took the cup also, after supper, saying, "This cup is the new covenant in my blood. Do this, as often as you drink it, in remembrance of me." For as often as you eat this bread and drink the cup, you proclaim the Lord's death until he comes.

Matt. 26:26–29 While they were eating, Jesus took a loaf of bread, and after blessing it he broke it, gave it to the disciples, and said, "Take, eat; this is my body." Then he took a cup, and after giving thanks he gave it to them, saying, "Drink from it, all of you; for this is my blood of the covenant, which is poured out for many for the forgiveness of sins. I tell you, I will never again drink of this fruit of the vine until that day when I drink it new with you in my Father's kingdom."

1 Cor. 10:16 The cup of blessing that we bless, is it not a sharing in the blood of Christ? The bread that we break, is it not a sharing in the body of Christ?

Question 46. Why do we pray to God?

Because we were created to live with God, who desires the prayers of our hearts. Our hearts long for God, for we need God's help and guidance every day.

Ps. 42:1–2 As a deer longs for flowing streams, so my soul longs for you, O God. My soul thirsts for God, for the living God. When shall I come and behold the face of God?

Matt. 6:5–8   And whenever you pray, do not be like the hypocrites; for they love to stand and pray in the synagogues and at the street corners, so that they may be seen by others. Truly I tell you, they have received their reward. But whenever you pray, go into your room and shut the door and pray to your Father who is in secret; and your Father who sees in secret will reward you. When you are praying, do not heap up empty phrases as the Gentiles do; for they think that they will be heard because of their many words. Do not be like them, for your Father knows what you need before you ask him.

Rom. 8:26–27   Likewise the Spirit helps us in our weakness; for we do not know how to pray as we ought, but that very Spirit intercedes with sighs too deep for words. And God, who searches the heart, knows what is the mind of the Spirit, because the Spirit intercedes for the saints according to the will of God.

Ps. 38:9   O Lord, all my longing is known to you; my sighing is not hidden from you.

Question 47. What do we do when we pray?

When we pray, we adore God, we confess our sins, we give God thanks, and we pray for the needs of others and ourselves.

Ps. 63:1, 3   O God, you are my God, I seek you, my soul thirsts for you; my flesh faints for you, as in a dry and weary land where there is no water. . . . Because your steadfast love is better than life, my lips will praise you. So I will bless you as long as I live; I will lift up my hands and call on your name.

Ps. 51:3–4, 10   For I know my transgressions, and my sin is ever before me. Against you, you alone, have I sinned. . . . Create in me a clean heart, O God, and put a new and right spirit within me.

Ps. 92:1–4   It is good to give thanks to the LORD, to sing praises to your name, O Most High; to declare your steadfast love in the morning, and your faithfulness by night, to the music of the lute and the harp, to the melody of the lyre. For you, O LORD, have made me glad by your work; at the works of your hands I sing for joy.

Phil. 1:3–5, 9–11   I thank my God every time I remember you, constantly praying with joy in every one of my prayers for all of you, because of your sharing in the gospel from the first day until now. . . . And this is my prayer, that your love may overflow more and more with knowledge and full insight to help you to determine what is best, so that in the day of Christ you may be pure and blameless, having produced the harvest of righteousness that comes through Jesus Christ for the glory and praise of God.

Question 48. How did Jesus teach his followers to pray?

He taught them the words of the Lord's Prayer.

Question 49. What is the Lord's Prayer?

Our Father in heaven,
hallowed be your name,
your kingdom come,
your will be done,
on earth as in heaven.

Give us today our daily bread,
Forgive us our sins
   as we forgive those who sin against us.
Save us from the time of trial
   and deliver us from evil.
For the kingdom, the power, and the glory are yours
   now and for ever. Amen.

Question 50. What do we mean when we pray to God as "Our Father"?

As Jesus taught us, we call upon God like little children who know that God cares for them and loves them. Because Jesus prayed to God as his Father, we too can pray to God in this way.

Matt. 18:1–5   At that time the disciples came to Jesus and asked, "Who is the greatest in the kingdom of heaven?" He called a child, whom he put among them, and said, "Truly I tell you, unless you change and become like children, you will never enter the kingdom of heaven. Whoever becomes humble like this child is the greatest in the kingdom of heaven. Whoever welcomes one such child in my name welcomes me."

Matt. 7:7–11   Ask, and it will be given you; search, and you will find; knock, and the door will be opened for you. For everyone who asks receives, and everyone who searches finds, and for everyone who knocks, the door will be opened. Is there anyone among you who, if your child asks for bread, will give a stone? Or if the child asks for a fish, will give a snake? If you then, who are evil, know how to give good gifts to your children, how much more will your Father in heaven give good things to those who ask him!

Rom. 8:15–16   When we cry, "Abba! Father!" it is that very Spirit bearing witness with our spirit that we are children of God. . . .

Gal. 4:6   And because you are children, God has sent the Spirit of his Son into our hearts, crying, "Abba! Father!"

Question 51. When we pray to God as our Father, do we mean that God is male?

No. Only creatures who have bodies can be male or female. But God is Spirit and has no body.

John 4:24   God is spirit, and those who worship him must worship in spirit and truth.

Gen. 1:27   So God created humankind in his image, in the image of God he created them; male and female he created them.

Isa. 49:15   Can a woman forget her nursing child, or show no compassion for the child of her womb? Even these may forget, yet I will not forget you.

Isa. 66:13   As a mother comforts her child, so I will comfort you; you shall be comforted in Jerusalem.

Matt. 23:37   Jerusalem, Jerusalem, the city that kills the prophets and stones those who are sent to it! How often have I desired to gather your children together as a hen gathers her brood under her wings, and you were not willing!

Matt. 23:9   And call no one your father on earth, for you have one Father—the one in heaven.

Question 52. What do we mean when we pray to God "in heaven"?

We mean that God draws near to us from beyond this world and hears our prayers.

1 Kings 8:27, 30   But will God indeed dwell on the earth? Even heaven and the highest heaven cannot contain you, much less this house that I have built! . . . Hear the plea of your servant and of your people Israel when they pray toward this place; O hear in heaven your dwelling place; heed and forgive.

Luke 2:13–14   And suddenly there was with the angel a multitude of the heavenly host, praising God and saying, "Glory to God in the highest heaven, and on earth peace among those whom he favors!"

Ps. 14:2   The LORD looks down from heaven on humankind to see if there are any who are wise, who seek after God.

1 Kings 22:19   Then Micaiah said, "Therefore hear the word of the LORD: I saw the LORD sitting on his throne, with all the host of heaven standing beside him to the right and to the left of him."

2 Kings 19:15   And Hezekiah prayed before the LORD, and said: "O LORD the God of Israel, who are enthroned above the cherubim, you are God, you alone, of all the kingdoms of the earth; you have made heaven and earth."

Question 53. What do we ask when we pray "Hallowed be your name"?

We pray that God's name will be honored in all the world and everywhere treated as holy, because God's name really stands for God.

Ex. 3:13–15   But Moses said to God, "If I come to the Israelites and say to them, 'The God of your ancestors has sent me to you,' and they ask me, 'What is his name?' what shall I say to them?" God said to Moses, "I AM WHO I AM." He said further, "Thus you shall say to the Israelites, 'I AM has sent me to you.' " God also said to Moses, "Thus you shall say to the Israelites, 'The LORD, the God of your ancestors, the God of Abraham, the God of Isaac, and the God of Jacob, has sent me to you': This is my name forever, and this my title for all generations."

1 Peter 1:15–16   Instead, as he who called you is holy, be holy yourselves in all your conduct; for it is written, "You shall be holy, for I am holy."

Lev. 20:26   You shall be holy to me; for I the LORD am holy, and I have separated you from the other peoples to be mine.

Num. 15:40   So you shall remember and do all my commandments, and you shall be holy to your God.

Deut. 5:11   You shall not make wrongful use of the name of the LORD your God, for the LORD will not acquit anyone who misuses his name.

Question 54. What do we ask when we pray "Your kingdom come, your will be done, on earth as in heaven"?

We ask God to fulfill God's purpose for the whole world. We also ask God to make us able and willing to accept God's will in all things, and to do our part in bringing about God's purpose.

Mark 14:36 He said, "Abba, Father, for you all things are possible; remove this cup from me; yet, not what I want, but what you want."

Ps. 103:19 The LORD has established his throne in the heavens, and his kingdom rules over all.

Rom. 14:17 For the kingdom of God is not food and drink but righteousness and peace and joy in the Holy Spirit.

Mark 14:25 Truly I tell you, I will never again drink of the fruit of the vine until that day when I drink it new in the kingdom of God.

Question 55. Why do we pray "Give us today our daily bread"?

Because all good things come from God. Even in our most ordinary needs, God cares for us completely.

Ex. 16:4 Then the LORD said to Moses, "I am going to rain bread from heaven for you, and each day the people shall go out and gather enough for that day."

Luke 12:22–24 He said to his disciples, "Therefore I tell you, do not worry about your life, what you will eat, or about your body, what you will wear. For life is more than food, and the body more than clothing. Consider the ravens: they neither sow nor reap, they have neither storehouse nor barn, and yet God feeds them. Of how much more value are you than the birds!"

James 1:17 Every generous act of giving, with every perfect gift, is from above, coming down from the Father of lights, with whom there is no variation or shadow due to change.

Question 56. What do we ask when we pray "Forgive us our sins"?

Telling God we are sorry, we ask God not to hold our sins against us, but to accept us again by grace.

Ex. 32:30–32 On the next day Moses said to the people, "You have sinned a great sin. But now I will go up to the LORD; perhaps I can make atonement for your sin." So Moses returned to the LORD and said, "Alas, this people has sinned a great sin; they have made for themselves gods of gold. But now, if you will only forgive their sin—but if not, blot me out of the book that you have written."

Luke 18:9–14 He also told this parable to some who trusted in themselves that they were righteous and regarded others with contempt: "Two men went up to the temple to pray, one a Pharisee and the other a tax collector. The Pharisee, standing by himself, was praying thus, 'God, I thank you that I am not like other people: thieves, rogues, adulterers, or even like this tax collector. I fast twice a week; I give a tenth of all my income.' But the tax collector, standing far off, would not even look up to heaven, but was beating his breast and saying, 'God, be merciful to me, a sinner!' I tell you, this man went down to his home justified rather than the other; for all who exalt themselves will be humbled, but all who humble themselves will be exalted."

Luke 24:47 Repentance and forgiveness of sins is to be proclaimed in his name to all nations, beginning from Jerusalem.

Ps. 86:5 For you, O LORD, are good and forgiving, abounding in steadfast love to all who call on you.

Ps. 25:18 Consider my affliction and my trouble, and forgive all my sins.

Question 57. Why do we continue with "as we forgive those who sin against us"?

Because we are to forgive others, just as God has forgiven us.

Matt. 18:32–33 You wicked slave! I forgave you all that debt because you pleaded with me. Should you not have had mercy on your fellow slave, as I had mercy on you?

Col. 3:13 Bear with one another and, if anyone has a complaint against another, forgive each other; just as the Lord has forgiven you, so you also must forgive.

Matt. 6:14–15 For if you forgive others their trespasses, your heavenly Father will also forgive you; but if you do not forgive others, neither will your Father forgive your trespasses.

Mark 11:25 Whenever you stand praying, forgive, if you have anything against anyone; so that your Father in heaven may also forgive you your trespasses.

Question 58. What do we ask when we pray "Save us from the time of trial and deliver us from evil"?

We ask God to protect us, especially when we most need it. We pray for God to free us from all desires that would lead us to sin, and to shelter us from the powers of evil that may threaten us.

Luke 4:1–2 Jesus, full of the Holy Spirit, returned from the Jordan and was led by the Spirit in the wilderness, where for forty days he was tempted by the devil.

1 Cor. 10:12–13 So if you think you are standing, watch out that you do not fall. No testing has overtaken you that is not common to everyone. God is faithful, and he will not let you be tested beyond your strength, but with the testing he will also provide the way out so that you may be able to endure it.

Ps. 34:4 I sought the LORD, and he answered me, and delivered me from all my fears.

Ps. 61:4 Let me abide in your tent forever, find refuge under the shelter of your wings.

Deut. 32:10–12 He sustained him in a desert land, in a howling wilderness waste; he shielded him, cared for him, guarded him as the apple of his eye. As an eagle stirs up its nest, and hovers over its young; as it spreads its wings, takes them up, and bears them aloft on its pinions, the LORD alone guided him. . . .

Question 59. What does it mean to pray "For the kingdom, the power, and the glory are yours now and for ever"?

We praise God for being able and willing to do everything we have asked in this prayer. We give ourselves over to God's wise and gracious rule, because we know that God can be trusted to make all things work together for good, now and forever.

Phil. 2:9–11   Therefore God also highly exalted him and gave him the name that is above every name, so that at the name of Jesus every knee should bend, in heaven and on earth and under the earth, and every tongue should confess that Jesus Christ is Lord, to the glory of God the Father.

Jude 1:24–25   Now to him who is able to keep you from falling, and to make you stand without blemish in the presence of his glory with rejoicing, to the only God our Savior, through Jesus Christ our Lord, be glory, majesty, power, and authority, before all time and now and forever. Amen.

Gen. 50:20   Even though you intended to do harm to me, God intended it for good, in order to preserve a numerous people, as he is doing today.

1 Chron. 29:11–12   Yours, O LORD, are the greatness, the power, the glory, the victory, and the majesty; for all that is in the heavens and on the earth is yours; yours is the kingdom, O LORD, and you are exalted as head above all. Riches and honor come from you, and you rule over all. In your hand are power and might; and it is in your hand to make great and to give strength to all.

Question 60. Why does our prayer end with "Amen"?

"Amen" means "so be it" or "let it be so." It expresses our complete confidence in God, who makes no promise that will not be kept and whose love endures forever.

Rev. 22:20   The one who testifies to these things says, "Surely I am coming soon." Amen. Come, Lord Jesus!

2 Cor. 1:20   For in him every one of God's promises is a "Yes." For this reason it is through him that we say the "Amen," to the glory of God.

Jer. 28:6   The prophet Jeremiah said, "Amen! May the LORD do so; may the LORD fulfill the words that you have prophesied, and bring back to this place from Babylon the vessels of the house of the LORD, and all the exiles."

1 Peter 5:11   To him be the power forever and ever. Amen.

The Study Catechism: Confirmation Version

In 1998 the 210th General Assembly of the Presbyterian Church (U.S.A.) approved two new catechisms for use as teaching tools for the church. The second of these is The Study Catechism, which was prepared in two versions: the Full Version and the shorter, somewhat simplified Confirmation Version. Both follow the traditional sequence of the Apostles' Creed, the Ten Commandments, and the Lord's Prayer. The Confirmation Version is designed to be used with youth during the confirmation process, while the Full Version can be used in the training of church officers, in adult study groups, in the education of new church members, or in many other settings.

THE STUDY CATECHISM:
CONFIRMATION VERSION

Question 1. What is God's purpose for your life?

God wills that I should live by the grace of the Lord Jesus Christ, for the love of God, and in the communion of the Holy Spirit.

2 Cor. 13:13   The grace of the Lord Jesus Christ, the love of God, and the communion of the Holy Spirit be with all of you.

Question 2. How do you live by the grace of the Lord Jesus Christ?

I am not my own. I have been bought with a price. The Lord Jesus Christ loved me and gave himself for me. I entrust myself completely to his care, giving thanks each day for his wonderful goodness.

1 Cor. 6:19–20   Or do you not know that your body is a temple of the Holy Spirit within you, which you have from God, and that you are not your own? For you were bought with a price; therefore glorify God in your body.

Gal. 2:20   It is no longer I who live, but it is Christ who lives in me. And the life I now live in the flesh I live by faith in the Son of God, who loved me and gave himself for me.

Ps. 136:1   O give thanks to the LORD, for he is good, for his steadfast love endures forever.

Question 3. How do you live for the love of God?

I love because God first loved me. Amazed by grace, I live for the Lord who died and rose again, triumphant over death, for my sake. Therefore, I take those around me to heart, especially those in need, knowing that Christ died for them no less than for me.

1 John 4:19   We love because he first loved us.

2 Cor. 5:15   And he died for all, so that those who live might live no longer for themselves, but for him who died and was raised for them.

27

Rom. 12:15–16   Rejoice with those who rejoice, weep with those who weep. Live in harmony with one another; do not be haughty, but associate with the lowly; do not claim to be wiser than you are.

Question 4. How do you live in the communion of the Holy Spirit?

By the Holy Spirit, I am made one with the Lord Jesus Christ. I am baptized into Christ's body, the church. As a member of this community, I trust in God's Word, share in the Lord's Supper, and turn to God in prayer. As I grow in grace and knowledge, I am led to do the good works that God intends for my life.

1 Cor. 12:27   Now you are the body of Christ and individually members of it.

Gal. 3:27   As many of you as were baptized into Christ have clothed yourselves with Christ.

1 Cor. 6:17, 19   But anyone united to the Lord becomes one spirit with him. . . . Or do you not know that your body is a temple of the Holy Spirit within you, which you have from God, and that you are not your own?

2 Peter 3:18   But grow in the grace and knowledge of our Lord and Savior Jesus Christ. To him be the glory both now and to the day of eternity. Amen.

Eph. 2:10   For we are what he has made us, created in Christ Jesus for good works, which God prepared beforehand to be our way of life.

I. The Apostles' Creed

Question 5. What does a Christian believe?

All that is promised in the gospel. A summary is found in the Apostles' Creed, which affirms the main content of the Christian faith.

John 20:31   But these are written so that you may come to believe that Jesus is the Messiah, the Son of God, and that through believing you may have life in his name.

Question 6. What is the first article of the Apostles' Creed?

"I believe in God the Father Almighty, Maker of heaven and earth."

Question 7. What do you believe when you confess your faith in "God the Father Almighty"?

That God is a God of love, and that God's love is powerful beyond measure.

Lam. 3:22   The steadfast love of the LORD never ceases, his mercies never come to an end.

Song 8:7   Many waters cannot quench love, neither can floods drown it. If one offered for love all the wealth of his house, it would be utterly scorned.

1 John 4:8   Whoever does not love does not know God, for God is love.

Question 8. How do you understand the love and power of God?

Through Jesus Christ. In his life of compassion, his death on the cross, and his resurrection from the dead, I see how vast is God's love for the world—a love that is ready to suffer for our sakes, yet so strong that nothing will prevail against it.

28

John 3:16   For God so loved the world that he gave his only Son, so that everyone who believes in him may not perish but may have eternal life.

Heb. 1:3   He is the reflection of God's glory and the exact imprint of God's very being, and he sustains all things by his powerful word.

1 John 4:9   God's love was revealed among us in this way: God sent his only Son into the world so that we might live through him.

Matt. 9:36   When he saw the crowds, he had compassion for them, because they were harassed and helpless, like sheep without a shepherd.

Ps. 106:8   Yet he saved them for his name's sake, so that he might make known his mighty power.

Question 9. What comfort do you receive from this truth?

This powerful and loving God is the one whose promises I may trust in all the circumstances of my life, and to whom I belong in life and in death.

Ps. 12:6   The promises of the LORD are promises that are pure, silver refined in a furnace on the ground, purified seven times.

Rom. 8:38–39   For I am convinced that neither death, nor life, nor angels, nor rulers, nor things present, nor things to come, nor powers, nor height, nor depth, nor anything else in all creation, will be able to separate us from the love of God in Christ Jesus our Lord.

Question 10. Do you make this confession by yourself?

No. With all those before me who have loved the Lord Jesus Christ, and with all who serve him on earth here and now, I confess my faith in this loving and powerful God.

Heb. 12:1   Therefore, since we are surrounded by so great a cloud of witnesses, let us also lay aside every weight and the sin that clings so closely, and let us run with perseverance the race that is set before us. . . .

Rom. 1:12   [I am longing to see you] so that we may be mutually encouraged by each other's faith, both yours and mine.

Question 11. When the creed speaks of "God the Father," does it mean that God is male?

No. Only creatures having bodies can be either male or female. But God has no body, since by nature God is Spirit. Holy Scripture reveals God as a living God beyond all sexual distinctions. Scripture uses diverse images for God, female as well as male.

Isa. 49:15   Can a woman forget her nursing child, or show no compassion for the child of her womb? Even these may forget, yet I will not forget you.

Isa. 66:13   As a mother comforts her child, so I will comfort you; you shall be comforted in Jerusalem.

Matt. 23:37   Jerusalem, Jerusalem, the city that kills the prophets and stones those who are sent to it! How often have I desired to gather your children together as a hen gathers her brood under her wings, and you were not willing!

Question 12. Why then does the creed speak of God the Father?

Because God is identified in the New Testament as the Father of our Lord Jesus Christ.

Rom. 1:7 To all God's beloved in Rome, who are called to be saints: Grace to you and peace from God our Father and the Lord Jesus Christ.

John 14:9–10 Jesus said to him, "Have I been with you all this time, Philip, and you still do not know me? Whoever has seen me has seen the Father. How can you say, 'Show us the Father'? Do you not believe that I am in the Father and the Father is in me? The words that I say to you I do not speak on my own; but the Father who dwells in me does his works."

John 17:24 Father, I desire that those also, whom you have given me, may be with me where I am, to see my glory, which you have given me because you loved me before the foundation of the world.

John 1:12 But to all who received him, who believed in his name, he gave power to become children of God. . . .

Gal. 4:6 And because you are children, God has sent the Spirit of his Son into our hearts, crying, "Abba! Father!"

Question 13. When you confess God as our Father, do you mean that men should dominate women?

No. All human beings, male or female, ought to conform their lives to the love, humility, and kindness of God. In fact God calls women and men to all ministries of the church. Any abuse or domination in human relationships is a direct violation of God's Fatherhood.

Gal. 3:28 There is no longer Jew or Greek, there is no longer slave or free, there is no longer male and female; for all of you are one in Christ Jesus.

Eph. 5:21 Be subject to one another out of reverence for Christ.

Question 14. If God's love is so powerful, why is there evil in the world?

No one can say why, for evil is a terrible mystery. Still, we know that God's triumph over evil is certain. Our Lord Jesus Christ, crucified and risen, is himself God's promise that suffering will come to an end, that death shall be no more, and that all things will be made new.

Ps. 23:4 Even though I walk through the darkest valley, I fear no evil; for you are with me; your rod and your staff—they comfort me.

1 Peter 1:3 Blessed be the God and Father of our Lord Jesus Christ! By his great mercy he has given us a new birth into a living hope through the resurrection of Jesus Christ from the dead.

2 Peter 3:13 But, in accordance with his promise, we wait for new heavens and a new earth, where righteousness is at home.

Rom. 8:21 The creation itself will be set free from its bondage to decay and will obtain the freedom of the glory of the children of God.

Job 19:25 For I know that my Redeemer lives, and that at the last he will stand upon the earth.

Question 15. What do you believe when you say that God is "Maker of heaven and earth"?

First, that God called heaven and earth, with all that is in them, into being out of nothing. Second, that God rules and supports the creation in perfect wisdom, according to God's eternal purpose.

> *Rev. 4:11*   You are worthy, our Lord and God, to receive glory and honor and power, for you created all things, and by your will they existed and were created.

> *Gen. 1:1*   In the beginning when God created the heavens and the earth, the earth was a formless void and darkness covered the face of the deep, while a wind from God swept over the face of the waters.

> *Heb. 11:3*   By faith we understand that the worlds were prepared by the word of God, so that what is seen was made from things that are not visible.

Question 16. Did God need to make the world?

No. God would still be God even if heaven and earth had never been made.

> *Acts 17:24–25*   The God who made the world and everything in it, he who is Lord of heaven and earth, does not live in shrines made by human hands, nor is he served by human hands, as though he needed anything, since he himself gives to all mortals life and breath and all things.

Question 17. Why, then, did God create the world?

God's creation of the world was an act of grace. God granted existence to the world simply in order to bless it. God created the world to reveal God's glory, to share the love and freedom at the heart of God's being, and to give us eternal life in fellowship with God.

> *Ps. 19:1*   The heavens are telling the glory of God; and the firmament proclaims his handiwork.

> *2 Cor. 3:17*   Now the Lord is the Spirit, and where the Spirit of the Lord is, there is freedom.

> *Ps. 67:6–7*   The earth has yielded its increase; God, our God, has blessed us. May God continue to bless us; let all the ends of the earth revere him.

> *Eph. 1:3–4*   Blessed be the God and Father of our Lord Jesus Christ, who has blessed us in Christ with every spiritual blessing in the heavenly places, just as he chose us in Christ before the foundation of the world to be holy and blameless before him in love.

> *John 3:36*   Whoever believes in the Son has eternal life; whoever disobeys the Son will not see life, but must endure God's wrath.

Question 18. Does your confession of God as Creator contradict the findings of modern science?

No. Natural science has much to teach us about the particular mechanisms of nature, but it is not equipped to answer questions about ultimate reality. Nothing basic to the Christian faith contradicts the findings of modern science, nor does anything essential to modern science contradict the Christian faith.

John 1:1–3   In the beginning was the Word, and the Word was with God, and the Word was God. He was in the beginning with God. All things came into being through him, and without him not one thing came into being.

Question 19. What does it mean to say that human beings are created in the image of God?

God created us to live together in love and freedom—with God, with one another, and with the world. We are created to be loving companions of others so that something of God's goodness may be reflected in our lives.

Gen. 1:26   Then God said, "Let us make humankind in our image, according to our likeness; and let them have dominion over the fish of the sea, and over the birds of the air, and over the cattle, and over all the wild animals of the earth, and over every creeping thing that creeps upon the earth."

Gen. 1:27   So God created humankind in his image, in the image of God he created them; male and female he created them.

Question 20. What does our creation in God's image reflect about God?

Our being created for loving relationships is a reflection of the Holy Trinity. In the mystery of the one God, the three divine persons—Father, Son, and Holy Spirit—live eternally in perfect love and freedom.

Luke 3:21–22   Now when all the people were baptized, and when Jesus also had been baptized and was praying, the heaven was opened, and the Holy Spirit descended upon him in bodily form like a dove. And a voice came from heaven, "You are my Son, the Beloved; with you I am well pleased."

John 1:18   No one has ever seen God. It is God the only Son, who is close to the Father's heart, who has made him known.

John 5:19   Jesus said to them, "Very truly, I tell you, the Son can do nothing on his own, but only what he sees the Father doing; for whatever the Father does, the Son does likewise."

John 17:21–22   As you, Father, are in me and I am in you, may they also be in us, so that the world may believe that you have sent me. The glory that you have given me I have given them, so that they may be one, as we are one. . . .

Question 21. What does our creation in God's image say about our responsibility for the earth?

We are responsible for seeing that the earth's gifts are used fairly and wisely. We must take care that no creature suffers from the abuse of what we are given, and that future generations may continue to enjoy the earth's abundance in praise to God.

Ps. 24:1   The earth is the LORD's and all that is in it, the world, and those who live in it. . . .

Ps. 89:11   The heavens are yours, the earth also is yours; the world and all that is in it—you have founded them.

Gen. 2:15   The LORD God took the man and put him in the garden of Eden to till it and keep it.

Gen. 1:26 Then God said, "Let us make humankind in our image, according to our likeness; and let them have dominion over the fish of the sea, and over the birds of the air, and over the cattle, and over all the wild animals of the earth, and over every creeping thing that creeps upon the earth."

Isa. 24:5 The earth lies polluted under its inhabitants; for they have transgressed laws, violated the statutes, broken the everlasting covenant.

Rom. 12:2 Do not be conformed to this world, but be transformed by the renewing of your minds, so that you may discern what is the will of God—what is good and acceptable and perfect.

Question 22. What is God's providence?

God not only preserves the world, but also continually rules over it. God cares for every creature and brings good out of evil, so that nothing evil is permitted to occur that God does not bend finally to the good.

Rom. 8:28 We know that all things work together for good for those who love God, who are called according to his purpose.

Ps. 103:19 The LORD has established his throne in the heavens, and his kingdom rules over all.

Ps. 145:17 The LORD is just in all his ways, and kind in all his doings.

Question 23. What comfort do you receive by trusting in God's providence?

The eternal Father of our Lord Jesus Christ watches over me each day of my life, blessing and guiding me wherever I may be. God strengthens me when I am faithful, comforts me when I am discouraged or sorrowful, raises me up if I fall, and brings me at last to eternal life.

Ps. 146:9 The LORD watches over the strangers; he upholds the orphan and the widow, but the way of the wicked he brings to ruin.

Isa. 58:11 The LORD will guide you continually, and satisfy your needs in parched places, and make your bones strong; and you shall be like a watered garden, like a spring of water, whose waters never fail.

Isa. 41:10 Do not fear, for I am with you, do not be afraid, for I am your God; I will strengthen you, I will help you, I will uphold you with my victorious right hand.

2 Cor. 1:3–5 Blessed be the God and Father of our Lord Jesus Christ, the Father of mercies and the God of all consolation, who consoles us in all our affliction, so that we may be able to console those who are in any affliction with the consolation with which we ourselves are consoled by God.

Ps. 30:5 For his anger is but for a moment; his favor is for a lifetime. Weeping may linger for the night, but joy comes with the morning.

Question 24. What is the second article of the Apostles' Creed?

"And I believe in Jesus Christ, his only Son, our Lord. He was conceived by the Holy Spirit, born of the Virgin Mary, suffered under Pontius Pilate, was crucified, dead and buried. He descended into hell. On the third day he rose again from the dead. He ascended into heaven and is seated at the right hand of the Father. He will come again to judge the living and the dead."

Question 25. What do you believe when you confess your faith in Jesus Christ as "God's only Son"?

No one else will ever be God incarnate. No one else will ever die for the sins of the world. Only Jesus Christ is such a person, only he could do such a work, and he in fact has done it.

Isa. 53:5 But he was wounded for our transgressions, crushed for our iniquities; upon him was the punishment that made us whole, and by his bruises we are healed.

John 1:29 The next day he saw Jesus coming toward him and declared, "Here is the Lamb of God who takes away the sin of the world!"

Col. 1:15–20 He is the image of the invisible God, the firstborn of all creation; for in him all things in heaven and on earth were created, things visible and invisible, whether thrones or dominions or rulers or powers—all things have been created through him and for him. He himself is before all things, and in him all things hold together. He is the head of the body, the church; he is the beginning, the firstborn from the dead, so that he might come to have first place in everything. For in him all the fullness of God was pleased to dwell, and through him God was pleased to reconcile to himself all things, whether on earth or in heaven, by making peace through the blood of his cross.

Luke 3:21–22 Now when all the people were baptized, and when Jesus also had been baptized and was praying, the heaven was opened, and the Holy Spirit descended upon him in bodily form like a dove. And a voice came from heaven, "You are my Son, the Beloved; with you I am well pleased."

John 1:14 And the Word became flesh and lived among us, and we have seen his glory, the glory as of a father's only son, full of grace and truth.

Question 26. What do you affirm when you confess your faith in Jesus Christ as "our Lord"?

That having been raised from the dead Christ reigns with compassion and justice over all things in heaven and on earth, especially over those who confess him by faith. By loving and serving him above all else, I give glory and honor to God.

1 Cor. 15:3–4 For I handed on to you as of first importance what I in turn had received: that Christ died for our sins in accordance with the scriptures, and that he was buried, and that he was raised on the third day in accordance with the scriptures. . . .

Rev. 11:15 Then the seventh angel blew his trumpet, and there were loud voices in heaven, saying, "The kingdom of the world has become the kingdom of our Lord and of his Messiah, and he will reign forever and ever."

Eph. 1:20–23 God put this power to work in Christ when he raised him from the dead and seated him at his right hand in the heavenly places, far above all rule and authority and power and dominion, and above every name that is named, not only in this age but also in the age to come. And he has put all things under his feet and has made him the head over all things for the church, which is his body, the fullness of him who fills all in all.

Phil. 2:9–11 Therefore God also highly exalted him and gave him the name that is above every name, so that at the name of Jesus every knee should bend, in heaven and on earth and under the earth, and every tongue should confess that Jesus Christ is Lord, to the glory of God the Father.

Question 27. How did the coming of Jesus confirm God's covenant with Israel?

God made a covenant with Israel, promising that God would be their God, that they would be God's people, and that through them all the peoples of the earth would be blessed. With the coming of Jesus the covenant was thrown open to the world. By faith in him, all peoples were welcomed into the covenant. This throwing open of the gates confirmed the promise that through Israel God's blessing would come to all.

Gen. 17:3–4 Then Abram fell on his face; and God said to him, "As for me, this is my covenant with you: You shall be the ancestor of a multitude of nations."

Gen. 12:1–3 Now the LORD said to Abram, "Go from your country and your kindred and your father's house to the land that I will show you. I will make of you a great nation, and I will bless you, and make your name great, so that you will be a blessing. I will bless those who bless you, and the one who curses you I will curse; and in you all the families of the earth shall be blessed."

Ex. 6:4–5 I also established my covenant with them, to give them the land of Canaan, the land in which they resided as aliens. I have also heard the groaning of the Israelites whom the Egyptians are holding as slaves, and I have remembered my covenant.

Gal. 3:14 . . . in order that in Christ Jesus the blessing of Abraham might come to the Gentiles, so that we might receive the promise of the Spirit through faith.

Jer. 30:22 And you shall be my people, and I will be your God.

1 Peter 2:9–10 But you are a chosen race, a royal priesthood, a holy nation, God's own people, in order that you might proclaim the mighty acts of him who called you out of darkness into his marvelous light. Once you were not a people, but now you are God's people; once you had not received mercy, but now you have received mercy.

Zech. 1:6 But my words and my statutes, which I commanded my servants the prophets, did they not overtake your ancestors? So they repented and said, "The LORD of hosts has dealt with us according to our ways and deeds, just as he planned to do."

Lev. 5:6 And you shall bring to the LORD, as your penalty for the sin that you have committed, . . . a sheep or a goat, as a sin offering; and the priest shall make atonement on your behalf for your sin.

Ps. 72:1, 4 Give the king your justice, O God, and your righteousness to a king's son. . . . May he defend the cause of the poor of the people, give deliverance to the needy, and crush the oppressor.

Question 28. Was the covenant with Israel an everlasting covenant?

Yes. Although for the most part Israel has not accepted Jesus as the Messiah, God has not rejected Israel. God still loves Israel, and God is their hope, "for the gifts and the calling of God are irrevocable" (Rom. 11:29).

Isa. 61:8   For I the LORD love justice, I hate robbery and wrongdoing; I will faithfully give them their recompense, and I will make an everlasting covenant with them.

Jer. 31:3   I have loved you with an everlasting love; therefore I have continued my faithfulness to you.

2 Sam. 23:5   Is not my house like this with God? For he has made with me an everlasting covenant, ordered in all things and secure. Will he not cause to prosper all my help and my desire?

Rom. 11:29   For the gifts and the calling of God are irrevocable.

Question 29. What do you affirm when you say he was "conceived by the Holy Spirit and born of the Virgin Mary"?

First, that being born of Mary, Jesus was truly a human being. Second, that our Lord's incarnation was a holy and mysterious event. Third, that he was set apart by his unique origin for the sake of accomplishing our salvation.

Luke 1:31   And now, you will conceive in your womb and bear a son, and you will name him Jesus.

Luke 1:35   The angel said to her, "The Holy Spirit will come upon you, and the power of the Most High will overshadow you; therefore the child to be born will be holy; he will be called Son of God."

Heb. 2:14   Since, therefore, the children share flesh and blood, he himself likewise shared the same things, so that through death he might destroy the one who has the power of death, that is, the devil. . . .

Phil. 2:5–7   Let the same mind be in you that was in Christ Jesus, who, though he was in the form of God, did not regard equality with God as something to be exploited, but emptied himself, taking the form of a slave, being born in human likeness.

Question 30. What is the significance of affirming that Jesus is truly God?

Only God can properly deserve worship. Only God can reveal to us who God is. And only God can save us from our sins. Being truly God, Jesus meets these conditions. He is the proper object of our worship, the self-revelation of God, and the Savior of the world.

John 20:28   Thomas answered him, "My Lord and my God!" Jesus said to him, "Have you believed because you have seen me? Blessed are those who have not seen and yet have come to believe."

Matt. 11:27   All things have been handed over to me by my Father; and no one knows the Son except the Father, and no one knows the Father except the Son and anyone to whom the Son chooses to reveal him.

1 John 4:14   And we have seen and do testify that the Father has sent his Son as the Savior of the world.

Question 31. What is the significance of affirming that Jesus is also truly a human being?

Being truly human, Jesus entered fully into our fallen situation and overcame it. He lived a life of pure obedience to God, even to the point of accepting a violent death. When we accept him by faith, he removes our disobedience and clothes us with his perfect righteousness.

Heb. 2:17–18   Therefore he had to become like his brothers and sisters in every respect, so that he might be a merciful and faithful high priest in the service of God, to make a sacrifice of atonement for the sins of the people. Because he himself was tested by what he suffered, he is able to help those who are being tested.

Heb. 4:15   For we do not have a high priest who is unable to sympathize with our weaknesses, but we have one who in every respect has been tested as we are, yet without sin.

Heb. 5:8–9   Although he was a Son, he learned obedience through what he suffered; and having been made perfect, he became the source of eternal salvation for all who obey him. . . .

Rom. 5:19   For just as by the one man's disobedience the many were made sinners, so by the one man's obedience the many will be made righteous.

Question 32. What do you affirm when you say that he "suffered under Pontius Pilate"?

First, that our Lord was rejected and abused by the authorities of that time, both religious and political. Second, and even more importantly, that he submitted to condemnation by an earthly judge so that we might be acquitted before our heavenly Judge.

Luke 18:32   For he will be handed over to the Gentiles; and he will be mocked and insulted and spat upon.

Isa. 53:3   He was despised and rejected by others; a man of suffering and acquainted with infirmity; and as one from whom others hide their faces he was despised, and we held him of no account.

Ps. 9:9   The LORD is a stronghold for the oppressed, a stronghold in times of trouble.

Luke 1:52   He has brought down the powerful from their thrones, and lifted up the lowly. . . .

2 Cor. 5:21   For our sake he made him to be sin who knew no sin, so that in him we might become the righteousness of God.

2 Tim. 4:8   From now on there is reserved for me the crown of righteousness, which the Lord, the righteous judge, will give me on that day, and not only to me but also to all who have longed for his appearing.

Question 33. What do you affirm when you say that he was "crucified, dead, and buried"?

From Christ's lonely and terrible death we learn that there is no sorrow he has not known, no grief he has not borne, and no price he was unwilling to pay in order to reconcile us to God.

Matt. 26:38–39   Then he said to them, "I am deeply grieved, even to death; remain here, and stay awake with me." And going a little farther, he threw himself on the ground and prayed, "My Father, if it is possible, let this cup pass from me; yet not what I want but what you want."

Isa. 53:5   But he was wounded for our transgressions, crushed for our iniquities; upon him was the punishment that made us whole, and by his bruises we are healed.

Gal. 3:13   Christ redeemed us from the curse of the law by becoming a curse for us—for it is written, "Cursed is everyone who hangs on a tree. . . ."

Heb. 2:9   But we do see Jesus, who for a little while was made lower than the angels, now crowned with glory and honor because of the suffering of death, so that by the grace of God he might taste death for everyone.

2 Cor. 5:19   In Christ God was reconciling the world to himself, not counting their trespasses against them, and entrusting the message of reconciliation to us.

Question 34. What do you affirm when you say that he "descended into hell"?

That our Lord took upon himself the full consequences of our sinfulness in order that we might be spared.

Mark 15:34   At three o'clock Jesus cried out with a loud voice, "Eloi, Eloi, lema sabachthani?" which means, "My God, my God, why have you forsaken me?"

Heb. 9:26   . . . for then he would have had to suffer again and again since the foundation of the world. But as it is, he has appeared once for all at the end of the age to remove sin by the sacrifice of himself.

Rom. 4:24–25   It will be reckoned to us who believe in him who raised Jesus our Lord from the dead, who was handed over to death for our trespasses and was raised for our justification.

Question 35. What do you affirm when you say that "on the third day he rose again from the dead"?

Our Lord could not be held by the power of death. Having died on the cross, he appeared to his followers, and revealed himself to them as the Lord and Savior of the world.

Acts 2:24   But God raised him up, having freed him from death, because it was impossible for him to be held in its power.

1 Cor. 15:3–4   For I handed on to you as of first importance what I in turn had received: that Christ died for our sins in accordance with the scriptures, and that he was buried, and that he was raised on the third day in accordance with the scriptures. . . .

Luke 24:36–40   While they were talking about this, Jesus himself stood among them and said to them, "Peace be with you." They were startled and terrified, and thought that they were seeing a ghost. He said to them, "Why are you frightened, and why do doubts arise in your hearts? Look at my hands and my feet; see that it is I myself. Touch me and see; for a ghost does not have flesh and bones as you see that I have." And when he had said this, he showed them his hands and his feet.

John 20:15–18   Jesus said to her, "Woman, why are you weeping? Whom are you looking for?" Supposing him to be the gardener, she said to him, "Sir, if you have carried him away, tell me where you have laid him, and I will take him away." Jesus said to her, "Mary!" She turned and said to him in Hebrew, "Rabbouni!" (which means teacher). Jesus said to her, "Do not hold on to me, because I have not yet ascended to the Father. But go to my brothers and say to them, 'I am ascending to my Father and your Father, to my God and your God.'" Mary Magdalene went and announced to the disciples, "I have seen the Lord"; and she told them that he had said these things to her.

1 Cor. 15:5–8   . . . and that he appeared to Cephas, then to the twelve. Then he appeared to more than five hundred brothers and sisters at one time, most of whom are still alive, though some have died. Then he appeared to James, then to all the apostles. Last of all, as to one untimely born, he appeared also to me.

John 20:27   Then he said to Thomas, "Put your finger here and see my hands. Reach out your hand and put it in my side. Do not doubt but believe."

Question 36. What do you affirm when you say that "he ascended into heaven and is seated at the right hand of the Father"?

First, that Christ has gone to be with his loving Father so that he is now hidden except to the eyes of faith. Second, however, that he is not cut off from us but is present here and now by grace. He reigns with divine authority, protecting us, guiding us, and interceding for us until he returns in glory.

Acts 1:6–11   So when they had come together, they asked him, "Lord, is this the time when you will restore the kingdom to Israel?" He replied, "It is not for you to know the times or periods that the Father has set by his own author- ity. But you will receive power when the Holy Spirit has come upon you; and you will be my witnesses in Jerusalem, in all Judea and Samaria, and to the ends of the earth." When he had said this, as they were watching, he was lifted up, and a cloud took him out of their sight. While he was going and they were gazing up toward heaven, suddenly two men in white robes stood by them. They said, "Men of Galilee, why do you stand looking up toward heaven? This Jesus, who has been taken up from you into heaven, will come in the same way as you saw him go into heaven."

Col. 3:1   So if you have been raised with Christ, seek the things that are above, where Christ is, seated at the right hand of God.

Question 37. How do you understand the words that "he will come again to judge the living and the dead"?

Like everyone else, I too must stand in fear and trembling before the judgment seat of Christ. But the Judge is the one who submitted to judgment for my sake. Nothing will be able to separate me from the love of God in Christ Jesus my Lord.

2 Cor. 5:10   For all of us must appear before the judgment seat of Christ, so that each may receive recompense for what has been done in the body, whether good or evil.

Eccl. 12:14   For God will bring every deed into judgment, including every secret thing, whether good or evil.

Acts 17:31 . . . because he has fixed a day on which he will have the world judged in righteousness by a man whom he has appointed, and of this he has given assurance to all by raising him from the dead.

Rom. 8:38–39 For I am convinced that neither death, not life, nor angels, nor rulers, nor things present, nor things to come, nor powers, nor height, nor depth, nor anything else in all creation, will be able to separate us from the love of God in Christ Jesus our Lord.

1 John 4:17 Love has been perfected among us in this: that we may have boldness on the day of judgment, because as he is, so are we in this world.

1 Cor. 3:12–15 Now if anyone builds on the foundation with gold, silver, precious stones, wood, hay, straw—the work of each builder will become visible, for the Day will disclose it, because it will be revealed with fire, and the fire will test what sort of work each has done. If what has been built on the foundation survives, the builder will receive a reward. If the work is burned up, the builder will suffer loss; the builder will be saved, but only as through fire.

Acts 10:42 He commanded us to preach to the people and to testify that he is the one ordained by God as judge of the living and the dead.

Question 38. Will all human beings be saved?

No one will be lost who can be saved. The limits to salvation, whatever they may be, are known only to God. Three truths above all are certain. God is a holy God who is not to be trifled with. No one will be saved except by grace alone. And no judge could possibly be more gracious than our Lord and Savior, Jesus Christ.

Heb. 10:31 It is a fearful thing to fall into the hands of the living God.

Rom. 11:32 For God has imprisoned all in disobedience so that he may be merciful to all.

Luke 15:4–7 Which one of you, having a hundred sheep and losing one of them, does not leave the ninety-nine in the wilderness and go after the one that is lost until he finds it? When he has found it, he lays it on his shoulders and rejoices. And when he comes home, he calls together his friends and neighbors, saying to them, "Rejoice with me, for I have found my sheep that was lost." Just so, I tell you, there will be more joy in heaven over one sinner who repents than over ninety-nine righteous persons who need no repentance.

Eph. 2:8 For by grace you have been saved through faith, and this is not your own doing; it is the gift of God. . . .

1 Tim. 2:3–4 This is right and is acceptable in the sight of God our Savior, who desires everyone to be saved and to come to the knowledge of the truth.

John 3:17–18 Indeed, God did not send the Son into the world to condemn the world, but in order that the world might be saved through him. Those who believe in him are not condemned; but those who do not believe are condemned already, because they have not believed in the name of the only Son of God.

Ezek. 18:32 For I have no pleasure in the death of anyone, says the Lord GOD. Turn, then, and live.

2 Cor. 5:14–15   For the love of Christ urges us on, because we are convinced that one has died for all; therefore all have died. And he died for all, so that those who live might live no longer for themselves, but for him who died and was raised for them.

Question 39. How should I treat non-Christians and people of other religions?

I should meet friendship with friendship, hostility with kindness, generosity with gratitude, persecution with forbearance, truth with agreement, and error with truth. I should express my faith by word and by deed. I should avoid compromising the truth on the one hand and being narrow-minded on the other. In short, I should welcome and accept these others in a way that honors and reflects the Lord's welcome and acceptance of me.

Rom. 15:7   Welcome one another, therefore, just as Christ has welcomed you, for the glory of God.

Luke 6:37   Do not judge, and you will not be judged; do not condemn, and you will not be condemned. Forgive, and you will be forgiven.

Matt. 5:44   But I say to you, Love your enemies and pray for those who persecute you. . . .

Eph. 4:25   So then, putting away falsehood, let all of us speak the truth to our neighbors, for we are members of one another.

Acts 13:47   For so the Lord has commanded us, saying, "I have set you to be a light for the Gentiles, so that you may bring salvation to the ends of the earth."

Rom. 12:21   Do not be overcome by evil, but overcome evil with good.

Rom. 13:10   Love does no wrong to a neighbor; therefore, love is the fulfilling of the law.

Question 40. How will God deal with the followers of other religions?

God offers salvation to all human beings through Jesus Christ. How God will deal with those who do not know or follow Christ, but who follow another tradition, we cannot finally say. We can say, however, that God is gracious and merciful, and that God will not deal with people in any other way than we see in Jesus Christ, who came as the Savior of the world.

Rev. 7:9   After this I looked, and there was a great multitude that no one could count, from every nation, from all tribes and peoples and languages, standing before the throne and before the Lamb, robed in white, with palm branches in their hands.

Ps. 103:8   The LORD is merciful and gracious, slow to anger and abounding in steadfast love.

John 3:19   And this is the judgment, that the light has come into the world, and people loved darkness rather than light because their deeds were evil.

Titus 2:11   For the grace of God has appeared, bringing salvation to all. . . .

Question 41. Is Christianity the only true religion?

By the grace of God, Christianity offers the truth of the gospel. Although other religions may contain various truths, no other can or does affirm the name of Jesus Christ as the hope of the world.

Matt. 7:3   Why do you see the speck in your neighbor's eye, but do not notice the log in your own eye?

James 1:26   If any think they are religious, and do not bridle their tongues but deceive their hearts, their religion is worthless.

James 1:27   Religion that is pure and undefiled before God, the Father, is this: to care for orphans and widows in their distress, and to keep oneself unstained by the world.

Acts 4:12   There is salvation in no one else, for there is no other name under heaven given among mortals by which we must be saved.

John 14:6   Jesus said to him, "I am the way, and the truth, and the life. No one comes to the Father except through me."

Rom. 1:16   For I am not ashamed of the gospel; it is the power of God for salvation to everyone who has faith, to the Jew first and also to the Greek.

2 Cor. 4:7   But we have this treasure in clay jars, so that it may be made clear that this extraordinary power belongs to God and does not come from us.

Question 42. What is the third article of the Apostles' Creed?

"I believe in the Holy Spirit, the holy catholic church, the communion of saints, the forgiveness of sins, the resurrection of the body, and the life everlasting. Amen."

Question 43. What do you believe when you confess your faith in the Holy Spirit?

The Holy Spirit is the divine person who enables us to love, know, and serve Jesus Christ.

John 14:26   But the Advocate, the Holy Spirit, whom the Father will send in my name, will teach you everything, and remind you of all that I have said to you.

1 Cor. 12:3   Therefore I want you to understand that no one speaking by the Spirit of God ever says "Let Jesus be cursed!" and no one can say "Jesus is Lord" except by the Holy Spirit.

Rom. 5:5   . . . and hope does not disappoint us, because God's love has been poured into our hearts through the Holy Spirit that has been given to us.

1 Cor. 6:17, 19   But anyone united to the Lord becomes one spirit with him. . . . Or do you not know that your body is a temple of the Holy Spirit within you, which you have from God, and that you are not your own?

1 Cor. 3:16   Do you not know that you are God's temple and that God's Spirit dwells in you?

John 4:24   God is spirit, and those who worship him must worship in spirit and truth.

Question 44. How do we receive the Holy Spirit?

By receiving the Word of God. The Spirit arrives with the Word, brings us to rebirth, and assures us of eternal life. The Spirit nurtures, corrects, and strengthens us with the truth of the Word.

Eph. 6:17   Take the helmet of salvation, and the sword of the Spirit, which is the word of God.

John 14:16–17   And I will ask the Father, and he will give you another Advocate, to be with you forever. This is the Spirit of truth, whom the world cannot receive, because it neither sees him nor knows him. You know him, because he abides with you, and he will be in you.

John 3:5–6   Jesus answered, "Very truly, I tell you, no one can enter the kingdom of God without being born of water and Spirit. What is born of the flesh is flesh, and what is born of the Spirit is spirit."

Luke 11:13   If you then, who are evil, know how to give good gifts to your children, how much more will the heavenly Father give the Holy Spirit to those who ask him!

1 Thess. 1:5   . . . because our message of the gospel came to you not in word only, but also in power and in the Holy Spirit and with full conviction; just as you know what kind of persons we proved to be among you for your sake.

John 16:8   And when he comes, he will prove the world wrong about sin and righteousness and judgment. . . .

Rom. 8:15–16   For you did not receive a spirit of slavery to fall back into fear, but you have received a spirit of adoption. When we cry, "Abba! Father!" it is that very Spirit bearing witness with our spirit that we are children of God. . . .

1 Peter 2:2   Like newborn infants, long for the pure, spiritual milk, so that by it you may grow into salvation. . . .

Question 45. What do you mean when you speak of "the Word of God"?

"Jesus Christ, as he is attested for us in Holy Scripture, is the one Word of God which we have to hear and which we have to trust and obey in life and in death" (Barmen Declaration, Article I).

John 1:1–5   In the beginning was the Word, and the Word was with God, and the Word was God. He was in the beginning with God. All things came into being through him, and without him not one thing came into being. What has come into being in him was life, and the life was the light of all people. The light shines in the darkness, and the darkness did not overcome it.

John 1:14   And the Word became flesh and lived among us, and we have seen his glory, the glory as of a father's only son, full of grace and truth.

Question 46. Isn't Holy Scripture also the Word of God?

Yes. Holy Scripture is also God's Word because of its focus, its function, and its founder. Its central focus is Jesus Christ, the living Word. Its basic function is to deepen our love, knowledge, and service of him as our Savior and Lord. And its dependable founder is the Holy Spirit, who spoke through the prophets and apostles, and who inspires us with eager desire for the truths that Scripture contains.

2 Tim. 3:16   All scripture is inspired by God and is useful for teaching, for reproof, for correction, and for training in righteousness. . . .

John 5:39   You search the scriptures because you think that in them you have eternal life; and it is they that testify on my behalf.

Question 47. Isn't preaching also the Word of God?

Yes. Preaching is God's Word when it is faithful to the witness of Holy Scripture. Faith comes by hearing God's Word in the form of faithful preaching and teaching.

> *Mark 16:15*   And he said to them, "Go into all the world and proclaim the good news to the whole creation."
>
> *2 Cor. 4:5*   For we do not proclaim ourselves; we proclaim Jesus Christ as Lord and ourselves as your slaves for Jesus' sake.
>
> *Rom. 1:15–16*   . . . hence my eagerness to proclaim the gospel to you also who are in Rome. For I am not ashamed of the gospel; it is the power of God for salvation to everyone who has faith, to the Jew first and also to the Greek.
>
> *Rom. 10:17*   So faith comes from what is heard, and what is heard comes through the word of Christ.

Question 48. What do you affirm when you speak of "the holy catholic church"?

The church is the community of all faithful people who have given their lives to Jesus Christ with thanksgiving. The church is holy because he is holy, and universal (or "catholic") in significance because he is universal in significance. Despite all its remaining imperfections here and now, the church is called to become ever more holy and catholic, for that is what it already is in Christ.

> *Gal. 2:20*   It is no longer I who live, but it is Christ who lives in me. And the life I now live in the flesh I live by faith in the Son of God, who loved me and gave himself for me.
>
> *1 Cor. 1:2*   To the church of God that is in Corinth, to those who are sanctified in Christ Jesus, called to be saints, together with all those who in every place call on the name of our Lord Jesus Christ, both their Lord and ours. . . .
>
> *Lev. 11:44*   For I am the LORD your God; sanctify yourselves therefore, and be holy, for I am holy.
>
> *1 Peter 1:15–16*   Instead, as he who called you is holy, be holy yourselves in all your conduct; for it is written, "You shall be holy, for I am holy."
>
> *Rev. 5:9*   They sing a new song: "You are worthy to take the scroll and to open its seals, for you were slaughtered and by your blood you ransomed for God saints from every tribe and language and people and nation. . . ."

Question 49. What is the mission of the church?

The mission of the church is to bear witness to God's love for the world in Jesus Christ.

> *Acts 1:8*   But you will receive power when the Holy Spirit has come upon you; and you will be my witnesses in Jerusalem, in all Judea and Samaria, and to the ends of the earth.
>
> *John 15:26–27*   When the Advocate comes, whom I will send to you from the Father, the Spirit of truth who comes from the Father, he will testify on my behalf. You also are to testify because you have been with me from the beginning.

Eph. 3:8–10   Although I am the very least of all the saints, this grace was given to me to bring to the Gentiles the news of the boundless riches of Christ, and to make everyone see what is the plan of the mystery hidden for ages in God who created all things; so that through the church the wisdom of God in its rich variety might now be made known to the rulers and authorities in the heavenly places.

Question 50. What forms does this mission take?

The church's mission takes a wide variety of forms, including evangelism, work for social justice, and ministries of care. Yet the center is always the same: Jesus Christ. In every case the church extends mercy and forgiveness to the needy in a way that points finally to him.

Luke 10:37   He said, "The one who showed him mercy." Jesus said to him, "Go and do likewise."

Eph. 4:32   Be kind to one another, tenderhearted, forgiving one another, as God in Christ has forgiven you.

Deut. 15:11   Since there will never cease to be some in need on the earth, I therefore command you, "Open your hand to the poor and needy neighbor in your land."

Acts 4:34   There was not a needy person among them, for as many as owned lands or houses sold them and brought the proceeds of what was sold.

Question 51. Who are the needy?

The hungry need bread, the homeless need a roof, the oppressed need justice, and the lonely need fellowship. At the same time—on another and deeper level—the hopeless need hope, sinners need forgiveness, and the world needs the gospel. On this level no one is excluded, and all the needy are one. Our mission as the church is to bring hope to a desperate world by declaring God's undying love—as one beggar tells another where to find bread.

Ps. 10:12   Rise up, O LORD; O God, lift up your hand; do not forget the oppressed.

Matt. 25:37–40   Then the righteous will answer him, "Lord, when was it that we saw you hungry and gave you food, or thirsty and gave you something to drink? And when was it that we saw you a stranger and welcomed you, or naked and gave you clothing? And when was it that we saw you sick or in prison and visited you?" And the king will answer them, "Truly I tell you, just as you did it to one of the least of these who are members of my family, you did it to me."

Jer. 9:23   Thus says the LORD: Do not let the wise boast in their wisdom, do not let the mighty boast in their might, do not let the wealthy boast in their wealth. . . ."

1 Cor. 9:16   If I proclaim the gospel, this gives me no ground for boasting, for an obligation is laid on me, and woe to me if I do not proclaim the gospel!

Eph. 6:19   Pray also for me, so that when I speak, a message may be given to me to make known with boldness the mystery of the gospel. . . .

Question 52. What do you affirm when you speak of "the communion of saints"?

All those who live in union with Christ, whether on earth or with God in heaven, are "saints." Our communion with Christ makes us members one of another. The ties that bind us in Christ are deeper than any other human relationship.

Eph. 2:19–20   So then you are no longer strangers and aliens, but you are citizens with the saints and also members of the household of God, built upon the foundation of the apostles and prophets, with Christ Jesus himself as the cornerstone.

Rom. 12:5   . . . so we, who are many, are one body in Christ, and individually we are members one of another.

Eph. 2:14   For he is our peace; in his flesh he has made both groups into one and has broken down the dividing wall, that is, the hostility between us.

1 Cor. 12:27   Now you are the body of Christ and individually members of it.

Gal. 3:28   There is no longer Jew or Greek, there is no longer slave or free, there is no longer male and female; for all of you are one in Christ Jesus.

Eph. 4:4   There is one body and one Spirit, just as you were called to the one hope of your calling. . . .

1 Cor. 12:4–7, 12–13   Now there are varieties of gifts, but the same Spirit; and there are varieties of services, but the same Lord; and there are varieties of activities, but it is the same God who activates all of them in everyone. To each is given the manifestation of the Spirit for the common good. . . . For just as the body is one and has many members, and all the members of the body, though many, are one body, so it is with Christ. For in the one Spirit we were all baptized into one body—Jews or Greeks, slaves or free—and we were all made to drink of one Spirit.

Question 53. How do you enter into communion with Christ and so with one another?

By the power of the Holy Spirit as it works through Word and Sacrament. The Scriptures acknowledge two sacraments as instituted by our Lord Jesus Christ—baptism and the Lord's Supper.

1 Cor. 10:17   Because there is one bread, we who are many are one body, for we all partake of the one bread.

1 Cor. 12:13   For in the one Spirit we were all baptized into one body—Jews or Greeks, slaves or free—and we were all made to drink of one Spirit.

Col. 3:16   Let the word of Christ dwell in you richly; teach and admonish one another in all wisdom; and with gratitude in your hearts sing psalms, hymns, and spiritual songs to God.

Question 54. What is a sacrament?

A sacrament is a special act of Christian worship, instituted by Christ, which uses a visible sign to proclaim the promise of the gospel for the forgiveness of sins and eternal life. In baptism the sign is that of water; in the Lord's Supper, that of bread and wine.

Mark 1:9–11   In those days Jesus came from Nazareth of Galilee and was baptized by John in the Jordan. And just as he was coming up out of the water, he saw the heavens torn apart and the Spirit descending like a dove on him. And a voice came from heaven, "You are my Son, the Beloved; with you I am well pleased."

Mark 14:22–25   While they were eating, he took a loaf of bread, and after blessing it he broke it, gave it to them, and said, "Take; this is my body." Then he took a cup, and after giving thanks he gave it to them, and all of them drank from it. He said to them, "This is my blood of the covenant, which is poured out for many. Truly I tell you, I will never again drink of the fruit of the vine until that day when I drink it new in the kingdom of God."

Question 55. What is baptism?

Baptism is the sign and seal through which we are joined to Christ.

Rom. 6:3–4   Do you not know that all of us who have been baptized into Christ Jesus were baptized into his death? Therefore we have been buried with him by baptism into death, so that, just as Christ was raised from the dead by the glory of the Father, so we too might walk in newness of life.

Gal. 3:27   As many of you as were baptized into Christ have clothed yourselves with Christ.

Rom. 4:11   He received the sign of circumcision as a seal of the righteousness that he had by faith while he was still uncircumcised. The purpose was to make him the ancestor of all who believe without being circumcised and who thus have righteousness reckoned to them. . . .

Question 56. What does it mean to be baptized?

My baptism means that I am joined to Jesus Christ forever. As I am baptized with water, he baptizes me with his Spirit, washing away all my sins and freeing me from their control. My baptism is a sign that one day I will rise with him in glory, and may walk with him even now in newness of life.

Col. 2:12   When you were buried with him in baptism, you were also raised with him through faith in the power of God, who raised him from the dead.

Mark 1:8   I have baptized you with water; but he will baptize you with the Holy Spirit.

1 Cor. 6:11   And this is what some of you used to be. But you were washed, you were sanctified, you were justified in the name of the Lord Jesus Christ and in the Spirit of our God.

Eph. 4:4–6   There is one body and one Spirit, just as you were called to the one hope of your calling, one Lord, one faith, one baptism, one God and Father of all, who is above all and through all and in all.

Question 57. Are infants also to be baptized?

Yes. Along with their believing parents, they are included in the great hope of the gospel and belong to the people of God. Forgiveness and faith are both promised to them through Christ's covenant with his people.

Gen. 17:7   I will establish my covenant between me and you, and your off-spring after you throughout their generations, for an everlasting covenant, to be God to you and to your offspring after you.

Acts 2:38–39   Peter said to them, "Repent, and be baptized every one of you in the name of Jesus Christ so that your sins may be forgiven; and you will receive the gift of the Holy Spirit. For the promise is for you, for your children, and for all who are far away, everyone whom the Lord our God calls to him."

Acts 16:15   When she and her household were baptized, she urged us, say-ing, "If you have judged me to be faithful to the Lord, come and stay at my home." And she prevailed upon us.

Acts 16:33   At the same hour of the night he took them and washed their wounds; then he and his entire family were baptized without delay.

Acts 18:8   Crispus, the official of the synagogue, became a believer in the Lord, together with all his household; and many of the Corinthians who heard Paul became believers and were baptized.

Question 58. Why are you baptized in the name of the Father, and of the Son, and of the Holy Spirit?

Because of the command Jesus gave his disciples. After he was raised from the dead, he appeared to them and said, "Go therefore and make disciples of all nations, baptizing them in the name of the Father and of the Son and of the Holy Spirit" (Matt. 28:19).

Matt. 28:16–20   Now the eleven disciples went to Galilee, to the mountain to which Jesus had directed them. When they saw him, they worshiped him; but some doubted. And Jesus came and said to them, "All authority in heaven and on earth has been given to me. Go therefore and make disciples of all nations, baptizing them in the name of the Father and of the Son and of the Holy Spirit, and teaching them to obey everything that I have commanded you. And remember, I am with you always, to the end of the age."

Matt. 3:16–17   And when Jesus had been baptized, just as he came up from the water, suddenly the heavens were opened to him and he saw the Spirit of God descending like a dove and alighting on him. And a voice from heaven said, "This is my Son, the Beloved, with whom I am well pleased."

1 Peter 1:2   [To those] who have been chosen and destined by God the Father and sanctified by the Spirit to be obedient to Jesus Christ and to be sprinkled with his blood: May grace and peace be yours in abundance.

1 Cor. 12:4–6   Now there are varieties of gifts, but the same Spirit; and there are varieties of services, but the same Lord; and there are varieties of activi-ties, but it is the same God who activates all of them in everyone.

Question 59. What is the meaning of this name?

It is the name of the Holy Trinity. The Father is God, the Son is God, and the Holy Spirit is God. And yet they are not three gods, but one God in three persons. We worship God in this mystery.

2 Cor. 13:13   The grace of the Lord Jesus Christ, the love of God, and the communion of the Holy Spirit be with all of you.

John 1:1–4   In the beginning was the Word, and the Word was with God, and the Word was God. He was in the beginning with God. All things came into being through him, and without him not one thing came into being. What has come into being in him was life, and the life was the light of all people.

Rom. 8:11   If the Spirit of him who raised Jesus from the dead dwells in you, he who raised Christ from the dead will give life to your mortal bodies also through his Spirit that dwells in you.

John 16:13–15   When the Spirit of truth comes, he will guide you into all the truth; for he will not speak on his own, but will speak whatever he hears, and he will declare to you the things that are to come. He will glorify me, because he will take what is mine and declare it to you. All that the Father has is mine. For this reason I said that he will take what is mine and declare it to you.

Question 60. What is the Lord's Supper?

The Lord's Supper is the sign and seal by which our communion with Christ is renewed.

1 Cor. 10:16   The cup of blessing that we bless, is it not a sharing in the blood of Christ? The bread that we break, is it not a sharing in the body of Christ?

Question 61. What does it mean to share in the Lord's Supper?

When we celebrate the Lord's Supper, the Lord Jesus Christ is truly present, pouring out his Spirit upon us. By his Spirit, the bread that we break and the cup that we bless share in his body and blood. As I receive the bread and the cup, remembering that Christ died even for me, I feed on him in my heart by faith with thanksgiving. His life becomes mine, and my life becomes his, to all eternity.

1 Cor. 11:23–26   For I received from the Lord what I also handed on to you, that the Lord Jesus on the night when he was betrayed took a loaf of bread, and when he had given thanks, he broke it and said, "This is my body that is for you. Do this in remembrance of me." In the same way he took the cup also, after supper, saying, "This cup is the new covenant in my blood. Do this, as often as you drink it, in remembrance of me." For as often as you eat this bread and drink the cup, you proclaim the Lord's death until he comes.

Mark 14:22–25   While they were eating, he took a loaf of bread, and after blessing it he broke it, gave it to them, and said, "Take; this is my body." Then he took a cup, and after giving thanks he gave it to them, and all of them drank from it. He said to them, "This is my blood of the covenant, which is poured out for many. Truly I tell you, I will never again drink of the fruit of the vine until that day when I drink it new in the kingdom of God."

Question 62. What do you mean when you speak of "the forgiveness of sins"?

Because of Jesus Christ, God no longer holds my sins against me. Christ alone is my righteousness and my life. Grace alone is the basis on which God has forgiven me in him. Faith alone is the means by which I receive Christ into my heart, and with him the forgiveness that makes me whole.

1 Cor. 1:30   He is the source of your life in Christ Jesus, who became for us wisdom from God, and righteousness and sanctification and redemption. . . .

1 Tim. 1:1   Paul, an apostle of Christ Jesus by the command of God our Savior and of Christ Jesus our hope . . .

Rom. 11:6   But if it is by grace, it is no longer on the basis of works, otherwise grace would no longer be grace.

Eph. 2:8   For by grace you have been saved through faith, and this is not your own doing; it is the gift of God. . . .

Rom. 5:15   But the free gift is not like the trespass. For if the many died through the one man's trespass, much more surely have the grace of God and the free gift in the grace of the one man, Jesus Christ, abounded for the many.

Rom. 4:16   For this reason it depends on faith, in order that the promise may rest on grace and be guaranteed to all his descendants, not only to the adherents of the law but also to those who share the faith of Abraham (for he is the father of all of us). . . .

Rom. 3:28   For we hold that a person is justified by faith apart from works prescribed by the law.

Question 63. Does forgiveness mean that God excuses sin?

No. God does not cease to be God. Although God is merciful to the sinner, God does not excuse the evil of sin. For to forgive is not to excuse.

Hab. 1:13   Your eyes are too pure to behold evil, and you cannot look on wrongdoing; why do you look on the treacherous, and are silent when the wicked swallow those more righteous than they?

Isa. 59:15   Truth is lacking, and whoever turns from evil is despoiled. The LORD saw it, and it displeased him that there was no justice.

Heb. 9:22   Indeed, under the law almost everything is purified with blood, and without the shedding of blood there is no forgiveness of sins.

Rom. 5:8–10   But God proves his love for us in that while we still were sinners Christ died for us. Much more surely then, now that we have been justified by his blood, will we be saved through him from the wrath of God. For if while we were enemies, we were reconciled to God through the death of his Son, much more surely, having been reconciled, will we be saved by his life.

1 Chron. 16:33   Then shall the trees of the forest sing for joy before the LORD, for he comes to judge the earth.

Question 64. Does your forgiveness of those who have harmed you depend on their repentance?

No. I am to forgive as I have been forgiven. Just as God's forgiveness of me does not depend on my first confessing and repenting of my sins, so my forgiveness of those who harm me does not depend on their doing so. However, when I forgive the person who has harmed me, I do not deny or excuse the harm that was done.

Col. 3:13   Bear with one another and, if anyone has a complaint against another, forgive each other; just as the Lord has forgiven you, so you also must forgive.

Mark 11:25 Whenever you stand praying, forgive, if you have anything against anyone; so that your Father in heaven may also forgive you your trespasses.

Col. 2:13 And when you were dead in trespasses and the uncircumcision of your flesh, God made you alive together with him, when he forgave us all our trespasses. . . .

Matt. 18:21–22 Then Peter came and said to him, "Lord, if another member of the church sins against me, how often should I forgive? As many as seven times?" Jesus said to him, "Not seven times, but, I tell you, seventy-seven times."

Heb. 12:14 Pursue peace with everyone, and the holiness without which no one will see the Lord.

Question 65. What do you mean when you speak of "the resurrection of the body"?

Because Christ lives, we will live also. Death is not the end of human life. The whole person, body and soul, will be raised from death to eternal life with God.

John 14:19 In a little while the world will no longer see me, but you will see me; because I live, you also will live.

John 11:25 Jesus said to her, "I am the resurrection and the life. Those who believe in me, even though they die, will live. . . ."

Rom. 6:5 For if we have been united with him in a death like his, we will certainly be united with him in a resurrection like his.

1 Cor. 15:21 For since death came through a human being, the resurrection of the dead has also come through a human being. . . .

1 Cor. 15:42 So it is with the resurrection of the dead. What is sown is perishable, what is raised is imperishable.

Col. 1:18 He is the head of the body, the church; he is the beginning, the firstborn from the dead, so that he might come to have first place in everything.

Question 66. What do you affirm when you speak of "the life everlasting"?

God does not will to be God without us, but instead grants to us creatures—fallen and mortal as we are—eternal life. Communion with Jesus Christ is eternal life itself.

John 3:16 For God so loved the world that he gave his only Son, so that everyone who believes in him may not perish but may have eternal life.

John 6:54 Those who eat my flesh and drink my blood have eternal life, and I will raise them up on the last day. . . .

John 17:3 And this is eternal life, that they may know you, the only true God, and Jesus Christ whom you have sent.

Rom. 6:22 But now that you have been freed from sin and enslaved to God, the advantage you get is sanctification. The end is eternal life.

Rom. 6:23 For the wages of sin is death, but the free gift of God is eternal life in Christ Jesus our Lord.

1 John 2:25 And this is what he has promised us, eternal life.

Matt. 25:34   Then the king will say to those at his right hand, "Come, you that are blessed by my Father, inherit the kingdom prepared for you from the foundation of the world. . . ."

Question 67. Won't heaven be a boring place?

No. Heaven is our true home, a world of love. There we shall at last see face to face what we now only glimpse as through a distant mirror. Our deepest, truest delights in this life are only a dim foreshadowing of the delights that await us in heaven.

John 14:2–3   In my Father's house there are many dwelling places. If it were not so, would I have told you that I go to prepare a place for you? And if I go and prepare a place for you, I will come again and will take you to myself, so that where I am, there you may be also.

Matt. 6:20   But store up for yourselves treasures in heaven, where neither moth nor rust consumes and where thieves do not break in and steal.

Matt. 8:11   I tell you, many will come from east and west and will eat with Abraham and Isaac and Jacob in the kingdom of heaven. . . .

Col. 1:5   . . . because of the hope laid up for you in heaven. You have heard of this hope before in the word of the truth, the gospel. . . .

1 Cor. 13:12   For now we see in a mirror, dimly, but then we will see face to face. Now I know only in part; then I will know fully, even as I have been fully known.

II. The Ten Commandments

Question 68. What are the Ten Commandments?

The Ten Commandments give a summary of God's law for our lives. They teach us how to live rightly with God and one another.

Deut. 10:4   Then he wrote on the tablets the same words as before, the ten commandments that the LORD had spoken to you on the mountain out of the fire on the day of the assembly; and the LORD gave them to me.

Matt. 19:17   And he said to him, "Why do you ask me about what is good? There is only one who is good. If you wish to enter into life, keep the commandments."

Question 69. Why should you obey this law?

Not to win God's love, for God already loves me. Not to earn my salvation, for Christ has earned it for me. Not to avoid being punished, for then I would obey out of fear. With gladness in my heart I should obey God's law out of gratitude, for God has blessed me by it and given it for my well-being.

Ps. 118:1   O give thanks to the LORD, for he is good; his steadfast love endures forever!

Col. 3:17   And whatever you do, in word or deed, do everything in the name of the Lord Jesus, giving thanks to God the Father through him.

Question 70. What is the first commandment?

You shall have no other gods before me (Ex. 20:3; Deut. 5:7).

> *Deut. 26:17* Today you have obtained the LORD's agreement: to be your God; and for you to walk in his ways, to keep his statutes, his commandments, and his ordinances, and to obey him.

> *Matt. 4:10* Jesus said to him, "Away with you, Satan! for it is written, 'Worship the Lord your God, and serve only him.'"

Question 71. What do you learn from this commandment?

No loyalty comes before my loyalty to God. I should worship and serve only God, expect all good from God alone, and love, fear, and honor God with all my heart.

> *Matt. 6:24* No one can serve two masters; for a slave will either hate the one and love the other, or be devoted to the one and despise the other. You cannot serve God and wealth.

> *Deut. 6:5* You shall love the LORD your God with all your heart, and with all your soul, and with all your might.

> *Prov. 9:10* The fear of the LORD is the beginning of wisdom, and the knowledge of the Holy One is insight.

> *Matt. 10:37* Whoever loves father or mother more than me is not worthy of me; and whoever loves son or daughter more than me is not worthy of me. . . .

Question 72. What is the second commandment?

You shall not make for yourself an idol (Ex. 20:4; Deut. 5:8).

Question 73. What do you learn from this commandment?

First, when I treat anything other than God as though it were God, I make it an idol. Second, when I assume that my own interests are more important than anything else, I make them into idols, and in effect I also make an idol of myself.

> *Deut. 6:14* Do not follow other gods, any of the gods of the peoples who are all around you. . . .

> *1 John 5:21* Little children, keep yourselves from idols.

> *Ex. 34:14* For you shall worship no other god, because the LORD, whose name is Jealous, is a jealous God.

> *1 Chron. 16:26* For all the gods of the peoples are idols, but the LORD made the heavens.

> *Rom. 1:22–23* Claiming to be wise, they became fools; and they exchanged the glory of the immortal God for images resembling a mortal human being or birds or four-footed animals or reptiles.

> *Phil. 2:4* Let each of you look not to your own interests, but to the interests of others.

Question 74. What is the third commandment?

You shall not make wrongful use of the name of the Lord your God (Ex. 20:7; Deut. 5:11).

Question 75. What do you learn from this commandment?

I should use God's name with reverence and awe. God's name is holy and deserves the highest honor from us. It is insulted when used carelessly, as in a curse or a pious cliché.

Ps. 29:2 Ascribe to the LORD the glory of his name; worship the LORD in holy splendor.

Rev. 15:3–4 And they sing the song of Moses, the servant of God, and the song of the Lamb: "Great and amazing are your deeds, Lord God the Almighty! Just and true are your ways, King of the nations! Lord, who will not fear and glorify your name? For you alone are holy. All nations will come and worship before you, for your judgments have been revealed."

Ps. 138:2 I bow down toward your holy temple and give thanks to your name for your steadfast love and your faithfulness; for you have exalted your name and your word above everything.

Eph. 4:29 Let no evil talk come out of your mouths, but only what is useful for building up, as there is need, so that your words may give grace to those who hear.

Ps. 103:1–2 Bless the LORD, O my soul, and all that is within me, bless his holy name. Bless the LORD, O my soul, and do not forget all his benefits. . . .

Question 76. What is the fourth commandment?

Remember the Sabbath day, and keep it holy (Ex. 20:8; Deut. 5:12).

Question 77. What do you learn from this commandment?

God requires a special day to be set apart so that worship can be at the center of my life. It is right to honor God with thanks and praise, and to hear and receive God's Word.

Rom. 10:8 But what does it say? "The word is near you, on your lips and in your heart" (that is, the word of faith that we proclaim). . . .

Deut. 5:12 Observe the sabbath day and keep it holy, as the LORD your God commanded you.

Gen. 2:3 So God blessed the seventh day and hallowed it, because on it God rested from all the work that he had done in creation.

Lev. 23:3 Six days shall work be done; but the seventh day is a sabbath of complete rest, a holy convocation; you shall do no work: it is a sabbath to the LORD throughout your settlements.

Acts 2:42, 46 They devoted themselves to the apostles' teaching and fellowship, to the breaking of bread and the prayers. . . . Day by day, as they spent much time together in the temple, they broke bread at home and ate their food with glad and generous hearts. . . .

Question 78. What is the best summary of the first four commandments?

These teach me how to live rightly with God. Jesus summed them up with the commandment he called the first and greatest: You shall love the Lord your God with all your heart, and with all your soul, and with all your mind (Matt. 22:37; Deut. 6:5).

Question 79. What is the fifth commandment?

Honor your father and your mother (Ex. 20:12; Deut. 5:16).

Question 80. What do you learn from this commandment?

Though I owe reverence to God alone, I owe genuine respect to my parents, both my mother and father. God wills me to listen to them, be thankful for the benefits I receive from them, and be considerate of their needs, especially in old age.

Eph. 5:21   Be subject to one another out of reverence for Christ.

Rom. 12:10   Love one another with mutual affection; outdo one another in showing honor.

Eph. 6:2   "Honor your father and mother"—this is the first commandment with a promise. . . .

Prov. 1:8   Hear, my child, your father's instruction, and do not reject your mother's teaching. . . .

Lev. 19:32   You shall rise before the aged, and defer to the old; and you shall fear your God: I am the LORD.

Luke 2:51   Then he went down with them and came to Nazareth, and was obedient to them. His mother treasured all these things in her heart.

Question 81. Are there limits to your obligation to obey them?

Yes. No mere human being is God. Blind obedience is not required, for everything should be tested by loyalty and obedience to God.

1 Peter 2:17   Honor everyone. Love the family of believers. Fear God. Honor the emperor.

Acts 5:29   But Peter and the apostles answered, "We must obey God rather than any human authority."

Question 82. What is the sixth commandment?

You shall not murder (Ex. 20:13; Deut. 5:17).

Question 83. What do you learn from this commandment?

God forbids anything that harms my neighbor unfairly. Murder or injury can be done not only by direct violence but also by an angry word or a clever plan, and not only by an individual but also by unjust social institutions. I should honor every human being, including my enemy, as a person made in God's image.

1 John 3:15   All who hate a brother or sister are murderers, and you know that murderers do not have eternal life abiding in them.

Prov. 24:17   Do not rejoice when your enemies fall, and do not let your heart be glad when they stumble. . . .

Rom. 12:19–20   Beloved, never avenge yourselves, but leave room for the wrath of God; for it is written, "Vengeance is mine, I will repay, says the Lord." No, "if your enemies are hungry, feed them; if they are thirsty, give them something to drink; for by doing this you will heap burning coals on their heads."

Col. 3:12–13   As God's chosen ones, holy and beloved, clothe yourselves with compassion, kindness, humility, meekness, and patience. Bear with one another and, if anyone has a complaint against another, forgive each other; just as the Lord has forgiven you, so you also must forgive.

Matt. 5:21–22   You have heard that it was said to those of ancient times, "You shall not murder"; and "whoever murders shall be liable to judgment." But I say to you that if you are angry with a brother or sister, you will be liable to judgment; and if you insult a brother or sister, you will be liable to the council; and if you say, "You fool," you will be liable to the hell of fire.

Matt. 26:52   Then Jesus said to him, "Put your sword back into its place; for all who take the sword will perish by the sword."

Question 84. What is the seventh commandment?

You shall not commit adultery (Ex. 20:14; Deut. 5:18).

Question 85. What do you learn from this commandment?

God requires fidelity and purity in sexual relations. Since love is God's great gift, God expects me not to corrupt it, or confuse it with momentary desire or the selfish fulfillment of my own pleasures. God forbids all sexual immorality, whether in married or in single life.

Eph. 5:3   But fornication and impurity of any kind, or greed, must not even be mentioned among you, as is proper among saints.

Matt. 5:27–29   You have heard that it was said, "You shall not commit adultery." But I say to you that everyone who looks at a woman with lust has already committed adultery with her in his heart. If your right eye causes you to sin, tear it out and throw it away; it is better for you to lose one of your members than for your whole body to be thrown into hell.

Heb. 13:4   Let marriage be held in honor by all, and let the marriage bed be kept undefiled; for God will judge fornicators and adulterers.

1 Thess. 4:3–4   For this is the will of God, your sanctification: that you abstain from fornication; that each one of you know how to control your own body in holiness and honor. . . .

Question 86. What is the eighth commandment?

You shall not steal (Ex. 20:15; Deut. 5:19).

Question 87. What do you learn from this commandment?

God forbids all theft and robbery, including schemes, tricks, or systems that unjustly take what belongs to someone else. God requires me not to be driven by greed, not to misuse or waste the gifts I have been given, and not to distrust the promise that God will supply my needs.

Job 20:19–20   For they have crushed and abandoned the poor, they have seized a house that they did not build. "They knew no quiet in their bellies; in their greed they let nothing escape."

Jer. 22:13   Woe to him who builds his house by unrighteousness, and his upper rooms by injustice; who makes his neighbors work for nothing, and does not give them their wages. . . .

Prov. 18:9   One who is slack in work is close kin to a vandal.

1 Tim. 6:9–10   But those who want to be rich fall into temptation and are trapped by many senseless and harmful desires that plunge people into ruin and destruction. For the love of money is a root of all kinds of evil, and in their eagerness to be rich some have wandered away from the faith and pierced themselves with many pains.

1 John 3:17   How does God's love abide in anyone who has the world's goods and sees a brother or sister in need and yet refuses help?

Luke 12:15   And he said to them, "Take care! Be on your guard against all kinds of greed; for one's life does not consist in the abundance of possessions."

Phil. 4:19   And my God will fully satisfy every need of yours according to his riches in glory in Christ Jesus.

Question 88. What is the ninth commandment?

You shall not bear false witness against your neighbor (Ex. 20:16; Deut. 5:20).

Question 89. What do you learn from this commandment?

God forbids me to damage the honor or reputation of my neighbor. I should not say false things against anyone for the sake of money, favor, or friendship, for the sake of revenge, or for any other reason. God requires me to speak well of my neighbor when I can, and to view the faults of my neighbor with tolerance when I cannot.

Zech. 8:16–17   These are the things that you shall do: Speak the truth to one another, render in your gates judgments that are true and make for peace, do not devise evil in your hearts against one another, and love no false oath; for all these are things that I hate, says the LORD."

1 Peter 3:16   Keep your conscience clear, so that, when you are maligned, those who abuse you for your good conduct in Christ may be put to shame.

Prov. 14:5   A faithful witness does not lie, but a false witness breathes out lies.

James 4:11   Do not speak evil against one another, brothers and sisters. Whoever speaks evil against another or judges another, speaks evil against the law and judges the law; but if you judge the law, you are not a doer of the law but a judge.

1 Peter 4:8   Above all, maintain constant love for one another, for love covers a multitude of sins.

Question 90. Does this commandment forbid racism and other forms of negative stereotyping?

Yes. In forbidding false witness against my neighbor, God forbids me to be prejudiced against people who belong to any vulnerable, different, or disfavored social group. Jews, women, homosexuals, racial and ethnic minorities, and national enemies are among those who have suffered terribly from being subjected to the slurs of social prejudice.

Rom. 3:13, 15   "Their throats are opened graves; they use their tongues to deceive." "The venom of vipers is under their lips." . . . "Their feet are swift to shed blood."

Prov. 31:8–9 Speak out for those who cannot speak, for the rights of all the destitute. Speak out, judge righteously, defend the rights of the poor and needy.

Matt. 7:1–2 Do not judge, so that you may not be judged. For with the judgment you make you will be judged, and the measure you give will be the measure you get.

Question 91. What is the tenth commandment?

You shall not covet what is your neighbor's (Ex. 20:17; Deut. 5:21).

Question 92. What do you learn from this commandment?

My whole heart should belong to God alone, not to money or the things of this world. "Coveting" means desiring something wrongfully. I should not resent the good fortune or success of my neighbor or allow envy to corrupt my heart.

Heb. 13:5 Keep your lives free from the love of money, and be content with what you have; for he has said, "I will never leave you or forsake you."

Gal. 5:26 Let us not become conceited, competing against one another, envying one another.

Question 93. What is the best summary of the last six commandments?

These teach me how to live rightly with my neighbor. Jesus summed them up with a commandment which is like the greatest one about loving God: You shall love your neighbor as yourself (Matt. 22:39; Lev. 19:18).

Question 94. Can you obey these commandments perfectly?

No. Yet there is more grace in God than sin in me. While I must confess my sins to God and resolve not to commit them, I can be confident that God is forgiving, and will give me the grace to grow in love and knowledge day by day.

Ps. 14:3 They have all gone astray, they are all alike perverse; there is no one who does good, no, not one.

Eph. 2:8 For by grace you have been saved through faith, and this is not your own doing; it is the gift of God . . .

Ps. 130:3–4 If you, O LORD, should mark iniquities, Lord, who could stand? But there is forgiveness with you, so that you may be revered.

Col. 1:13–14 He has rescued us from the power of darkness and transferred us into the kingdom of his beloved Son, in whom we have redemption, the forgiveness of sins.

1 John 1:8 If we say that we have no sin, we deceive ourselves, and the truth is not in us.

III. The Lord's Prayer

Question 95. What is prayer?

Prayer means calling upon God whose Spirit is always present with us. In prayer we approach God with reverence, confidence, and humility. Prayer involves both addressing God in praise, confession, thanksgiving, and supplication, and listening for God's word within our hearts. When we adore God, we are filled with wonder, love, and praise before God's heavenly glory. When we confess our sins to God, we ask for forgiveness with sorry hearts. When we give thanks to God, we acknowledge God's great goodness in all that has been provided for us. Finally, when we call upon God to hear our requests, we affirm that God is always near to us in times of need and sorrow.

Ps. 48:1   Great is the LORD and greatly to be praised in the city of our God.

Ps. 96:8–9   Ascribe to the LORD the glory due his name; bring an offering, and come into his courts. Worship the LORD in holy splendor; tremble before him, all the earth.

James 5:16   Therefore confess your sins to one another, and pray for one another, so that you may be healed. The prayer of the righteous is powerful and effective.

1 John 1:9   If we confess our sins, he who is faithful and just will forgive us our sins and cleanse us from all unrighteousness.

Ps. 107:8   Let them thank the LORD for his steadfast love, for his wonderful works to humankind.

Ps. 75:1   We give thanks to you, O God; we give thanks; your name is near. People tell of your wondrous deeds.

Ps. 50:15   Call on me in the day of trouble; I will deliver you, and you shall glorify me.

Ps. 145:18   The LORD is near to all who call on him, to all who call on him in truth.

Eph. 6:18   Pray in the Spirit at all times in every prayer and supplication. To that end keep alert and always persevere in supplication for all the saints.

Question 96. What is the purpose of prayer?

Prayer brings us into communion with God. The more our lives are rooted in prayer, the more we sense how wonderful God is in grace, purity, majesty, and love. Prayer means offering our lives completely to God, submitting ourselves to God's will, and waiting faithfully for God's grace. Through prayer God frees us from anxiety, equips us for service, and deepens our faith.

Ps. 62:8   Trust in him at all times, O people; pour out your heart before him; God is a refuge for us.

Ps. 139:1   O LORD, you have searched me and known me.

Phil. 4:6   Do not worry about anything, but in everything by prayer and supplication with thanksgiving let your requests be made known to God.

Matt. 7:7–8   Ask, and it will be given you; search, and you will find; knock, and the door will be opened for you. For everyone who asks receives, and everyone who searches finds, and for everyone who knocks, the door will be opened.

Question 97. What prayer serves as our rule or pattern?

Our rule or pattern is found in the Lord's Prayer, which Jesus taught to his disciples:

Our Father in heaven,
   hallowed be your name,
   your kingdom come,
   your will be done,
     on earth as in heaven.
Give us today our daily bread.
Forgive us our sins
   as we forgive those who sin against us.
Save us from the time of trial
   and deliver us from evil.
For the kingdom, the power, and the glory
   are yours now and for ever. Amen.

These words express everything that we may desire and expect from God.

Question 98. What is meant by addressing God as "Our Father in heaven"?

When we pray to God as "our Father in heaven," we draw near with childlike reverence and place ourselves securely in God's hands. We express our confidence that God cares for us, and that nothing on earth is beyond the reach of God's grace.

> *Rom. 8:15–16*   For you did not receive a spirit of slavery to fall back into fear, but you have received a spirit of adoption. When we cry, "Abba! Father!" it is that very Spirit bearing witness with our spirit that we are children of God. . . .

> *Jer. 23:23–24*   Am I a God near by, says the LORD, and not a God far off? Who can hide in secret places so that I cannot see them? says the LORD. Do I not fill heaven and earth? says the LORD.

> *Acts 17:24–25*   The God who made the world and everything in it, he who is Lord of heaven and earth, does not live in shrines made by human hands, nor is he served by human hands, as though he needed anything, since he himself gives to all mortals life and breath and all things.

Question 99. What is meant by the first petition, "Hallowed be your name"?

This petition is placed first, because it expresses the goal and purpose of the whole prayer. When we pray for God's name to be "hallowed," we ask that we will know and glorify God as God really is, and that all things will truly come to serve God.

> *Jer. 9:23–24*   Thus says the LORD: Do not let the wise boast in their wisdom, do not let the mighty boast in their might, do not let the wealthy boast in their wealth; but let those who boast boast in this, that they understand and know me, that I am the LORD; I act with steadfast love, justice, and righteousness in the earth, for in these things I delight, says the LORD.

> *Rom. 11:36*   For from him and through him and to him are all things. To him be the glory forever. Amen.

> *Ps. 115:1*   Not to us, O LORD, not to us, but to your name give glory, for the sake of your steadfast love and your faithfulness.

Question 100. What is meant by the second petition, "Your kingdom come"?

We ask God to come and rule among us through faith, love, and justice. We pray for both the church and the world, that God will rule in our hearts through faith, in our personal relationships through love, and in our institutional affairs through justice.

Ps. 68:1 Let God rise up, let his enemies be scattered; let those who hate him flee before him.

2 Thess. 3:1 Finally, brothers and sisters, pray for us, so that the word of the Lord may spread rapidly and be glorified everywhere, just as it is among you. . . .

Rev. 22:20 The one who testifies to these things says, "Surely I am coming soon." Amen. Come, Lord Jesus!

Rom. 8:22–24 We know that the whole creation has been groaning in labor pains until now; and not only the creation, but we ourselves, who have the first fruits of the Spirit, groan inwardly while we wait for adoption, the redemption of our bodies. For in hope we were saved. Now hope that is seen is not hope. For who hopes for what is seen?

1 Cor. 15:20, 28 But in fact Christ has been raised from the dead, the first fruits of those who have died. . . . When all things are subjected to him, then the Son himself will also be subjected to the one who put all things in subjection under him, so that God may be all in all.

Question 101. What is meant by the third petition, "Your will be done, on earth as in heaven"?

Of course, God's will is always done and will surely come to pass, whether we desire it or not. But the phrase "on earth as in heaven" means that we ask for the grace to do God's will on earth in the way that it is done in heaven—gladly and from the heart. We yield ourselves, in life and in death, to God's will.

Ps. 119:34–36 Give me understanding, that I may keep your law and observe it with my whole heart. Lead me in the path of your commandments, for I delight in it. Turn my heart to your decrees, and not to selfish gain.

Ps. 103:20, 22 Bless the LORD, O you his angels, you mighty ones who do his bidding, obedient to his spoken word. . . . Bless the LORD, all his works, in all places of his dominion. Bless the LORD, O my soul.

Luke 22:42 Father, if you are willing, remove this cup from me; yet, not my will but yours be done.

Rom. 12:2 Do not be conformed to this world, but be transformed by the renewing of your minds, so that you may discern what is the will of God— what is good and acceptable and perfect.

Question 102. What is meant by the fourth petition, "Give us today our daily bread"?

We ask God to supply all our needs, for we know that God, who cares for us in every area of our life, has promised to give us temporal as well as spiritual blessings. God commands us to pray each day for all that we need and no more, so that we will learn to rely completely on God.

Prov. 30:8 Remove far from me falsehood and lying; give me neither poverty nor riches; feed me with the food that I need. . . .

Ps. 90:17   Let the favor of the Lord our God be upon us, and prosper for us the work of our hands—O prosper the work of our hands!

Ps. 55:22   Cast your burden on the LORD, and he will sustain you; he will never permit the righteous to be moved.

Ps. 72:4   May he defend the cause of the poor of the people, give deliverance to the needy, and crush the oppressor.

Ps. 104:27–28   These all look to you to give them their food in due season; when you give to them, they gather it up; when you open your hand, they are filled with good things.

Question 103. What is meant by the fifth petition, "Forgive us our sins as we forgive those who sin against us"?

We pray that a new and right spirit will be put within us. We ask for the grace to treat others with the same mercy we have received from God. We ask that we will not resent or strike back at those who harm us, but that our hearts will be knit together with the merciful heart of God.

Matt. 18:33   Should you not have had mercy on your fellow slave, as I had mercy on you?

Matt. 6:14–15   For if you forgive others their trespasses, your heavenly Father will also forgive you; but if you do not forgive others, neither will your Father forgive your trespasses.

Ps. 51:10   Create in me a clean heart, O God, and put a new and right spirit within me.

1 John 2:1–2   My little children, I am writing these things to you so that you may not sin. But if anyone does sin, we have an advocate with the Father, Jesus Christ the righteous; and he is the atoning sacrifice for our sins, and not for ours only but also for the sins of the whole world.

Question 104. What is meant by the final petition, "Save us from the time of trial and deliver us from evil"?

We ask God to protect us from all that threatens to hurt or destroy us. We pray for the ability to resist sin and evil in our own lives, and for the grace to endure suffering in trust and without bitterness when it is unavoidable. We ask for the grace to believe in the love of God that will finally swallow up all the evil and hatred in the world.

2 Cor. 4:8   We are afflicted in every way, but not crushed; perplexed, but not driven to despair. . . .

Eph. 3:19   . . . and to know the love of Christ that surpasses knowledge, so that you may be filled with all the fullness of God.

Matt. 26:41   Stay awake and pray that you may not come into the time of trial; the spirit indeed is willing, but the flesh is weak.

Question 105. What is meant by the closing doxology, "For the kingdom, the power, and the glory are yours now and for ever"?

We give God thanks and praise for the kingdom more powerful than all enemies, for the power perfected in the weakness of love, and for the glory that includes our well-being and that of the whole creation, both now and to all eternity.

Rev. 5:12   Worthy is the Lamb that was slaughtered to receive power and wealth and wisdom and might and honor and glory and blessing!

Rev. 4:11   You are worthy, our Lord and God, to receive glory and honor and power, for you created all things, and by your will they existed and were created.

1 Chron. 29:11, 13   Yours, O LORD, are the greatness, the power, the glory, the victory, and the majesty; for all that is in the heavens and on the earth is yours; yours is the kingdom, O LORD, and you are exalted as head above all. . . . And now, our God, we give thanks to you and praise your glorious name.

Question 106. What is meant by the word "Amen"?

"Amen" means "so be it" or "let it be so." It expresses our complete confidence in the triune God, the God of the covenant with Israel as fulfilled through our Lord Jesus Christ, who makes no promise that will not be kept, and whose mercy endures forever.

Rev. 22:20   The one who testifies to these things says, "Surely I am coming soon." Amen. Come, Lord Jesus!

2 Cor. 1:20   For in him every one of God's promises is a "Yes." For this reason it is through him that we say the "Amen," to the glory of God.

2 Tim. 2:13   If we are faithless, he remains faithful—for he cannot deny himself.

The Study Catechism: Full Version

In 1998 the 210th General Assembly of the Presbyterian Church (U.S.A.) approved two new catechisms for use as teaching tools for the church. The second of these is the Study Catechism, which was divided into two versions: the Full Version and the shorter, somewhat simplified Confirmation Version. Both follow the traditional sequence of the Apostles' Creed, the Ten Commandments, and the Lord's Prayer. The Confirmation Version is designed to be used with youth during the confirmation process, while the Full Version can be used in the training of church officers, in adult study groups, in the education of new church members, or in many other settings.

THE STUDY CATECHISM:
FULL VERSION

Question 1. What is God's purpose for your life?

God wills that I should live by the grace of the Lord Jesus Christ, for the love of God, and in the communion of the Holy Spirit.

> *2 Cor. 13:13* The grace of the Lord Jesus Christ, the love of God, and the communion of the Holy Spirit be with all of you.

Question 2. How do you live by the grace of the Lord Jesus Christ?

I am not my own. I have been bought with a price. The Lord Jesus Christ loved me and gave himself for me. I entrust myself completely to his care, giving thanks each day for his wonderful goodness.

> *1 Cor. 6:19–20* Or do you not know that your body is a temple of the Holy Spirit within you, which you have from God, and that you are not your own? For you were bought with a price; therefore glorify God in your body.

> *Gal. 2:20* It is no longer I who live, but it is Christ who lives in me. And the life I now live in the flesh I live by faith in the Son of God, who loved me and gave himself for me.

> *Ps. 136:1* O give thanks to the LORD, for he is good, for his steadfast love endures forever.

Question 3. How do you live for the love of God?

I love because God first loved me. God loves me in Christ with a love that never ends. Amazed by grace, I no longer live for myself. I live for the Lord who died and rose again, triumphant over death, for my sake. Therefore, I take those around me to heart, especially those in particular need, knowing that Christ died for them no less than for me.

> *1 John 4:19* We love because he first loved us.

64

2 Cor. 5:15   And he died for all, so that those who live might live no longer for themselves, but for him who died and was raised for them.

Rom. 12:15–16   Rejoice with those who rejoice, weep with those who weep. Live in harmony with one another; do not be haughty, but associate with the lowly; do not claim to be wiser than you are.

Question 4. How do you live in the communion of the Holy Spirit?

By the Holy Spirit, I am made one with the Lord Jesus Christ. I am baptized into Christ's body, the church, along with all others who confess him by faith. As a member of this community, I trust in God's Word, share in the Lord's Supper, and turn to God constantly in prayer. As I grow in grace and knowledge, I am led to do the good works that God intends for my life.

1 Cor. 12:27   Now you are the body of Christ and individually members of it.

Gal. 3:27   As many of you as were baptized into Christ have clothed yourselves with Christ.

1 Cor. 6:17, 19   But anyone united to the Lord becomes one spirit with him. ... Or do you not know that your body is a temple of the Holy Spirit within you, which you have from God, and that you are not your own?

2 Peter 3:18   But grow in the grace and knowledge of our Lord and Savior Jesus Christ. To him be the glory both now and to the day of eternity. Amen.

Eph. 2:10   For we are what he has made us, created in Christ Jesus for good works, which God prepared beforehand to be our way of life.

I. The Apostles' Creed

Question 5. What does a Christian believe?

All that is promised in the gospel. A summary is found in the Apostles' Creed, which affirms the main content of the Christian faith.

John 20:31   But these are written so that you may come to believe that Jesus is the Messiah, the Son of God, and that through believing you may have life in his name.

Question 6. What is the first article of the Apostles' Creed?

"I believe in God the Father Almighty, Maker of heaven and earth."

Question 7. What do you believe when you confess your faith in "God the Father Almighty"?

That God is a God of love, and that God's love is powerful beyond measure.

Lam. 3:22   The steadfast love of the LORD never ceases, his mercies never come to an end.

Song 8:7   Many waters cannot quench love, neither can floods drown it. If one offered for love all the wealth of his house, it would be utterly scorned.

1 John 4:8   Whoever does not love does not know God, for God is love.

Question 8. How do you understand the love and power of God?

Through Jesus Christ. In his life of compassion, his death on the cross, and his resurrection from the dead, I see how vast is God's love for the world—a love that is ready to suffer for our sakes, yet so strong that nothing will prevail against it.

John 3:16 For God so loved the world that he gave his only Son, so that everyone who believes in him may not perish but may have eternal life.

Heb. 1:3 He is the reflection of God's glory and the exact imprint of God's very being, and he sustains all things by his powerful word.

1 John 4:9 God's love was revealed among us in this way: God sent his only Son into the world so that we might live through him.

Matt. 9:36 When he saw the crowds, he had compassion for them, because they were harassed and helpless, like sheep without a shepherd.

Ps. 106:8 Yet he saved them for his name's sake, so that he might make known his mighty power.

Question 9. What comfort do you receive from this truth?

This powerful and loving God is the one whose promises I may trust in all the circumstances of my life, and to whom I belong in life and in death.

Ps. 12:6 The promises of the LORD are promises that are pure, silver refined in a furnace on the ground, purified seven times.

Rom. 8:38–39 For I am convinced that neither death, nor life, nor angels, nor rulers, nor things present, nor things to come, nor powers, nor height, nor depth, nor anything else in all creation, will be able to separate us from the love of God in Christ Jesus our Lord.

Question 10. Do you make this confession only as an individual?

No. With the apostles, prophets, and martyrs, with all those through the ages who have loved the Lord Jesus Christ, and with all who strive to serve him on earth here and now, I confess my faith in the God of loving power and powerful love.

Heb. 12:1 Therefore, since we are surrounded by so great a cloud of witnesses, let us also lay aside every weight and the sin that clings so closely, and let us run with perseverance the race that is set before us. . . .

Rom. 1:12 . . . so that we may be mutually encouraged by each other's faith, both yours and mine.

Question 11. When the creed speaks of "God the Father," does it mean that God is male?

No. Only creatures having bodies can be either male or female. But God has no body, since by nature God is Spirit. Holy Scripture reveals God as a living God beyond all sexual distinctions. Scripture uses diverse images for God, female as well as male. We read, for example, that God will no more forget us than a woman can forget her nursing child (Isa. 49:15). " 'As a mother comforts her child, so will I comfort you,' says the Lord" (Isa. 66:13).

Isa. 49:15 Can a woman forget her nursing child, or show no compassion for the child of her womb? Even these may forget, yet I will not forget you.

Isa. 66:13 As a mother comforts her child, so I will comfort you; you shall be comforted in Jerusalem.

Matt. 23:37 Jerusalem, Jerusalem, the city that kills the prophets and stones those who are sent to it! How often have I desired to gather your children together as a hen gathers her brood under her wings, and you were not willing!

Question 12. Why then does the creed speak of God the Father?

First, because God is identified in the New Testament as the Father of our Lord Jesus Christ. Second, because Jesus Christ is the eternal Son of this Father. Third, because when we are joined to Christ through faith, we are adopted as sons and daughters into the relationship he enjoys with his Father.

Rom. 1:7 To all God's beloved in Rome, who are called to be saints: Grace to you and peace from God our Father and the Lord Jesus Christ.

John 14:9–10 Jesus said to him, "Have I been with you all this time, Philip, and you still do not know me? Whoever has seen me has seen the Father. How can you say, 'Show us the Father'? Do you not believe that I am in the Father and the Father is in me? The words that I say to you I do not speak on my own; but the Father who dwells in me does his works.

John 17:24 Father, I desire that those also, whom you have given me, may be with me where I am, to see my glory, which you have given me because you loved me before the foundation of the world.

John 1:12 But to all who received him, who believed in his name, he gave power to become children of God. . . .

Gal. 4:6 And because you are children, God has sent the Spirit of his Son into our hearts, crying, "Abba! Father!"

Question 13. When you confess the God and Father of our Lord Jesus Christ, are you elevating men over women and endorsing male domination?

No. Human power and authority are trustworthy only as they reflect God's mercy and kindness, not abusive patterns of domination. As Jesus taught his disciples, "The greatest among you will be your servant" (Matt. 23:11). God the Father sets the standard by which all misuses of power are exposed and condemned. "Call no one your father on earth," said Jesus, "for you have one Father—the one in heaven" (Matt. 23:9). In fact God calls women and men to all ministries of the church.

Gal. 3:28 There is no longer Jew or Greek, there is no longer slave or free, there is no longer male and female; for all of you are one in Christ Jesus.

Eph. 5:21 Be subject to one another out of reverence for Christ.

Question 14. If God's love is powerful beyond measure, why is there so much evil in the world?

No one can say why, for evil is a terrible abyss beyond all rational explanation. Its ultimate origin is obscure. Its enormity perplexes us. Nevertheless, we boldly affirm that God's triumph over evil is certain. In Jesus Christ God suffers with us, knowing all our sorrows. In raising him from the dead, God gives new hope to the world. Our Lord Jesus Christ, crucified and risen, is himself God's promise that suffering will come to an end, that death shall be no more, and that all things will be made new.

Ps. 23:4 Even though I walk through the darkest valley, I fear no evil; for you are with me; your rod and your staff—they comfort me.

1 Peter 1:3 Blessed be the God and Father of our Lord Jesus Christ! By his great mercy he has given us a new birth into a living hope through the resurrection of Jesus Christ from the dead.

2 Peter 3:13 But, in accordance with his promise, we wait for new heavens and a new earth, where righteousness is at home.

Rom. 8:21 The creation itself will be set free from its bondage to decay and will obtain the freedom of the glory of the children of God.

Job 19:25 For I know that my Redeemer lives, and that at the last he will stand upon the earth. . . .

Question 15. What do you believe when you say that God is "Maker of heaven and earth"?

First, that God called heaven and earth, with all that is in them, into being out of nothing simply by the power of God's Word. Second, that by that same power all things are upheld and governed in perfect wisdom, according to God's eternal purpose.

Rev. 4:11 You are worthy, our Lord and God, to receive glory and honor and power, for you created all things, and by your will they existed and were created.

Gen. 1:1 In the beginning when God created the heavens and the earth, the earth was a formless void and darkness covered the face of the deep, while a wind from God swept over the face of the waters.

Heb. 11:3 By faith we understand that the worlds were prepared by the word of God, so that what is seen was made from things that are not visible.

Question 16. What does it mean to say that we human beings are created in the image of God?

That God created us to live together in love and freedom—with God, with one another, and with the world. Our distinctive capacities—reason, imagination, volition, and so on—are given primarily for this purpose. We are created to be loving companions of others so that something of God's goodness may be reflected in our lives.

Gen. 1:26 Then God said, "Let us make humankind in our image, according to our likeness; and let them have dominion over the fish of the sea, and over the birds of the air, and over the cattle, and over all the wild animals of the earth, and over every creeping thing that creeps upon the earth."

Gen. 1:27 So God created humankind in his image, in the image of God he created them; male and female he created them.

Question 17. What does our creation in God's image reflect about God's reality?

Our being created in and for relationship is a reflection of the Holy Trinity. In the mystery of the one God, the three divine persons—Father, Son, and Holy Spirit—live in, with, and for one another eternally in perfect love and freedom.

Luke 3:21–22   Now when all the people were baptized, and when Jesus also had been baptized and was praying, the heaven was opened, and the Holy Spirit descended upon him in bodily form like a dove. And a voice came from heaven, "You are my Son, the Beloved; with you I am well pleased."

John 1:18   No one has ever seen God. It is God the only Son, who is close to the Father's heart, who has made him known.

John 5:19   Jesus said to them, "Very truly, I tell you, the Son can do nothing on his own, but only what he sees the Father doing; for whatever the Father does, the Son does likewise."

John 17:21–22   As you, Father, are in me and I am in you, may they also be in us, so that the world may believe that you have sent me. The glory that you have given me I have given them, so that they may be one, as we are one. . . .

Question 18. What does our creation in God's image reflect about God's love for us?

We are created to live wholeheartedly for God. When we honor our Creator as the source of all good things, we are like mirrors reflecting back the great beam of love that God shines on us. We are also created to honor God by showing love toward other human beings.

Ps. 9:1   I will give thanks to the LORD with my whole heart; I will tell of all your wonderful deeds.

1 John 4:7   Beloved, let us love one another, because love is from God; everyone who loves is born of God and knows God.

1 John 4:11   Beloved, since God loved us so much, we also ought to love one another.

Matt. 5:14–16   You are the light of the world. A city built on a hill cannot be hid. No one after lighting a lamp puts it under the bushel basket, but on the lampstand, and it gives light to all in the house. In the same way, let your light shine before others, so that they may see your good works and give glory to your Father in heaven.

Question 19. As creatures made in God's image, what responsibility do we have for the earth?

God commands us to care for the earth in ways that reflect God's loving care for us. We are responsible for ensuring that earth's gifts be used fairly and wisely, that no creature suffers from the abuse of what we are given, and that future generations may continue to enjoy the abundance and goodness of the earth in praise to God.

Ps. 24:1   The earth is the LORD's and all that is in it, the world, and those who live in it. . . .

Ps. 89:11   The heavens are yours, the earth also is yours; the world and all that is in it—you have founded them.

Gen. 2:15   The LORD God took the man and put him in the garden of Eden to till it and keep it.

Gen. 1:26   Then God said, "Let us make humankind in our image, according to our likeness; and let them have dominion over the fish of the sea, and over the birds of the air, and over the cattle, and over all the wild animals of the earth, and over every creeping thing that creeps upon the earth."

Isa. 24:5   The earth lies polluted under its inhabitants; for they have transgressed laws, violated the statutes, broken the everlasting covenant.

Rom. 12:2   Do not be conformed to this world, but be transformed by the renewing of your minds, so that you may discern what is the will of God— what is good and acceptable and perfect.

Question 20. Was the image of God lost when we turned from God by falling into sin?

Yes and no. Sin means that all our relations with others have become distorted and confused. Although we did not cease to be with God, our fellow human beings, and other creatures, we did cease to be for them; and although we did not lose our distinctive human capacities completely, we did lose the ability to use them rightly, especially in relation to God. Having ruined our connection with God by disobeying God's will, we are persons with hearts curved in upon ourselves. We have become slaves to the sin of which we are guilty, helpless to save ourselves, and are free, so far as freedom remains, only within the bounds of sin.

John 8:34   Jesus answered them, "Very truly, I tell you, everyone who commits sin is a slave to sin."

Romans 3:23   All have sinned and fall short of the glory of God. . . .

Romans 3:10   There is no one who is righteous, not even one. . . .

Romans 1:21   Though they knew God, they did not honor him as God or give thanks to him, but they became futile in their thinking, and their senseless minds were darkened.

Isa. 59:1–3   See, the LORD's hand is not too short to save, nor his ear too dull to hear. Rather, your iniquities have been barriers between you and your God, and your sins have hidden his face from you so that he does not hear. For your hands are defiled with blood, and your fingers with iniquity; your lips have spoken lies, your tongue mutters wickedness.

Question 21. What does it mean to say that Jesus Christ is the image of God?

Despite our turning from God, God did not turn from us, but instead sent Jesus Christ in the fullness of time to restore our broken humanity. Jesus lived completely for God, by giving himself completely for us, even to the point of dying for us. By living so completely for others, he manifested what he was—the perfect image of God. When by grace we are conformed to him through faith, our humanity is renewed according to the divine image that we lost.

Isa. 65:2   I held out my hands all day long to a rebellious people, who walk in a way that is not good, following their own devices. . . .

Phil. 2:8   He humbled himself and became obedient to the point of death— even death on a cross.

Col. 1:15   He is the image of the invisible God, the firstborn of all creation. . . .

Rom. 8:29   For those whom he foreknew he also predestined to be conformed to the image of his Son, in order that he might be the firstborn within a large family.

Question 22. What do you understand by God's providence?

That God not only preserves the world but also continually attends to it, ruling and sustaining it with wise and benevolent care. God is concerned for every creature: "The eyes of all look to you, and you give them their food in due season. You open your hand, you satisfy the desire of every living thing" (Ps. 145:15). In particular, God provides for the world by bringing good out of evil, so that nothing evil is permitted to occur that God does not bend finally to the good. Scripture tells us, for example, how Joseph said to his brothers: "As for you, you meant evil against me; but God meant it for good, to bring it about that many people should be kept alive, as they are today" (Gen. 50:20).

Rom. 8:28   We know that all things work together for good for those who love God, who are called according to his purpose.

Ps. 103:19   The LORD has established his throne in the heavens, and his kingdom rules over all.

Ps. 145:17   The LORD is just in all his ways, and kind in all his doings.

Question 23. What comfort do you receive by trusting in God's providence?

The eternal Father of our Lord Jesus Christ watches over me each day of my life, blessing and guiding me wherever I may be. God strengthens me when I am faithful, comforts me when discouraged or sorrowful, raises me up if I fall, and brings me at last to eternal life. Entrusting myself wholly to God's care, I receive the grace to be patient in adversity, thankful in the midst of blessing, courageous against injustice, and confident that no evil afflicts me that God will not turn to my good.

Ps. 146:9   The LORD watches over the strangers; he upholds the orphan and the widow, but the way of the wicked he brings to ruin.

Isa. 58:11   The LORD will guide you continually, and satisfy your needs in parched places, and make your bones strong; and you shall be like a watered garden, like a spring of water, whose waters never fail.

Isa. 41:10   Do not fear, for I am with you, do not be afraid, for I am your God; I will strengthen you, I will help you, I will uphold you with my victorious right hand.

2 Cor. 1:3–5   Blessed be the God and Father of our Lord Jesus Christ, the Father of mercies and the God of all consolation, who consoles us in all our affliction, so that we may be able to console those who are in any affliction with the consolation with which we ourselves are consoled by God.

Ps. 30:5   For his anger is but for a moment; his favor is for a lifetime. Weeping may linger for the night, but joy comes with the morning.

Question 24. What difference does your faith in God's providence make when you struggle against bitterness and despair?

When I suffer harm or adversity, my faith in God's providence upholds me against bitterness and despair. It reminds me when hope disappears that my heartache and pain are contained by a larger purpose and a higher power than I can presently discern. Even in grief, shame, and loss, I can still cry out to God in lament, waiting on God to supply my needs, and to bring me healing and comfort.

Ps. 42:11 Why are you cast down, O my soul, and why are you disquieted within me? Hope in God; for I shall again praise him, my help and my God.

2 Cor. 4:8–10 We are afflicted in every way, but not crushed; perplexed, but not driven to despair; persecuted, but not forsaken; struck down, but not destroyed; always carrying in the body the death of Jesus, so that the life of Jesus may also be made visible in our bodies.

Ps. 13:1–2 How long, O LORD? Will you forget me forever? How long will you hide your face from me? How long must I bear pain in my soul, and have sorrow in my heart all day long? How long shall my enemy be exalted over me?

Job 7:11 Therefore I will not restrain my mouth; I will speak in the anguish of my spirit; I will complain in the bitterness of my soul.

Question 25. Did God need the world in order to be God?

No. God would still be God, eternally perfect and inexhaustibly rich, even if no creatures had ever been made. Yet without God, all created beings would simply fail to exist. Creatures can neither come into existence, nor continue, nor find fulfillment apart from God. God, however, is self-existent and self-sufficient.

Acts 17:24–25 The God who made the world and everything in it, he who is Lord of heaven and earth, does not live in shrines made by human hands, nor is he served by human hands, as though he needed anything, since he himself gives to all mortals life and breath and all things.

John 1:16 From his fullness we have all received, grace upon grace.

John 5:26 For just as the Father has life in himself, so he has granted the Son also to have life in himself. . . .

Eph. 1:22 And he has put all things under his feet and has made him the head over all things for the church . . .

Question 26. Why then did God create the world?

God's decision to create the world was an act of grace. In this decision God chose to grant existence to the world simply in order to bless it. God created the world to reveal God's glory, to share the love and freedom at the heart of God's triune being, and to give us eternal life in fellowship with God.

Ps. 19:1 The heavens are telling the glory of God; and the firmament proclaims his handiwork.

2 Cor. 3:17 Now the Lord is the Spirit, and where the Spirit of the Lord is, there is freedom.

Ps. 67:6–7 The earth has yielded its increase; God, our God, has blessed us. May God continue to bless us; let all the ends of the earth revere him.

Eph. 1:3–4 Blessed be the God and Father of our Lord Jesus Christ, who has blessed us in Christ with every spiritual blessing in the heavenly places, just as he chose us in Christ before the foundation of the world to be holy and blameless before him in love.

John 3:36 Whoever believes in the Son has eternal life; whoever disobeys the Son will not see life, but must endure God's wrath.

Question 27. Does your confession of God as Creator contradict the findings of modern science?

No. My confession of God as Creator answers three questions: Who?, How?, and Why? It affirms that (a) the triune God, who is self-sufficient, (b) called the world into being out of nothing by the creative power of God's Word (c) for the sake of sharing love and freedom. Natural science has much to teach us about the particular mechanisms and processes of nature, but it is not in a position to answer these questions about ultimate reality, which point to mysteries that science as such is not equipped to explore. Nothing basic to the Christian faith contradicts the findings of modern science, nor does anything essential to modern science contradict the Christian faith.

> *John 1:1–3*   In the beginning was the Word, and the Word was with God, and the Word was God. He was in the beginning with God. All things came into being through him, and without him not one thing came into being.

Question 28. What is the second article of the Apostles' Creed?

"And I believe in Jesus Christ, his only Son, our Lord. He was conceived by the Holy Spirit, born of the Virgin Mary, suffered under Pontius Pilate, was crucified, dead and buried. He descended into hell. On the third day he rose again from the dead. He ascended into heaven and is seated at the right hand of the Father. He will come again to judge the living and the dead."

Question 29. What do you believe when you confess your faith in Jesus Christ as "God's only Son"?

That Jesus Christ is a unique person who was sent to do a unique work.

> *Luke 3:21–22*   Now when all the people were baptized, and when Jesus also had been baptized and was praying, the heaven was opened, and the Holy Spirit descended upon him in bodily form like a dove. And a voice came from heaven, "You are my Son, the Beloved; with you I am well pleased."

> *Luke 12:49–50*   I came to bring fire to the earth, and how I wish it were already kindled! I have a baptism with which to be baptized, and what stress I am under until it is completed!

> *John 1:14*   And the Word became flesh and lived among us, and we have seen his glory, the glory as of a father's only son, full of grace and truth.

Question 30. How do you understand the uniqueness of Jesus Christ?

No one else will ever be God incarnate. No one else will ever die for the sins of the world. Only Jesus Christ is such a person, only he could do such a work, and he in fact has done it.

> *Isa. 53:5*   But he was wounded for our transgressions, crushed for our iniquities; upon him was the punishment that made us whole, and by his bruises we are healed.

> *John 1:29*   The next day he saw Jesus coming toward him and declared, "Here is the Lamb of God who takes away the sin of the world!"

> *Col. 1:15–20*   He is the image of the invisible God, the firstborn of all creation; for in him all things in heaven and on earth were created, things visible

and invisible, whether thrones or dominions or rulers or powers—all things have been created through him and for him. He himself is before all things, and in him all things hold together. He is the head of the body, the church; he is the beginning, the firstborn from the dead, so that he might come to have first place in everything. For in him all the fullness of God was pleased to dwell, and through him God was pleased to reconcile to himself all things, whether on earth or in heaven, by making peace through the blood of his cross.

Question 31. What do you affirm when you confess your faith in Jesus Christ as "our Lord"?

That having been raised from the dead he reigns with compassion and justice over all things in heaven and on earth, especially over those who confess him by faith; and that by loving and serving him above all else, I give glory and honor to God.

1 Cor. 15:3–4   For I handed on to you as of first importance what I in turn had received: that Christ died for our sins in accordance with the scriptures, and that he was buried, and that he was raised on the third day in accordance with the scriptures. . . .

Rev. 11:15   Then the seventh angel blew his trumpet, and there were loud voices in heaven, saying, "The kingdom of the world has become the kingdom of our Lord and of his Messiah, and he will reign forever and ever."

Eph. 1:20–23   God put this power to work in Christ when he raised him from the dead and seated him at his right hand in the heavenly places, far above all rule and authority and power and dominion, and above every name that is named, not only in this age but also in the age to come. And he has put all things under his feet and has made him the head over all things for the church, which is his body, the fullness of him who fills all in all.

Phil. 2:9–11   Therefore God also highly exalted him and gave him the name that is above every name, so that at the name of Jesus every knee should bend, in heaven and on earth and under the earth, and every tongue should confess that Jesus Christ is Lord, to the glory of God the Father.

Question 32. What do you affirm when you say he was "conceived by the Holy Spirit and born of the Virgin Mary"?

First, that being born of a woman, Jesus was truly a human being. Second, that our Lord's incarnation was a holy and mysterious event, brought about solely by free divine grace surpassing any human possibilities. Third, that from the very beginning of his life on earth, he was set apart by his unique origin for the sake of accomplishing our salvation.

Luke 1:31   And now, you will conceive in your womb and bear a son, and you will name him Jesus.

Luke 1:35   The angel said to her, "The Holy Spirit will come upon you, and the power of the Most High will overshadow you; therefore the child to be born will be holy; he will be called Son of God."

Heb. 2:14   Since, therefore, the children share flesh and blood, he himself likewise shared the same things, so that through death he might destroy the one who has the power of death, that is, the devil. . . .

Phil. 2:5–7 Let the same mind be in you that was in Christ Jesus, who, though he was in the form of God, did not regard equality with God as something to be exploited, but emptied himself, taking the form of a slave, being born in human likeness.

Question 33. What is the significance of affirming that Jesus is truly God?

Only God can properly deserve worship. Only God can reveal to us who God is. And only God can save us from our sins. Being truly God, Jesus meets these conditions. He is the proper object of our worship, the self–revelation of God, and the Savior of the world.

John 20:28 Thomas answered him, "My Lord and my God!" Jesus said to him, "Have you believed because you have seen me? Blessed are those who have not seen and yet have come to believe."

Matt. 11:27 All things have been handed over to me by my Father; and no one knows the Son except the Father, and no one knows the Father except the Son and anyone to whom the Son chooses to reveal him.

1 John 4:14 And we have seen and do testify that the Father has sent his Son as the Savior of the world.

Question 34. What is the significance of affirming that Jesus is also truly a human being?

Being truly human, Jesus entered fully into our fallen situation and overcame it from within. By his pure obedience, he lived a life of unbroken unity with God, even to the point of accepting a violent death. As sinners at war with grace, this is precisely the kind of life we fail to live. When we accept him by faith, he removes our disobedience and clothes us with his perfect righteousness.

Heb. 2:17–18 Therefore he had to become like his brothers and sisters in every respect, so that he might be a merciful and faithful high priest in the service of God, to make a sacrifice of atonement for the sins of the people. Because he himself was tested by what he suffered, he is able to help those who are being tested.

Heb. 4:15 For we do not have a high priest who is unable to sympathize with our weaknesses, but we have one who in every respect has been tested as we are, yet without sin.

Heb. 5:8–9 Although he was a Son, he learned obedience through what he suffered; and having been made perfect, he became the source of eternal salvation for all who obey him. . . .

Rom. 5:19 For just as by the one man's disobedience the many were made sinners, so by the one man's obedience the many will be made righteous.

Question 35. How can Jesus be truly God and yet also truly human at the same time?

The mystery of Jesus Christ's divine-human unity passes our understanding; only faith given by the Holy Spirit enables us to affirm it. When Holy Scripture depicts Jesus as someone with divine power, status, and authority, it presupposes his humanity. And when it depicts him as someone with human weakness, neediness, and mortality, it presupposes his deity. We cannot understand how this should be, but we can trust that the God who made heaven and earth is free to become God incarnate and thus to be God with us in this wonderful and awe-inspiring way.

Mark 1:27   They were all amazed, and they kept on asking one another, "What is this? A new teaching—with authority! He commands even the unclean spirits, and they obey him."

Mark 4:41   And they were filled with great awe and said to one another, "Who then is this, that even the wind and the sea obey him?"

Matt. 28:18   And Jesus came and said to them, "All authority in heaven and on earth has been given to me."

Luke 22:44   In his anguish he prayed more earnestly, and his sweat became like great drops of blood falling down on the ground.

Job 5:9   He does great things and unsearchable, marvelous things without number.

Question 36. How did God use the people of Israel to prepare the way for the coming of Jesus?

God made a covenant with Israel, promising that God would be their light and their salvation, that they would be God's people, and that through them all the peoples of the earth would be blessed. Therefore, no matter how often Israel turned away from God, God still cared for them and acted on their behalf. In particular, God sent them prophets, priests, and kings. Each of these was "anointed" by God's Spirit—prophets, to declare God's word; priests, to make sacrifice for the people's sins; and kings, to rule justly in the fear of God, upholding the poor and needy, and defending the people from their enemies.

Gen. 17:3–4   Then Abram fell on his face; and God said to him, "As for me, this is my covenant with you: You shall be the ancestor of a multitude of nations."

Gen. 12:1–3   Now the LORD said to Abram, "Go from your country and your kindred and your father's house to the land that I will show you. I will make of you a great nation, and I will bless you, and make your name great, so that you will be a blessing. I will bless those who bless you, and the one who curses you I will curse; and in you all the families of the earth shall be blessed."

Ex. 6:4–5   I also established my covenant with them, to give them the land of Canaan, the land in which they resided as aliens. I have also heard the groaning of the Israelites whom the Egyptians are holding as slaves, and I have remembered my covenant.

Gal. 3:14   . . . in order that in Christ Jesus the blessing of Abraham might come to the Gentiles, so that we might receive the promise of the Spirit through faith.

Jer. 30:22   And you shall be my people, and I will be your God.

1 Peter 2:9–10   But you are a chosen race, a royal priesthood, a holy nation, God's own people, in order that you might proclaim the mighty acts of him who called you out of darkness into his marvelous light. Once you were not a people, but now you are God's people; once you had not received mercy, but now you have received mercy.

Zech. 1:6   But my words and my statutes, which I commanded my servants the prophets, did they not overtake your ancestors? So they repented and said, "The LORD of hosts has dealt with us according to our ways and deeds, just as he planned to do."

Lev. 5:6   And you shall bring to the LORD, as your penalty for the sin that you have committed, . . . a sheep or a goat, as a sin offering; and the priest shall make atonement on your behalf for your sin.

Ps. 72:1, 4   Give the king your justice, O God, and your righteousness to a king's son. . . . May he defend the cause of the poor of the people, give deliverance to the needy, and crush the oppressor.

Question 37. Was the covenant with Israel an everlasting covenant?

Yes. With the coming of Jesus the covenant with Israel was expanded and confirmed. By faith in him Gentiles were welcomed into the covenant. This throwing open of the gates confirmed the promise that through Israel God's blessing would come to all peoples. Although for the most part Israel has not accepted Jesus as the Messiah, God has not rejected Israel. God still loves Israel, and God is their hope, "for the gifts and the calling of God are irrevocable" (Rom. 11:29). The God who has reached out to unbelieving Gentiles will not fail to show mercy to Israel as the people of the everlasting covenant.

Isa. 61:8   For I the LORD love justice, I hate robbery and wrongdoing; I will faithfully give them their recompense, and I will make an everlasting covenant with them.

Jer. 31:3   I have loved you with an everlasting love; therefore I have continued my faithfulness to you.

2 Sam. 23:5   Is not my house like this with God? For he has made with me an everlasting covenant, ordered in all things and secure. Will he not cause to prosper all my help and my desire?

Rom. 11:29   For the gifts and the calling of God are irrevocable.

Question 38. Why was the title "Christ," which means "anointed one," applied to Jesus?

Jesus Christ was the definitive prophet, priest, and king. All of the Lord's anointed in Israel anticipated and led finally to him. In assuming these offices Jesus not only transformed them, but also realized the purpose of Israel's election for the sake of the world.

2 Cor. 1:20   For in him every one of God's promises is a "Yes." For this reason it is through him that we say the "Amen," to the glory of God.

Acts 10:37–38   That message spread throughout Judea, beginning in Galilee after the baptism that John announced. . . .

Luke 4:16–19   When he came to Nazareth, where he had been brought up, he went to the synagogue on the sabbath day, as was his custom. He stood up to read, and the scroll of the prophet Isaiah was given to him. He unrolled the scroll and found the place where it was written: "The Spirit of the Lord is upon me, because he has anointed me to bring good news to the poor. He has sent me to proclaim release to the captives and recovery of sight to the blind, to let the oppressed go free, to proclaim the year of the Lord's favor."

Question 39. How did Jesus Christ fulfill the office of prophet?

He was God's Word to a dying and sinful world; he embodied the love he proclaimed. His life, death, and resurrection became the great Yes that continues to be spoken despite how often we have said No. When we receive this Word by faith, Christ himself enters our hearts, that he may dwell in us forever, and we in him.

> *Acts 3:20, 22* ... so that times of refreshing may come from the presence of the Lord, and that he may send the Messiah appointed for you, that is, Jesus. ... Moses said, "The Lord your God will raise up for you from your own people a prophet like me. You must listen to whatever he tells you."

> *John 1:18* No one has ever seen God. It is God the only Son, who is close to the Father's heart, who has made him known.

> *Eph. 3:17* ... and that Christ may dwell in your hearts through faith, as you are being rooted and grounded in love.

Question 40. How did Jesus Christ fulfill the office of priest?

He was the Lamb of God that took away the sin of the world; he became our priest and sacrifice in one. Confronted by our hopelessness in sin and death, Christ interceded by offering himself—his entire person and work—in order to reconcile us to God.

> *Heb. 4:14* Since, then, we have a great high priest who has passed through the heavens, Jesus, the Son of God, let us hold fast to our confession.

> *John 1:29* The next day he saw Jesus coming toward him and declared, "Here is the Lamb of God who takes away the sin of the world!"

> *Heb. 2:17* Therefore he had to become like his brothers and sisters in every respect, so that he might be a merciful and faithful high priest in the service of God, to make a sacrifice of atonement for the sins of the people.

> *Eph. 1:7* In him we have redemption through his blood, the forgiveness of our trespasses, according to the riches of his grace. ...

Question 41. How did Jesus Christ fulfill the office of king?

He was the Lord who took the form of a servant; he perfected royal power in weakness. With no sword but the sword of righteousness, and no power but the power of love, Christ defeated sin, evil, and death by reigning from the cross.

> *John 19:19* Pilate also had an inscription written and put on the cross. It read, "Jesus of Nazareth, the King of the Jews."

> *Phil. 2:5–8* Let the same mind be in you that was in Christ Jesus, who, though he was in the form of God, did not regard equality with God as something to be exploited, but emptied himself, taking the form of a slave, being born in human likeness. And being found in human form, he humbled himself and became obedient to the point of death—even death on a cross.

> *1 Cor. 1:25* For God's foolishness is wiser than human wisdom, and God's weakness is stronger than human strength.

John 12:32   And I, when I am lifted up from the earth, will draw all people to myself.

Question 42. What do you affirm when you say that he "suffered under Pontius Pilate"?

First, that our Lord was humiliated, rejected, and abused by the temporal authorities of his day, both religious and political. Christ thus aligned himself with all human beings who are oppressed, tortured, or otherwise shamefully treated by those with worldly power. Second, and even more importantly, that our Lord, though innocent, submitted himself to condemnation by an earthly judge so that through him we ourselves, though guilty, might be acquitted before our heavenly Judge.

Luke 18:32   For he will be handed over to the Gentiles; and he will be mocked and insulted and spat upon.

Isa. 53:3   He was despised and rejected by others; a man of suffering and acquainted with infirmity; and as one from whom others hide their faces he was despised, and we held him of no account.

Ps. 9:9   The LORD is a stronghold for the oppressed, a stronghold in times of trouble.

Luke 1:52   He has brought down the powerful from their thrones, and lifted up the lowly. . . .

2 Cor. 5:21   For our sake he made him to be sin who knew no sin, so that in him we might become the righteousness of God.

2 Tim. 4:8   From now on there is reserved for me the crown of righteousness, which the Lord, the righteous judge, will give me on that day, and not only to me but also to all who have longed for his appearing.

Question 43. What do you affirm when you say that he was "crucified, dead, and buried"?

That when our Lord passed through the door of real human death, he showed us that there is no sorrow he has not known, no grief he has not borne, and no price he was unwilling to pay in order to reconcile us to God.

Matt. 26:38–39   Then he said to them, "I am deeply grieved, even to death; remain here, and stay awake with me." And going a little farther, he threw himself on the ground and prayed, "My Father, if it is possible, let this cup pass from me; yet not what I want but what you want."

Isa. 53:5   But he was wounded for our transgressions, crushed for our iniquities; upon him was the punishment that made us whole, and by his bruises we are healed.

Gal. 3:13   Christ redeemed us from the curse of the law by becoming a curse for us—for it is written, "Cursed is everyone who hangs on a tree. . . ."

Heb. 2:9   But we do see Jesus, who for a little while was made lower than the angels, now crowned with glory and honor because of the suffering of death, so that by the grace of God he might taste death for everyone.

2 Cor. 5:19   In Christ God was reconciling the world to himself, not counting their trespasses against them, and entrusting the message of reconciliation to us.

Question 44. What do you affirm when you say that he "descended into hell"?

That our Lord took upon himself the full consequences of our sinfulness, even the agony of abandonment by God, in order that we might be spared.

Mark 15:34 At three o'clock Jesus cried out with a loud voice, "Eloi, Eloi, lema sabachthani?" which means, "My God, my God, why have you forsaken me?"

Heb. 9:26 . . . for then he would have had to suffer again and again since the foundation of the world. But as it is, he has appeared once for all at the end of the age to remove sin by the sacrifice of himself.

Rom. 4:24–25 It will be reckoned to us who believe in him who raised Jesus our Lord from the dead, who was handed over to death for our trespasses and was raised for our justification.

Question 45. Why did Jesus have to suffer as he did?

Because grace is more abundant—and sin more serious—than we suppose. However cruelly we may treat one another, all sin is primarily against God. God condemns sin, yet never judges apart from grace. In giving Jesus Christ to die for us, God took the burden of our sin into God's own self to remove it once and for all. The cross in all its severity reveals an abyss of sin swallowed up by the suffering of divine love.

Rom. 8:1, 3–4 There is therefore now no condemnation for those who are in Christ Jesus. . . . For God has done what the law, weakened by the flesh, could not do: by sending his own Son in the likeness of sinful flesh, and to deal with sin, he condemned sin in the flesh, so that the just requirement of the law might be fulfilled in us, who walk not according to the flesh but according to the Spirit.

1 Cor. 1:18 For the message about the cross is foolishness to those who are perishing, but to us who are being saved it is the power of God.

Rom. 5:8 But God proves his love for us in that while we still were sinners Christ died for us.

Col. 1:20 And through him God was pleased to reconcile to himself all things, whether on earth or in heaven, by making peace through the blood of his cross.

James 2:13 For judgment will be without mercy to anyone who has shown no mercy; mercy triumphs over judgment.

Question 46. What do you affirm when you say that "on the third day he rose again from the dead"?

That our Lord could not be held by the power of death. Having died on the cross, he appeared to his followers, triumphant from the grave, in a new, exalted kind of life. In showing them his hands and his feet, the one who was crucified revealed himself to them as the Lord and Savior of the world.

Acts 2:24 But God raised him up, having freed him from death, because it was impossible for him to be held in its power.

1 Cor. 15:3–4   For I handed on to you as of first importance what I in turn had received: that Christ died for our sins in accordance with the scriptures, and that he was buried, and that he was raised on the third day in accordance with the scriptures. . . .

Luke 24:36–40   While they were talking about this, Jesus himself stood among them and said to them, "Peace be with you." They were startled and terrified, and thought that they were seeing a ghost. He said to them, "Why are you frightened, and why do doubts arise in your hearts? Look at my hands and my feet; see that it is I myself. Touch me and see; for a ghost does not have flesh and bones as you see that I have." And when he had said this, he showed them his hands and his feet.

John 20:15–18   Jesus said to her, "Woman, why are you weeping? Whom are you looking for?" Supposing him to be the gardener, she said to him, "Sir, if you have carried him away, tell me where you have laid him, and I will take him away." Jesus said to her, "Mary!" She turned and said to him in Hebrew, "Rabbouni!" (which means Teacher). Jesus said to her, "Do not hold on to me, because I have not yet ascended to the Father. But go to my brothers and say to them, 'I am ascending to my Father and your Father, to my God and your God.' " Mary Magdalene went and announced to the disciples, "I have seen the Lord"; and she told them that he had said these things to her.

1 Cor. 15:5–8   . . . and that he appeared to Cephas, then to the twelve. Then he appeared to more than five hundred brothers and sisters at one time, most of whom are still alive, though some have died. Then he appeared to James, then to all the apostles. Last of all, as to one untimely born, he appeared also to me.

John 20:27   Then he said to Thomas, "Put your finger here and see my hands. Reach out your hand and put it in my side. Do not doubt but believe."

Question 47. What do you affirm when you say that "he ascended into heaven and is seated at the right hand of the Father"?

First, that Christ has gone to be with the Father, hidden except to the eyes of faith. Second, however, that Christ is not cut off from us in the remote past, or in some place from which he cannot reach us, but is present to us here and now by grace. He reigns with divine authority, protecting us, guiding us, and interceding for us until he returns in glory.

Acts 1:6–11   So when they had come together, they asked him, "Lord, is this the time when you will restore the kingdom to Israel?" He replied, "It is not for you to know the times or periods that the Father has set by his own authority. But you will receive power when the Holy Spirit has come upon you; and you will be my witnesses in Jerusalem, in all Judea and Samaria, and to the ends of the earth." When he had said this, as they were watching, he was lifted up, and a cloud took him out of their sight. While he was going and they were gazing up toward heaven, suddenly two men in white robes stood by them. They said, "Men of Galilee, why do you stand looking up toward heaven? This Jesus, who has been taken up from you into heaven, will come in the same way as you saw him go into heaven."

Col. 3:1   So if you have been raised with Christ, seek the things that are above, where Christ is, seated at the right hand of God.

Question 48. How do you understand the words that "he will come again to judge the living and the dead"?

Like everyone else, I too must stand in fear and trembling before the judgment seat of Christ. But the Judge is the one who submitted to judgment for my sake. Nothing will be able to separate me from the love of God in Christ Jesus my Lord. All the sinful failures that cause me shame will perish as through fire, while any good I may have done will be received with gladness by God.

2 Cor. 5:10   For all of us must appear before the judgment seat of Christ, so that each may receive recompense for what has been done in the body, whether good or evil.

Eccl. 12:14   For God will bring every deed into judgment, including every secret thing, whether good or evil.

Acts 17:31   He has fixed a day on which he will have the world judged in righteousness by a man whom he has appointed, and of this he has given assurance to all by raising him from the dead.

Rom. 8:38–39   For I am convinced that neither death, nor life, nor angels, nor rulers, nor things present, nor things to come, nor powers, nor height, nor depth, nor anything else in all creation, will be able to separate us from the love of God in Christ Jesus our Lord.

1 John 4:17   Love has been perfected among us in this: that we may have boldness on the day of judgment, because as he is, so are we in this world.

1 Cor. 3:12–15   Now if anyone builds on the foundation with gold, silver, precious stones, wood, hay, straw—the work of each builder will become visible, for the Day will disclose it, because it will be revealed with fire, and the fire will test what sort of work each has done. If what has been built on the foundation survives, the builder will receive a reward. If the work is burned up, the builder will suffer loss; the builder will be saved, but only as through fire.

Acts 10:42   He commanded us to preach to the people and to testify that he is the one ordained by God as judge of the living and the dead.

Question 49. Will all human beings be saved?

No one will be lost who can be saved. The limits to salvation, whatever they may be, are known only to God. Three truths above all are certain. God is a holy God who is not to be trifled with. No one will be saved except by grace alone. And no judge could possibly be more gracious than our Lord and Savior, Jesus Christ.

Heb. 10:31   It is a fearful thing to fall into the hands of the living God.

Rom. 11:32   For God has imprisoned all in disobedience so that he may be merciful to all.

Luke 15:4–7   Which one of you, having a hundred sheep and losing one of them, does not leave the ninety-nine in the wilderness and go after the one that is lost until he finds it? When he has found it, he lays it on his shoulders and rejoices. And when he comes home, he calls together his friends and neighbors, saying to them, "Rejoice with me, for I have found my sheep that was lost." Just so, I tell you, there will be more joy in heaven over one sinner who repents than over ninety-nine righteous persons who need no repentance.

Eph. 2:8   For by grace you have been saved through faith, and this is not your own doing; it is the gift of God. . . .

1 Tim. 2:3–4   This is right and is acceptable in the sight of God our Savior, who desires everyone to be saved and to come to the knowledge of the truth.

John 3:17–18   Indeed, God did not send the Son into the world to condemn the world, but in order that the world might be saved through him. Those who believe in him are not condemned; but those who do not believe are condemned already, because they have not believed in the name of the only Son of God.

Ezek. 18:32   For I have no pleasure in the death of anyone, says the Lord GOD. Turn, then, and live.

2 Cor. 5:14–15   For the love of Christ urges us on, because we are convinced that one has died for all; therefore all have died. And he died for all, so that those who live might live no longer for themselves, but for him who died and was raised for them.

Question 50. Is Christianity the only true religion?

Religion is a complex matter. When used as a means to promote self-justification, war-mongering, or prejudice, it is a form of sin. Too often all religions—and not least Christianity—have been twisted in this way. Nevertheless, by grace, despite all disobedience, Christianity offers the truth of the gospel. Although other religions may enshrine various truths, no other can or does affirm the name of Jesus Christ as the hope of the world.

Matt. 7:3   Why do you see the speck in your neighbor's eye, but do not notice the log in your own eye?

James 1:26   If any think they are religious, and do not bridle their tongues but deceive their hearts, their religion is worthless.

James 1:27   Religion that is pure and undefiled before God, the Father, is this: to care for orphans and widows in their distress, and to keep oneself unstained by the world.

Acts 4:12   There is salvation in no one else, for there is no other name under heaven given among mortals by which we must be saved.

John 14:6   Jesus said to him, "I am the way, and the truth, and the life. No one comes to the Father except through me."

Rom. 1:16   For I am not ashamed of the gospel; it is the power of God for salvation to everyone who has faith, to the Jew first and also to the Greek.

2 Cor. 4:7   But we have this treasure in clay jars, so that it may be made clear that this extraordinary power belongs to God and does not come from us.

Question 51. How will God deal with the followers of other religions?

God has made salvation available to all human beings through Jesus Christ, crucified and risen. How God will deal with those who do not know or follow Christ, but who follow another tradition, we cannot finally say. We can say, however, that

God is gracious and merciful, and that God will not deal with people in any other way than we see in Jesus Christ, who came as the Savior of the world.

Rev. 7:9   After this I looked, and there was a great multitude that no one could count, from every nation, from all tribes and peoples and languages, standing before the throne and before the Lamb, robed in white, with palm branches in their hands.

Ps. 103:8   The LORD is merciful and gracious, slow to anger and abounding in steadfast love.

John 3:19   And this is the judgment, that the light has come into the world, and people loved darkness rather than light because their deeds were evil.

Titus 2:11   For the grace of God has appeared, bringing salvation to all. . . .

Question 52. How should I treat non-Christians and people of other religions?

As much as I can, I should meet friendship with friendship, hostility with kindness, generosity with gratitude, persecution with forbearance, truth with agreement, and error with truth. I should express my faith with humility and devotion as the occasion requires, whether silently or openly, boldly or meekly, by word or by deed. I should avoid compromising the truth on the one hand and being narrow-minded on the other. In short, I should always welcome and accept these others in a way that honors and reflects the Lord's welcome and acceptance of me.

Rom. 15:7   Welcome one another, therefore, just as Christ has welcomed you, for the glory of God.

Luke 6:37   Do not judge, and you will not be judged; do not condemn, and you will not be condemned. Forgive, and you will be forgiven.

Matt. 5:44   But I say to you, Love your enemies and pray for those who persecute you. . . .

Eph. 4:25   So then, putting away falsehood, let all of us speak the truth to our neighbors, for we are members of one another.

Acts 13:47   For so the Lord has commanded us, saying, "I have set you to be a light for the Gentiles, so that you may bring salvation to the ends of the earth."

Rom. 12:21   Do not be overcome by evil, but overcome evil with good.

Rom. 13:10   Love does no wrong to a neighbor; therefore, love is the fulfilling of the law.

Question 53. What is the third article of the Apostles' Creed?

"I believe in the Holy Spirit, the holy catholic church, the communion of saints, the forgiveness of sins, the resurrection of the body, and the life everlasting. Amen."

Question 54. What do you believe when you confess your faith in the Holy Spirit?

Apart from the Holy Spirit, our Lord can neither be loved, nor known, nor served. The Holy Spirit is the personal bond by which Jesus Christ unites us to himself, the teacher who opens our hearts to Christ, and the comforter who leads us to repentance, empowering us to live in Christ's service. As the work of the one Holy Spirit, our love, knowledge, and service of Christ are all inseparably related.

John 14:26 But the Advocate, the Holy Spirit, whom the Father will send in my name, will teach you everything, and remind you of all that I have said to you.

1 Cor. 12:3 Therefore I want you to understand that no one speaking by the Spirit of God ever says "Let Jesus be cursed!" and no one can say "Jesus is Lord" except by the Holy Spirit.

Rom. 5:5 And hope does not disappoint us, because God's love has been poured into our hearts through the Holy Spirit that has been given to us.

1 Cor. 6:17, 19 But anyone united to the Lord becomes one spirit with him. . . . Or do you not know that your body is a temple of the Holy Spirit within you, which you have from God, and that you are not your own?

1 Cor. 3:16 Do you not know that you are God's temple and that God's Spirit dwells in you?

John 4:24 God is spirit, and those who worship him must worship in spirit and truth.

Question 55. How do we receive the Holy Spirit?

By receiving the Word of God. As the midwife of the new creation, the Spirit arrives with the Word, brings us to rebirth, and assures us of eternal life. The Spirit nurtures, corrects, and strengthens us with the pure spiritual milk of the Word (1 Peter 2:2).

Eph. 6:17 Take the helmet of salvation, and the sword of the Spirit, which is the word of God.

John 14:16–17 And I will ask the Father, and he will give you another Advocate, to be with you forever. This is the Spirit of truth, whom the world cannot receive, because it neither sees him nor knows him. You know him, because he abides with you, and he will be in you.

John 3:5–6 Jesus answered, "Very truly, I tell you, no one can enter the kingdom of God without being born of water and Spirit. What is born of the flesh is flesh, and what is born of the Spirit is spirit."

Luke 11:13 If you then, who are evil, know how to give good gifts to your children, how much more will the heavenly Father give the Holy Spirit to those who ask him!

1 Thess. 1:5 . . . because our message of the gospel came to you not in word only, but also in power and in the Holy Spirit and with full conviction; just as you know what kind of persons we proved to be among you for your sake.

John 16:8 And when he comes, he will prove the world wrong about sin and righteousness and judgment. . . .

Rom. 8:15–16 For you did not receive a spirit of slavery to fall back into fear, but you have received a spirit of adoption. When we cry, "Abba! Father!" it is that very Spirit bearing witness with our spirit that we are children of God. . .
1 Peter 2:2 Like newborn infants, long for the pure, spiritual milk, so that by it you may grow into salvation. . . .

Question 56. What do you mean when you speak of "the Word of God"?

"Jesus Christ, as he is attested for us in Holy Scripture, is the one Word of God which we have to hear and which we have to trust and obey in life and in death" (Barmen Declaration, Article I).

> *John 1:1–5* In the beginning was the Word, and the Word was with God, and the Word was God. He was in the beginning with God. All things came into being through him, and without him not one thing came into being. What has come into being in him was life, and the life was the light of all people. The light shines in the darkness, and the darkness did not overcome it.

> *John 1:14* And the Word became flesh and lived among us, and we have seen his glory, the glory as of a father's only son, full of grace and truth.

Question 57. Isn't Holy Scripture also the Word of God?

Yes. Holy Scripture is also God's Word because of its content, its function, and its origin. Its central content is Jesus Christ, the living Word. Its basic function, is to deepen our love, knowledge, and service of him as our Savior and Lord. And its ultimate origin is in the Holy Spirit, who spoke through the prophets and apostles, and who inspires us with eager desire for the truths that Scripture contains.

> *2 Tim. 3:16* All scripture is inspired by God and is useful for teaching, for reproof, for correction, and for training in righteousness. . . .

> *John 5:39* You search the scriptures because you think that in them you have eternal life; and it is they that testify on my behalf.

Question 58. Isn't preaching also the Word of God?

Yes. Preaching and other forms of Christian witness are also God's Word when they are faithful to the witness of Holy Scripture. By the power of the Spirit, preaching actually gives to us what it proclaims—the real presence of our Lord Jesus Christ. Faith comes by hearing God's Word in the form of faithful proclamation.

> *Mark 16:15* And he said to them, "Go into all the world and proclaim the good news to the whole creation."

> *2 Cor. 4:5* For we do not proclaim ourselves; we proclaim Jesus Christ as Lord and ourselves as your slaves for Jesus' sake.

> *Rom. 1:15–16* . . . hence my eagerness to proclaim the gospel to you also who are in Rome. For I am not ashamed of the gospel; it is the power of God for salvation to everyone who has faith, to the Jew first and also to the Greek.

> *Rom. 10:17* So faith comes from what is heard, and what is heard comes through the word of Christ.

Question 59. Does the Holy Spirit ever speak apart from God's Word in its written and proclaimed forms?

Since the Spirit is not given to the church without the Word, true proclamation depends on Scripture. Since the Word cannot be grasped without the Spirit, true interpretation depends on prayer. However, as the wind blows where it will, so may the Spirit speak or work in people's lives in unexpected or indirect ways, yet always according to the Word, never contradicting or diluting it.

John 3:8   The wind blows where it chooses, and you hear the sound of it, but you do not know where it comes from or where it goes. So it is with everyone who is born of the Spirit.

Acts 8:29–31   Then the Spirit said to Philip, "Go over to this chariot and join it." So Philip ran up to it and heard him reading the prophet Isaiah. He asked, "Do you understand what you are reading?" He replied, "How can I, unless someone guides me?" And he invited Philip to get in and sit beside him.

Eph. 6:18   Pray in the Spirit at all times in every prayer and supplication. To that end keep alert and always persevere in supplication for all the saints.

2 Peter 1:20–21   First of all you must understand this, that no prophecy of scripture is a matter of one's own interpretation, because no prophecy ever came by human will, but men and women moved by the Holy Spirit spoke from God.

Question 60. Aren't people without faith sometimes wiser than those who have faith?

Yes. The important question for the church is not so much where an insight may come from as the norm by which to test it. Truth is where one finds it, whether inside or outside the church, and whether supporting or contradicting one's own most cherished opinions. Our faithful discernment of what is true, however, depends finally on God's Word as conveyed in Holy Scripture. The church is therefore reformed and always being reformed according to the Word of God.

Titus 1:9   He must have a firm grasp of the word that is trustworthy in accordance with the teaching, so that he may be able both to preach with sound doctrine and to refute those who contradict it.

Luke 16:8b   For the children of this age are more shrewd in dealing with their own generation than are the children of light.

Isaiah 45:4   For the sake of my servant Jacob, and Israel my chosen, I call you by your name, I surname you, though you do not know me.

Num. 22:28   Then the Lord opened the mouth of the donkey, and it said to Balaam, "What have I done to you, that you have struck me these three times?"

Question 61. Doesn't modern critical scholarship undermine your belief that Holy Scripture is a form of God's Word?

No. The methods of modern scholarship are a good servant but a bad master. They are neither to be accepted nor rejected uncritically. Properly used they help us rightly and richly interpret Scripture; improperly used they can usurp the place of faith (or establish an alternative faith). Wise interpreters use these methods in the service of faithful witness and understanding. The methods of modern scholarship remain a useful tool, while Holy Scripture remains reliable in all essential matters of faith and practice.

Prov. 1:5–6   Let the wise also hear and gain in learning, and the discerning acquire skill, to understand a proverb and a figure, the words of the wise and their riddles.

Prov. 10:14   The wise lay up knowledge, but the babbling of a fool brings ruin near.

1 Cor. 1:20, 25   Where is the one who is wise? Where is the scribe? Where is the debater of this age? Has not God made foolish the wisdom of the world? . . . For God's foolishness is wiser than human wisdom, and God's weakness is stronger than human strength.

Question 62. What do you affirm when you speak of "the holy catholic church"?

The church is the company of all faithful people who have given their lives to Jesus Christ, as he has given and gives himself to them. Since Christ cannot be separated from his people, the church is holy because he is holy, and universal (or "catholic") in significance because he is universal in significance. Despite all its remaining imperfections here and now, the church is called to become ever more holy and catholic, for that is what it already is in Christ.

Gal. 2:20   It is no longer I who live, but it is Christ who lives in me. And the life I now live in the flesh I live by faith in the Son of God, who loved me and gave himself for me.

1 Cor. 1:2   To the church of God that is in Corinth, to those who are sanctified in Christ Jesus, called to be saints, together with all those who in every place call on the name of our Lord Jesus Christ, both their Lord and ours . . .

Lev. 11:44   For I am the LORD your God; sanctify yourselves therefore, and be holy, for I am holy.

1 Peter 1:15–16   Instead, as he who called you is holy, be holy yourselves in all your conduct; for it is written, "You shall be holy, for I am holy."

Rev. 5:9   They sing a new song: "You are worthy to take the scroll and to open its seals, for you were slaughtered and by your blood you ransomed for God saints from every tribe and language and people and nation. . . ."

Question 63. What is the mission of the church?

The mission of the church is to bear witness to God's love for the world in Jesus Christ.

Acts 1:8   But you will receive power when the Holy Spirit has come upon you; and you will be my witnesses in Jerusalem, in all Judea and Samaria, and to the ends of the earth.

John 15:26–27   When the Advocate comes, whom I will send to you from the Father, the Spirit of truth who comes from the Father, he will testify on my behalf. You also are to testify because you have been with me from the beginning.

Eph. 3:8–10   Although I am the very least of all the saints, this grace was given to me to bring to the Gentiles the news of the boundless riches of Christ, and to make everyone see what is the plan of the mystery hidden for ages in God who created all things; so that through the church the wisdom of God in its rich variety might now be made known to the rulers and authorities in the heavenly places.

Question 64. What forms does this mission take?

The forms are as various as the forms of God's love, yet the center is always Jesus Christ. The church is faithful to its mission when it extends mercy and forgiveness to the needy in ways that point finally to him. For in the end it is always by Christ's mercy that the needs of the needy are met.

Luke 10:37 He said, "The one who showed him mercy." Jesus said to him, "Go and do likewise."

Eph. 4:32 Be kind to one another, tenderhearted, forgiving one another, as God in Christ has forgiven you.

Deut. 15:11 Since there will never cease to be some in need on the earth, I therefore command you, "Open your hand to the poor and needy neighbor in your land."

Acts 4:34 There was not a needy person among them, for as many as owned lands or houses sold them and brought the proceeds of what was sold.

Question 65. Who are the needy?

The hungry need bread, the homeless need a roof, the oppressed need justice, and the lonely need fellowship. At the same time—on another and deeper level—the hopeless need hope, sinners need forgiveness, and the world needs the gospel. On this level no one is excluded, and all the needy are one. Our mission as the church is to bring hope to a desperate world by declaring God's undying love—as one beggar tells another where to find bread.

Ps. 10:12 Rise up, O LORD; O God, lift up your hand; do not forget the oppressed.

Matt. 25:37–40 Then the righteous will answer him, "Lord, when was it that we saw you hungry and gave you food, or thirsty and gave you something to drink? And when was it that we saw you a stranger and welcomed you, or naked and gave you clothing? And when was it that we saw you sick or in prison and visited you?" And the king will answer them, "Truly I tell you, just as you did it to one of the least of these who are members of my family, you did it to me."

Jer. 9:23 Thus says the LORD: Do not let the wise boast in their wisdom, do not let the mighty boast in their might, do not let the wealthy boast in their wealth. . . .

1 Cor. 9:16 If I proclaim the gospel, this gives me no ground for boasting, for an obligation is laid on me, and woe to me if I do not proclaim the gospel!

Eph. 6:19 Pray also for me, so that when I speak, a message may be given to me to make known with boldness the mystery of the gospel. . . .

Question 66. What do you affirm when you speak of "the communion of saints"?

All those who live in union with Christ, whether on earth or with God in heaven, are "saints." Our communion with Christ makes us members one of another. As by his death he removed our separation from God, so by his Spirit he removes all that divides us from each other. Breaking down every wall of hostility, he makes us, who are many, one body in himself. The ties that bind us in Christ are deeper than any other human relationship.

Eph. 2:19–20 So then you are no longer strangers and aliens, but you are citizens with the saints and also members of the household of God, built upon the foundation of the apostles and prophets, with Christ Jesus himself as the cornerstone.

Rom. 12:5 . . . so we, who are many, are one body in Christ, and individually we are members one of another.

Eph. 2:14 For he is our peace; in his flesh he has made both groups into one and has broken down the dividing wall, that is, the hostility between us.

1 Cor. 12:27 Now you are the body of Christ and individually members of it.

Gal. 3:28 There is no longer Jew or Greek, there is no longer slave or free, there is no longer male and female; for all of you are one in Christ Jesus.

Eph. 4:4 There is one body and one Spirit, just as you were called to the one hope of your calling. . . .

1 Cor. 12:4–7, 12–13 Now there are varieties of gifts, but the same Spirit; and there are varieties of services, but the same Lord; and there are varieties of activities, but it is the same God who activates all of them in everyone. To each is given the manifestation of the Spirit for the common good. . . . For just as the body is one and has many members, and all the members of the body, though many, are one body, so it is with Christ. For in the one Spirit we were all baptized into one body—Jews or Greeks, slaves or free—and we were all made to drink of one Spirit.

Question 67. How do you enter into communion with Christ and so with one another?

By the power of the Holy Spirit as it works through Word and Sacrament. Because the Spirit uses them for our salvation, Word and Sacrament are called "means of grace." The Scriptures acknowledge two sacraments as instituted by our Lord Jesus Christ—baptism and the Lord's Supper.

1 Cor. 10:17 Because there is one bread, we who are many are one body, for we all partake of the one bread.

1 Cor. 12:13 For in the one Spirit we were all baptized into one body—Jews or Greeks, slaves or free—and we were all made to drink of one Spirit.

Col. 3:16 Let the word of Christ dwell in you richly; teach and admonish one another in all wisdom; and with gratitude in your hearts sing psalms, hymns, and spiritual songs to God.

Question 68. What is a sacrament?

A sacrament is a special act of Christian worship, instituted by Christ, which uses a visible sign to proclaim the promise of the gospel for the forgiveness of sins and eternal life. The sacramental sign seals this promise to believers by grace and brings to them what is promised. In baptism the sign is that of water; in the Lord's Supper, that of bread and wine.

Mark 1:9–11 In those days Jesus came from Nazareth of Galilee and was baptized by John in the Jordan. And just as he was coming up out of the water, he saw the heavens torn apart and the Spirit descending like a dove on him. And a voice came from heaven, "You are my Son, the Beloved; with you I am well pleased."

Mark 14:22–25 While they were eating, he took a loaf of bread, and after blessing it he broke it, gave it to them, and said, "Take; this is my body." Then he took a cup, and after giving thanks he gave it to them, and all of them drank from it. He said to them, "This is my blood of the covenant, which is poured out for many. Truly I tell you, I will never again drink of the fruit of the vine until that day when I drink it new in the kingdom of God."

Question 69. How do you understand the relationship between the word of promise and the sacramental sign?

Take away the word of promise, and the water is merely water, or the bread and wine, merely bread and wine. But add water, or bread and wine, to the word of promise, and it becomes a visible word. In this form it does what by grace the word always does: it brings the salvation it promises, and conveys to faith the real presence of our Lord Jesus Christ. The sacraments are visible words which uniquely assure and confirm that no matter how greatly I may have sinned, Christ died also for me, and comes to live in me and with me.

Luke 24:30–31 When he was at the table with them, he took bread, blessed and broke it, and gave it to them. Then their eyes were opened, and they recognized him; and he vanished from their sight.

1 Cor. 10:16 The cup of blessing that we bless, is it not a sharing in the blood of Christ? The bread that we break, is it not a sharing in the body of Christ?

Matt. 28:20 . . . teaching them to obey everything that I have commanded you. And remember, I am with you always, to the end of the age.

Col. 1:27 To them God chose to make known how great among the Gentiles are the riches of the glory of this mystery, which is Christ in you, the hope of glory.

Question 70. What is the main difference between baptism and the Lord's Supper?

While I receive baptism only once, I receive the Lord's Supper again and again. Being unrepeatable, baptism indicates not only that Christ died for our sins once and for all, but that by grace we are also united with him once and for all through faith. Being repeatable, the Lord's Supper indicates that as we turn unfilled to him again and again, our Lord continually meets us in the power of the Holy Spirit to renew and deepen our faith.

Acts 2:41 So those who welcomed his message were baptized, and that day about three thousand persons were added.

John 6:33 For the bread of God is that which comes down from heaven and gives life to the world.

John 6:51 I am the living bread that came down from heaven. Whoever eats of this bread will live forever; and the bread that I will give for the life of the world is my flesh.

John 6:56 Those who eat my flesh and drink my blood abide in me, and I in them.

1 Cor. 11:26 For as often as you eat this bread and drink the cup, you proclaim the Lord's death until he comes.

Question 71. What is baptism?

Baptism is the sign and seal through which we are joined to Christ.

> *Rom. 6:3–4* Do you not know that all of us who have been baptized into Christ Jesus were baptized into his death? Therefore we have been buried with him by baptism into death, so that, just as Christ was raised from the dead by the glory of the Father, so we too might walk in newness of life.

> *Gal. 3:27* As many of you as were baptized into Christ have clothed yourselves with Christ.

> *Rom. 4:11* He received the sign of circumcision as a seal of the righteousness that he had by faith while he was still uncircumcised. The purpose was to make him the ancestor of all who believe without being circumcised and who thus have righteousness reckoned to them. . . .

Question 72. What does it mean to be baptized?

My baptism means that I am joined to Jesus Christ forever. I am baptized into his death and resurrection, along with all who have received him by faith. As I am baptized with water, he baptizes me with his Spirit, washing away all my sins and freeing me from their control. My baptism is a sign that one day I will rise with him in glory, and may walk with him even now in newness of life.

> *Col. 2:12* . . . When you were buried with him in baptism, you were also raised with him through faith in the power of God, who raised him from the dead.

> *Mark 1:8* I have baptized you with water; but he will baptize you with the Holy Spirit.

> *1 Cor. 6:11* And this is what some of you used to be. But you were washed, you were sanctified, you were justified in the name of the Lord Jesus Christ and in the Spirit of our God.

> *Eph. 4:4–6* There is one body and one Spirit, just as you were called to the one hope of your calling, one Lord, one faith, one baptism, one God and Father of all, who is above all and through all and in all.

Question 73. Are infants also to be baptized?

Yes. Along with their believing parents, they are included in the great hope of the gospel and belong to the people of God. Forgiveness and faith are both promised to them as gifts through Christ's covenant with his people. These children are therefore to be received into the community by baptism, nurtured in the Word of God, and confirmed at an appropriate time by their own profession of faith.

> *Gen. 17:7* I will establish my covenant between me and you, and your offspring after you throughout their generations, for an everlasting covenant, to be God to you and to your offspring after you.

> *Acts 2:38–39* Peter said to them, "Repent, and be baptized every one of you in the name of Jesus Christ so that your sins may be forgiven; and you will receive the gift of the Holy Spirit. For the promise is for you, for your children, and for all who are far away, everyone whom the Lord our God calls to him."

Acts 16:15 When she and her household were baptized, she urged us, saying, "If you have judged me to be faithful to the Lord, come and stay at my home." And she prevailed upon us.

Acts 16:33 At the same hour of the night he took them and washed their wounds; then he and his entire family were baptized without delay.

Acts 18:8 Crispus, the official of the synagogue, became a believer in the Lord, together with all his household; and many of the Corinthians who heard Paul became believers and were baptized.

Question 74. Should infants be baptized if their parents or guardians have no relation to the church?

No. It would be irresponsible to baptize an infant without at least one Christian parent or guardian who promises to nurture the infant in the life of the community and to instruct it in the Christian faith.

Eph. 6:4 And, fathers, do not provoke your children to anger, but bring them up in the discipline and instruction of the Lord.

2 Tim. 1:5 I am reminded of your sincere faith, a faith that lived first in your grandmother Lois and your mother Eunice and now, I am sure, lives in you.

1 Cor. 7:14 For the unbelieving husband is made holy through his wife, and the unbelieving wife is made holy through her husband. Otherwise, your children would be unclean, but as it is, they are holy.

Question 75. In what name are you baptized?

In the name of the Trinity. After he was raised from the dead, our Lord appeared to his disciples and said to them, "Go therefore and make disciples of all nations, baptizing them in the name of the Father and of the Son and of the Holy Spirit" (Matt. 28:19).

Matt. 28:16–20 Now the eleven disciples went to Galilee, to the mountain to which Jesus had directed them. When they saw him, they worshiped him; but some doubted. And Jesus came and said to them, "All authority in heaven and on earth has been given to me. Go therefore and make disciples of all nations, baptizing them in the name of the Father and of the Son and of the Holy Spirit, and teaching them to obey everything that I have commanded you. And remember, I am with you always, to the end of the age."

Matt. 3:16–17 And when Jesus had been baptized, just as he came up from the water, suddenly the heavens were opened to him and he saw the Spirit of God descending like a dove and alighting on him. And a voice from heaven said, "This is my Son, the Beloved, with whom I am well pleased."

1 Peter 1:2 [To those] who have been chosen and destined by God the Father and sanctified by the Spirit to be obedient to Jesus Christ and to be sprinkled with his blood: May grace and peace be yours in abundance.

1 Cor. 12:4–6 Now there are varieties of gifts, but the same Spirit; and there are varieties of services, but the same Lord; and there are varieties of activities, but it is the same God who activates all of them in everyone.

Question 76. What is the meaning of this name?

It is the name of the Holy Trinity. The Father is God, the Son is God, and the Holy Spirit is God. And yet they are not three gods, but one God in three persons. We worship God in this mystery.

2 Cor. 13:13   The grace of the Lord Jesus Christ, the love of God, and the communion of the Holy Spirit be with all of you.

John 1:1–4   In the beginning was the Word, and the Word was with God, and the Word was God. He was in the beginning with God. All things came into being through him, and without him not one thing came into being. What has come into being in him was life, and the life was the light of all people.

Rom. 8:11   If the Spirit of him who raised Jesus from the dead dwells in you, he who raised Christ from the dead will give life to your mortal bodies also through his Spirit that dwells in you.

John 16:13–15   When the Spirit of truth comes, he will guide you into all the truth; for he will not speak on his own, but will speak whatever he hears, and he will declare to you the things that are to come. He will glorify me, because he will take what is mine and declare it to you. All that the Father has is mine. For this reason I said that he will take what is mine and declare it to you.

Question 77. What is the Lord's Supper?

The Lord's Supper is the sign and seal by which our communion with Christ is renewed.

1 Cor. 10:16   The cup of blessing that we bless, is it not a sharing in the blood of Christ? The bread that we break, is it not a sharing in the body of Christ?

Question 78. What does it mean to share in the Lord's Supper?

When we celebrate the Lord's Supper, the Lord Jesus Christ is truly present, pouring out his Spirit upon us. By his Spirit, the bread that we break and the cup that we bless share in our Lord's own body and blood. Through them he once offered our life to God; through them he now offers his life to us. As I receive the bread and the cup, remembering that Christ died even for me, I feed on him in my heart by faith with thanksgiving, and enter his risen life, so that his life becomes mine, and my life becomes his, to all eternity.

1 Cor. 11:23–26   For I received from the Lord what I also handed on to you, that the Lord Jesus on the night when he was betrayed took a loaf of bread, and when he had given thanks, he broke it and said, "This is my body that is for you. Do this in remembrance of me." In the same way he took the cup also, after supper, saying, "This cup is the new covenant in my blood. Do this, as often as you drink it, in remembrance of me." For as often as you eat this bread and drink the cup, you proclaim the Lord's death until he comes.

Mark 14:22–25   While they were eating, he took a loaf of bread, and after blessing it he broke it, gave it to them, and said, "Take; this is my body." Then he took a cup, and after giving thanks he gave it to them, and all of them drank from it. He said to them, "This is my blood of the covenant, which is poured out for many. Truly I tell you, I will never again drink of the fruit of the vine until that day when I drink it new in the kingdom of God."

Question 79. Who may receive the Lord's Supper?

All baptized Christians who rejoice in so great a gift, who confess their sins, and who draw near with faith intending to lead a new life, may receive the Lord's Supper. This includes baptized children who have expressed a desire to participate and who have been instructed in the meaning of the sacrament in a way they can understand.

> *Luke 13:29*   Then people will come from east and west, from north and south, and will eat in the kingdom of God.

> *1 Cor 11:28*   Examine yourselves, and only then eat of the bread and drink of the cup.

> *Phil. 4:4*   Rejoice in the Lord always; again I will say, Rejoice.

Question 80. What do you mean when you speak of "the forgiveness of sins"?

That because of Jesus Christ, God no longer holds my sins against me. Christ alone is my righteousness and my life; Christ is my only hope. Grace alone, not my merits, is the basis on which God has forgiven me in him. Faith alone, not my works, is the means by which I receive Christ into my heart, and with him the forgiveness that makes me whole. Christ alone, grace alone, and faith alone bring the forgiveness I receive through the gospel.

> *1 Cor. 1:30*   He is the source of your life in Christ Jesus, who became for us wisdom from God, and righteousness and sanctification and redemption. . . .

> *1 Tim. 1:1*   Paul, an apostle of Christ Jesus by the command of God our Savior and of Christ Jesus our hope. . . .

> *Rom. 11:6*   But if it is by grace, it is no longer on the basis of works, otherwise grace would no longer be grace.

> *Eph. 2:8*   For by grace you have been saved through faith, and this is not your own doing; it is the gift of God. . . .

> *Rom. 5:15*   But the free gift is not like the trespass. For if the many died through the one man's trespass, much more surely have the grace of God and the free gift in the grace of the one man, Jesus Christ, abounded for the many.

> *Rom. 4:16*   For this reason it depends on faith, in order that the promise may rest on grace and be guaranteed to all his descendants, not only to the adherents of the law but also to those who share the faith of Abraham (for he is the father of all of us). . . .

> *Rom. 3:28*   For we hold that a person is justified by faith apart from works prescribed by the law.

Question 81. Does forgiveness mean that God condones sin?

No. God does not cease to be God. Although God is merciful, God does not condone what God forgives. In the death and resurrection of Christ, God judges what God abhors—everything hostile to love—by abolishing it at the very roots. In this judgment the unexpected occurs: good is brought out of evil, hope out of hopelessness, and life out of death. God spares sinners and turns them from enemies into friends. The uncompromising judgment of God is revealed in the suffering love of the cross.

Hab. 1:13   Your eyes are too pure to behold evil, and you cannot look on wrongdoing; why do you look on the treacherous, and are silent when the wicked swallow those more righteous than they?

Isa. 59:15   Truth is lacking, and whoever turns from evil is despoiled. The Lord saw it, and it displeased him that there was no justice.

Heb. 9:22   Indeed, under the law almost everything is purified with blood, and without the shedding of blood there is no forgiveness of sins.

Rom. 5:8–10   But God proves his love for us in that while we still were sinners Christ died for us. Much more surely then, now that we have been justified by his blood, will we be saved through him from the wrath of God. For if while we were enemies, we were reconciled to God through the death of his Son, much more surely, having been reconciled, will we be saved by his life.

1 Chron. 16:33   Then shall the trees of the forest sing for joy before the LORD, for he comes to judge the earth.

Question 82. Does your forgiveness of those who have harmed you depend on their repentance?

No. I am to forgive as I have been forgiven. The gospel is the astonishing good news that while we were yet sinners Christ died for us. Just as God's forgiveness of me is unconditional, and so precedes my confession of sin and repentance, so my forgiveness of those who have harmed me does not depend on their confessing and repenting of their sin. However, when I forgive the person who has done me harm, giving up any resentment or desire to retaliate, I do not condone the harm that was done or excuse the evil of the sin.

Col. 3:13   Bear with one another and, if anyone has a complaint against another, forgive each other; just as the Lord has forgiven you, so you also must forgive.

Mark 11:25   Whenever you stand praying, forgive, if you have anything against anyone; so that your Father in heaven may also forgive you your trespasses.

Col. 2:13   And when you were dead in trespasses and the uncircumcision of your flesh, God made you alive together with him, when he forgave us all our trespasses. . . .

Matt. 18:21–22   Then Peter came and said to him, "Lord, if another member of the church sins against me, how often should I forgive? As many as seven times?" Jesus said to him, "Not seven times, but, I tell you, seventy-seven times."

Heb. 12:14   Pursue peace with everyone, and the holiness without which no one will see the Lord.

Question 83. How can you forgive those who have really hurt you?

I cannot love my enemies, I cannot pray for those who persecute me, I cannot even be ready to forgive those who have really hurt me, without the grace that comes from above. I cannot be conformed to the image of God's Son, apart from the power of God's Word and Spirit. Yet I am promised that I can do all things through Christ who strengthens me.

Luke 6:27–28   But I say to you that listen, Love your enemies, do good to those who hate you, bless those who curse you, pray for those who abuse you.

James 1:17   Every generous act of giving, with every perfect gift, is from above, coming down from the Father of lights, with whom there is no variation or shadow due to change.

Rom. 8:29   For those whom he foreknew he also predestined to be conformed to the image of his Son, in order that he might be the firstborn within a large family.

Phil. 4:13   I can do all things through him who strengthens me.

Question 84. What do you mean when you speak of "the resurrection of the body"?

Because Christ lives, we will live also. The resurrection of the body celebrates our eternal value to God as living persons, each one with a unique and distinctive identity. Indeed, the living Savior who goes before us was once heard, seen, and touched in person, after the discovery of his empty tomb. The resurrection of the body means hope for the whole person, because it is in the unity of body and soul, not in soul alone, that I belong in life and in death to my faithful Savior Jesus Christ.

John 14:19   In a little while the world will no longer see me, but you will see me; because I live, you also will live.

John 11:25   Jesus said to her, "I am the resurrection and the life. Those who believe in me, even though they die, will live. . . ."

Rom. 6:5   For if we have been united with him in a death like his, we will certainly be united with him in a resurrection like his.

1 Cor. 15:21   For since death came through a human being, the resurrection of the dead has also come through a human being. . . .

1 Cor. 15:42   So it is with the resurrection of the dead. What is sown is perishable, what is raised is imperishable.

Col. 1:18   He is the head of the body, the church; he is the beginning, the firstborn from the dead, so that he might come to have first place in everything.

Question 85. What is the nature of resurrection hope?

Resurrection hope is a hope for the transformation of this world, not a hope for escape from it. It is the hope that evil in all its forms will be utterly eradicated, that past history will be redeemed, and that all the things that ever were will be made new. It is the hope of a new creation, a new heaven, and a new earth, in which God is really honored as God, human beings are truly loving, and peace and justice reign on earth.

Isa. 11:6   The wolf shall live with the lamb, the leopard shall lie down with the kid, the calf and the lion and the fatling together, and a little child shall lead them.

Rev. 21:1   Then I saw a new heaven and a new earth; for the first heaven and the first earth had passed away, and the sea was no more.

Isa. 65:17   For I am about to create new heavens and a new earth; the former things shall not be remembered or come to mind.

2 Peter 3:13 But, in accordance with his promise, we wait for new heavens and a new earth, where righteousness is at home.

2 Cor. 5:17 So if anyone is in Christ, there is a new creation: everything old has passed away; see, everything has become new!

Question 86. Does resurrection hope mean that we don't have to take action to relieve the suffering of this world?

No. When the great hope is truly alive, small hopes arise even now for alleviating the sufferings of the present time. Reconciliation—with God, with one another, and with oneself—is the great hope God has given to the world. While we commit to God the needs of the whole world in our prayers, we also know that we are commissioned to be instruments of God's peace. When hostility, injustice, and suffering are overcome here and now, we anticipate the end of all things—the life that God brings out of death, which is the meaning of resurrection hope.

Ps. 27:13 I believe that I shall see the goodness of the LORD in the land of the living.

Ps. 33:20–22 Our soul waits for the LORD; he is our help and shield. Our heart is glad in him, because we trust in his holy name. Let your steadfast love, O Lord, be upon us, even as we hope in you.

Rom. 14:19 Let us then pursue what makes for peace and for mutual upbuilding.

Deut. 30:19 I call heaven and earth to witness against you today that I have set before you life and death, blessings and curses. Choose life so that you and your descendants may live. . . .

Luke 1:78–79 By the tender mercy of our God, the dawn from on high will break upon us, to give light to those who sit in darkness and in the shadow of death, to guide our feet into the way of peace.

Question 87. What do you affirm when you speak of "the life everlasting"?

That God does not will to be God without us, but instead grants to us creatures—fallen and mortal as we are—eternal life. Communion with Jesus Christ is eternal life itself. In him we were chosen before the foundation of the world. By him the eternal covenant with Israel was taken up, embodied, and fulfilled. To him we are joined by the Holy Spirit through faith and adopted as children, the sons and daughters of God. Through him we are raised from death to new life. For him we shall live to all eternity.

John 3:16 For God so loved the world that he gave his only Son, so that everyone who believes in him may not perish but may have eternal life.

John 6:54 Those who eat my flesh and drink my blood have eternal life, and I will raise them up on the last day. . . .

John 17:3 And this is eternal life, that they may know you, the only true God, and Jesus Christ whom you have sent.

Rom. 6:22 But now that you have been freed from sin and enslaved to God, the advantage you get is sanctification. The end is eternal life.

Rom. 6:23 For the wages of sin is death, but the free gift of God is eternal life in Christ Jesus our Lord.

1 John 2:25   And this is what he has promised us, eternal life.

Matt. 25:34   Then the king will say to those at his right hand, "Come, you that are blessed by my Father, inherit the kingdom prepared for you from the foundation of the world. . . ."

Question 88. Won't heaven be a boring place?

No. Heaven is our true home, a world of love. There the Spirit shall be poured out into every heart in perfect love. There the Father and the Son are united in the loving bond of the Spirit. There we shall be united with them and one another. There we shall at last see face to face what we now only glimpse as through a distant mirror. Our deepest, truest delights in this life are only a dim foreshadowing of the delights that await us in heaven. "You show me the path of life. In your presence there is fullness of joy; in your right hand are pleasures forevermore" (Ps. 16:11).

John 14:2–3   In my Father's house there are many dwelling places. If it were not so, would I have told you that I go to prepare a place for you? And if I go and prepare a place for you, I will come again and will take you to myself, so that where I am, there you may be also.

Matt. 6:20   But store up for yourselves treasures in heaven, where neither moth nor rust consumes and where thieves do not break in and steal.

Matt. 8:11   I tell you, many will come from east and west and will eat with Abraham and Isaac and Jacob in the kingdom of heaven. . . .

Col. 1:5   . . . because of the hope laid up for you in heaven. You have heard of this hope before in the word of the truth, the gospel. . . .

1 Cor. 13:12   For now we see in a mirror, dimly, but then we will see face to face. Now I know only in part; then I will know fully, even as I have been fully known.

II. The Ten Commandments

Question 89. What are the Ten Commandments?

The Ten Commandments give a summary of God's law for our lives. They teach us how to live rightly with God and one another.

Deut. 10:4   Then he wrote on the tablets the same words as before, the ten commandments that the LORD had spoken to you on the mountain out of the fire on the day of the assembly; and the LORD gave them to me.

Matt. 19:17   And he said to him, "Why do you ask me about what is good? There is only one who is good. If you wish to enter into life, keep the commandments."

Question 90. Why did God give this law?

After rescuing the people of Israel from their slavery in Egypt, God led them to Mount Sinai, where they received the law through Moses. It was the great charter of liberty for Israel, a people chosen to live in covenant with God and to serve as a light to the nations. It remains the charter of liberty for all who would love, know, and serve the Lord today.

Ex. 20:2   I am the LORD your God, who brought you out of the land of Egypt, out of the house of slavery. . . .

Deut. 11:1   You shall love the LORD your God, therefore, and keep his charge, his decrees, his ordinances, and his commandments always.

Luke 1:74–75   . . . that we, being rescued from the hands of our enemies, might serve him without fear, in holiness and righteousness before him all our days.

Question 91. Why should you obey this law?

Not to win God's love, for God already loves me. Not to earn my salvation, for Christ has earned it for me. Not to avoid being punished, for then I would obey out of fear. With gladness in my heart I should obey God's law out of gratitude, for God has blessed me by it and given it for my well-being.

Ps. 118:1   O give thanks to the LORD, for he is good; his steadfast love endures forever!

Col. 3:17   And whatever you do, in word or deed, do everything in the name of the Lord Jesus, giving thanks to God the Father through him.

Question 92. What are the uses of God's law?

God's law has three uses. First, it shows me how grievously I fail to live according to God's will, driving me to pray for God's mercy. Second, it functions to restrain even the worst of sinners through the fear of punishment. Finally, it teaches me how to live a life which bears witness to the gospel, and spurs me on to do so.

Rom. 3:20   For "no human being will be justified in his sight" by deeds prescribed by the law, for through the law comes the knowledge of sin.

Rom. 7:7   What then should we say? That the law is sin? By no means! Yet, if it had not been for the law, I would not have known sin. I would not have known what it is to covet if the law had not said, "You shall not covet."

Prov. 6:23   For the commandment is a lamp and the teaching a light, and the reproofs of discipline are the way of life. . . .

Phil. 1:27a   Only, live your life in a manner worthy of the gospel of Christ. . . .

Question 93. What is the first commandment?

"You shall have no other gods before me" (Ex. 20:3; Deut. 5:7).

Deut. 26:17   Today you have obtained the LORD's agreement: to be your God; and for you to walk in his ways, to keep his statutes, his commandments, and his ordinances, and to obey him.

Matt. 4:10   Jesus said to him, "Away with you, Satan! for it is written, 'Worship the Lord your God, and serve only him.'"

Question 94. What do you learn from this commandment?

No loyalty comes before my loyalty to God. I should worship and serve only God, expect all good from God alone, and love, fear, and honor God with all my heart.

Matt. 6:24   No one can serve two masters; for a slave will either hate the one and love the other, or be devoted to the one and despise the other. You cannot serve God and wealth.

Deut. 6:5   You shall love the LORD your God with all your heart, and with all your soul, and with all your might.

Prov. 9:10   The fear of the LORD is the beginning of wisdom, and the knowledge of the Holy One is insight.

Matt. 10:37   Whoever loves father or mother more than me is not worthy of me; and whoever loves son or daughter more than me is not worthy of me. . . .

Question 95. What is the second commandment?

"You shall not make for yourself an idol" (Ex. 20:4; Deut. 5:8).

Question 96. What do you learn from this commandment?

First, when I treat anything other than God as though it were God, I practice idolatry. Second, when I assume that my own interests are more important than anything else, I make them into idols, and in effect make an idol of myself.

Deut. 6:14   Do not follow other gods, any of the gods of the peoples who are all around you. . . .

1 John 5:21 Little children, keep yourselves from idols.

Ex. 34:14   For you shall worship no other god, because the LORD, whose name is Jealous, is a jealous God.

1 Chron. 16:26   For all the gods of the peoples are idols, but the LORD made the heavens.

Rom. 1:22–23   Claiming to be wise, they became fools; and they exchanged the glory of the immortal God for images resembling a mortal human being or birds or four-footed animals or reptiles.

Phil. 2:4   Let each of you look not to your own interests, but to the interests of others.

Question 97. What is the third commandment?

"You shall not make wrongful use of the name of the Lord your God" (Ex. 20:7; Deut. 5:11).

Question 98. What do you learn from this commandment?

I should use God's name with reverence and awe. God's name is taken in vain when used to support wrong. It is insulted when used carelessly, as in a curse or a pious cliché.

Ps. 29:2   Ascribe to the LORD the glory of his name; worship the Lord in holy splendor.

Rev. 15:3–4   And they sing the song of Moses, the servant of God, and the song of the Lamb: "Great and amazing are your deeds, Lord God the Almighty! Just and true are your ways, King of the nations! Lord, who will not fear and glorify your name? For you alone are holy. All nations will come and worship before you, for your judgments have been revealed."

Ps. 138:2   I bow down toward your holy temple and give thanks to your name for your steadfast love and your faithfulness; for you have exalted your name and your word above everything.

Eph. 4:29   Let no evil talk come out of your mouths, but only what is useful for building up, as there is need, so that your words may give grace to those who hear.

Ps. 103:1–2   Bless the LORD, O my soul, and all that is within me, bless his holy name. Bless the LORD, O my soul, and do not forget all his benefits. . . .

Question 99. What is the fourth commandment?

"Remember the Sabbath day, and keep it holy" (Ex. 20:8; Deut. 5:12).

Question 100. What do you learn from this commandment?

God requires a special day to be set apart so that worship can be at the center of my life. It is right to honor God with thanks and praise, and to hear and receive God's Word, so that I may have it in my heart and on my lips, and put it into practice in my life.

Rom. 10:8   But what does it say? "The word is near you, on your lips and in your heart" (that is, the word of faith that we proclaim). . . .

Deut. 5:12   Observe the sabbath day and keep it holy, as the LORD your God commanded you.

Gen. 2:3   So God blessed the seventh day and hallowed it, because on it God rested from all the work that he had done in creation.

Lev. 23:3   Six days shall work be done; but the seventh day is a sabbath of complete rest, a holy convocation; you shall do no work: it is a sabbath to the LORD throughout your settlements.

Acts 2:42, 46   They devoted themselves to the apostles' teaching and fellowship, to the breaking of bread and the prayers. . . . Day by day, as they spent much time together in the temple, they broke bread at home and ate their food with glad and generous hearts. . . .

Question 101. Why set aside one day a week as a day of rest?

First, working people should not be taken advantage of by their employers (Deut. 5:14). My job should not be my tyrant, for my life is more than my work. Second, God requires me to put time aside for the regular study of Holy Scripture and for prayer, not only by myself but also with others, not least those in my own household.

Deut. 5:14   But the seventh day is a sabbath to the LORD your God; you shall not do any work—you, or your son or your daughter, or your male or female slave, or your ox or your donkey, or any of your livestock, or the resident alien in your towns, so that your male and female slave may rest as well as you.

Ex. 31:17   It is a sign forever between me and the people of Israel that in six days the LORD made heaven and earth, and on the seventh day he rested, and was refreshed.

Question 102. Why do we Christians usually gather on the first day of the week?

In worshiping together on the first day of the week, we celebrate our Lord's resurrection, so that the new life Christ brought us might begin to fill our whole lives.

Mark 16:2   And very early on the first day of the week, when the sun had risen, they went to the tomb.

Acts 20:7   On the first day of the week, when we met to break bread, Paul was holding a discussion with them; since he intended to leave the next day, he continued speaking until midnight.

Acts 4:33   With great power the apostles gave their testimony to the resurrection of the Lord Jesus, and great grace was upon them all.

Question 103. What is the best summary of the first four commandments?

These teach me how to live rightly with God. Jesus summed them up with the commandment he called the first and greatest: "You shall love the Lord your God with all your heart, and with all your soul, and with all your mind" (Matt. 22:37; Deut. 6:5).

Question 104. What is the fifth commandment?

"Honor your father and your mother" (Ex. 20:12; Deut. 5:16).

Question 105. What do you learn from this commandment?

Though I owe reverence to God alone, I owe genuine respect to my parents, both my mother and father. God wills me to listen to them, be thankful for the benefits I receive from them, and be considerate of their needs, especially in old age.

Eph. 5:21   Be subject to one another out of reverence for Christ.

Rom. 12:10   Love one another with mutual affection; outdo one another in showing honor.

Eph. 6:2   "Honor your father and mother"—this is the first commandment with a promise. . . .

Prov. 1:8   Hear, my child, your father's instruction, and do not reject your mother's teaching. . . .

Lev. 19:32   You shall rise before the aged, and defer to the old; and you shall fear your God: I am the LORD.

Luke 2:51   Then he went down with them and came to Nazareth, and was obedient to them. His mother treasured all these things in her heart.

Question 106. Are there limits to your obligation to obey them?

Yes. No mere human being is God. Blind obedience is not required, for everything should be tested by loyalty and obedience to God. When it seems as though I should not obey, I should always be alert to possible self-deception on my part and should pray that we may all walk in the truth of God's will.

1 Peter 2:17   Honor everyone. Love the family of believers. Fear God. Honor the emperor.

Acts 5:29   But Peter and the apostles answered, "We must obey God rather than any human authority."

Question 107. What is the sixth commandment?

"You shall not murder" (Ex. 20:13; Deut. 5:17).

Question 108. What do you learn from this commandment?

God forbids anything that harms my neighbor unfairly. Murder or injury can be done not only by direct violence but also by an angry word or a clever plan, and not only by an individual but also by unjust social institutions. I should honor every human being, including my enemy, as a person made in God's image.

1 John 3:15   All who hate a brother or sister are murderers, and you know that murderers do not have eternal life abiding in them.

Prov. 24:17   Do not rejoice when your enemies fall, and do not let your heart be glad when they stumble. . . .

Rom. 12:19–20   Beloved, never avenge yourselves, but leave room for the wrath of God; for it is written, "Vengeance is mine, I will repay, says the Lord." No, "if your enemies are hungry, feed them; if they are thirsty, give them something to drink; for by doing this you will heap burning coals on their heads."

Col. 3:12–13   As God's chosen ones, holy and beloved, clothe yourselves with compassion, kindness, humility, meekness, and patience. Bear with one another and, if anyone has a complaint against another, forgive each other; just as the Lord has forgiven you, so you also must forgive.

Matt. 5:21–22   You have heard that it was said to those of ancient times, "You shall not murder"; and "whoever murders shall be liable to judgment." But I say to you that if you are angry with a brother or sister, you will be liable to judgment; and if you insult a brother or sister, you will be liable to the council; and if you say, "You fool," you will be liable to the hell of fire.

Matt. 26:52   Then Jesus said to him, "Put your sword back into its place; for all who take the sword will perish by the sword."

Question 109. What is the seventh commandment?

"You shall not commit adultery" (Ex. 20:14; Deut. 5:18).

Question 110. What do you learn from this commandment?

God requires fidelity and purity in sexual relations. Since love is God's great gift, God expects me not to corrupt it, or confuse it with momentary desire or the selfish fulfillment of my own pleasures. God forbids all sexual immorality, whether in married or in single life.

Eph. 5:3   But fornication and impurity of any kind, or greed, must not even be mentioned among you, as is proper among saints.

Matt. 5:27–29   You have heard that it was said, "You shall not commit adultery." But I say to you that everyone who looks at a woman with lust has already committed adultery with her in his heart. If your right eye causes you to sin, tear it out and throw it away; it is better for you to lose one of your members than for your whole body to be thrown into hell.

Heb. 13:4   Let marriage be held in honor by all, and let the marriage bed be kept undefiled; for God will judge fornicators and adulterers.

1 Thess. 4:3–4   For this is the will of God, your sanctification: that you abstain from fornication; that each one of you know how to control your own body in holiness and honor. . . .

Question 111. What is the eighth commandment?

"You shall not steal" (Ex. 20:15; Deut. 5:19).

Question 112. What do you learn from this commandment?

God forbids all theft and robbery, including schemes, tricks, or systems that unjustly take what belongs to someone else. God requires me not to be driven by greed, not to misuse or waste the gifts I have been given, and not to distrust the promise that God will supply my needs.

Job 20:19–20   For they have crushed and abandoned the poor, they have seized a house that they did not build. "They knew no quiet in their bellies; in their greed they let nothing escape."

Jer. 22:13   Woe to him who builds his house by unrighteousness, and his upper rooms by injustice; who makes his neighbors work for nothing, and does not give them their wages. . . .

Prov. 18:9   One who is slack in work is close kin to a vandal.

1 Tim. 6:9–10   But those who want to be rich fall into temptation and are trapped by many senseless and harmful desires that plunge people into ruin and destruction. For the love of money is a root of all kinds of evil, and in their eagerness to be rich some have wandered away from the faith and pierced themselves with many pains.

1 John 3:17   How does God's love abide in anyone who has the world's goods and sees a brother or sister in need and yet refuses help?

Luke 12:15   And he said to them, "Take care! Be on your guard against all kinds of greed; for one's life does not consist in the abundance of possessions."

Phil. 4:19   And my God will fully satisfy every need of yours according to his riches in glory in Christ Jesus.

Question 113. What is the ninth commandment?

"You shall not bear false witness against your neighbor" (Ex. 20:16; Deut. 5:20).

Question 114. What do you learn from this commandment?

God forbids me to damage the honor or reputation of my neighbor. I should not say false things against anyone for the sake of money, favor, or friendship, for the sake of revenge, or for any other reason. God requires me to speak the truth, to speak well of my neighbor when I can, and to view the faults of my neighbor with tolerance when I cannot.

Zech. 8:16–17   These are the things that you shall do: Speak the truth to one another, render in your gates judgments that are true and make for peace, do not devise evil in your hearts against one another, and love no false oath; for all these are things that I hate, says the LORD.

1 Peter 3:16   Keep your conscience clear, so that, when you are maligned, those who abuse you for your good conduct in Christ may be put to shame.

Prov. 14:5   A faithful witness does not lie, but a false witness breathes out lies.

James 4:11   Do not speak evil against one another, brothers and sisters. Whoever speaks evil against another or judges another, speaks evil against the law and judges the law; but if you judge the law, you are not a doer of the law but a judge.

1 Peter 4:8   Above all, maintain constant love for one another, for love covers a multitude of sins.

Question 115. Does this commandment forbid racism and other forms of negative stereotyping?

Yes. In forbidding false witness against my neighbor, God forbids me to be prejudiced against people who belong to any vulnerable, different, or disfavored social group. Jews, women, homosexuals, racial and ethnic minorities, and national enemies are among those who have suffered terribly from being subjected to the slurs of social prejudice. Negative stereotyping is a form of falsehood that invites actions of humiliation, abuse, and violence as forbidden by the commandment against murder.

Rom. 3:13, 15   "Their throats are opened graves; they use their tongues to deceive." "The venom of vipers is under their lips." . . . "Their feet are swift to shed blood." . . .

Prov. 31:8–9   Speak out for those who cannot speak, for the rights of all the destitute. Speak out, judge righteously, defend the rights of the poor and needy.

Matt. 7:1–2   Do not judge, so that you may not be judged. For with the judgment you make you will be judged, and the measure you give will be the measure you get.

Question 116. What is the tenth commandment?

"You shall not covet what is your neighbor's" (Ex. 20:17; Deut. 5:21).

Question 117. What do you learn from this commandment?

My whole heart should belong to God alone, not to money or the things of this world. "Coveting" means desiring something wrongfully. I should not resent the good fortune or success of my neighbor or allow envy to corrupt my heart.

Heb. 13:5   Keep your lives free from the love of money, and be content with what you have; for he has said, "I will never leave you or forsake you."

Gal. 5:26   Let us not become conceited, competing against one another, envying one another.

Question 118. What is the best summary of the last six commandments?

These teach me how to live rightly with my neighbor. Jesus summed them up with the commandment which is like the greatest one about loving God: "You shall love your neighbor as yourself" (Matt. 22:39; Lev. 19:18).

Question 119. Can you obey these commandments perfectly?

No. I am at once a forgiven sinner and a forgiven sinner. As a sinner without excuse, I fail to obey these commandments as God requires. "For whoever keeps the whole law but fails in one point has become accountable for all of it" (James 2:10). I should not adjust the law to my failures, nor reduce my failures before God. Yet there is more grace in God than sin in me. While I should not cease to pray to God for mercy, I can be confident that God is forgiving and that I will be set free from all my sins. By grace I can confess my sins, repent of them, and grow in love and knowledge day by day.

Ps. 14:3 They have all gone astray, they are all alike perverse; there is no one who does good, no, not one.

Eph. 2:8 For by grace you have been saved through faith, and this is not your own doing; it is the gift of God. . . .

Ps. 130:3–4 If you, O Lord, should mark iniquities, Lord, who could stand? But there is forgiveness with you, so that you may be revered.

Col. 1:13–14 He has rescued us from the power of darkness and transferred us into the kingdom of his beloved Son, in whom we have redemption, the forgiveness of sins.

1 John 1:8 If we say that we have no sin, we deceive ourselves, and the truth is not in us.

III. The Lord's Prayer

Question 120. What is prayer?

Prayer means calling upon God whose Spirit is always present with us. In prayer we approach God with reverence, confidence, and humility. Prayer involves both addressing God in praise, confession, thanksgiving, and supplication, and listening for God's word within our hearts. When we adore God, we are filled with wonder, love, and praise before God's heavenly glory, not least when we find it hidden in the cross of Golgotha. When confessing our guilt to God, we ask for forgiveness with humble and sorry hearts, remembering that God is gracious as well as holy. When giving thanks to God, we acknowledge God's great goodness, rejoicing in God for all that is so wonderfully provided for us. Finally, when calling upon God to hear our requests, we affirm that God draws near in every need and sorrow of life, and ask God to do so again.

Ps. 48:1 Great is the Lord and greatly to be praised in the city of our God.

Ps. 96:8–9 Ascribe to the Lord the glory due his name; bring an offering, and come into his courts. Worship the Lord in holy splendor; tremble before him, all the earth.

James 5:16 Therefore confess your sins to one another, and pray for one another, so that you may be healed. The prayer of the righteous is powerful and effective.

1 John 1:9 If we confess our sins, he who is faithful and just will forgive us our sins and cleanse us from all unrighteousness.

Ps. 107:8 Let them thank the Lord for his steadfast love, for his wonderful works to humankind.

Ps. 75:1 We give thanks to you, O God; we give thanks; your name is near. People tell of your wondrous deeds.

Ps. 50:15 Call on me in the day of trouble; I will deliver you, and you shall glorify me.

Ps. 145:18   The LORD is near to all who call on him, to all who call on him in truth.

Eph. 6:18   Pray in the Spirit at all times in every prayer and supplication. To that end keep alert and always persevere in supplication for all the saints.

Question 121. What is the purpose of prayer?

Prayer brings us into communion with God. The more our lives are rooted in prayer, the more we sense how wonderful God is in grace, purity, majesty, and love. Prayer means offering our lives completely to God, submitting ourselves to God's will, and waiting faithfully for God's grace. Through prayer God frees us from anxiety, equips us for service, and deepens our faith.

Ps. 62:8   Trust in him at all times, O people; pour out your heart before him; God is a refuge for us.

Ps. 139:1   O LORD, you have searched me and known me.

Phil. 4:6   Do not worry about anything, but in everything by prayer and supplication with thanksgiving let your requests be made known to God.

Matt. 7:7–8   Ask, and it will be given you; search, and you will find; knock, and the door will be opened for you. For everyone who asks receives, and everyone who searches finds, and for everyone who knocks, the door will be opened.

Question 122. How does God respond to our prayers?

God takes all our prayers into account, weighing them with divine wisdom, and responding to them by a perfect will. Although for the time being God's answers may seem beyond our understanding, or sometimes even bitter, we know nonetheless that they are always determined by the grace of our Lord Jesus Christ. God answers our prayers, particularly for temporal blessings, only in ways that are compatible with the larger purposes of God's glory and our salvation. Communion with God is finally the answer within the answers to all our prayers.

1 John 5:14   And this is the boldness we have in him, that if we ask anything according to his will, he hears us.

James 1:17   Every generous act of giving, with every perfect gift, is from above, coming down from the Father of lights, with whom there is no variation or shadow due to change.

Matt. 6:33   But strive first for the kingdom of God and his righteousness, and all these things will be given to you as well.

Question 123. What encourages us to pray each day?

The God who has adopted us as children is the God who encourages and commands us to pray. When we pray, we respond with love to that greater love which meets us from above. Before we enter into prayer, God is ready to grant all that we need. We may turn to God with confidence each day, not because we are worthy, but simply because of God's grace. By praying we acknowledge that we depend on grace for all that is good, beautiful, life-giving, and true.

Isa. 65:24   Before they call I will answer, while they are yet speaking I will hear.

Luke 11:12–13 Or if the child asks for an egg, will [you] give a scorpion? If you then, who are evil, know how to give good gifts to your children, how much more will the heavenly Father give the Holy Spirit to those who ask him!

Phil. 4:8 Finally, beloved, whatever is true, whatever is honorable, whatever is just, whatever is pure, whatever is pleasing, whatever is commendable, if there is any excellence and if there is anything worthy of praise, think about these things.

Eph. 3:20–21 Now to him who by the power at work within us is able to accomplish abundantly far more than all we can ask or imagine, to him be glory in the church and in Christ Jesus to all generations, forever and ever. Amen.

Question 124. What prayer serves as our rule or pattern?

Our rule or pattern is found in the Lord's Prayer, which Jesus taught to his disciples:

> Our Father in heaven,
>   hallowed be your name,
>   your kingdom come,
>   your will be done,
>   on earth as in heaven.
> Give us today our daily bread.
> Forgive us our sins
>   as we forgive those who sin against us.
> Save us from the time of trial
>   and deliver us from evil.
> For the kingdom, the power, and the
>   glory are yours
>   now and for ever. Amen.

These words express everything that we may desire and expect from God.

Question 125. What is the design of the Lord's Prayer?

The Lord's Prayer falls into two parts, preceded by an opening address, and concluded by a "doxology" or word of praise. Each part consists of three petitions. The first part concerns God's glory; the second part, our salvation. The first part involves our love for God; the second part, God's love for us. The petitions in part one will not be fulfilled perfectly until the life to come; those in part two relate more directly to our present needs here and now.

Question 126. What is meant by addressing God as "Our Father in heaven"?

By addressing God as "our Father," we draw near with childlike reverence and place ourselves securely in God's hands. Although God is certainly everywhere, God is said to exist and dwell "in heaven." For while God is free to enter into the closest relationship with the creature, God does not belong to the order of created beings. "Heaven" is the seat of divine authority, the place from which God reigns in glory and brings salvation to earth. Our opening address expresses our confidence that we rest securely in God's intimate care and that nothing on earth lies beyond the reach of God's grace.

Rom. 8:15–16   For you did not receive a spirit of slavery to fall back into fear, but you have received a spirit of adoption. When we cry, "Abba! Father!" it is that very Spirit bearing witness with our spirit that we are children of God. . . .

Jer. 23:23–24   Am I a God near by, says the LORD, and not a God far off? Who can hide in secret places so that I cannot see them? says the LORD. Do I not fill heaven and earth? says the LORD.

Acts 17:24–25   The God who made the world and everything in it, he who is Lord of heaven and earth, does not live in shrines made by human hands, nor is he served by human hands, as though he needed anything, since he himself gives to all mortals life and breath and all things.

Question 127. What is meant by the first petition, "Hallowed be your name"?

This petition is placed first, because it comprehends the goal and purpose of the whole prayer. The glory of God's name is the highest concern in all that we pray and do. God's "name" stands for God's being as well as for God's attributes and works. When we pray for this name to be "hallowed," we ask that we and all others will know and glorify God as God really is and that all things will be so ordered that they serve God truly for God's sake.

Jer. 9:23–24   Thus says the LORD: Do not let the wise boast in their wisdom, do not let the mighty boast in their might, do not let the wealthy boast in their wealth; but let those who boast boast in this, that they understand and know me, that I am the LORD; I act with steadfast love, justice, and righteousness in the earth, for in these things I delight, says the LORD.

Rom. 11:36   For from him and through him and to him are all things. To him be the glory forever. Amen.

Ps. 115:1   Not to us, O LORD, not to us, but to your name give glory, for the sake of your steadfast love and your faithfulness.

Question 128. What is meant by the second petition, "Your kingdom come"?

We are asking God to come and rule among us through faith, love, and justice— and not through any one of them without the others. We pray for both the church and the world, that God will rule in our hearts through faith, in our personal relationships through love, and in our institutional affairs through justice. We ask especially that the gospel will not be withheld from us, but rightly preached and received. We pray that the church will be upheld and increase, particularly when in distress; and that all the world will more and more submit to God's reign, until that day when crying and pain are no more, and we live forever with God in perfect peace.

Ps. 68:1   Let God rise up, let his enemies be scattered; let those who hate him flee before him.

2 Thess. 3:1   Finally, brothers and sisters, pray for us, so that the word of the Lord may spread rapidly and be glorified everywhere, just as it is among you. . . .

Rev. 22:20   The one who testifies to these things says, "Surely I am coming soon." Amen. Come, Lord Jesus!

Rom. 8:22–24   We know that the whole creation has been groaning in labor pains until now; and not only the creation, but we ourselves, who have the first fruits of the Spirit, groan inwardly while we wait for adoption, the redemption of our bodies. For in hope we were saved. Now hope that is seen is not hope. For who hopes for what is seen?

1 Cor. 15:20, 28   But in fact Christ has been raised from the dead, the first fruits of those who have died. . . . When all things are subjected to him, then the Son himself will also be subjected to the one who put all things in subjection under him, so that God may be all in all.

Question 129. What is meant by the third petition, "Your will be done, on earth as in heaven"?

Of course, God's will is always done and will surely come to pass, whether we desire it or not. But the phrase "on earth as in heaven" means that we ask for the grace to do God's will on earth in the way that it is done in heaven—gladly and from the heart. We thus ask that all opposition to God's will might be removed from the earth, and especially from our own hearts. We ask for the freedom to conform our desires and deeds more fully to God's, so that we might be completely delivered from our sin. We yield ourselves, in life and in death, to God's will.

Ps. 119:34–36   Give me understanding, that I may keep your law and observe it with my whole heart. Lead me in the path of your commandments, for I delight in it. Turn my heart to your decrees, and not to selfish gain.

Ps. 103:20, 22   Bless the LORD, O you his angels, you mighty ones who do his bidding, obedient to his spoken word. . . . Bless the LORD, all his works, in all places of his dominion. Bless the LORD, O my soul.

Luke 22:42   Father, if you are willing, remove this cup from me; yet, not my will but yours be done.

Rom. 12:2   Do not be conformed to this world, but be transformed by the renewing of your minds, so that you may discern what is the will of God— what is good and acceptable and perfect.

Question 130. What is meant by the fourth petition, "Give us today our daily bread"?

We ask God to provide for all our needs, for we know that God, who cares for us in every area of our life, has promised us temporal as well as spiritual blessings. God commands us to pray each day for all that we need and no more, so that we will learn to rely completely on God. We pray that we will use what we are given wisely, remembering especially the poor and the needy. Along with every living creature we look to God, the source of all generosity, to bless us and nourish us, according to the divine good pleasure.

Prov. 30:8   Remove far from me falsehood and lying; give me neither poverty nor riches; feed me with the food that I need. . . .

Ps. 90:17   Let the favor of the Lord our God be upon us, and prosper for us the work of our hands—O prosper the work of our hands!

Ps. 55:22   Cast your burden on the LORD, and he will sustain you; he will never permit the righteous to be moved.

Ps. 72:4   May he defend the cause of the poor of the people, give deliverance to the needy, and crush the oppressor.

Ps. 104:27–28   These all look to you to give them their food in due season; when you give to them, they gather it up; when you open your hand, they are filled with good things.

Question 131. What is meant by the fifth petition, "Forgive us our sins as we forgive those who sin against us"?

We pray that a new and right spirit will be put within us. We ask for the grace to treat others, especially those who harm us, with the same mercy that we have received from God. We remember that not one day goes by when we do not need to turn humbly to God for our own forgiveness. We know that our reception of this forgiveness can be blocked by our unwillingness to forgive others. We ask that we will not delight in doing evil, nor in avenging any wrong, but that we will survive all cruelty without bitterness and overcome evil with good, so that our hearts will be knit together with the mercy and forgiveness of God.

Matt. 18:33   Should you not have had mercy on your fellow slave, as I had mercy on you?

Matt. 6:14–15   For if you forgive others their trespasses, your heavenly Father will also forgive you; but if you do not forgive others, neither will your Father forgive your trespasses.

Ps. 51:10   Create in me a clean heart, O God, and put a new and right spirit within me.

1 John 2:1–2   My little children, I am writing these things to you so that you may not sin. But if anyone does sin, we have an advocate with the Father, Jesus Christ the righteous; and he is the atoning sacrifice for our sins, and not for ours only but also for the sins of the whole world.

Question 132. What is meant by the final petition, "Save us from the time of trial and deliver us from evil"?

We ask God to protect us from our own worst impulses and from all external powers of destruction in the world. We ask that we might not yield to despair in the face of seemingly hopeless circumstances. We pray for the grace to remember and believe, despite our unbelief, that no matter how bleak the world may sometimes seem, there is nonetheless a depth of love which is deeper than our despair, and that this love—which delivered Israel from slavery in Egypt and raised our Lord Jesus from the dead—will finally swallow up forever all that would now seem to defeat it.

2 Cor. 4:8   We are afflicted in every way, but not crushed; perplexed, but not driven to despair. . . .

Eph. 3:19   . . . and to know the love of Christ that surpasses knowledge, so that you may be filled with all the fullness of God.

Matt. 26:41   Stay awake and pray that you may not come into the time of trial; the spirit indeed is willing, but the flesh is weak.

Question 133. What is meant by the closing doxology, "For the kingdom, the power and the glory are yours now and for ever"?

We give God thanks and praise for the kingdom more powerful than all enemies, for the power perfected in the weakness of love, and for the glory that includes our well-being and that of the whole creation, both now and to all eternity. We give thanks and praise to God as made known through Christ our Lord.

Rev. 5:12 Worthy is the Lamb that was slaughtered to receive power and wealth and wisdom and might and honor and glory and blessing!

Rev. 4:11 You are worthy, our Lord and God, to receive glory and honor and power, for you created all things, and by your will they existed and were created.

1 Chron. 29:11, 13 Yours, O LORD, are the greatness, the power, the glory, the victory, and the majesty; for all that is in the heavens and on the earth is yours; yours is the kingdom, O LORD, and you are exalted as head above all. . . . And now, our God, we give thanks to you and praise your glorious name.

Question 134. What is meant by the word "Amen"?

"Amen" means "so be it" or "let it be so." It expresses our complete confidence in the triune God, the God of the covenant with Israel as fulfilled through our Lord Jesus Christ, who makes no promise that will not be kept, and whose steadfast love and mercy endures forever.

Rev. 22:20 The one who testifies to these things says, "Surely I am coming soon." Amen. Come, Lord Jesus!

2 Cor. 1:20 For in him every one of God's promises is a "Yes." For this reason it is through him that we say the "Amen," to the glory of God.

2 Tim. 2:13 If we are faithless, he remains faithful—for he cannot deny himself.

The Heidelberg Catechism

The Reformation was not a single movement. Soon after Luther posted his Ninety-five Theses, reform movements sprang up throughout Europe. Tension between Lutherans and Reformed Christians was intense. Because the Reformed did not affirm the real, bodily presence of Christ in bread and wine, Lutherans believed that they were desecrating the Lord's Supper.

Acting to end the controversy, Frederick the Elector, ruler of the Palatinate, asked two young men of Heidelberg—Zacharias Ursinus, professor of theology, and Kaspar Olevianus, preacher to the city—to prepare a catechism acceptable to both sides. They revised an earlier catechism that Ursinus had written, using its outline and some ninety of its questions and answers. Completed in 1562, the Heidelberg Catechism was published in January of the following year.

Each question of the catechism is personal, addressed to "you." Each answer draws as much as possible on biblical language. The catechism's tone is irenic, showing nothing of the controversy that called it forth. Its theology is both catholic, universal in appeal, and evangelical, setting forth the gospel of Jesus Christ. The influence of the Heidelberg Catechism in the church's preaching and teaching continues to be felt in Germany, Austria, the Netherlands, Hungary, parts of eastern Europe, Scotland, Canada, and the United States.

THE HEIDELBERG CATECHISM[1]

LORD'S DAY 1

Q. 1. What is your only comfort, in life and in death?

A. That I belong—body and soul, in life and in death—not to myself but to my faithful Savior, Jesus Christ, who at the cost of his own blood has fully paid for all my sins and has completely freed me from the dominion of the devil; that he protects me so well that without the will of my Father in heaven not a hair can fall from my head; indeed, that everything must fit his purpose for my salvation. Therefore, by his Holy Spirit, he also assures me of eternal life, and makes me wholeheartedly willing and ready from now on to live for him.

Q. 2. How many things must you know that you may live and die in the blessedness of this comfort?

A. Three. First, the greatness of my sin and wretchedness. Second, how I am freed from all my sins and their wretched consequences. Third, what gratitude I owe to God for such redemption.

PART I
Of Man's Misery

LORD'S DAY 2

Q. 3. Where do you learn of your sin and its wretched consequences?

A. From the Law of God.

---

[1]Reprinted from *The Heidelberg Catechism, 1563–1963. 400th Anniversary Edition.* Copyright 1962. United Church Press. Used by permission.

Q. 4. What does the Law of God require of us?

A. Jesus Christ teaches this in a summary in Matthew 22:37–40: "You shall love the Lord your God with all your heart, and with all your soul, and with all your mind. This is the great and first commandment. And a second is like it, you shall love your neighbor as yourself. On these two commandments depend all the law and the prophets." (Cf. Luke 10:27.)

Q. 5. Can you keep all this perfectly?

A. No, for by nature I am prone to hate God and my neighbor.

LORD'S DAY 3

Q. 6. Did God create man evil and perverse like this?

A. No. On the contrary, God created man good and in his image, that is, in true righteousness and holiness, so that he might rightly know God his Creator, love him with his whole heart, and live with him in eternal blessedness, praising and glorifying him.

Q. 7. Where, then, does this corruption of human nature come from?

A. From the fall and disobedience of our first parents, Adam and Eve, in the Garden of Eden; whereby our human life is so poisoned that we are all conceived and born in the state of sin.

Q. 8. But are we so perverted that we are altogether unable to do good and prone to do evil?

A. Yes, unless we are born again through the Spirit of God.

LORD'S DAY 4

Q. 9. Is not God unjust in requiring of man in his Law what he cannot do?

A. No, for God so created man that he could do it. But man, upon the instigation of the devil, by deliberate disobedience, has cheated himself and all his descendants out of these gifts.

Q. 10. Will God let man get by with such disobedience and defection?

A. Certainly not, for the wrath of God is revealed from heaven, both against our inborn sinfulness and our actual sins, and he will punish them according to his righteous judgment in time and in eternity, as he has declared: "Cursed be everyone who does not abide by all things written in the book of the Law, and do them."

Q. 11. But is not God also merciful?

A. God is indeed merciful and gracious, but he is also righteous. It is his righteousness which requires that sin committed against the supreme majesty of God be punished with extreme, that is, with eternal punishment of body and soul.

PART II
Of Man's Redemption

LORD'S DAY 5

Q. 12. Since, then, by the righteous judgment of God we have deserved temporal and eternal punishment, how may we escape this punishment, come again to grace, and be reconciled to God?

A. God wills that his righteousness be satisfied; therefore, payment in full must be made to his righteousness, either by ourselves or by another.

Q. 13. Can we make this payment ourselves?

A. By no means. On the contrary, we increase our debt each day.

Q. 14. Can any mere creature make the payment for us?

A. No one. First of all, God does not want to punish any other creature for man's debt. Moreover, no mere creature can bear the burden of God's eternal wrath against sin and redeem others from it.

Q. 15. Then what kind of mediator and redeemer must we seek?

A. One who is a true and righteous man and yet more powerful than all creatures, that is, one who is at the same time true God.

LORD'S DAY 6

Q. 16. Why must he be a true and righteous man?

A.Because God's righteousness requires that man who has sinned should make reparation for sin, but the man who is himself a sinner cannot pay for others.

Q. 17. Why must he at the same time be true God?

A. So that by the power of his divinity he might bear as a man the burden of God's wrath, and recover for us and restore to us righteousness and life.

Q. 18. Who is this mediator who is at the same time true God and a true and perfectly righteous man?

A. Our Lord Jesus Christ, who is freely given to us for complete redemption and righteousness.

Q. 19. Whence do you know this?

A. From the holy gospel, which God himself revealed in the beginning in the Garden of Eden, afterward proclaimed through the holy patriarchs and prophets and foreshadowed through the sacrifices and other rites of the Old Covenant, and finally fulfilled through his own well-beloved Son.

LORD'S DAY 7

Q. 20. Will all men, then, be saved through Christ as they became lost through Adam?

A. No. Only those who, by true faith, are incorporated into him and accept all his benefits.

116

Q. 21. What is true faith?

A. It is not only a certain knowledge by which I accept as true all that God has revealed to us in his Word, but also a wholehearted trust which the Holy Spirit creates in me through the gospel, that, not only to others, but to me also God has given the forgiveness of sins, everlasting righteousness and salvation, out of sheer grace solely for the sake of Christ's saving work.

Q. 22. What, then, must a Christian believe?

A. All that is promised us in the gospel, a summary of which is taught us in the articles of the Apostles' Creed, our universally acknowledged confession of faith.

Q. 23. What are these articles?

A. I believe in God the Father Almighty, Maker of Heaven and earth; And in Jesus Christ, his only-begotten Son, our Lord; who was conceived by the Holy Spirit, born of the Virgin Mary; suffered under Pontius Pilate, was crucified, dead, and buried; he descended into hell; the third day he rose again from the dead; he ascended into heaven, and sits at the right hand of God the Father Almighty; from thence he shall come to judge the living and the dead.
I believe in the Holy Spirit; the holy catholic Church; the communion of saints; the forgiveness of sins; the resurrection of the body; and the life everlasting.

LORD'S DAY 8

Q. 24. How are these articles divided?

A. Into three parts: The first concerns God the Father and our creation; the second, God the Son and our redemption; and the third, God the Holy Spirit and our sanctification.

Q. 25. Since there is only one Divine Being, why do you speak of three, Father, Son, and Holy Spirit?

A. Because God has thus revealed himself in his Word, that these three distinct persons are the one, true, eternal God.

Of God the Father

LORD'S DAY 9

Q. 26. What do you believe when you say: "I believe in God the Father Almighty, Maker of heaven and earth"?

A. That the eternal Father of our Lord Jesus Christ, who out of nothing created heaven and earth with all that is in them, who also upholds and governs them by his eternal counsel and providence, is for the sake of Christ his Son my God and my Father. I trust in him so completely that I have no doubt that he will provide me with all things necessary for body and soul. Moreover, whatever evil he sends upon me in this troubled life he will turn to my good, for he is able to do it, being almighty God, and is determined to do it, being a faithful Father.

117

Q. 27. What do you understand by the providence of God?

A. The almighty and ever-present power of God whereby he still upholds, as it were by his own hand, heaven and earth together with all creatures, and rules in such a way that leaves and grass, rain and drought, fruitful and unfruitful years, food and drink, health and sickness, riches and poverty, and everything else, come to us not by chance but by his fatherly hand.

Q. 28. What advantage comes from acknowledging God's creation and providence?

A. We learn that we are to be patient in adversity, grateful in the midst of blessing, and to trust our faithful God and Father for the future, assured that no creature shall separate us from his love, since all creatures are so completely in his hand that without his will they cannot even move.

Of God the Son

Q. 29. Why is the Son of God called JESUS, which means SAVIOR?

A. Because he saves us from our sins, and because salvation is to be sought or found in no other.

Q. 30. Do those who seek their salvation and well-being from saints, by their own efforts, or by other means really believe in the only Savior Jesus?

A. No. Rather, by such actions they deny Jesus, the only Savior and Redeemer, even though they boast of belonging to him. It therefore follows that either Jesus is not a perfect Savior, or those who receive this Savior with true faith must possess in him all that is necessary for their salvation.

Q. 31. Why is he called CHRIST, that is, the ANOINTED ONE?

A. Because he is ordained by God the Father and anointed with the Holy Spirit to be our chief Prophet and Teacher, fully revealing to us the secret purpose and will of God concerning our redemption; to be our only High Priest, having redeemed us by the one sacrifice of his body and ever interceding for us with the Father; and to be our eternal King, governing us by his Word and Spirit, and defending and sustaining us in the redemption he has won for us.

Q. 32. But why are you called a Christian?

A. Because through faith I share in Christ and thus in his anointing, so that I may confess his name, offer myself a living sacrifice of gratitude to him, and fight against sin and the devil with a free and good conscience throughout this life and hereafter rule with him in eternity over all creatures.

Q. 33. Why is he called God's only-begotten son, since we also are God's children?

A. Because Christ alone is God's own eternal Son, whereas we are accepted for his sake as children of God by grace.

Q. 34. Why do you call him our Lord?

A. Because, not with gold or silver but at the cost of his blood, he has redeemed us body and soul from sin and all the dominion of the devil, and has bought us for his very own.

LORD'S DAY 14

Q. 35. What is the meaning of: "Conceived by the Holy Spirit, born of the Virgin Mary"?

A. That the eternal Son of God, who is and remains true and eternal God, took upon himself our true manhood from the flesh and blood of the Virgin Mary through the action of the Holy Spirit, so that he might also be the true seed of David, like his fellow men in all things, except for sin.

Q. 36. What benefit do you receive from the holy conception and birth of Christ?

A. That he is our Mediator, and that, in God's sight, he covers over with his innocence and perfect holiness the sinfulness in which I have been conceived.

LORD'S DAY 15

Q. 37. What do you understand by the word "suffered"?

A. That throughout his life on earth, but especially at the end of it, he bore in body and soul the wrath of God against the sin of the whole human race, so that by his suffering, as the only expiatory sacrifice, he might redeem our body and soul from everlasting damnation, and might obtain for us God's grace, righteousness, and eternal life.

Q. 38. Why did he suffer "under Pontius Pilate" as his judge?

A. That he, being innocent, might be condemned by an earthly judge, and thereby set us free from the judgment of God which, in all its severity, ought to fall upon us.

Q. 39. Is there something more in his having been crucified than if he had died some other death?

A. Yes, for by this I am assured that he took upon himself the curse which lay upon me, because the death of the cross was cursed by God.

LORD'S DAY 16

Q. 40. Why did Christ have to suffer "death"?

A. Because the righteousness and truth of God are such that nothing else could make reparation for our sins except the death of the Son of God.

Q. 41. Why was he "buried"?

A. To confirm the fact that he was really dead.

119

Q. 42. Since, then, Christ died for us, why must we also die?

A. Our death is not a reparation for our sins, but only a dying to sin and an entering into eternal life.

Q. 43. What further benefit do we receive from the sacrifice and death of Christ on the cross?

A.That by his power our old self is crucified, put to death, and buried with him, so that the evil passions of our mortal bodies may reign in us no more, but that we may offer ourselves to him as a sacrifice of thanksgiving.

Q. 44. Why is there added: "He descended into hell"?

A. That in my severest tribulations I may be assured that Christ my Lord has redeemed me from hellish anxieties and torment by the unspeakable anguish, pains, and terrors which he suffered in his soul both on the cross and before.

LORD'S DAY 17

Q. 45. What benefit do we receive from "the resurrection" of Christ?

A. First, by his resurrection he has overcome death that he might make us share in the righteousness which he has obtained for us through his death. Second, we too are now raised by his power to a new life. Third, the resurrection of Christ is a sure pledge to us of our blessed resurrection.

LORD'S DAY 18

Q. 46. How do you understand the words: "He ascended into heaven"?

A. That Christ was taken up from the earth into heaven before the eyes of his disciples and remains there on our behalf until he comes again to judge the living and the dead.

Q. 47. Then, is not Christ with us unto the end of the world, as he has promised us?

A. Christ is true man and true God. As a man he is no longer on earth, but in his divinity, majesty, grace, and Spirit, he is never absent from us.

Q. 48. But are not the two natures in Christ separated from each other in this way, if the humanity is not wherever the divinity is?

A. Not at all; for since divinity is incomprehensible and everywhere present, it must follow that the divinity is indeed beyond the bounds of the humanity which it has assumed, and is nonetheless ever in that humanity as well, and remains personally united to it.

Q. 49. What benefit do we receive from Christ's ascension into heaven?

A. First, that he is our Advocate in the presence of his Father in heaven. Second, that we have our flesh in heaven as a sure pledge that he, as the Head, will also take us, his members, up to himself. Third, that he sends us his Spirit as a counterpledge by whose power we seek what is above, where Christ is, sitting at the right hand of God, and not things that are on earth.

Q. 50. Why is there added: "And sits at the right hand of God"?

A. Because Christ ascended into heaven so that he might manifest himself there as the Head of his Church, through whom the Father governs all things.

Q. 51. What benefit do we receive from this glory of Christ, our Head?

A. First, that through his Holy Spirit he pours out heavenly gifts upon us, his members. Second, that by his power he defends and supports us against all our enemies.

Q. 52. What comfort does the return of Christ "to judge the living and the dead" give you?

A. That in all affliction and persecution I may await with head held high the very Judge from heaven who has already submitted himself to the judgment of God for me and has removed all the curse from me; that he will cast all his enemies and mine into everlasting condemnation, but he shall take me, together with all his elect, to himself into heavenly joy and glory.

The Holy Spirit

Q. 53. What do you believe concerning "the Holy Spirit"?

A. First, that, with the Father and the Son, he is equally eternal God; second, that God's Spirit is also given to me, preparing me through a true faith to share in Christ and all his benefits, that he comforts me and will abide with me forever.

Q. 54. What do you believe concerning "the Holy Catholic Church"?

A. I believe that, from the beginning to the end of the world, and from among the whole human race, the Son of God, by his Spirit and his Word, gathers, protects, and preserves for himself, in the unity of the true faith, a congregation chosen for eternal life. Moreover, I believe that I am and forever will remain a living member of it.

Q. 55. What do you understand by "the communion of saints"?

A. First, that believers one and all, as partakers of the Lord Christ, and all his treasures and gifts, shall share in one fellowship. Second, that each one ought to know that he is obliged to use his gifts freely and with joy for the benefit and welfare of other members.

Q. 56. What do you believe concerning "the forgiveness of sins"?

A. That, for the sake of Christ's reconciling work, God will no more remember my sins or the sinfulness with which I have to struggle all my life long; but that he graciously imparts to me the righteousness of Christ so that I may never come into condemnation.

Q. 57. What comfort does "the resurrection of the body" give you?

A. That after this life my soul shall be immediately taken up to Christ, its Head, and that this flesh of mine, raised by the power of Christ, shall be reunited with my soul, and be conformed to the glorious body of Christ.

Q. 58. What comfort does the article concerning "the life everlasting" give you?

A. That, since I now feel in my heart the beginning of eternal joy, I shall possess, after this life, perfect blessedness, which no eye has seen, nor ear heard, nor the heart of man conceived, and thereby praise God forever.

Q. 59. But how does it help you now that you believe all this?

A. That I am righteous in Christ before God, and an heir of eternal life.

Q. 60. How are you righteous before God?

A. Only by true faith in Jesus Christ. In spite of the fact that my conscience accuses me that I have grievously sinned against all the commandments of God, and have not kept any one of them, and that I am still ever prone to all that is evil, nevertheless, God, without any merit of my own, out of pure grace, grants me the benefits of the perfect expiation of Christ, imputing to me his righteousness and holiness as if I had never committed a single sin or had ever been sinful, having fulfilled myself all the obedience which Christ has carried out for me, if only I accept such favor with a trusting heart.

Q. 61. Why do you say that you are righteous by faith alone?

A. Not because I please God by virtue of the worthiness of my faith, but because the satisfaction, righteousness, and holiness of Christ alone are my righteousness before God, and because I can accept it and make it mine in no other way than by faith alone.

Q. 62. But why cannot our good works be our righteousness before God, or at least a part of it?

A. Because the righteousness which can stand before the judgment of God must be absolutely perfect and wholly in conformity with the divine Law. But even our best works in this life are all imperfect and defiled with sin.

Q. 63. Will our good works merit nothing, even when it is God's purpose to reward them in this life, and in the future life as well?

A. This reward is not given because of merit, but out of grace.

Q. 64. But does not this teaching make people careless and sinful?

A. No, for it is impossible for those who are ingrafted into Christ by true faith not to bring forth the fruit of gratitude.

The Holy Sacraments

Q. 65. Since, then, faith alone makes us share in Christ and all his benefits, where does such faith originate?

A. The Holy Spirit creates it in our hearts by the preaching of the holy gospel, and confirms it by the use of the holy Sacraments.

Q. 66. What are the Sacraments?

A. They are visible, holy signs and seals instituted by God in order that by their use he may the more fully disclose and seal to us the promise of the gospel, namely, that because of the one sacrifice of Christ accomplished on the cross he graciously grants us the forgiveness of sins and eternal life.

Q. 67. Are both the Word and the Sacraments designed to direct our faith to the one sacrifice of Jesus Christ on the cross as the only ground of our salvation?

A. Yes, indeed, for the Holy Spirit teaches in the gospel and confirms by the holy Sacraments that our whole salvation is rooted in the one sacrifice of Christ offered for us on the cross.

Q. 68. How many Sacraments has Christ instituted in the New Testament?

A. Two, holy Baptism and the holy Supper.

Holy Baptism

Q. 69. How does holy Baptism remind and assure you that the one sacrifice of Christ on the cross avails for you?

A. In this way: Christ has instituted this external washing with water and by it has promised that I am as certainly washed with his blood and Spirit from the uncleanness of my soul and from all my sins, as I am washed externally with water which is used to remove the dirt from my body.

Q. 70. What does it mean to be washed with the blood and Spirit of Christ?

A. It means to have the forgiveness of sins from God, through grace, for the sake of Christ's blood which he shed for us in his sacrifice on the cross, and also to be renewed by the Holy Spirit and sanctified as members of Christ, so that we may more and more die unto sin and live in a consecrated and blameless way.

Q. 71. Where has Christ promised that we are as certainly washed with his blood and Spirit as with the water of baptism?

A. In the institution of Baptism which runs thus: "Go therefore and make disciples of all nations, baptizing them in the name of the Father and of the Son and of the Holy Spirit." "He who believes and is baptized will be saved: but he who does not believe will be condemned." This promise is also repeated where the Scriptures call baptism "the water of rebirth" and the washing away of sins.

123

Q. 72. Does merely the outward washing with water itself wash away sins?

A. No; for only the blood of Jesus Christ and the Holy Spirit cleanse us from all sins.

Q. 73. Then why does the Holy Spirit call baptism the water of rebirth and the washing away of sins?

A. God does not speak in this way except for a strong reason. Not only does he teach us by Baptism that just as the dirt of the body is taken away by water, so our sins are removed by the blood and Spirit of Christ; but more important still, by the divine pledge and sign he wishes to assure us that we are just as truly washed from our sins spiritually as our bodies are washed with water.

Q. 74. Are infants also to be baptized?

A. Yes, because they, as well as their parents, are included in the covenant and belong to the people of God. Since both redemption from sin through the blood of Christ and the gift of faith from the Holy Spirit are promised to these children no less than to their parents, infants are also by baptism, as a sign of the covenant, to be incorporated into the Christian church and distinguished from the children of unbelievers. This was done in the Old Covenant by circumcision. In the New Covenant baptism has been instituted to take its place.

The Holy Supper

Q. 75. How are you reminded and assured in the Holy Supper that you participate in the one sacrifice of Christ on the cross and in all his benefits?

A. In this way: Christ has commanded me and all believers to eat of this broken bread, and to drink of this cup in remembrance of him. He has thereby promised that his body was offered and broken on the cross for me, and his blood was shed for me, as surely as I see with my eyes that the bread of the Lord is broken for me, and that the cup is shared with me. Also, he has promised that he himself as certainly feeds and nourishes my soul to everlasting life with his crucified body and shed blood as I receive from the hand of the minister and actually taste the bread and the cup of the Lord which are given to me as sure signs of the body and blood of Christ.

Q. 76. What does it mean to eat the crucified body of Christ and to drink his shed blood?

A. It is not only to embrace with a trusting heart the whole passion and death of Christ, and by it to receive the forgiveness of sins and eternal life. In addition, it is to be so united more and more to his blessed body by the Holy Spirit dwelling both in Christ and in us that, although he is in heaven and we are on earth, we are nevertheless flesh of his flesh and bone of his bone, always living and being governed by one Spirit, as the members of our bodies are governed by one soul.

Q. 77. Where has Christ promised that he will feed and nourish believers with his body and blood just as surely as they eat of this broken bread and drink of this cup?

A. In the institution of the holy Supper which reads: The Lord Jesus on the night when he was betrayed took bread, and when he had given thanks, he broke it, and said, "this is my body which is for you. Do this in remembrance of me." In the same way also the cup, after supper, saying, "this cup is the new covenant in my blood. Do this, as often as you drink it, in remembrance of me." For as often as you eat this bread and drink the cup, you proclaim the Lord's death until he comes. This promise is also repeated by the apostle Paul: When we bless "the cup of blessing," is it not a means of sharing in the blood of Christ? When we break the bread, is it not a means of sharing the body of Christ? Because there is one loaf, we, many as we are, are one body; for it is one loaf of which we all partake.

LORD'S DAY 29

Q. 78. Do the bread and wine become the very body and blood of Christ?

A. No, for as the water in baptism is not changed into the blood of Christ, nor becomes the washing away of sins by itself, but is only a divine sign and confirmation of it, so also in the Lord's Supper the sacred bread does not become the body of Christ itself, although, in accordance with the nature and usage of sacraments, it is called the body of Christ.

Q. 79. Then why does Christ call the bread his body, and the cup his blood, or the New Covenant in his blood, and why does the apostle Paul call the Supper "a means of sharing" in the body and blood of Christ?

A. Christ does not speak in this way except for a strong reason. He wishes to teach us by it that as bread and wine sustain this temporal life so his crucified body and shed blood are the true food and drink of our souls for eternal life. Even more, he wishes to assure us by this visible sign and pledge that we come to share in his true body and blood through the working of the Holy Spirit as surely as we receive with our mouth these holy tokens in remembrance of him, and that all his sufferings and his death are our own as certainly as if we had ourselves suffered and rendered satisfaction in our own persons.

LORD'S DAY 30

Q. 80. What difference is there between the Lord's Supper and the papal Mass?[2]

A. The Lord's Supper testifies to us that we have complete forgiveness of all our sins through the one sacrifice of Jesus Christ which he himself has accomplished on the cross once for all; (and that through the Holy Spirit we are incorporated into Christ, who is now in heaven with his true body at the right hand of the Father and is there to be worshiped). But the Mass teaches that the living and the dead do not have forgiveness of sins through the sufferings of Christ unless Christ is again offered for them daily by the priest (and that Christ is bodily under the form of bread and wine and is therefore to be worshiped in them). Therefore the Mass is fundamentally a complete denial of the once for all sacrifice and passion of Jesus Christ (and as such an idolatry to be condemned).

---

[2]This question first appeared in part in the second edition. The sections in parentheses were added in the third.

Q. 81. Who ought to come to the table of the Lord?

A. Those who are displeased with themselves for their sins, and who nevertheless trust that these sins have been forgiven them and that their remaining weakness is covered by the passion and death of Christ, and who also desire more and more to strengthen their faith and improve their life. The impenitent and hypocrites, however, eat and drink judgment to themselves.

Q. 82. Should those who show themselves to be unbelievers and enemies of God by their confession and life be admitted to this Supper?

A. No, for then the covenant of God would be profaned and his wrath provoked against the whole congregation. According to the ordinance of Christ and his apostles, therefore, the Christian church is under obligation, by the office of the keys, to exclude such persons until they amend their lives.

LORD'S DAY 31

Q. 83. What is the office of the keys?

A. The preaching of the holy gospel and Christian discipline. By these two means the kingdom of heaven is opened to believers and shut against unbelievers.

Q. 84. How is the kingdom of heaven opened and shut by the preaching of the holy gospel?

A. In this way: The kingdom of heaven is opened when it is proclaimed and openly testified to believers, one and all, according to the command of Christ, that as often as they accept the promise of the gospel with true faith all their sins are truly forgiven them by God for the sake of Christ's gracious work. On the contrary, the wrath of God and eternal condemnation fall upon all unbelievers and hypocrites as long as they do not repent. It is according to this witness of the gospel that God will judge the one and the other in this life and in the life to come.

Q. 85. How is the kingdom of heaven shut and opened by Christian discipline?

A. In this way: Christ commanded that those who bear the Christian name in an unchristian way either in doctrine or in life should be given brotherly admonition. If they do not give up their errors or evil ways, notification is given to the church or to those ordained for this by the church. Then, if they do not change after this warning, they are forbidden to partake of the holy Sacraments and are thus excluded from the communion of the church and by God himself from the kingdom of Christ. However, if they promise and show real amendment, they are received again as members of Christ and of the church.

PART III
Thankfulness

LORD'S DAY 32

Q. 86. Since we are redeemed from our sin and its wretched consequences by grace through Christ without any merit of our own, why must we do good works?

126

A. Because just as Christ has redeemed us with his blood he also renews us through his Holy Spirit according to his own image, so that with our whole life we may show ourselves grateful to God for his goodness and that he may be glorified through us; and further, so that we ourselves may be assured of our faith by its fruits and by our reverent behavior may win our neighbors to Christ.

Q. 87. Can those who do not turn to God from their ungrateful, impenitent life be saved?

A. Certainly not! Scripture says, "Surely you know that the unjust will never come into possession of the kingdom of God. Make no mistake: no fornicator or idolater, none who are guilty either of adultery or of homosexual perversion, no thieves or grabbers or drunkards or slanderers or swindlers, will possess the kingdom of God."

LORD'S DAY 33

Q. 88. How many parts are there to the true repentance or conversion of man?

A. Two: the dying of the old self and the birth of the new.

Q. 89. What is the dying of the old self?

A. Sincere sorrow over our sins and more and more to hate them and to flee from them.

Q. 90. What is the birth of the new self?

A. Complete joy in God through Christ and a strong desire to live according to the will of God in all good works.

Q. 91. But what are good works?

A. Only those which are done out of true faith, in accordance with the Law of God, and for his glory, and not those based on our own opinion or on the traditions of men.

LORD'S DAY 34

Q. 92. What is the law of God?

A. God spoke all these words saying:

FIRST COMMANDMENT

"I am the Lord your God, who brought you out of the land of Egypt, out of the house of bondage. You shall have no other gods before Me."

SECOND COMMANDMENT

"You shall not make yourself a graven image, or any likeness of anything that is in heaven above, or that is in the earth beneath, or that is in the water under the earth; you shall not bow down to them or serve them; for I the Lord your God am a jealous God, visiting the iniquity of the fathers upon the children to the third and fourth generation of those who hate Me, but showing steadfast love to thousands of those who love Me and keep My commandments."

THIRD COMMANDMENT

"You shall not take the name of the Lord your God in vain; for the Lord will not hold him guiltless who takes His name in vain."

FOURTH COMMANDMENT

"Remember the sabbath day, to keep it holy. Six days you shall labor, and do all your work; but the seventh day is a sabbath to the Lord your God; in it you shall not do any work, you, or your son, or your daughter, your manservant, or your maidservant, or your cattle, or the sojourner who is within your gates; for in six days the Lord made heaven and earth, the sea, and all that is in them, and rested the seventh day; therefore the Lord blessed the sabbath day and hallowed it."

FIFTH COMMANDMENT

"Honor your father and your mother, that your days may be long in the land which the Lord your God gives you."

SIXTH COMMANDMENT

"You shall not kill."

SEVENTH COMMANDMENT

"You shall not commit adultery."

EIGHTH COMMANDMENT

"You shall not steal."

NINTH COMMANDMENT

"You shall not bear false witness against your neighbor."

TENTH COMMANDMENT

"You shall not covet your neighbor's house; you shall not covet your neighbor's wife, or his manservant, or his maidservant, or his ox, or his ass, or anything that is your neighbor's."

Q. 93. How are these commandments divided?

A. Into two tables, the first of which teaches us in four commandments how we ought to live in relation to God; the other, in six commandments, what we owe to our neighbor.

Q. 94. What does the Lord require in the first commandment?

A. That I must avoid and flee all idolatry, sorcery, enchantments, invocation of saints or other creatures because of the risk of losing my salvation. Indeed, I ought properly to acknowledge the only true God, trust in him alone, in humility and patience expect all good from him only, and love, fear and honor him with my whole heart. In short, I should rather turn my back on all creatures than do the least thing against his will.

Q. 95. What is idolatry?

A. It is to imagine or possess something in which to put one's trust in place of or beside the one true God who has revealed himself in his Word.

LORD'S DAY 35

Q. 96. What does God require in the second commandment?

A. That we should not represent him or worship him in any other manner than he has commanded in his word.

Q. 97. Should we, then, not make any images at all?

A. God cannot and should not be pictured in any way. As for creatures, although they may indeed be portrayed, God forbids making or having any likeness of them in order to worship them, or to use them to serve him.

Q. 98. But may not pictures be tolerated in churches in place of books for unlearned people?

A. No, for we must not try to be wiser than God who does not want his people to be taught by means of lifeless idols, but through the living preaching of his Word.

LORD'S DAY 36

Q. 99. What is required in the third commandment?

A. That we must not profane or abuse the name of God by cursing, by perjury, or by unnecessary oaths. Nor are we to participate in such horrible sins by keeping quiet and thus giving silent consent. In a word, we must not use the holy name of God except with fear and reverence so that he may be rightly confessed and addressed by us, and be glorified in all our words and works.

Q. 100. Is it, therefore, so great a sin to blaspheme God's name by cursing and swearing that God is also angry with those who do not try to prevent and forbid it as much as they can?

A. Yes, indeed; for no sin is greater or provokes his wrath more than the profaning of his name. That is why he commanded it to be punished with death.

LORD'S DAY 37

Q. 101. But may we not swear oaths by the name of God in a devout manner?

A. Yes, when the civil authorities require it of their subjects, or when it is otherwise needed to maintain and promote fidelity and truth, to the glory of God and the welfare of our neighbor. Such oath-taking is grounded in God's Word and has therefore been rightly used by God's people under the Old and New Covenants.

Q. 102. May we also swear by the saints or other creatures?

A. No; for a lawful oath is a calling upon God, as the only searcher of hearts, to bear witness to the truth, and to punish me if I swear falsely. No creature deserves such honor.

LORD'S DAY 38

Q. 103. What does God require in the fourth commandment?

A. First, that the ministry of the gospel and Christian education be maintained, and that I diligently attend church, especially on the Lord's day, to hear the Word of God, to participate in the holy Sacraments, to call publicly upon the Lord, and to give Christian service to those in need. Second, that I cease from my evil works all the days of my life, allow the Lord to work in me through his Spirit, and thus begin in this life the eternal Sabbath.

LORD'S DAY 39

Q. 104. What does God require in the fifth commandment?

A. That I show honor, love, and faithfulness to my father and mother and to all who are set in authority over me; that I submit myself with respectful obedience to all their careful instruction and discipline; and that I also bear patiently their failures, since it is God's will to govern us by their hand.

LORD'S DAY 40

Q. 105. What does God require in the sixth commandment?

A. That I am not to abuse, hate, injure, or kill my neighbor, either with thought, or by word or gesture, much less by deed, whether by myself or through another, but to lay aside all desire for revenge; and that I do not harm myself or willfully expose myself to danger. This is why the authorities are armed with the means to prevent murder.

Q. 106. But does this commandment speak only of killing?

A. In forbidding murder God means to teach us that he abhors the root of murder, which is envy, hatred, anger, and desire for revenge, and that he regards all these as hidden murder.

Q. 107. Is it enough, then, if we do not kill our neighbor in any of these ways?

A. No; for when God condemns envy, hatred, and anger, he requires us to love our neighbor as ourselves, to show patience, peace, gentleness, mercy, and friendliness toward him, to prevent injury to him as much as we can, also to do good to our enemies.

LORD'S DAY 41

Q. 108. What does the seventh commandment teach us?

A. That all unchastity is condemned by God, and that we should therefore detest it from the heart, and live chaste and disciplined lives, whether in holy wedlock or in single life.

Q. 109. Does God forbid nothing more than adultery and such gross sins in this commandment?

A. Since both our body and soul are a temple of the Holy Spirit, it is his will that we keep both pure and holy. Therefore he forbids all unchaste actions, gestures, words, thoughts, desires and whatever may excite another person to them.

LORD'S DAY 42

Q. 110. What does God forbid in the eighth commandment?

A. He forbids not only the theft and robbery which civil authorities punish, but God also labels as theft all wicked tricks and schemes by which we seek to get for ourselves our neighbor's goods, whether by force or under the pretext of right, such as false weights and measures, deceptive advertising or merchandising, counterfeit money, exorbitant interest, or any other means forbidden by God. He also forbids all greed and misuse and waste of his gifts.

Q. 111. But what does God require of you in this commandment?

A. That I work for the good of my neighbor wherever I can and may, deal with him as I would have others deal with me, and do my work well so that I may be able to help the poor in their need.

LORD'S DAY 43

Q. 112. What is required in the ninth commandment?

A. That I do not bear false witness against anyone, twist anyone's words, be a gossip or a slanderer, or condemn anyone lightly without a hearing. Rather I am required to avoid, under penalty of God's wrath, all lying and deceit as the works of the devil himself. In judicial and all other matters I am to love the truth, and to speak and confess it honestly. Indeed, insofar as I am able, I am to defend and promote my neighbor's good name.

LORD'S DAY 44

Q. 113. What is required in the tenth commandment?

A. That there should never enter our heart even the least inclination or thought contrary to any commandment of God, but that we should always hate sin with our whole heart and find satisfaction and joy in all righteousness.

Q. 114. But can those who are converted to God keep these commandments perfectly?

A. No, for even the holiest of them make only a small beginning in obedience in this life. Nevertheless, they begin with serious purpose to conform not only to some, but to all the commandments of God.

Q. 115. Why, then, does God have the ten commandments preached so strictly since no one can keep them in this life?

A. First, that all our life long we may become increasingly aware of our sinfulness, and therefore more eagerly seek forgiveness of sins and righteousness in Christ. Second, that we may constantly and diligently pray to God for the grace of the Holy Spirit, so that more and more we may be renewed in the image of God, until we attain the goal of full perfection after this life.

Prayer

LORD'S DAY 45

Q. 116. Why is prayer necessary for Christians?

A. Because it is the chief part of the gratitude which God requires of us, and because God will give his grace and Holy Spirit only to those who sincerely beseech him in prayer without ceasing, and who thank him for these gifts.

131

Q. 117. What is contained in a prayer which pleases God and is heard by him?

A. First, that we sincerely call upon the one true God, who has revealed himself to us in his Word, for all that he has commanded us to ask of him. Then, that we thoroughly acknowledge our need and evil condition so that we may humble ourselves in the presence of his majesty. Third, that we rest assured that, in spite of our unworthiness, he will certainly hear our prayer for the sake of Christ our Lord, as he has promised us in his Word.

Q. 118. What has God commanded us to ask of him?

A. All things necessary for soul and body which Christ the Lord has included in the prayer which he himself taught us.

Q. 119. What is the Lord's Prayer?

A. "Our Father who art in heaven, hallowed be thy name. Thy kingdom come, thy will be done, on earth as it is in heaven. Give us this day our daily bread; and forgive us our debts, as we also have forgiven our debtors; and lead us not into temptation, but deliver us from evil, for thine is the kingdom and the power and the glory, forever. Amen."

Our Lord's Prayer

LORD'S DAY 46

Q. 120. Why has Christ commanded us to address God: "Our Father"?

A. That at the very beginning of our prayer he may awaken in us the childlike reverence and trust toward God which should be the motivation of our prayer, which is that God has become our Father through Christ and will much less deny us what we ask him in faith than our human fathers will refuse us earthly things.

Q. 121. Why is there added: "who art in heaven"?

A. That we may have no earthly conception of the heavenly majesty of God, but that we may expect from his almighty power all things that are needed for body and soul.

LORD'S DAY 47

Q. 122. What is the first petition?

A. "Hallowed be thy name." That is: help us first of all to know thee rightly, and to hallow, glorify, and praise thee in all thy works through which there shine thine almighty power, wisdom, goodness, righteousness, mercy, and truth. And so order our whole life in thought, word, and deed that thy name may never be blasphemed on our account, but may always be honored and praised.

LORD'S DAY 48

Q. 123. What is the second petition?

A. "Thy kingdom come." That is: so govern us by thy Word and Spirit that we may more and more submit ourselves unto thee. Uphold and increase thy church. Destroy the works of the devil, every power that raises itself against thee, and all wicked schemes thought up against thy holy Word, until the full coming of thy kingdom in which thou shalt be all in all.

LORD'S DAY 49

Q. 124. What is the third petition?

A. "Thy will be done, on earth as it is in heaven." That is: grant that we and all men may renounce our own will and obey thy will, which alone is good, without grumbling, so that everyone may carry out his office and calling as willingly and faithfully as the angels in heaven.

LORD'S DAY 50

Q. 125. What is the fourth petition?

A. "Give us this day our daily bread." That is: be pleased to provide for all our bodily needs so that thereby we may acknowledge that thou art the only source of all that is good, and that without thy blessing neither our care and labor nor thy gifts can do us any good. Therefore, may we withdraw our trust from all creatures and place it in thee alone.

LORD'S DAY 51

Q. 126. What is the fifth petition?

A. "And forgive us our debts, as we also have forgiven our debtors." That is: be pleased, for the sake of Christ's blood, not to charge to us, miserable sinners, our many transgressions, nor the evil which still clings to us. We also find this witness of thy grace in us, that it is our sincere intention heartily to forgive our neighbor.

LORD'S DAY 52

Q. 127. What is the sixth petition?

A. "And lead us not into temptation, but deliver us from evil." That is: since we are so weak that we cannot stand by ourselves for one moment, and besides, since our sworn enemies, the devil, the world, and our own sin, ceaselessly assail us, be pleased to preserve and strengthen us through the power of thy Holy Spirit so that we may stand firm against them, and not be defeated in this spiritual warfare, until at last we obtain complete victory.

Q. 128. How do you close this prayer?

A. "For thine is the kingdom and the power and the glory, forever." That is: we ask all this of thee because, as our King, thou art willing and able to give us all that is good since thou hast power over all things, and that by this not we ourselves but thy holy name may be glorified forever.

Q. 129. What is the meaning of the little word "Amen"?

A. Amen means: this shall truly and certainly be. For my prayer is much more certainly heard by God than I am persuaded in my heart that I desire such things from him.

The Westminster Standards

The Westminster Standards include the Westminster Confession of Faith and both the Larger and Shorter Catechisms. These documents were produced by the Westminster Assembly (1647). Though it didn't play a major role in the future of Protestantism in England, the Westminster Confession of Faith was for centuries the most influential confessional document among English-speaking Presbyterians.

The Larger Catechism was designed for public exposition from the pulpit, while the Shorter Catechism was written for the education of children. Both deal with questions of God, Christ, the Christian life, the Ten Commandments, the sacraments, and the Lord's Prayer. Unlike most earlier catechisms, neither contains a section on the Apostles' Creed. The most famous section is the first question and answer of the Shorter Catechism: "What is the chief end of man? Man's chief end is to glorify God, and to enjoy him forever."

THE SHORTER CATECHISM

Q. 1. What is the chief end of man?

A. Man's chief end is to glorify God,[1] and to enjoy him forever.[2]

Q. 2. What rule hath God given to direct us how we may glorify and enjoy him?

A. The Word of God which is contained in the Scriptures of the Old and New Testaments is the only rule to direct us how we may glorify and enjoy him.[1]

Q. 3. What do the Scriptures principally teach?

A. The Scriptures principally teach what man is to believe concerning God, and what duty God requires of man.[1]

Q. 4. What is God?

A. God is a Spirit,[1] infinite, eternal and unchangeable, in his being,[2] wisdom,[3] power,[4] holiness,[5] justice,[6] goodness,[7] and truth.[8]

Q. 5. Are there more Gods than one?

A. There is but one only, the living and true God.[1]

Q. 6. How many Persons are there in the Godhead?

A. There are three Persons in the Godhead: the Father, the Son, and the Holy Ghost; and these three are one God, the same in substance, equal in power and glory.[1]

Q. 7. What are the decrees of God?

A. The decrees of God are his eternal purpose, according to the counsel of his will, whereby, for his own glory, he hath foreordained whatsoever comes to pass.[1]

Q. 8. How doth God execute his decrees?

A. God executeth his decrees in the works of creation and providence.[1]

Q. 9. What is the work of creation?

A. The work of creation is God's making all things of nothing, by the word of his power, in the space of six days, and all very good.[1]

Q. 10. How did God create man?

A. God created man male and female, after his own image,[1] in knowledge, righteousness, and holiness,[2] with dominion over the creatures.[3]

Q. 11. What are God's works of providence?

A. God's works of providence are his most holy,[1] wise,[2] and powerful preserving[3] and governing all his creatures, and all their actions.[4]

Q. 12. What special act of providence did God exercise towards man, in the estate wherein he was created?

A. When God created man, he entered into a covenant of life with him, upon condition of perfect obedience;[1] forbidding him to eat of the tree of knowledge of good and evil, upon the pain of death.[2]

Q. 13. Did our first parents continue in the estate wherein they were created?

A. Our first parents, being left to the freedom of their own will, fell from the estate wherein they were created, by sinning against God.[1]

Q. 14. What is sin?

A. Sin is any want of conformity unto, or transgression of, the law of God.[1]

Q. 15. What was the sin whereby our first parents fell from the estate wherein they were created?

A. The sin whereby our first parents fell from the estate wherein they were created was their eating the forbidden fruit.[1]

Q. 16. Did all mankind fall in Adam's first transgression?

A. The covenant being made with Adam, not only for himself, but for his posterity,[1] all mankind, descending from him by ordinary generation, sinned in him, and fell with him, in his first transgression.[2]

Q. 17. Into what estate did the Fall bring mankind?

A. The Fall brought mankind into an estate of sin and misery.[1]

Q. 18. Wherein consists the sinfulness of that estate whereinto man fell?

A. The sinfulness of that estate whereinto man fell consists in: the guilt of Adam's first sin,[1] the want of original righteousness, and the corruption of his whole nature, which is commonly called original sin;[2] together with all actual transgressions which proceed from it.[3]

Q. 19. What is the misery of that estate whereinto man fell?

A. All mankind, by their fall, lost communion with God,[1] are under his wrath and curse,[2] and so made liable to all miseries of this life, to death itself, and to the pains of hell forever.[3]

Q. 20. Did God leave all mankind to perish in the estate of sin and misery?

A. God, having out of his mere good pleasure, from all eternity, elected some to everlasting life,[1] did enter into a covenant of grace, to deliver them out of the estate of sin and misery, and to bring them into an estate of salvation by a Redeemer.[2]

Q. 21. Who is the Redeemer of God's elect?

A. The only Redeemer of God's elect is the Lord Jesus Christ,[1] who, being the eternal Son of God, became man,[2] and so was, and continueth to be, God and man, in two distinct natures, and one Person forever.[3]

Q. 22. How did Christ, being the Son of God, become man?

A. Christ, the Son of God, became man, by taking to himself a true body and a reasonable soul,[1] being conceived by the power of the Holy Ghost, in the womb of the Virgin Mary, and born of her,[2] yet without sin.[3]

Q. 23.What offices doth Christ execute as our Redeemer?

A. Christ, as our Redeemer, executeth the offices of a prophet,[1] of a priest,[2] and of a king, both in his estate of humiliation and exaltation.[3]

Q. 24. How doth Christ execute the office of a prophet?

A. Christ executeth the office of a prophet in revealing to us,[1] by his Word and Spirit, the will of God for our salvation.[2]

Q. 25. How doth Christ execute the office of a priest?

A. Christ executeth the office of a priest in his once offering up of himself a sacrifice to satisfy divine justice,[1] and reconcile us to God,[2] and in making continual intercession for us.[3]

Q. 26. How doth Christ execute the office of a king?

A. Christ executeth the office of a king in subduing us to himself,[1] in ruling and defending us,[2] and in restraining and conquering all his and our enemies.[3]

Q. 27. Wherein did Christ's humiliation consist?

A. Christ's humiliation consisted in his being born, and that in a low condition,[1] made under the law,[2] undergoing the miseries of this life,[3] the wrath of God,[4] and the cursed death of the cross;[5] in being buried, and continuing under the power of death for a time.[6]

Q. 28. Wherein consisteth Christ's exaltation?

A. Christ's exaltation consisteth in his rising again from the dead on the third day,[1] in ascending up into heaven, in sitting at the right hand of God the Father,[2] and in coming to judge the world at the last day.[3]

Q. 29. How are we made partakers of the redemption purchased by Christ?

A. We are made partakers of the redemption purchased by Christ by the effectual application of it to us by his Holy Spirit.[1]

Q. 30. How doth the Spirit apply to us the redemption purchased by Christ?

A. The Spirit applieth to us the redemption purchased by Christ by working faith in us,[1] and thereby uniting us to Christ in our effectual calling.[2]

Q. 31. What is effectual calling?

A. Effectual calling is the work of God's Spirit,[1] whereby, convincing us of our sin and misery,[2] enlightening our minds in the knowledge of Christ,[3] and renewing our wills,[4] he doth persuade and enable us to embrace Jesus Christ, freely offered to us in the gospel.[5]

Q. 32. What benefits do they that are effectually called partake of in this life?

A. They that are effectually called do in this life partake of justification,[1] adoption,[2] sanctification, and the several benefits which, in this life, do either accompany or flow from them.[3]

Q. 33. What is justification?

A. Justification is an act of God's free grace, wherein he pardoneth all our sins,[1] and accepteth us as righteous in his sight,[2] only for the righteousness of Christ imputed to us,[3] and received by faith alone.[4]

Q. 34. What is adoption?

A. Adoption is an act of God's free grace,[1] whereby we are received into the number, and have a right to all the privileges, of the sons of God.[2]

Q. 35. What is sanctification?

A. Sanctification is the work of God's free grace,[1] whereby we are renewed in the whole man after the image of God,[2] and are enabled more and more to die unto sin and live unto righteousness.[3]

Q. 36. What are the benefits which in this life do accompany or flow from justification, adoption, and sanctification?

A.The benefits which in this life do accompany or flow from justification, adoption, and sanctification are: assurance of God's love, peace of conscience, joy in the Holy Ghost,[1] increase of grace,[2] and perseverance therein to the end.[3]

Q. 37. What benefits do believers receive from Christ at death?

A. The souls of believers are at their death made perfect in holiness, and do immediately pass into glory;[1] and their bodies, being still united to Christ,[2] do rest in their graves till the resurrection.[3]

Q. 38. What benefits do believers receive from Christ at the resurrection?

A.At the resurrection, believers, being raised up in glory,[1] shall be openly acknowledged and acquitted in the Day of Judgment,[2] and made perfectly blessed in the full enjoying of God[3] to all eternity.[4]

Q. 39. What is the duty which God requireth of man?

A.The duty which God requireth of man is obedience to his revealed will.[1]

Q. 40. What did God at first reveal to man for the rule of his obedience?

A. The rule which God at first revealed to man for his obedience was the moral law.[1]

Q. 41. Where is the moral law summarily comprehended?

A. The moral law is summarily comprehended in the Ten Commandments.[1]

Q. 42. What is the sum of the Ten Commandments?

A. The sum of the Ten Commandments is: to love the Lord our God with all our heart, with all our soul, with all our strength, and with all our mind; and our neighbor as ourselves.[1]

Q. 43. What is the preface to the Ten Commandments?

A. The preface to the Ten Commandments is in these words: "I am the Lord thy God, which have brought thee out of the land of Egypt, out of the house of bondage."[1]

Q. 44. What doth the preface to the Ten Commandments teach us?

A. The preface to the Ten Commandments teacheth us that because God is the Lord, and our God and Redeemer, therefore we are bound to keep all his commandments.

Q. 45. Which is the First Commandment?

A. The First Commandment is, "Thou shalt have no other gods before me."[1]

Q. 46. What is required in the First Commandment?

A. The First Commandment requireth us[1] to know and acknowledge God to be the only true God, and our God;[2] and to worship and glorify him accordingly.[3]

Q. 47. What is forbidden in the First Commandment?

A. The First Commandment forbiddeth the denying,[1] or not worshiping and glorifying, the true God as God,[2] and our God;[3] and the giving of that worship and glory to any other which is due to him alone.[4]

Q. 48. What are we specially taught by these words, "before me," in the First Commandment?

A. These words, "before me," in the First Commandment teach us that God, who seeth all things, taketh notice of, and is much displeased with, the sin of having any other god.[1]

Q. 49. Which is the Second Commandment?

A. The Second Commandment is, "Thou shalt not make unto thee any graven image, or any likeness of any thing that is in heaven above, or that is in the earth beneath, or that is in the water under the earth: thou shalt not bow down thyself to them, nor serve them: for I the Lord thy God am a jealous God, visiting the iniquity of the fathers upon the children unto the third and fourth generation of them that hate me; and showing mercy unto thousands of them that love me, and keep my commandments."[1]

Q. 50. What is required in the Second Commandment?

A.The Second Commandment requireth the receiving, observing, and keeping pure and entire all such religious worship and ordinances as God hath appointed in his Word.[1]

Q. 51. What is forbidden in the Second Commandment?

A. The Second Commandment forbiddeth the worshiping of God by images,[1] or any other way not appointed in his Word.[2]

Q. 52. What are the reasons annexed to the Second Commandment?

A. The reasons annexed to the Second Commandment are: God's sovereignty over us,[1] his propriety in us,[2] and the zeal he hath to his own worship.[3]

Q. 53. Which is the Third Commandment?

A. The Third Commandment is, "Thou shalt not take the name of the Lord thy God in vain: for the Lord will not hold him guiltless that taketh his name in vain."[1]

Q. 54. What is required in the Third Commandment?

A. The Third Commandment requireth the holy and reverent use of God's names,[1] titles, attributes,[2] ordinances,[3] Word,[4] and works.[5]

Q. 55. What is forbidden in the Third Commandment?

A. The Third Commandment forbiddeth all profaning or abusing of anything whereby God maketh himself known.[1]

Q. 56. What is the reason annexed to the Third Commandment?

A. The reason annexed to the Third Commandment is that, however the breakers of this commandment may escape punishment from men, yet the Lord our God will not suffer them to escape his righteous judgment.[1]

Q. 57. Which is the Fourth Commandment?

A. The Fourth Commandment is, "Remember the Sabbath day, to keep it holy. Six days shalt thou labor, and do all thy work: but the seventh day is the Sabbath of the Lord thy God: in it thou shalt not do any work, thou, nor thy son, nor thy daughter, thy manservant, nor thy maidservant, nor thy cattle, nor thy stranger that is within thy gates: for in six days the Lord made heaven and earth, the sea, and all that in them is, and rested the seventh day: wherefore the Lord blessed the Sabbath day, and hallowed it."[1]

Q. 58. What is required in the Fourth Commandment?

A. The Fourth Commandment requireth the keeping holy to God such set times as he hath appointed in his Word; expressly one whole day in seven, to be a holy Sabbath to himself.[1]

Q. 59. Which day of the seven hath God appointed to be the weekly Sabbath?

A. From the beginning of the world to the resurrection of Christ, God appointed the seventh day of the week to be the weekly Sabbath;[1] and the first day of the week ever since, to continue to the end of the world, which is the Christian Sabbath.[2]

Q. 60. How is the Sabbath to be sanctified?

A. The Sabbath is to be sanctified by a holy resting all that day, even from such worldly employments and recreations as are lawful on other days;[1] and spending the whole time in the public and private exercises of God's worship,[2] except so much as is to be taken up in the works of necessity and mercy.[3]

Q. 61. What is forbidden in the Fourth Commandment?

A.The Fourth Commandment forbiddeth the omission, or careless performance, of the duties required,[1] and the profaning the day by idleness, or doing that which is in itself sinful,[2] or by unnecessary thoughts, words, or works, about our worldly employments or recreations.[3]

Q. 62. What are the reasons annexed to the Fourth Commandment?

A.The reasons annexed to the Fourth Commandment are: God's allowing us six days of the week for our own employments,[1] his challenging a special propriety in the seventh,[2] his own example,[3] and his blessing the Sabbath Day.[4]

Q. 63. Which is the Fifth Commandment?

A.The Fifth Commandment is, "Honor thy father and thy mother: that thy days may be long upon the land which the Lord thy God giveth thee."[1]

Q. 64. What is required in the Fifth Commandment?

A. The Fifth Commandment requireth the preserving the honor, and performing the duties, belonging to everyone in their several places and relations, as superiors, inferiors, or equals.[1]

Q. 65. What is forbidden in the Fifth Commandment?

A. The Fifth Commandment forbiddeth the neglecting of, or doing anything against, the honor and duty which belongeth to everyone in their several places and relations.[1]

Q. 66. What is the reason annexed to the Fifth Commandment?

A. The reason annexed to the Fifth Commandment is a promise of long life and prosperity (as far as it shall serve for God's glory, and their own good) to all such as keep this commandment.[1]

Q. 67. Which is the Sixth Commandment?

A. The Sixth Commandment is, "Thou shalt not kill."[1]

Q. 68. What is required in the Sixth Commandment?

A. The Sixth Commandment requireth all lawful endeavors to preserve our own life,[1] and the life of others.[2]

Q. 69. What is forbidden in the Sixth Commandment?

A. The Sixth Commandment forbiddeth the taking away of our own life,[1] or the life of our neighbor unjustly,[2] or whatsoever tendeth thereunto.[3]

Q. 70. Which is the Seventh Commandment?

A. The Seventh Commandment is, "Thou shalt not commit adultery."[1]

Q. 71. What is required in the Seventh Commandment?

A. The Seventh Commandment requireth the preservation of our own[1] and our neighbor's chastity,[2] in heart,[3] speech,[4] and behavior.[5]

Q. 72. What is forbidden in the Seventh Commandment?

A.The Seventh Commandment forbiddeth all unchaste thoughts,[1] words,[2] and actions.[3]

Q. 73. Which is the Eighth Commandment?

A. The Eighth Commandment is, "Thou shalt not steal."[1]

Q. 74. What is required in the Eighth Commandment?

A. The Eighth Commandment requireth the lawful procuring and furthering the wealth and outward estate of ourselves[1] and others.[2]

Q. 75. What is forbidden in the Eighth Commandment?

A. The Eighth Commandment forbiddeth whatsoever doth, or may, unjustly hinder our own,[1] or our neighbor's, wealth or outward estate.[2]

Q. 76. Which is the Ninth Commandment?

A. The Ninth Commandment is, "Thou shalt not bear false witness against thy neighbor."[1]

Q. 77. What is required in the Ninth Commandment?

A. The Ninth Commandment requireth the maintaining and promoting of truth between man and man,[1] and of our own[2] and our neighbor's good name,[3] especially in witness-bearing.[4]

Q. 78. What is forbidden in the Ninth Commandment?

A. The Ninth Commandment forbiddeth whatsoever is prejudicial to truth,[1] or injurious to our own or our neighbor's good name.[2]

Q. 79. Which is the Tenth Commandment?

A. The Tenth Commandment is, "Thou shalt not covet thy neighbor's house, thou shalt not covet thy neighbor's wife, nor his manservant, nor his maidservant, nor his ox, nor his ass, nor any thing that is thy neighbor's."[1]

Q. 80. What is required in the Tenth Commandment?

A. The Tenth Commandment requireth full contentment with our own condition,[1] with a right and charitable frame of spirit toward our neighbor and all that is his.[2]

Q. 81. What is forbidden in the Tenth Commandment?

A. The Tenth Commandment forbiddeth all discontentment with our own estate,[1] envying or grieving at the good of our neighbor,[2] and all inordinate motions and affections to anything that is his.[3]

Q. 82. Is any man able perfectly to keep the commandments of God?

A. No mere man, since the Fall, is able, in this life, perfectly to keep the commandments of God,[1] but doth daily break them, in thought,[2] word,[3] and deed.[4]

Q. 83. Are all transgressions of the law equally heinous?

A. Some sins in themselves, and by reason of several aggravations, are more heinous in the sight of God than others.[1]

Q. 84. What doth every sin deserve?

A. Every sin deserveth God's wrath and curse, both in this life and that which is to come.[1]

Q. 85. What doth God require of us, that we may escape his wrath and curse, due to us for sin?

A. To escape the wrath and curse of God, due to us for sin, God requireth of us faith in Jesus Christ, repentance unto life,[1] with the diligent use of all the outward means whereby Christ communicateth to us the benefits of redemption.[2]

Q. 86. What is faith in Jesus Christ?

A. Faith in Jesus Christ is a saving grace,[1] whereby we receive[2] and rest upon him alone for salvation,[3] as he is offered to us in the gospel.[4]

Q. 87. What is repentance unto life?

A. Repentance unto life is a saving grace,[1] whereby a sinner, out of a true sense of his sin,[2] and apprehension of the mercy of God in Christ,[3] doth, with grief and hatred of his sin, turn from it unto God,[4] with full purpose of, and endeavor after, new obedience.[5]

Q. 88. What are the outward means whereby Christ communicateth to us the benefits of redemption?

A. The outward and ordinary means whereby Christ communicateth to us the benefits of redemption are his ordinances, especially the Word, sacraments, and prayer,[1] all which are made effectual to the elect for salvation.

Q. 89. How is the Word made effectual to salvation?

A. The Spirit of God maketh the reading, but especially the preaching, of the Word an effectual means of convincing and converting sinners,[1] and of building them up in holiness and comfort, through faith unto salvation.[2]

Q. 90. How is the Word to be read and heard, that it may become effectual to salvation?

A. That the Word may become effectual to salvation we must attend thereunto with diligence,[1] preparation,[2] and prayer;[3] receive it with faith[4] and love;[5] lay it up in our hearts;[6] and practice it in our lives.[7]

Q. 91. How do the sacraments become effectual means of salvation?

A. The sacraments become effectual means of salvation, not from any virtue in them, or in him that doth administer them, but only by the blessing of Christ, and the working of his Spirit in them that by faith receive them.[1]

Q. 92. What is a sacrament?

A. A sacrament is a holy ordinance instituted by Christ, wherein, by sensible signs, Christ and the benefits of the new covenant are represented,[1] sealed, and applied to believers.[2]

Q. 93. Which are the sacraments of the New Testament?

A. The sacraments of the New Testament are Baptism[1] and the Lord's Supper.[2]

Q. 94. What is Baptism?

A. Baptism is a sacrament, wherein the washing with water, in the name of the Father, and of the Son, and of the Holy Ghost,[1] doth signify and seal our ingrafting into Christ, and partaking of the benefits of the covenant of grace,[2] and our engagement to be the Lord's.[3]

Q. 95. To whom is Baptism to be administered?

A. Baptism is not to be administered to any that are out of the visible Church, till they profess their faith in Christ and obedience to him;[1] but the infants of such as are members of the visible Church are to be baptized.[2]

Q. 96. What is the Lord's Supper?

A. The Lord's Supper is a sacrament, wherein by giving and receiving bread and wine, according to Christ's appointment, his death is showed forth;[1] and the worthy receivers are, not after a corporal and carnal manner, but by faith, made partakers of his body and blood, with all his benefits, to their spiritual nourishment and growth in grace.[2]

Q. 97. What is required to the worthy receiving of the Lord's Supper?

A. It is required of them that would worthily partake of the Lord's Supper that they examine themselves, of their knowledge to discern the Lord's body,[1] of their faith to feed upon him,[2] of their repentance,[3] love,[4] and new obedience;[5] lest, coming unworthily, they eat and drink judgment to themselves.[6]

Q. 98. What is prayer?

A. Prayer is an offering up of our desires unto God,[1] for things agreeable to his will,[2] in the name of Christ,[3] with confession of our sins,[4] and thankful acknowledgment of his mercies.[5]

Q. 99. What rule hath God given for our direction in prayer?

A. The whole Word of God is of use to direct us in prayer;[1] but the special rule of direction is that form of prayer which Christ taught his disciples, commonly called "the Lord's Prayer."[2]

Q. 100. What doth the preface of the Lord's Prayer teach us?

A. The preface of the Lord's Prayer, which is, "Our Father which art in heaven," teacheth us to draw near to God with all holy reverence and confidence, as children to a father, able and ready to help us;[1] and that we should pray with and for others.[2]

Q. 101. What ao we pray for in the first petition?

A. In the first petition, which is, "Hallowed be thy name," we pray that God would enable us, and others, to glorify him in all that whereby he maketh himself known,[1] and that he would dispose all things to his own glory.[2]

Q. 102. What do we pray for in the second petition?

A. In the second petition, which is, "Thy kingdom come," we pray that Satan's kingdom may be destroyed,[1] and that the Kingdom of grace may be advanced, ourselves and others brought into it, and kept in it,[2] and that the Kingdom of glory may be hastened.[3]

Q. 103. What do we pray for in the third petition?

A. In the third petition, which is, "Thy will be done in earth, as it is in heaven," we pray that God, by his grace, would make us able and willing to know, obey, and submit to his will in all things,[1] as the angels do in heaven.[2]

Q. 104. What do we pray for in the fourth petition?

A. In the fourth petition, which is, "Give us this day our daily bread," we pray that, of God's free gift, we may receive a competent portion of the good things of this life,[1] and enjoy his blessing with them.[2]

Q. 105. What do we pray for in the fifth petition?

A. In the fifth petition, which is, "And forgive us our debts, as we forgive our debtors," we pray that God, for Christ's sake, would freely pardon all our sins;[1] which we are the rather encouraged to ask because by his grace we are enabled from the heart to forgive others.[2]

Q. 106. What do we pray for in the sixth petition?

A. In the sixth petition, which is, "And lead us not into temptation, but deliver us from evil," we pray that God would either keep us from being tempted to sin[1] or support and deliver us when we are tempted.[2]

Q. 107. What doth the conclusion of the Lord's Prayer teach us?

A. The conclusion of the Lord's Prayer, which is, "For thine is the kingdom, and the power, and the glory, forever. Amen," teacheth us to take our encouragement in prayer from God only,[1] and in our prayers to praise him, ascribing Kingdom, power, and glory to him;[2] and in testimony of our desire and assurance to be heard, we say, "Amen."[3]

THE TEN COMMANDMENTS

EXODUS, CH. 20

GOD spake all these words, saying, I am the Lord thy God, which have brought thee out of the land of Egypt, out of the house of bondage.

    I. Thou shalt have no other gods before me.

    II. Thou shalt not make unto thee any graven image, or any likeness of any thing that is in heaven above, or that is in the earth beneath, or that is in the water under the earth: thou shalt not bow down thyself to them, nor serve them: for I the Lord thy God am a jealous God, visiting the iniquity of the fathers upon the children unto the third and fourth generation of them that hate me; and showing mercy unto thousands of them that love me, and keep my commandments.

    III. Thou shalt not take the name of the Lord thy God in vain: for the Lord will not hold him guiltless that taketh his name in vain.

    IV. Remember the Sabbath day, to keep it holy. Six days shalt thou labor, and do all thy work: but the seventh day is the Sabbath of the Lord thy God: in it thou shalt not do any work, thou, nor thy son, nor thy daughter, thy manservant, nor thy maidservant, nor thy cattle, nor thy stranger that is within thy gates: for in six days the Lord made heaven and earth, the sea, and all that in them is, and rested the seventh day: wherefore the Lord blessed the seventh day, and hallowed it.

    V. Honor thy father and thy mother: that thy days may be long upon the land which the Lord thy God giveth thee.

    VI. Thou shalt not kill.

VII. Thou shalt not commit adultery.

VIII. Thou shalt not steal.

IX. Thou shalt not bear false witness against thy neighbor.

X. Thou shalt not covet thy neighbor's house, thou shalt not covet thy neighbor's wife, nor his manservant, nor his maidservant, nor his ox, nor his ass, nor any thing that is thy neighbor's.

THE LORD'S PRAYER

MATTHEW, CH. 6

Our Father which art in heaven, hallowed be thy name. Thy kingdom come. Thy will be done in earth, as it is in heaven. Give us this day our daily bread. And forgive us our debts, as we forgive our debtors. And lead us not into temptation, but deliver us from evil: For thine is the kingdom, and the power, and the glory, forever. Amen.

THE APOSTLES' CREED

I BELIEVE in God the Father Almighty, Maker of heaven and earth;

And in Jesus Christ his only Son our Lord; who was conceived by the Holy Ghost, born of the Virgin Mary, suffered under Pontius Pilate, was crucified, dead, and buried; he descended into hell;[1] the third day he rose again from the dead; he ascended into heaven, and sitteth on the right hand of God the Father Almighty; from thence he shall come to judge the quick and the dead.

I believe in the Holy Ghost; the holy catholic Church; the communion of saints; the forgiveness of sins; the resurrection of the body; and the life everlasting. Amen.

Q. 1.
    1. I Cor. 10:31; Rom. 11:36.
    2. Ps. 73:24–26; John 17:22, 24.
Q. 2.
    1. Gal. 1:8, 9; Isa. 8:20; Luke 16:29, 31; II Tim. 3:15–17.
Q. 3.
    1. Micah 6:8; John 20:31; John 3:16.
Q. 4.
    1. John 4:24.
    2. Ps. 90:2; Mal. 3:6; James 1:17; I Kings 8:27; Jer. 23:24; Isa. 40:22.
    3. Ps. 147:5; Rom. 16:27.
    4. Gen. 17:1; Rev. 19:16.
    5. Isa. 57:15; John 17:11; Rev. 4:8.
    6. Deut. 32:4.
    7. Ps. 100:5; Rom. 2:4.
    8. Exod. 34:6; Ps. 117:2.
Q. 5.
    1. Deut. 6:4; Jer. 10:10.
Q. 6.
    1. II Cor. 13:14; Matt. 28:19; Matt. 3:16, 17.
Q. 7.
    1. Eph. 1:11; Acts 4:27, 28; Ps. 33:11; Eph. 2:10; Rom. 9:22,23; 11:33.
Q. 8.
    1. Rev. 4:11; Eph. 1:11.
Q. 9.
    1. Heb. 11:3; Rev. 4:11; Gen. 1:1–31.
Q.10.
    1. Gen. 1:27.
    2. Col. 3:10; Eph. 4:24.
    3. Gen. 1:28.
Q.11.
    1. Ps. 145:17.
    2. Ps. 104:24.
    3. Heb. 1:3.
    4. Ps. 103:19; Matt. 10:29, 30; Job, Chapters 38–41.
Q.12.
    1. Compare Gen. 2:16, 17 with Rom. 5:12–14; Rom. 10:5; Luke 10:25–28, and with the covenants made with Noah and Abraham.
    2. Gen. 2:17.
Q.13.
    1. Gen. 3:6–8, 13; II Cor. 11:3.
Q.14.
    1. I John 3:4; James 4:17; Rom. 3:23.
Q.15.
    1. See proof to Answer 13. Gen. 3:6.
Q.16.
    1. Acts 17:26. See under Question 12.
    2. Gen. 2:17. Compare Rom. 5:12–20; I Cor. 15:21, 22.
Q.17.
    1. Rom. 5:12; Gal. 3:10.
Q.18.
    1. Rom. 5:12, 19; I Cor. 15:22.

   2. Rom. 5:6; Eph. 2:1–3; Rom. 8:7, 8; Gen. 6:5; Rom. 3:10–20; Ps. 51:5; 58:3.

   3. James 1:14, 15; Matt. 15:19.

Q.19.

   1. Gen. 3:8, 24.

   2. Eph. 2:3.

   3. Rom. 5:14; Rom. 6:23.

Q.20.

   1. Eph. 1:4–7.

   2. Titus 3:4–7; Titus 1:2; Gal. 3:21; Rom. 3:20–22.

Q.21.

   1. I Tim. 2:5.

   2. John 1:1, 14; John 10:30; Phil. 2:6; Gal. 4:4.

   3. See texts just cited; also Phil. 2:5–11.

Q.22.

   1. John 1:14; Heb. 2:14; Matt. 26:38.

   2. Luke 1:31, 35, 41, 42; Gal. 4:4.

   3. Heb. 4:15; Heb. 7:26.

Q.23.

   1. Acts 3:22; Luke 4:18, 21.

   2. Heb. 5:5, 6; Heb. 4:14, 15.

   3. Rev. 19:16; Isa. 9:6, 7; Ps. 2:6.

Q.24.

   1. John 1:1, 4.

   2. John 15:15; John 20:31; II Peter 1:21; John 14:26.

Q.25.

   1. Heb. 9:14, 28; Rom. 3:26; Rom. 10:4.

   2. Heb. 2:17.

   3. Heb. 7:25.

Q.26.

   1. Ps. 110:3.

   2. Isa. 33:22.

   3. I Cor. 15:25; Acts 12:17; 18:9, 10.

Q.27.

   1. Luke 2:7; Phil. 2:6–8; II Cor. 8:9.

   2. Gal. 4:4.

   3. Isa. 53:3.

   4. Matt. 27:46; Luke 22:41–44.

   5. Gal. 3:13; Phil. 2:8.

   6. I Cor. 15:3, 4.

Q.28.

   1. See last quoted text.

   2. Acts 1:9; Eph. 1:19, 20.

   3. Acts 1:11; Acts 17:31.

Q.29.

   1. John 1:12, 13; John 3:5, 6; Titus 3:5, 6.

Q.30.

   1. Eph. 2:8.

   2. John 15:5; I Cor. 6:17; I Cor. 1:9; I Peter 5:10.

Q.31.

   1. II Tim. 1:8, 9; Eph. 1:18–20.

   2. Acts 2:37.

   3. Acts 26:18.

4. Ezek. 11:19; Ezek. 36:26, 27.

5. John 6:44, 45; Phil. 2:13; Deut. 30:6; Eph. 2:5.

Q.32.

    1. Rom. 8:30.

    2. Eph. 1:5.

    3. I Cor. 1:30.

Q.33.

    1. Eph. 1:7.

    2. II Cor. 5:19, 21; Rom. 4:5; Rom. 3:22, 24, 25.

    3. Rom. 5:17–19; Rom. 4:6–8.

    4. Rom. 5:1; Acts 10:43; Gal. 2:16; Phil. 3:9.

Q.34.

    1. I John 3:1.

    2. John 1:12; Rom. 8:17.

Q.35.

    1. II Thess. 2:13.

    2. Eph. 4:23, 24.

    3. Rom. 6:4, 6, 14; Rom. 8:4.

Q.36.

    1. Rom. 5:1, 2, 5; Rom. 14:17.

    2. Col. 1:10, 11; Prov. 4:18; Eph. 3:16–18; II Peter 3:18.

    3. Jer. 32:40; I John 2:19, 27; Rev. 14:21; I Peter 1:5; I John 5:13.

Q.37.

    1. Luke 23:43; Luke 16:23; Phil. 1:23; II Cor. 5:6–8.

    2. I Thess. 4:14.

    3. Rom. 8:23; I Thess. 4:14.

Q.38.

    1. I Cor. 15:42, 43.

    2. Matt. 25:33, 34; Matt. 10:32.

    3. Ps. 16:11; I Cor. 2:9.

    4. I Thess. 4:17. See preceding context.

Q.39.

    1. Deut. 29:29; Micah 6:8; I Sam. 15:22.

Q.40.

    1. Rom. 2:14, 15; Rom. 10:5.

Q.41.

    1. Matt. 19:17–19.

Q. 42

    1. Matt. 22:37–40.

Q.43.

    1. Exod. 20:2.

Q.45.

    1. Exod. 20:3.

Q.46.

    1. The exposition of the Ten Commandments found in answers to Questions 46–81 are deductions from the commandments themselves and the rules set forth in the Larger Catechism, Q. 99. The texts under the specifications are given to show that they are in accord with the general teaching of the Scriptures.

    2. I Chron. 28:9; Deut. 26:17.

    3. Matt. 4:10; Ps. 95:6, 7; Ps. 29:2.

Q.47.

    1. Ps. 14:1.

2. Rom. 1:20, 21.
3. Ps. 81:11.
4. Rom. 1:25.

Q.48.
1. I Chron. 28:9; Ps. 44:20, 21.

Q.49.
1. Exod. 20:4–6.

Q.50.
1. Deut. 12:32; Deut. 32:46; Matt. 28:20.

Q.51.
1. Deut. 4:15, 16; See verses 17–19; Acts 17:29.
2. Deut. 12:30–32.

Q.52.
1. Ps. 95:2, 3.
2. Ps. 45:11.
3. Exod. 34:14.

Q.53.
1. Exod. 20:7.

Q.54.
1. Ps. 29:2; Matt. 6:9.
2. Rev. 15:3, 4.
3. Mal. 1:14.
4. Ps. 138:2.
5. Ps. 107:21, 22.

Q.55.
1. Mal. 2:2; Isa. 5:12.

Q.56.
1. Deut. 28:58, 59.

Q.57.
1. Exod. 20:8–11.

Q.58.
1. Lev. 19:30; Deut. 5:12; Isa. 56:2–7.

Q.59.
1. Gen. 2:3; Luke 23:56.
2. Acts 20:7; I Cor. 16:1, 2; John 20:19–26.

Q.60.
1. Lev. 23:3; Exod. 16:25–29; Jer. 17:21, 22.
2. Ps. 92:1, 2. (A Psalm or Song for the sabbath day) Luke 4:16; Isa. 58:13; Acts 20:7.
3. Matt. 12:11, 12. See context.

Q.61.
1. Ezek. 22:26; Mal. 1:13; Amos 8:5.
2. Ezek. 23:38.
3. Isa. 58:13; Jer. 17:24, 27.

Q.62.
1. Exod. 31:15, 16.
2. Lev. 23:3.
3. Exod. 31:17.
4. Gen. 2:3.

Q.63.
1. Exod. 20:12.

Q.64.
1. Eph. 5:21, 22; Eph. 6:1, 5, 9; Rom. 13:1; Rom. 12:10.

Q.65.
    1. Rom. 13:7, 8.
Q.66.
    1. Eph. 6:2, 3.
Q.67.
    1. Exod. 20:13.
Q.68.
    1. Eph. 5:29; Matt. 10:23.
    2. Ps. 82:3, 4; Job 29:13; I Kings 18:4.
Q.69.
    1. Acts 16:28.
    2. Gen. 9:6.
    3. Matt. 5:22; I John 3:15; Gal. 5:15; Prov. 24:11, 12; Exod. 21:18–32.
Q.70.
    1. Exod. 20:14.
Q.71.
    1. I Thess. 4:4, 5.
    2. I Cor. 7:2; Eph. 5:11, 12.
    3. Matt. 5:28.
    4. Eph. 4:29; Col. 4:6.
    5. I Peter 3:2.
Q.72.
    1. Matt. 5:28.
    2. Eph. 5:4.
    3. Eph. 5:3.
Q.73.
    1. Exod. 20:15.
Q.74.
    1. II Thess. 3:10–12; Rom. 12:17; Prov. 27:23.
    2. Lev. 25:35; Phil. 2:4; Prov. 13:4; Prov. 20:4; Prov. 24:30–34.
Q.75.
    1. I Tim. 5:8.
    2. Eph. 4:28; Prov. 21:16; II Thess. 3:7–10.
Q.76.
    1. Exod. 20:16.
Q.77.
    1. Zech. 8:16.
    2. I Peter 3:16; Acts 25:10.
    3. III John 12.
    4. Prov. 14:5, 25.
Q.78.
    1. Prov. 19:5; Prov. 6:16–19.
    2. Luke 3:14; Ps. 15:3.
Q.79.
    1. Exod. 20:17.
Q.80.
    1. Heb. 13:5.
    2. Rom. 12:15; Phil. 2:4; I Cor. 13:4–6.
Q.81.
    1. I Cor. 10:10.
    2. Gal. 5:26.
    3. Col. 3:5.

Q.82.
    1. I Kings 8:46; I John 1:8–2:6.
    2. Gen. 8:21.
    3. James 3:8.
    4. James 3:2.
Q.83.
    1. Ps. 19:13; John 19:11.
Q.84.
    1. Gal. 3:10; Matt. 25:41.
Q.85.
    1. Acts 20:21; Mark 1:15; John 3:18.
    2. See under Question 88 below.
Q.86.
    1. Heb. 10:39.
    2. John 1:12.
    3. Phil. 3:9.
    4. John 6:40.
Q.87.
    1. Acts 11:18.
    2. Acts 2:37.
    3. Joel 2:13.
    4. II Cor. 7:11; Jer. 31:18, 19; Acts 26:18.
    5. Ps. 119:59.
Q.88.
    1. Matt. 28:19, 20; Acts 2:41, 42.
Q.89.
    1. Ps. 19:7, Ps. 119:130; Heb. 4:12.
    2. I Thess. 1:6; Rom. 1:16; Rom. 16:25; Acts 20:32.
Q.90.
    1. Prov. 8:34.
    2. Luke 8:18; I Peter 2:1, 2.
    3. Ps. 119:18.
    4. Heb. 4:2.
    5. II Thess. 2:10.
    6. Ps. 119:11.
    7. Luke 8:15; James 1:25.
Q.91.
    1. I Peter 3:21; Acts 8:13, 23.See intervening context. I Cor. 3:7; I Cor. 6:11; I Cor. 12:13.
Q.92.
    1. Matt. 28:19; Matt. 26:26–28.
    2. Rom. 4:11.
Q.93.
    1. Matt. 28:19.
    2. I Cor. 11:23.
Q.94.
    1. See Matt. 28:19 cited under Question 93 above.
    2. Gal. 3:27; Rom. 6:3.
    3. Rom. 6:4.
Q.95.
    1. Acts 2:41.
    2. Gen. 17:7, 10; Gal. 3:17, 18, 29; Acts 2:38, 39.

Q.96.
1. Matt. 26:26, 27; I Cor. 11:26.
2. I Cor. 10:16; Eph. 3:17.
Q.97.
1. I Cor. 11:28, 29.
2. John 6:53–56.
3. Zech. 12:10.
4. I John 4:19; Gal. 5:6.
5. Rom. 6:4; Rom. 6:17–22.
6. I Cor. 11:27.
Q.98.
1. Ps. 62:8; Ps. 10:17.
2. I John 5:14; Matt. 26:39; John 6:38.
3. John 16:23.
4. Dan. 9:4.
5. Phil. 4:6.
Q.99.
1. II Tim. 3:16, 17; I John 5:14.
2. Matt. 6:9.
Q.100.
1. Isa. 64:9; Luke 11:13; Rom. 8:15.
2. Eph. 6:18; Acts 12:5; Zech. 8:21.
Q.101.
1. Ps. 67:1–3; II Thess. 3:1; Ps. 145.
2. Isa. 64:1, 2; Rom. 11:36.
Q.102.
1. Ps. 68:1.
2. II Thess. 3:1; Ps. 51:18; 67:1–3; Rom. 10:1.
3. Rev. 22:20; II Peter 3:11–13.
Q.103.
1. Ps. 119:35–36; Acts 21:14.
2. Ps. 103:20–22.
Q.104.
1. Prov. 30:8.
2. I Tim. 4:4, 5; Prov. 10:22.
Q.105.
1. Ps. 51:1; Rom 3:24, 25.
2. Luke 11:4; Matt. 18:35; Matt. 6:14, 15.
Q.106.
1. Matt. 26:41; Ps. 19:13.
2. I Cor. 10:13; Ps. 51:10, 12.
Q.107.
1. Dan. 9:18, 19.
2. I Chron. 29:11–13.
3. Rev. 22:20, 21; I Cor. 14:16.
The Apostles' Creed
1. *I.e.* Continued in the state of the dead, and under the power of death, until the third day. See the answer to Question 50 in the Larger Catechism.

THE LARGER CATECHISM

Q. 1. What is the chief and highest end of man?

A. Man's chief and highest end is to glorify God,[1] and fully to enjoy him forever.[2]

Q. 2. How doth it appear that there is a God?

A. The very light of nature in man, and the works of God, declare plainly that there is a God;[1] but his Word and Spirit only, do sufficiently and effectually reveal him unto men for their salvation.[2]

Q. 3. What is the Word of God?

A. The holy Scriptures of the Old and New Testaments are the Word of God, the only rule of faith and obedience.[1]

Q. 4. How doth it appear that the Scriptures are the Word of God?

A. The Scriptures manifest themselves to be the Word of God, by their majesty and purity; by the consent of all the parts, and the scope of the whole, which is to give all glory to God; by their light and power to convince and convert sinners, to comfort and build up believers unto salvation.[1] But the Spirit of God, bearing witness by and with the Scriptures in the heart of man, is alone able fully to persuade it that they are the very word of God.[2]

Q. 5. What do the Scriptures principally teach?

A. The Scriptures principally teach, what man is to believe concerning God, and what duty God requires of man.[1]

What Man Ought to Believe Concerning God

Q. 6. What do the Scriptures make known of God?

A. The Scriptures make known what God is,[1] the persons in the Godhead,[2] his decrees,[3] and the execution of his decrees.[4]

Q. 7. What is God?

A. God is a Spirit,[1] in and of himself infinite in being,[2] glory, blessedness, and perfection;[3] all-sufficient, [4] eternal,[5] unchangeable,[6] incomprehensible,[7] everywhere present,[8] almighty;[9] knowing all things,[10] most wise,[11] most holy,[12] most just,[13] most merciful and gracious, long-suffering, and abundant in goodness and truth.[14]

Q. 8. Are there more Gods than one?

A. There is but one only, the living and true God.[1]

Q. 9. How many persons are there in the Godhead?

A. There be three persons in the Godhead: the Father, the Son, and the Holy Ghost; and these three are one true, eternal God, the same in substance, equal in power and glory; although distinguished by their personal properties.[1]

Q. 10. What are the personal properties of the three persons in the Godhead?

A. It is proper to the Father to beget his Son,[1] and to the Son to be begotten of the Father,[2] and to the Holy Ghost to proceed from the Father and the Son, from all eternity.[3]

Q. 11. How doth it appear that the Son and the Holy Ghost are equal with the Father?

A. The Scriptures manifest that the Son and the Holy Ghost are God equal with the Father, ascribing unto them such names,[1] attributes,[2] works,[3] and worship,[4] as are proper to God only.

Q. 12. What are the decrees of God?

A. God's decrees are the wise, free, and holy acts of the counsel of his will, whereby, from all eternity, he hath, for his own glory, unchangeably foreordained whatsoever comes to pass in time,[1] especially concerning angels and men.

Q. 13. What hath God especially decreed concerning angels and men?

A. God, by an eternal and immutable decree, out of his mere love, for the praise of his glorious grace, to be manifested in due time, hath elected some angels to glory;[1] and, in Christ, hath chosen some men to eternal life, and the means thereof;[2] and also, according to his sovereign power, and the unsearchable counsel of his own will (whereby he extendeth or withholdeth favor as he pleaseth) hath passed by, and foreordained the rest to dishonor and wrath, to be for their sin inflicted, to the praise of the glory of his justice.[3]

Q. 14. How doth God execute his decrees?

A. God executeth his decrees in the works of creation and providence, according to his infallible foreknowledge, and the free and immutable counsel of his own will.[1]

Q. 15. What is the work of creation?

A. The work of creation is that wherein God did in the beginning, by the word of his power, make of nothing, the world and all things therein for himself, within the space of six days, and all very good.[1]

Q. 16. How did God create angels?

A. God created all the angels, spirits,[1] immortal,[2] holy,[3] excelling in knowledge,[4] mighty in power;[5] to execute his commandments, and to praise his name,[6] yet subject to change.[7]

Q. 17. How did God create man?

A. After God had made all other creatures, he created man, male and female;[1] formed the body of the man of the dust of the ground,[2] and the woman of the rib of man;[3] endued them with living, reasonable, and immortal souls;[4] made them after his own image,[5] in knowledge,[6] righteousness and holiness,[7] having the law of God written in their hearts,[8] and power to fulfill it, with dominion over the creatures;[9] yet subject to fall.[10]

Q. 18. What are God's works of providence?

A. God's works of providence are his most holy,[1] wise,[2] and powerful preserving,[3] and governing all his creatures;[4] ordering them, and all their actions,[5] to his own glory.[6]

Q. 19. What is God's providence toward the angels?

A. God by his providence permitted some of the angels, willfully and irrecoverably, to fall into sin and damnation,[1] limiting and ordering that, and all their sins, to his own glory;[2] and established the rest in holiness and happiness;[3] employing them all, at his pleasure, in the administrations of his power, mercy, and justice.[4]

Q. 20. What was the providence of God toward man in the estate in which he was created?

A. The providence of God toward man in the estate in which he was created was, the placing him in paradise, appointing him to dress it, giving him liberty to eat of the fruit of the earth,[1] putting the creatures under his dominion,[2] ordaining marriage for his help,[3] affording him communion with himself,[4] and instituting the Sabbath;[5] entering into a covenant of life with him, upon condition of personal, perfect, and perpetual obedience,[6] of which the tree of life was a pledge; and forbidding to eat of the tree of the knowledge of good and evil, upon pain of death.[7]

Q. 21. Did man continue in that estate wherein God at first Created him?

A. Our first parents, being left to the freedom of their own will, through the temptation of Satan, transgressed the commandment of God, in eating the forbidden fruit, and thereby fell from the estate of innocency wherein they were created.[1]

Q. 22. Did all mankind fall in that first transgression?

A. The covenant being made with Adam, as a public person, not for himself only, but for his posterity, all mankind, descending from him by ordinary generation,[1] sinned in him, and fell with him in that first transgression.[2]

Q. 23. Into what estate did the Fall bring mankind?

A. The Fall brought mankind into an estate of sin and misery.[1]

Q. 24. What is sin?

A. Sin is any want of conformity unto, or transgression of, any law of God, given as a rule to the reasonable creature.[1]

Q. 25. Wherein consists the sinfulness of that estate whereinto man fell?

A. The sinfulness of that estate whereinto man fell, consisteth in the guilt of Adam's first sin,[1] the want of that righteousness wherein he was created, and the corruption of his nature, whereby he is utterly indisposed, disabled, and made opposite unto all that is spiritually good, and wholly inclined to all evil, and that continually;[2] which is commonly called original sin, and from which do proceed all actual transgressions.[3]

Q. 26. How is original sin conveyed from our first parents unto their posterity?

A. Original sin is conveyed from our first parents unto their posterity by natural generation, so as all that proceed from them in that way, are conceived and born in sin.[1]

Q. 27. What misery did the Fall bring upon mankind?

A. The Fall brought upon mankind the loss of communion with God,[1] his displeasure and curse; so as we are by nature children of wrath,[2] bondslaves to Satan,[3] and justly liable to all punishments in this world and that which is to come.[4]

Q. 28. What are the punishments of sin in this world?

A. The punishments of sin in this world, are either inward, as blindness of mind,[1] a reprobate sense,[2] strong delusions,[3] hardness of heart,[4] horror of conscience,[5] and vile affections:[6] or outward, as the curse of God upon the creatures for our sake,[7] and all other evils that befall us in our bodies, names, estates, relations, and employments;[8] together with death itself.[9]

Q. 29. What are the punishments of sin in the world to come?

A. The punishments of sin in the world to come are everlasting separation from the comfortable presence of God, and most grievous torments in soul and body, without intermission, in hell fire forever.[1]

Q. 30. Doth God leave all mankind to perish in the estate of sin and misery?

A. God doth not leave all men to perish in the estate of sin and misery, into which they fell by the breach of the first covenant, commonly called the covenant of works;[1] but of his mere love and mercy delivereth his elect out of it, and bringeth them into an estate of salvation by the second covenant, commonly called the covenant of grace.[2]

Q. 31. With whom was the covenant of grace made?

A. The covenant of grace was made with Christ as the second Adam, and in him with all the elect as his seed.[1]

Q. 32. How is the grace of God manifested in the second covenant?

A. The grace of God is manifested in the second covenant, in that he freely provideth and offereth to sinners a mediator,[1] and life and salvation by him;[2] and requiring faith as the condition to interest them in him,[3] promiseth and giveth his Holy Spirit to all his elect, to work in them that faith, with all other saving graces;[4] and to enable them unto all holy obedience,[5] as the evidence of the truth of their faith[6] and of their thankfulness to God,[7] and as the way which he hath appointed them to salvation.[8]

Q. 33. Was the covenant of grace always administered after one and the same manner?

A.The covenant of grace was not always administered after the same manner, but the administrations of it under the Old Testament were different from those under the New.[1]

Q. 34. How was the covenant of grace administered under the Old Testament?

A. The covenant of grace was administered under the Old Testament, by promises,[1] prophecies,[2] sacrifices,[3] circumcision,[4] the passover,[5] and other types and ordinances; which did all foresignify Christ then to come, and were for that time sufficient to build up the elect in faith in the promised Messiah,[6] by whom they then had full remission of sin and eternal salvation.[7]

Q. 35. How is the covenant of grace administered under the New Testament?

A. Under the New Testament, when Christ the substance was exhibited, the same covenant of grace was, and still is to be, administered in the preaching of the Word,[1] and the administration of the sacraments of Baptism,[2] and the Lord's Supper;[3] in which grace and salvation are held forth in more fullness, evidence, and efficacy to all nations.[4]

Q. 36. Who is the Mediator of the covenant of grace?

A. The only Mediator of the covenant of grace is the Lord Jesus Christ,[1] who being the eternal Son of God, of one substance and equal with the Father, in the fullness of time became man, and so was, and continues to be, God and man, in two entire distinct natures, and one person, forever.[2]

Q. 37. How did Christ, being the Son of God, become man?

A. Christ, the Son of God, became man by taking to himself a true body, and a reasonable soul,[1] being conceived by the power of the Holy Ghost, in the womb of the Virgin Mary, of her substance, and born of her,[2] yet without sin.[3]

Q. 38. Why was it requisite that the Mediator should be God?

A. It was requisite that the Mediator should be God; that he might sustain and keep the human nature from sinking under the infinite wrath of God, and the power of death; give worth and efficacy to his sufferings, obedience, and intercession; and to satisfy God's justice, procure his favor, purchase a peculiar people, give his Spirit to them, conquer all their enemies, and bring them to everlasting salvation.[1]

Q. 39. Why was it requisite that the Mediator should be man?

A. It was requisite that the Mediator should be man; that he might advance our nature, perform obedience to the law,[1] suffer and make intercession for us in our nature,[2] have a fellow feeling of our infirmities;[3] that we might receive the adoption of sons,[4] and have comfort and access with boldness unto the throne of grace.[5]

Q. 40. Why was it requisite that the Mediator should be God and man in one person?

A. It was requisite that the Mediator who was to reconcile God and man, should himself be both God and man, and this in one person; that the proper works of each nature might be accepted of God for us, and relied on by us, as the works of the whole person.[1]

Q. 41. Why was our Mediator called Jesus?

A. Our Mediator was called Jesus, because he saveth his people from their sins.[1]

Q. 42. Why was our Mediator called Christ?

A. Our Mediator was called Christ, because he was anointed with the Holy Ghost above measure;[1] and so set apart, and fully furnished with all authority and ability,[2] to execute the office of prophet,[3] priest,[4] and king of his church, in the estate both of his humiliation and exaltation.[5]

Q. 43. How doth Christ execute the office of a prophet?

A. Christ executeth the office of a prophet, in his revealing to the church in all ages,[1] by his Spirit and Word,[2] in divers ways of administration, the whole will of God, in all things concerning their edification and salvation.[3]

Q. 44. How doth Christ execute the office of a priest?

A. Christ executeth the office of a priest, in his once offering himself a sacrifice without spot to God,[1] to be a reconciliation for the sins of his people;[2] and in making continual intercession for them.[3]

Q. 45. How doth Christ execute the office of a king?

A. Christ executeth the office of a king, in calling out of the world a people to himself;[1] and giving them officers,[2] laws,[3] and censures, by which he visibly governs them;[4] in bestowing saving grace upon his elect,[5] rewarding their obedience,[6] and correcting them for their sins,[7] preserving and supporting them under all their temptations and sufferings;[8] restraining and overcoming all their enemies,[9] and powerfully ordering all things for his own glory,[10] and their good;[11] and also in taking vengeance on the rest, who know not God, and obey not the gospel.[12]

Q. 46. What was the estate of Christ's humiliation?

A. The estate of Christ's humiliation was that low condition, wherein he, for our sakes, emptying himself of his glory, took upon him the form of a servant, in his conception and birth, life, death, and after his death until his resurrection.[1]

Q. 47. How did Christ humble himself in his conception and birth?

A. Christ humbled himself in his conception and birth, in that, being from all eternity the Son of God in the bosom of the Father, he was pleased in the fullness of time to become the Son of man, made of a woman of low estate, and to be born to her, with divers circumstances of more than ordinary abasement.[1]

Q. 48. How did Christ humble himself in his life?

A. Christ humbled himself in his life, by subjecting himself to the law,[1] which he perfectly fulfilled,[2] and by conflicting with the indignities of the world,[3] temptations of Satan,[4] and infirmities in his flesh; whether common to the nature of man, or particularly accompanying that his low condition.[5]

Q. 49. How did Christ humble himself in his death?

A. Christ humbled himself in his death, in that having been betrayed by Judas,[1] forsaken by his disciples,[2] scorned and rejected by the world,[3] condemned by Pilate, and tormented by his persecutors;[4] having also conflicted with the terrors of death and the powers of darkness, felt and borne the weight of God's wrath,[5] he laid down his life an offering for sin,[6] enduring the painful, shameful, and cursed death of the cross.[7]

Q. 50. Wherein consisted Christ's humiliation after his death?

A. Christ's humiliation after his death consisted in his being buried,[1] and continuing in the state of the dead, and under the power of death till the third day,[2] which hath been otherwise expressed in these words: "He descended into hell."

Q. 51. What was the estate of Christ's exaltation?

A. The estate of Christ's exaltation comprehendeth his resurrection,[1] ascension,[2] sitting at the right hand of the Father,[3] and his coming again to judge the world.[4]

Q. 52. How was Christ exalted in his resurrection?

A. Christ was exalted in his resurrection, in that, not having seen corruption in death (of which it was not possible for him to be held),[1] and having the very same body in which he suffered, with the essential properties thereof[2] (but without mortality and other common infirmities belonging to this life), really united to his soul,[3] he rose again from the dead the third day by his own power;[4] whereby he declared himself to be the Son of God,[5] to have satisfied divine justice,[6] to have vanquished death and him that had the power of it,[7] and to be Lord of quick and dead.[8] All which he did as a public person,[9] the head of his church,[10] for their justification,[11] quickening in grace,[12] support against enemies,[13] and to assure them of their resurrection from the dead at the last day.[14]

Q. 53. How was Christ exalted in his ascension?

A. Christ was exalted in his ascension, in that having, after his resurrection, often appeared unto, and conversed with his apostles, speaking to them of the things pertaining to the Kingdom of God,[1] and giving them commission to preach the gospel to all nations;[2] forty days after his resurrection, he, in our nature, and as our head, triumphing over enemies, visibly went up into the highest heavens,[3] there to receive gifts for men,[4] to raise up our affections thither,[5] and to prepare a place for us,[6] where himself is, and shall continue till his second coming at the end of the world.[7]

Q. 54. How is Christ exalted in his sitting at the right hand of God?

A. Christ is exalted in his sitting at the right hand of God, in that as God-man he is advanced to the highest favor with God the Father,[1] with all fullness of joy,[2] glory,[3] and power over all things in heaven and earth;[4] and doth gather and defend his church, and subdue their enemies; furnisheth his ministers and people with gifts and graces,[5] and maketh intercession for them.[6]

Q. 55. How doth Christ make intercession?

A. Christ maketh intercession, by his appearing in our nature continually before the Father in heaven,[1] in the merit of his obedience and sacrifice on earth;[2] declaring his will to have it applied to all believers;[3] answering all accusations against them;[4] and procuring for them quiet of conscience, notwithstanding daily failings,[5] access with boldness to the throne of grace,[6] and acceptance of their persons[7] and services.[8]

Q. 56. How is Christ to be exalted in his coming again to judge the world?

A. Christ is to be exalted in his coming again to judge the world, in that he, who was unjustly judged and condemned by wicked men, shall come again at the last day in great power, and in the full manifestation of his own glory, and of his Father's, with all his holy angels, with a shout, with the voice of the archangel, and with the trumpet of God, to judge the world in righteousness.[1]

Q. 57. What benefits hath Christ procured by his mediation?

A. Christ by his mediation hath procured redemption, with all other benefits of the covenant of grace.[1]

Q. 58. How do we come to be made partakers of the benefits which Christ hath procured?

A. We are made partakers of the benefits which Christ hath procured, by the application of them unto us, which is the work especially of God the Holy Ghost.[1]

Q. 59. Who are made partakers of redemption through Christ?

A. Redemption is certainly applied, and effectually communicated, to all those for whom Christ hath purchased it;[1] who are in time by the Holy Ghost enabled to believe in Christ, according to the gospel.[2]

Q. 60. Can they who have never heard the gospel, and so know not Jesus Christ nor believe in him, be saved by their living according to the light of nature?

A. They who having never heard the gospel, know not Jesus Christ, and believe not in him, cannot be saved,[1] be they never so diligent to frame their lives according to the light of nature,[2] or the laws of that religion which they profess;[3] neither is there salvation in any other, but in Christ alone,[4] who is the Saviour only of his body the church.[5]

Q. 61. Are all they saved who hear the gospel, and live in the church?

A. All that hear the gospel, and live in the visible church, are not saved; but only they who are true members of the church invisible.[1]

Q. 62. What is the visible church?

A. The visible church is a society made up of all such as in all ages and places of the world do profess the true religion,[1] and of their children.[2]

Q. 63. What are the special privileges of the visible church?

A. The visible church hath the privilege of being under God's special care and government;[1] of being protected and preserved in all ages, notwithstanding the opposition of all enemies;[2] and of enjoying the communion of saints, the ordinary means of salvation,[3] and offers of grace by Christ, to all members of it, in the ministry of the gospel, testifying that whosoever believes in him shall be saved,[4] and excluding none that will come unto him.[5]

Q. 64. What is the invisible church?

A. The invisible church is the whole number of the elect, that have been, are, or shall be gathered into one under Christ the head.[1]

Q. 65. What special benefits do the members of the invisible church enjoy by Christ?

A. The members of the invisible church, by Christ, enjoy union and communion with him in grace and glory.[1]

Q. 66. What is that union which the elect have with Christ?

A. The union which the elect have with Christ is the work of God's grace,[1] whereby they are spiritually and mystically, yet really and inseparably, joined to Christ as their head and husband;[2] which is done in their effectual calling.[3]

Q. 67. What is effectual calling?

A. Effectual calling is the work of God's almighty power and grace,[1] whereby (out of his free and especial love to his elect, and from nothing in them moving him thereunto)[2] he doth in his accepted time invite and draw them to Jesus Christ, by his Word and Spirit;[3] savingly enlightening their minds,[4] renewing and powerfully determining their wills,[5] so as they (although in themselves dead in sin) are hereby made willing and able, freely to answer his call, and to accept and embrace the grace offered and conveyed therein.[6]

Q. 68. Are the elect only effectually called?

A. All the elect, and they only, are effectually called;[1] although others may be, and often are, outwardly called by the ministry of the Word,[2] and have some common operations of the Spirit,[3] who, for their willful neglect and contempt of the grace offered to them, being justly left in their unbelief, do never truly come to Jesus Christ.[4]

Q. 69. What is the communion in grace, which the members of the invisible church have with Christ?

A. The communion in grace, which the members of the invisible church have with Christ, is their partaking of the virtue of his mediation, in their justification,[1] adoption,[2] sanctification, and whatever else in this life manifests their union with him.[3]

Q. 70. What is justification?

A. Justification is an act of God's free grace unto sinners, in which he pardoneth all their sin, accepteth and accounteth their persons righteous in his sight;[1] not for anything wrought in them, or done by them,[2] but only for the perfect obedience and full satisfaction of Christ, by God imputed to them[3] and received by faith alone.[4]

Q. 71. How is justification an act of God's free grace?

A. Although Christ by his obedience and death, did make a proper, real, and full satisfaction to God's justice in the behalf of them that are justified: yet inasmuch as God accepteth the satisfaction from a surety, which he might have demanded of them; and did provide this surety, his only Son, imputing his righteousness to them, and requiring nothing of them for their justification, but faith, which also is his gift, their justification is to them of free grace.[1]

Q. 72. What is justifying faith?

A. Justifying faith is a saving grace,[1] wrought in the heart of a sinner, by the Spirit and the Word of God;[2] whereby he, being convinced of his sin and misery, and of the disability in himself and all other creatures to recover him out of his lost condition,[3] not only assenteth to the truth of the promise of the gospel,[4] but receiveth and resteth upon Christ and his righteousness therein held forth, for pardon of sin,[5] and for the accepting and accounting of his person righteous in the sight of God for salvation.[6]

Q. 73. How doth faith justify a sinner in the sight of God?

A. Faith justifies a sinner in the sight of God, not because of those other graces which do always accompany it, or of good works that are the fruits of it;[1] nor as if the grace of faith, or any act thereof, were imputed to him for justification;[2] but only as it is an instrument, by which he receiveth and applieth Christ and his righteousness.[3]

Q. 74. What is adoption?

A. Adoption is an act of the free grace of God,[1] in and for his only Son Jesus Christ,[2] whereby all those that are justified are received into the number of his children,[3] have his name put upon them,[4] the Spirit of his Son given to them,[5] are under his Fatherly care and dispensations,[6] admitted to all the liberties and privileges of the sons of God, made heirs of all the promises, and fellow heirs with Christ in glory.[7]

Q. 75. What is sanctification?

A. Sanctification is a work of God's grace, whereby they, whom God hath, before the foundation of the world, chosen to be holy, are, in time, through the powerful operation of his Spirit, applying the death and resurrection of Christ unto them, renewed in their whole man after the image of God;[1] having the seeds of repentance unto life, and all other saving graces, put into their hearts,[2] and those graces so stirred up, increased and strengthened,[3] as that they more and more die unto sin, and rise into newness of life.[4]

Q. 76. What is repentance unto life?

A. Repentance unto life is a saving grace,[1] wrought in the heart of a sinner by the Spirit and Word of God,[2] whereby out of the sight and sense, not only of the danger,[3] but also of the filthiness and odiousness of his sins,[4] and upon the apprehension of God's mercy in Christ to such as are penitent,[5] he so grieves for, and hates his sins,[6] as that he turns from them all to God,[7] purposing and endeavoring constantly to walk with him in all the ways of new obedience.[8]

Q. 77. Wherein do justification and sanctification differ?

A. Although sanctification be inseparably joined with justification,[1] yet they differ in that God, in justification, imputeth the righteousness of Christ;[2] in sanctification, his Spirit infuseth grace, and enableth to the exercise thereof;[3] in the former, sin is pardoned;[4] in the other, it is subdued;[5] the one doth equally free all believers from the revenging wrath of God, and that perfectly in this life, that they never fall into condemnation;[6] the other is neither equal in all,[7] nor in this life perfect in any,[8] but growing up to perfection.[9]

Q. 78. Whence ariseth the imperfection of sanctification in believers?

A. The imperfection of sanctification in believers ariseth from the remnants of sin abiding in every part of them, and the perpetual lusting of the flesh against the Spirit; whereby they are often foiled with temptations, and fall into many sins,[1] are hindered in all their spiritual service,[2] and their best works are imperfect and defiled in the sight of God.[3]

Q. 79. May not true believers, by reason of their imperfections, and the many temptations and sins they are overtaken with, fall away from the state of grace?

A. True believers, by reason of the unchangeable love of God,[1] and his decree and covenant to give them perseverance,[2] their inseparable union with Christ,[3] his continual intercession for them,[4] and the Spirit and seed of God abiding in them,[5] can neither totally nor finally fall away from the state of grace, but are kept by the power of God through faith unto salvation.[6]

Q. 80. Can true believers be infallibly assured that they are in the estate of grace, and that they shall persevere therein unto salvation?

A. Such as truly believe in Christ, and endeavor to walk in all good conscience before him, may, without extraordinary revelation, by faith grounded upon the truth of God's promises, and by the Spirit enabling them to discern in themselves those graces to which the promises of life are made, and bearing witness with their spirits that they are the children of God, be infallibly assured that they are in the estate of grace, and shall persevere therein unto salvation.[1]

Q. 81. Are all true believers at all times assured of their present being in the estate of grace, and that they shall be saved?

A. Assurance of grace and salvation not being of the essence of faith, true believers may wait long before they obtain it;[1] and, after the enjoyment thereof, may have it weakened and intermitted, through manifold distempers, sins, temptations, and desertions;[2] yet are they never left without such a presence and support of the Spirit of God, as keeps them from sinking into utter despair.[3]

Q. 82. What is the communion in glory which the members of the invisible church have with Christ?

A. The communion in glory which the members of the invisible church have with Christ, is in this life,[1] immediately after death,[2] and at last perfected at the resurrection and day of judgment.[3]

Q. 83. What is the communion in glory with Christ, which the members of the invisible church enjoy in this life?

A. The members of the invisible church have communicated to them, in this life, the first fruits of glory with Christ, as they are members of him their head, and so in him are interested in that glory which he is fully possessed of;[1] and as an earnest thereof, enjoy the sense of God's love,[2] peace of conscience, joy in the Holy Ghost, and hope of glory;[3] As, on the contrary, the sense of God's revenging wrath, horror of conscience, and a fearful expectation of judgment, are to the wicked the beginning of the torment which they shall endure after death.[4]

Q. 84. Shall all men die?

A. Death being threatened as the wages of sin,[1] it is appointed unto all men once to die;[2] for that all have sinned.[3]

Q. 85. Death being the wages of sin, why are not the righteous delivered from death, seeing all their sins are forgiven in Christ?

A. The righteous shall be delivered from death itself at the last day, and even in death are delivered from the sting and curse of it;[1] so that although they die, yet it is out of God's love,[2] to free them perfectly from sin and misery,[3] and to make them capable of further communion with Christ in glory, which they then enter upon.[4]

Q. 86. What is the communion in glory with Christ, which the members of the invisible church enjoy immediately after death?

A. The communion in glory with Christ, which the members of the invisible church enjoy immediately after death, is in that their souls are then made perfect in holiness, and received into the highest heavens, where they behold the face of God in light and glory;[1] waiting for the full redemption of their bodies,[2] which even in death continue united to Christ,[3] and rest in their graves as in their beds, till at the last day they be again united to their souls.[4] Whereas the souls of the wicked are at their death cast into hell, where they remain in torments and utter darkness; and their bodies kept in their graves, as in their prisons, until the resurrection and judgment of the great day.[5]

Q. 87. What are we to believe concerning the resurrection?

A. We are to believe that, at the last day, there shall be a general resurrection of the dead, both of the just and unjust;[1] when they that are then found alive shall in a moment be changed; and the selfsame bodies of the dead which are laid in the grave, being then again united to their souls forever, shall be raised up by the power of Christ.[2] The bodies of the just, by the Spirit of Christ, and by virtue of his resurrection as their head, shall be raised in power, spiritual, and incorruptible, and made like to his glorious body:[3] and the bodies of the wicked shall be raised up in dishonor by him as an offended judge.[4]

Q. 88. What shall immediately follow after the resurrection?

A. Immediately after the resurrection shall follow the general and final judgment of angels and men,[1] the day and hour whereof no man knoweth, that all may watch and pray, and be ever ready for the coming of the Lord.[2]

Q. 89. What shall be done to the wicked at the day of judgment?

A. At the day of judgment, the wicked shall be set on Christ's left hand,[1] and upon clear evidence, and full conviction of their own consciences,[2] shall have the fearful but just sentence of condemnation pronounced against them;[3] and thereupon shall be cast out from the favorable presence of God, and the glorious fellowship with Christ, his saints, and all his holy angels, into hell, to be punished with unspeakable torments both of body and soul, with the devil and his angels forever.[4]

Q. 90. What shall be done to the righteous at the day of judgment?

A. At the day of judgment, the righteous, being caught up to Christ in the clouds,[1] shall be set on his right hand, and, there openly acknowledged and acquitted,[2] shall join with him in the judging of reprobate angels and men;[3] and shall be received into heaven,[4] where they shall be fully and forever freed from all sin and misery;[5] filled with inconceivable joy;[6] made perfectly holy and happy both in body and soul, in the company of innumerable saints and angels,[7] but especially in the immediate vision and fruition of God the Father, of our Lord Jesus Christ, and of the Holy Spirit, to all eternity.[8] And this is the perfect and full communion, which the members of the invisible Church shall enjoy with Christ in glory, at the resurrection and day of judgment.

Having Seen What the Scriptures Principally
Teach Us to Believe Concerning God, It Follows
to Consider What They Require as the Duty of Man

Q. 91. What is the duty which God requireth of man?

A. The duty which God requireth of man is obedience to his revealed will.[1]

Q. 92. What did God at first reveal unto man as the rule of his obedience?

A. The rule of obedience revealed to Adam in the estate of innocence, and to all mankind in him, besides a special command, not to eat of the fruit of the tree of the knowledge of good and evil, was the moral law.[1]

Q. 93. What is the moral law?

A. The moral law is the declaration of the will of God to mankind, directing and binding everyone to personal, perfect, and perpetual conformity and obedience thereunto, in the frame and disposition of the whole man, soul and body, and in performance of all those duties of holiness and righteousness which he oweth to God and man:[1] promising life upon the fulfilling, and threatening death upon the breach of it.[2]

Q. 94. Is there any use of the moral law to man since the Fall?

A. Although no man since the Fall can attain to righteousness and life by the moral law,[1] yet there is great use thereof, as well common to all men, as peculiar either to the unregenerate, or the regenerate.[2]

Q. 95. Of what use is the moral law to all men?

A. The moral law is of use to all men, to inform them of the holy nature and will of God,[1] and of their duty binding them to walk accordingly;[2] to convince them of their disability to keep it, and of the sinful pollution of their nature, hearts, and lives,[3] to humble them in the sense of their sin and misery,[4] and thereby help them to a clearer sight of the need they have of Christ,[5] and of the perfection of his obedience.

Q. 96. What particular use is there of the moral law to unregenerate men?

A. The moral law is of use to unregenerate men, to awaken their consciences to flee from the wrath to come,[1] and to drive them to Christ;[2] or, upon their continuance in the estate and way of sin, to leave them inexcusable,[3] and under the curse thereof.[4]

Q. 97. What special use is there of the moral law to the regenerate?

A. Although they that are regenerate and believe in Christ be delivered from the moral law as a covenant of works, so as thereby they are neither justified nor condemned: yet, besides the general uses thereof common to them with all men, it is of special use to show them how much they are bound to Christ for his fulfilling it, and enduring the curse thereof, in their stead and for their good;[1] and thereby to provoke them to more thankfulness, and to express the same in their greater care to conform themselves thereunto as the rule of their obedience.[2]

Q. 98. Wherein is the moral law summarily comprehended?

A. The moral law is summarily comprehended in the Ten Commandments,[1] which were delivered by the voice of God upon Mount Sinai, and written by him on two tables of stone;[2] and are recorded in the twentieth chapter of Exodus; the first four commandments containing our duty to God, and the other six our duty to man.

Q. 99. What rules are to be observed for the right understanding of the Ten Commandments?

A. For the right understanding of the Ten Commandments, these rules are to be observed:

1. That the law is perfect, and bindeth everyone to full conformity in the whole man unto the righteousness thereof, and unto entire obedience forever; so as to require the utmost perfection of every duty, and to forbid the least degree of every sin.[1]

2. That it is spiritual, and so reacheth the understanding, will, affections, and all other powers of the soul; as well as words, works, and gestures.[1]

3. That one and the same thing, in divers respects, is required or forbidden in several commandments.[1]

4. That as, where a duty is commanded, the contrary sin is forbidden;[1] and where a sin is forbidden, the contrary duty is commanded;[2] so, where a promise is annexed, the contrary threatening is included;[3] and where a threatening is annexed, the contrary promise is included.[4]

5. That what God forbids, is at no time to be done;[1] what he commands is always our duty;[2] and yet every particular duty is not to be done at all times.[3]

6. That, under one sin or duty, all of the same kind are forbidden or commanded; together with all the causes, means, occasions, and appearances thereof, and provocations thereunto.[1]

7. That what is forbidden or commanded to ourselves, we are bound, according to our places, to endeavor that it may be avoided or performed by others, according to the duty of their places.[1]

8. That in what is commanded to others, we are bound, according to our places and callings, to be helpful to them:[1] and to take heed of partaking with others in what is forbidden them.[2]

Q. 100. What special things are we to consider in the Ten Commandments?

A. We are to consider in the Ten Commandments: the preface, the substances of the commandments themselves, and the several reasons annexed to some of them the more to enforce them.

Q. 101. What is the preface to the Ten Commandments?

A. The preface to the Ten Commandments is contained in these words: "I am the Lord thy God, which have brought thee out of the land of Egypt, out of the house of bondage."[1] Wherein God manifesteth his sovereignty, as being Jehovah, the eternal, immutable, and almighty God; having his being in and of himself, and giving being to all his words and works; and that he is a God in covenant, as with Israel of old, so with all his people; who as he brought them out of their bondage in Egypt, so he delivered us from our spiritual thralldom; and that therefore we are bound to take him for our God alone, and to keep all his commandments.

Q. 102. What is the sum of the four Commandments which contain our duty to God?

A. The sum of the four Commandments containing our duty to God is, to love the Lord our God with all our heart, and with all our soul, and with all our strength, and with all our mind.[1]

Q. 103. Which is the First Commandment?

A. The First Commandment is, "Thou shalt have no other gods before me."[1]

Q. 104. What are the duties required in the First Commandment?

A. The duties required in the First Commandment[1] are: the knowing and acknowledging of God to be the only true God, and our God;[2] and to worship and glorify him accordingly;[3] by thinking,[4] meditating,[5] remembering,[6] highly esteeming,[7] honoring,[8] adoring,[9] choosing,[10] loving,[11] desiring,[12] fearing of him;[13] believing him;[14] trusting,[15] hoping,[16] delighting,[17] rejoicing in him;[18] being zealous for him;[19] calling upon him, giving all praise and thanks,[20] and yielding all obedience and submission to him with the whole man;[21] being careful in all things to please him,[22] and sorrowful when in anything he is offended;[23] and walking humbly with him.[24]

Q. 105. What are the sins forbidden in the First Commandment?

A. The sins forbidden in the First Commandment are: atheism, in denying or not having a God;[1] idolatry, in having or worshiping more gods than one, or any with, or instead of the true God;[2] the not having and vouching him for God, and our God;[3] the omission or neglect of anything due to him, required in this commandment;[4] ignorance,[5] forgetfulness,[6] misapprehensions, false opinions,[7] unworthy and wicked thoughts of him;[8] bold and curious searchings into his secrets;[9] all profaneness,[10] hatred of God,[11] self-love,[12] self-seeking,[13] and all other inordinate and immoderate setting of our mind, will, or affections upon other things, and taking them off from him in whole or in part;[14] vain credulity,[15] unbelief,[16] heresy,[17] misbelief,[18] distrust,[19] despair,[20] incorrigibleness, and insensibleness under judgments,[21] hardness of heart,[22] pride,[23] presumption,[24] carnal security,[25] tempting of God;[26] using unlawful means,[27] and trusting in lawful means;[28] carnal delights and joys,[29] corrupt, blind, and indiscreet zeal;[30] lukewarmness,[31] and deadness in the things of God;[32] estranging ourselves, and apostatizing from God;[33] praying or giving any religious worship to saints, angels, or any other creatures;[34] all compacts and consulting with the devil,[35] and hearkening to his suggestions;[36] making men the lords of our faith and conscience;[37] slighting and despising God, and his commands;[38] resisting and grieving of his Spirit,[39] discontent and impatience at his dispensations, charging him foolishly for the evils he inflicts on us;[40] and ascribing the praise of any good, we either are, have, or can do, to fortune, idols,[41] ourselves,[42] or any other creature.[43]

Q. 106. What are we especially taught by these words "before me," in the First Commandment?

A. These words "before me," or "before my face," in the First Commandment, teach us, that God, who seeth all things, taketh special notice of, and is much displeased with, the sin of having any other God; that so it may be an argument to dissuade from it, and to aggravate it as a most impudent provocation;[1] as also to persuade us to do as in his sight, whatever we do in his service.[2]

Q. 107. Which is the Second Commandment?

A. The Second Commandment is, "Thou shalt not make unto thee any graven image, or any likeness of any thing that is in heaven above, or that is in the earth beneath, or that is in the water under the earth: thou shalt not bow down thyself to them, nor serve them: for I the Lord thy God am a jealous God, visiting the iniquity of the fathers upon the children unto the third and fourth generation of them that hate me; and shewing mercy unto thousands of them that love me, and keep my commandments."[1]

Q. 108. What are the duties required in the Second Commandment?

A. The duties required in the Second Commandment are: the receiving, observing, and keeping pure and entire, all such religious worship and ordinances as God hath instituted in his Word;[1] particularly prayer and thanksgiving in the name of Christ;[2] the reading, preaching, and hearing of the Word;[3] the administration and receiving of the sacraments;[4] church government and discipline;[5] the ministry and maintenance thereof;[6] religious fasting;[7] swearing by the name of God;[8] and vowing unto him:[9] as also the disapproving, detesting, opposing all false worship;[10] and, according to each one's place and calling, removing it, and all monuments of idolatry.[11]

Q. 109. What are the sins forbidden in the Second Commandment?

A. The sins forbidden in the Second Commandment are: all devising,[1] counseling,[2] commanding,[3] using,[4] and any wise approving any religious worship not instituted by God himself;[5] the making any representation of God, of all, or of any of the three Persons, either inwardly in our mind, or outwardly in any kind of image or likeness of any creature whatsoever;[6] all worshiping of it,[7] or God in it or by it;[8] the making of any representation of feigned deities,[9] and all worship of them, or service belonging to them;[10] all superstitious devices,[11] corrupting the worship of God,[12] adding to it, or taking from it,[13] whether invented and taken up of ourselves,[14] or received by tradition from others,[15] though under the title of antiquity,[16] custom,[17] devotion,[18] good intent, or any other pretense whatsoever;[19] simony,[20] sacrilege;[21] all neglect,[22] contempt,[23] hindering,[24] and opposing the worship and ordinances which God hath appointed.[25]

Q. 110. What are the reasons annexed to the Second Commandment, the more to enforce it?

A. The reasons annexed to the Second Commandment, the more to enforce it, contained in these words, "For I the Lord thy God am a jealous God, visiting the iniquity of the fathers upon the children unto the third and fourth generation of them that hate me; and shewing mercy unto thousands of them that love me, and keep my commandments;"[1] are, besides God's sovereignty over us, and propriety in us, his revengeful indignation against all false worship,[2] as being a spiritual whoredom;[3] accounting the breakers of this Commandment such as hate him, and threatening to punish them unto divers generations,[4] and esteeming the observers of it such as love him and keep his commandments, and promising mercy to them unto many generations.[5]

Q. 111. Which is the Third Commandment?

A. The Third Commandment is, "Thou shalt not take the name of the Lord thy God in vain; for the Lord will not hold him guiltless that taketh his name in vain."[1]

Q. 112. What is required in the Third Commandment?

A. The Third Commandment requires, that the name of God, his titles, attributes,[1] ordinances,[2] the word,[3] sacraments,[4] prayer,[5] oaths,[6] vows,[7] lots,[8] his works,[9] and whatsoever else there is whereby he makes himself known, be holily and reverently used in thought,[10] meditation,[11] word,[12] and writing;[13] by an holy profession,[14] and answerable conversation,[15] to the glory of God,[16] and the good of ourselves[17] and others.[18]

Q. 113. What are the sins forbidden in the Third Commandment?

A. The sins forbidden in the Third Commandment are: the not using of God's name as is required;[1] and the abuse of it in an ignorant,[2] vain,[3] irreverent, profane,[4] superstitious,[5] or wicked mentioning or otherwise using the titles, attributes,[6] ordinances,[7] or works;[8] by blasphemy;[9] perjury;[10] all sinful cursing,[11] oaths,[12] vows,[13] and lots;[14] violating our oaths and vows, if lawful;[15] and fulfilling them, if of things unlawful;[16] murmuring and quarreling at,[17] curious prying into,[18] and misapplying of God's decrees[19] and providence;[20] misinterpreting,[21] misapplying,[22] or any way perverting the Word, or any part of it,[23] to profane jests,[24] curious and unprofitable questions, vain janglings, or the maintaining of false doctrines;[25] abusing it, the creatures, or anything contained under the name of God, to charms,[26] or sinful lusts and practices;[27] the maligning,[28] scorning,[29] reviling,[30] or any way opposing of God's truth, grace, and ways;[31] making profession of religion in hypocrisy, or for sinister ends;[32] being ashamed of it,[33] or a shame to it, by uncomfortable,[34] unwise,[35] unfruitful,[36] and offensive walking[37] or backsliding from it.[38]

Q. 114. What reasons are annexed to the Third Commandment?

A. The reasons annexed to the Third Commandment, in these words, "the Lord thy God," and, "for the Lord will not hold him guiltless that taketh his name in vain,"[1] are because he is the Lord and our God, therefore his name is not to be profaned, or any way abused by us;[2] especially because he will be so far from acquitting and sparing the transgressors of this Commandment, as that he will not

169

suffer them to escape his righteous judgment,[3] albeit many such escape the censures and punishments of men.[4]

Q. 115. Which is the Fourth Commandment?

A. The Fourth Commandment is, "Remember the sabbath day, to keep it holy. Six days shalt thou labour, and do all thy work: but the seventh day is the sabbath of the Lord thy God: in it thou shalt not do any work, thou, nor thy son, nor thy daughter, thy manservant, nor thy maidservant, nor thy cattle, nor thy stranger that is within thy gates; for in six days the Lord made heaven and earth, the sea, and all that in them is, and rested the seventh day: wherefore the Lord blessed the sabbath day, and hallowed it."[1]

Q. 116. What is required in the Fourth Commandment?

A. The Fourth Commandment requireth of all men the sanctifying or keeping holy to God such set times as he hath appointed in his Word, expressly one whole day in seven;[1] which was the seventh from the beginning of the world to the resurrection of Christ,[2] and the first day of the week ever since, and so to continue to the end of the world; which is the Christian Sabbath,[3] and in the New Testament called "the Lord's Day."

Q. 117. How is the Sabbath or Lord's Day to be sanctified?

A. The Sabbath, or Lord's Day, is to be sanctified by an holy resting all that day,[1] not only from such works as are at all times sinful, but even from such worldly employments and recreations as are on other days lawful;[2] and making it our delight to spend the whole time (except so much of it as is to be taken up in works of necessity and mercy)[3] in the public and private exercise of God's worship.[4] And, to that end, we are to prepare our hearts, and with such foresight, diligence, and moderation, to dispose, and seasonably to dispatch our worldly business, that we may be the more free and fit for the duties of the day.[5]

Q. 118. Why is the charge of keeping the Sabbath more specially directed to governors of families and other superiors?

A. The charge of keeping the Sabbath is more specially directed to governors of families and other superiors, because they are bound not only to keep it themselves, but to see that it be observed by all those that are under their charge; and because they are prone ofttimes to hinder them by employments of their own.[1]

Q. 119. What are the sins forbidden in the Fourth Commandment?

A. The sins in the Fourth Commandment are: all omissions of the duties required,[1] all careless, negligent, and unprofitable performing of them, and being weary of them;[2] all profaning the day by idleness, and doing that which is in itself sinful;[3] and by all needless works, words, and thoughts about our worldly employments and recreations.[4]

Q. 120. What are the reasons annexed to the Fourth Commandment, the more to enforce it?

A. The reasons annexed to the Fourth Commandment, the more to enforce it, are taken from the equity of it, God allowing us six days of seven for our own affairs, and reserving but one for himself, in these words, "Six days shalt thou labour, and do all thy work;"[1] from God's challenging a special propriety in that day. "The seventh day is the sabbath of the Lord thy God;"[2] from the example of God who "in six days . . . made heaven and earth, the sea, and all that in them is, and rested the seventh day"; and from that blessing which God put upon that day, not only in sanctifying it to be a holy day for his service, but in ordaining it to be a means of blessing to us in our sanctifying it, "wherefore the Lord blessed the sabbath day, and hallowed it."[3]

Q. 121. Why is the word "remember" set in the beginning of the Fourth Commandment?

A. The word "remember" is set in the beginning of the Fourth Commandment,[1] partly because of the great benefit of remembering it, we being thereby helped in our preparation to keep it;[2] and, in keeping it, better to keep all the rest of the Commandments[3] and to continue a thankful remembrance of the two great benefits of creation and redemption, which contain a short abridgement of religion:[4] and partly because we are ready to forget it,[5] for that there is less light of nature for it, and yet it restraineth our natural liberty in things at other times lawful;[6] that it cometh but once in seven days, and many worldly businesses come between, and too often take off our minds from thinking of it, either to prepare for it, or to sanctify it;[7] and that Satan with his instruments much labor to blot out the glory, and even the memory of it, and to bring in all irreligion and impiety.[8]

Q. 122. What is the sum of the six Commandments which contain our duty to man?

A. The sum of the six Commandments which contain our duty to man is, to love our neighbor as ourselves,[1] and to do to others what we would have them to do to us.[2]

Q. 123. Which is the Fifth Commandment?

A. The Fifth Commandment is, "Honour thy father and thy mother: that thy days may be long upon the land which the Lord thy God giveth thee."[1]

Q. 124. Who are meant by "father" and "mother," in the Fifth Commandment?

A. By "father" and "mother" in the Fifth Commandment, are meant not only natural parents, but all superiors in age[1] and gifts;[2] and especially such as by God's ordinance are over us in place of authority, whether in family,[3] church,[4] or commonwealth.[5]

Q. 125. Why are superiors styled "father" and "mother"?

A. Superiors are styled "father" and "mother" both to teach them in all duties towards their inferiors, like natural parents, to express love and tenderness to them, according to their several relations,[1] and to work inferiors to a greater willingness and cheerfulness in performing their duties to their superiors, as to their parents.[2]

Q. 126. What is the general scope of the Fifth Commandment?

A. The general scope of the Fifth Commandment is, the performance of those duties which we mutually owe in our several relations, as inferiors, superiors, or equals.[1]

Q. 127. What is the honor which inferiors owe to superiors?

A. The honor which inferiors owe to their superiors is: all due reverence in heart,[1] word,[2] and behavior;[3] prayer and thanksgiving for them;[4] imitation of their virtues and graces;[5] willing obedience to their lawful commands and counsels,[6] due submission to their corrections;[7] fidelity to,[8] defense and maintenance of their persons and authority, according to their several ranks, and the nature of their places;[9] bearing with their infirmities, and covering them in love,[10] that so they may be an honor to them and to their government.[11]

Q. 128. What are the sins of inferiors against their superiors?

A. The sins of inferiors against their superiors are: all neglect of the duties required toward them;[1] envying at,[2] contempt of,[3] and rebellion[4] against their persons[5] and places,[6] in their lawful counsels,[7] commands, and corrections;[8] cursing, mocking,[9] and all such refractory and scandalous carriage, as proves a shame and dishonor to them and their government.[10]

Q. 129. What is required of superiors towards their inferiors?

A. It is required of superiors, according to that power they receive from God, and that relation wherein they stand, to love,[1] pray for,[2] and bless their inferiors;[3] to instruct,[4] counsel, and admonish them;[5] countenancing,[6] commending, and rewarding such as do well;[7] and discountenancing,[8] reproving, and chastising such as do ill;[9] protecting, and providing for them all things necessary for soul and body;[10] and, by grave, wise, holy, and exemplary carriage, to procure glory to God,[11] honor to themselves,[12] and so to preserve that authority which God hath put upon them.[13]

Q. 130. What are the sins of superiors?

A. The sins of superiors are, besides the neglect of the duties required of them[1] an inordinate seeking of themselves,[2] their own glory,[3] ease, profit or pleasure;[4] commanding things unlawful,[5] or not in the power of inferiors to perform;[6] counseling,[7] encouraging,[8] or favoring them in that which is evil;[9] dissuading, discouraging, or discountenancing them in that which is good;[10] correcting them unduly;[11] careless exposing or leaving them to wrong, temptation, and danger;[12] provoking them to wrath;[13] or any way dishonoring themselves, or lessening their authority, by an unjust, indiscreet, rigorous, or remiss behavior.[14]

Q. 131. What are the duties of equals?

A. The duties of equals are: to regard the dignity and worth of each other,[1] in giving honor to go one before another,[2] and to rejoice in each other's gifts and advancement as their own.[3]

Q. 132. What are the sins of equals?

A. The sins of equals are, besides the neglect of the duties required,[1] the undervaluing of the worth,[2] envying the gifts,[3] grieving at the advancement or prosperity one of another,[4] and usurping preeminence one over another.[5]

Q. 133. What is the reason annexed to the Fifth Commandment the more to enforce it?

A. The reason annexed to the Fifth Commandment in these words, "that thy days may be long upon the land which the Lord thy God giveth thee,"[1] is an express promise of long life and prosperity, as far as it shall serve for God's glory and their own good, to all such as keep this Commandment.[2]

Q. 134. Which is the Sixth Commandment?

A. The Sixth Commandment is, "Thou shalt not kill."[1]

Q. 135. What are the duties required in the Sixth Commandment?

A. The duties required in the Sixth Commandment are: all careful studies and lawful endeavors, to preserve the life of ourselves[1] and others,[2] by resisting all thoughts and purposes,[3] subduing all passions,[4] and avoiding all occasions,[5] temptations,[6] and practices, which tend to the unjust taking away the life of any;[7] by just defense thereof against violence;[8] patient bearing of the hand of God,[9] quietness of mind,[10] cheerfulness of spirit,[11] a sober use of meat,[12] drink,[13] physic,[14] sleep,[15] labor,[16] and recreation;[17] by charitable thoughts,[18] love,[19] compassion,[20] meekness, gentleness, kindness;[21] peaceable,[22] mild, and courteous speeches and behavior,[23] forbearance, readiness to be reconciled, patient bearing and forgiving of injuries, and requiting good for evil;[24] comforting and succoring the distressed, and protecting and defending the innocent.[25]

Q. 136. What are the sins forbidden in the Sixth Commandment?

A. The sins forbidden in the Sixth Commandment are: all taking away the life of ourselves,[1] or of others,[2] except in case of public justice,[3] lawful war,[4] or necessary defense;[5] the neglecting or withdrawing the lawful or necessary means of preservation of life;[6] sinful anger,[7] hatred,[8] envy,[9] desire of revenge;[10] all excessive passions;[11] distracting cares;[12] immoderate use of meat, drink,[13] labor,[14] and recreation;[15] provoking words;[16] oppression,[17] quarreling,[18] striking, wounding,[19] and whatsoever else tends to the destruction of the life of any.[20]

Q. 137. Which is the Seventh Commandment?

A. The Seventh Commandment is, "Thou shalt not commit adultery."[1]

Q. 138. What are the duties required in the Seventh Commandment?

A. The duties required in the Seventh Commandment are: chastity in body, mind, affections,[1] words,[2] and behavior,[3] and the preservation of it in ourselves and others;[4] watchfulness over the eyes and all the senses;[5] temperance,[6] keeping of chaste company,[7] modesty in apparel,[8] marriage by those that have not the gift of continency,[9] conjugal love,[10] and cohabitation;[11] diligent labor in our callings;[12] shunning of all occasions of uncleanness, and resisting temptations thereunto.[13]

Q. 139. What are the sins forbidden in the Seventh Commandment?

A. The sins forbidden in the Seventh Commandment, besides the neglect of the duties required,[1] are: adultery, fornication,[2] rape, incest,[3] sodomy, and all unnatural lusts;[4] all unclean imaginations, thoughts, purposes, and affections;[5] all corrupt or filthy communications, or listening thereto;[6] wanton looks,[7] impudent or light behavior, immodest apparel,[8] prohibiting of lawful,[9] and dispensing with unlawful marriages;[10] allowing, tolerating, keeping of stews, and resorting to them;[11] entangling vows of single life,[12] undue delay of marriage;[13] having more wives or husbands than one at the same time;[14] unjust divorce[15] or desertion;[16]

idleness, gluttony, drunkenness,[17] unchaste company;[18] lascivious songs, books, pictures, dancings, stageplays,[19] and all other provocations to, or acts of, uncleanness either in ourselves or others.[20]

Q. 140. Which is the Eighth Commandment?

A. The Eighth Commandment is, "Thou shalt not steal."[1]

Q. 141. What are the duties required in the Eighth Commandment?

A.The duties required in the Eighth Commandment are: truth, faithfulness, and justice in contracts and commerce between man and man;[1] rendering to everyone his due;[2] restitution of goods unlawfully detained from the right owners thereof;[3] giving and lending freely, according to our abilities, and the necessities of others;[4] moderation of our judgments, wills, and affections, concerning worldly goods;[5] a provident care and study to get,[6] keep, use, and dispose of those things which are necessary and convenient for the sustentation of our nature, and suitable to our condition;[7] a lawful calling,[8] and a diligence in it;[9] frugality;[10] avoiding unnecessary lawsuits,[11] and suretyship, or other like engagements;[12] and an endeavor by all just and lawful means to procure, preserve, and further the wealth and outward estate of others, as well as our own.[13]

Q. 142. What are the sins forbidden in the Eighth Commandment?

A. The sins forbidden in the Eighth Commandment besides the neglect of duties required,[1] are: theft,[2] robbery,[3] man-stealing,[4] and receiving anything that is stolen;[5] fraudulent dealing,[6] false weights and measures,[7] removing landmarks,[8] injustice and unfaithfulness in contracts between man and man,[9] or in matters of trust;[10] oppression,[11] extortion, usury,[12] bribery,[13] vexatious lawsuits,[14] unjust enclosures and depopulations;[15] engrossing commodities to enhance the price,[16] unlawful callings,[17] and all other unjust or sinful ways of taking or withholding from our neighbor what belongs to him, or of enriching ourselves;[18] covetousness,[19] inordinate prizing and affecting worldly goods;[20] distrustful and distracting cares and studies in getting, keeping, and using them;[21] envying at the prosperity of others;[22] as likewise idleness,[23] prodigality, wasteful gaming, and all other ways whereby we do unduly prejudice our own outward estate;[24] and defrauding ourselves of the due use and comfort of that estate which God hath given us.[25]

Q. 143. Which is the Ninth Commandment?

A. The Ninth Commandment is, "Thou shalt not bear false witness against thy neighbour."[1]

Q. 144. What are the duties required in the Ninth Commandment?

A. The duties required in the Ninth Commandment are: the preserving and promoting of truth between man and man,[1] and the good name of our neighbor, as well as our own;[2] appearing and standing for the truth;[3] and from the heart, sincerely,[4] freely,[5] clearly,[6] and fully,[7] speaking the truth, and only the truth, in matters of judgment and justice,[8] and in all other things whatsoever;[9] a charitable esteem of our neighbors,[10] loving, desiring, and rejoicing in their good name;[11] sorrowing for,[12] and covering of their infirmities;[13] freely acknowledging of their gifts and graces,[14] defending their innocency;[15] a ready receiving of good report,[16] and unwillingness to admit of an evil report concerning them;[17] discouraging talebearers,[18] flatterers,[19] and slanderers;[20] love and care of our own good name, and defending it when need requireth;[21] keeping of lawful promises;[22] studying and practicing of whatsoever things are true, honest, lovely, and of good report.[23]

Q. 145. What are the sins forbidden in the Ninth Commandment?

A. The sins forbidden in the Ninth Commandment are: all prejudicing of the truth, and the good name of our neighbors as well as our own,[1] especially in public judicature;[2] giving false evidence,[3] suborning false witnesses,[4] wittingly appearing and pleading for an evil cause, outfacing and overbearing the truth;[5] passing unjust sentence,[6] calling evil good, and good evil; rewarding the wicked according to the work of the righteous, and the righteous according to the work of the wicked;[7] forgery,[8] concealing the truth, undue silence in a just cause,[9] and holding our peace when iniquity calleth for either a reproof from ourselves,[10] or complaint to others;[11] speaking the truth unseasonably,[12] or maliciously to a wrong end,[13] or perverting it to a wrong meaning,[14] or in doubtful and equivocal expression, to the prejudice of truth or justice;[15] speaking untruth,[16] lying,[17] slandering,[18] backbiting,[19] detracting,[20] talebearing,[21] whispering,[22] scoffing,[23] reviling;[24] rash,[25] harsh,[26] and partial censuring;[27] misconstruing intentions, words, and actions;[28] flattering,[29] vainglorious boasting,[30] thinking or speaking too highly or too meanly of ourselves or others; denying the gifts and graces of God;[31] aggravating smaller faults;[32] hiding, excusing, or extenuating of sins, when called to a free confession;[33] unnecessarily discovering of infirmities;[34] raising false rumors;[35] receiving and countenancing evil reports,[36] and stopping our ears against just defense;[37] evil suspicion;[38] envying or grieving at the deserved credit of any;[39] endeavoring or desiring to impair it,[40] rejoicing in their disgrace and infamy;[41] scornful contempt,[42] fond admiration,[43] breach of lawful promises;[44] neglecting such things as are of good report;[45] and practicing or not avoiding ourselves, or not hindering what we can in others, such things as procure an ill name.[46]

Q. 146. Which is the Tenth Commandment?

A. The Tenth Commandment is, "Thou shalt not covet thy neighbour's house, thou shalt not covet thy neighbour's wife, nor his manservant, nor his maidservant, nor his ox, nor his ass, nor any thing that is thy neighbour's."[1]

Q. 147. What are the duties required in the Tenth Commandment?

A. The duties required in the Tenth Commandment are: such a full contentment with our own condition,[1] and such a charitable frame of the whole soul towards our neighbor, as that all our inward motions and affections touching him, tend unto and further all that good which is his.[2]

Q. 148. What are the sins forbidden in the Tenth Commandment?

A. The sins forbidden in the Tenth Commandment are: discontentment with our own estate;[1] envying,[2] and grieving at the good of our neighbor,[3] together with all inordinate motions and affections to anything that is his.[4]

Q. 149. Is any man able perfectly to keep the Commandments of God?

A. No man is able, either of himself,[1] or by any grace received in this life, perfectly to keep the Commandments of God;[2] but doth daily break them in thought,[3] word, and deed.[4]

Q. 150. Are all transgressions of the law of God equally heinous in themselves, and in the sight of God?

A. All transgressions of the law of God are not equally heinous; but some sins in themselves, and by reason of several aggravations, are more heinous in the sight of God than others.[1]

Q. 151. What are those aggravations that make some sins more heinous than others?

A. Sins receive their aggravations,

1. From the persons offending:[1] if they be of riper age, greater experience, or grace;[2] eminent for profession,[3] gifts,[4] place, office,[5] guides to others,[6] and whose example is likely to be followed by others.[7]

2. From the parties offended:[8] if immediately against God,[9] his attributes,[10] and worship;[11] against Christ, and his grace:[12] the Holy Spirit, his witness, and workings;[13] against superiors, men of eminency,[14] and such as we stand especially related and engaged unto;[15] against any of the saints,[16] particularly weak brethren, the souls of them or any other;[17] and the common good of all or many.[18]

3. From the nature and quality of the offense:[19] if it be against the express letter of the law,[20] break many commandments, contain in it many sins:[21] if not only conceived in the heart, but break forth in words and actions,[22] scandalize others,[23] and admit no reparation:[24] if against means,[25] mercies,[26] judgments,[27] light of nature,[28] conviction of conscience,[29] public or private admonition,[30] censures of the church,[31] civil punishments;[32] and our prayers, purposes, promises, vows, covenants, and engagements to God or men:[33] if done deliberately, willfully,[34] presumptuously, impudently, boastingly,[35] maliciously,[36] frequently,[37] obstinately,[38] with light,[39] continuance,[40] or relapsing after repentance.[41]

4. From circumstances of time,[42] and place:[43] if on the Lord's Day,[44] or other times of divine worship;[45] or immediately before,[46] or after these,[47] or other helps to prevent or remedy such miscarriages;[48] if in public, or in the presence of others, who are thereby likely to be provoked or defiled.[49]

Q. 152. What doth every sin deserve at the hands of God?

A. Every sin, even the least,[1] being against the sovereignty,[2] goodness,[3] and holiness of God,[4] and against his righteous law,[5] deserveth his wrath and curse,[6] both in this life,[7] and that which is to come;[8] and cannot be expiated but by the blood of Christ.[9]

Q. 153. What doth God require of us, that we may escape his wrath and curse due to us by reason of the transgression of the law?

A. That we may escape the wrath and curse of God due to us by reason of the transgression of the law, he requireth of us repentance towards God, and faith towards our Lord Jesus Christ,[1] and the diligent use of the outward means whereby Christ communicates to us the benefits of his mediation.[2]

Q. 154. What are the outward means whereby Christ communicates to us the benefits of his mediation?

A. The outward and ordinary means, whereby Christ communicates to his church the benefits of his mediation, are all his ordinances, especially the Word, sacraments, and prayer, all which are made effectual to the elect for their salvation.[1]

Q. 155. How is the Word made effectual to salvation?

A. The Spirit of God maketh the reading, but especially the preaching of the Word, an effectual means of enlightening, convincing, and humbling sinners,[1] of driving them out of themselves, and drawing them unto Christ,[2] of conforming them to his image,[3] and subduing them to his will;[4] of strengthening them against temptations and corruptions;[5] of building them up in grace,[6] and establishing their hearts in holiness and comfort through faith unto salvation.[7]

Q. 156. Is the Word of God to be read by all?

A. Although all are not permitted to read the Word publicly to the congregation, yet all sorts of people are bound to read it apart by themselves,[1] and with their families;[2] to which end, the Holy Scriptures are to be translated out of the original into the language of every people unto whom they come.[3]

Q. 157. How is the Word of God to be read?

A. The Holy Scriptures are to be read with an high and reverent esteem of them;[1] with a firm persuasion that they are the very Word of God,[2] and that he only can enable us to understand them;[3] with desire to know, believe, and obey, the will of God revealed in them;[4] with diligence,[5] and attention to the matter and scope of them;[6] with meditation,[7] application,[8] self-denial,[9] and prayer.[10]

Q. 158. By whom is the Word of God to be preached?

A. The Word of God is to be preached only by such as are sufficiently gifted,[1] and also duly approved and called to that office.[2]

Q. 159. How is the Word of God to be preached by those that are called thereunto?

A. They that are called to labor in the ministry of the Word are to preach sound doctrine,[1] diligently, in season, and out of season;[2] plainly,[3] not in the enticing word of man's wisdom, but in demonstration of the Spirit, and of power;[4] faithfully,[5] making known the whole counsel of God;[6] wisely,[7] applying themselves to the necessities and capacities of the hearers;[8] zealously,[9] with fervent love to God,[10] and the souls of his people;[11] sincerely,[12] aiming at his glory,[13] and their conversion,[14] edification,[15] and salvation.[16]

Q. 160. What is required of those that hear the Word preached?

A. It is required of those that hear the Word preached, that they attend upon it with diligence,[1] preparation,[2] and prayer;[3] examine what they hear by the Scriptures;[4] receive the truth with faith,[5] love,[6] meekness,[7] and readiness of mind,[8] as the Word of God;[9] meditate,[10] and confer of it;[11] hide it in their hearts,[12] and bring forth the fruit of it in their lives.[13]

Q. 161. How do the sacraments become effectual means of salvation?

A. The sacraments become effectual means of salvation, not by any power in themselves or any virtue derived from the piety or intention of him by whom they are administered; but only by the working of the Holy Ghost, and the blessing of Christ by whom they are instituted.[1]

Q. 162. What is a sacrament?

A. A sacrament is an holy ordinance instituted by Christ in his church,[1] to signify, seal and exhibit[2] unto those that are within the covenant of grace,[3] the benefits of his mediation;[4] to strengthen and increase their faith and all other graces;[5] to oblige them to obedience;[6] to testify and cherish their love and communion one with another,[7] and to distinguish them from those that are without.[8]

Q. 163. What are the parts of a sacrament?

A. The parts of a sacrament are two: the one, an outward and sensible sign used according to Christ's own appointment; the other, an inward and spiritual grace thereby signified.[1]

Q. 164. How many sacraments hath Christ instituted under the New Testament?

A. Under the New Testament Christ hath instituted in his church only two sacraments, baptism, and the Lord's Supper.[1]

Q. 165. What is Baptism?

A. Baptism is a sacrament of the New Testament, wherein Christ hath ordained the washing with water in the name of the Father, and of the Son, and of the Holy Ghost,[1] to be a sign and seal of ingrafting into himself,[2] of remission of sins by his blood,[3] and regeneration by his Spirit;[4] of adoption,[5] and resurrection unto everlasting life:[6] and whereby the parties baptized are solemnly admitted into the visible church,[7] and enter into an open and professed engagement to be wholly and only the Lord's.[8]

Q. 166. Unto whom is Baptism to be administered?

A. Baptism is not to be administered to any that are out of the visible church, and so strangers from the covenant of promise, till they profess their faith in Christ, and obedience to him;[1] but infants descending from parents, either both or but one of them, professing faith in Christ, and obedience to him, are, in that respect, within the covenant, and are to be baptized.[2]

Q. 167. How is our Baptism to be improved by us?

A. The needful but much neglected duty of improving our Baptism, is to be performed by us all our life long, especially in the time of temptation,[1] and when we are present at the administration of it to others, by serious and thankful consideration of the nature of it and of the ends for which Christ instituted it, the privileges and benefits conferred and sealed thereby, and our solemn vow made therein;[2] by being humbled for our sinful defilement, our falling short of, and walking contrary to, the grace of Baptism and our engagements;[3] by growing up to assurance of pardon of sin, and of all other blessings sealed to us in that sacrament;[4] by drawing strength from the death and resurrection of Christ, into whom we are baptized, for the mortifying of sin, and quickening of grace;[5] and by endeavoring to live by faith,[6] to have our conversation in holiness and righteousness,[7] as those that have therein given up their names to Christ, and to walk in brotherly love, as being baptized by the same Spirit into one body.[8]

Q. 168. What is the Lord's Supper?

A. The Lord's Supper is a sacrament of the New Testament, wherein by giving and receiving bread and wine according to the appointment of Jesus Christ, his death is showed forth;[1] and they that worthily communicate, feed upon his body and blood to their spiritual nourishment and growth in grace;[2] have their union and communion with him confirmed; testify and renew their thankfulness and engagement to God,[3] and their mutual love and fellowship each with other, as members of the same mystical body.[4]

Q. 169. How hath Christ appointed bread and wine to be given and received in the sacrament of the Lord's Supper?

A. Christ hath appointed the ministers of his Word in the administration of this sacrament of the Lord's Supper, to set apart the bread and wine from common use by the word of institution, thanksgiving, and prayer; to take and break the bread, and to give both the bread and the wine to the communicants; who are by the same appointment to take and eat the bread, and to drink the wine; in thankful remembrance that the body of Christ was broken and given, and his blood shed for them.[1]

Q. 170. How do they that worthily communicate in the Lord's Supper feed upon the body and blood of Christ therein?

A. As the body and the blood of Christ are not corporally or carnally present in, with, or under the bread and wine in the Lord's Supper;[1] and yet are spiritually present to the faith of the receiver, no less truly and really than the elements themselves are to their outward senses;[2] so they that worthily communicate in the sacrament of the Lord's Supper, do therein feed upon the body and blood of Christ, not after a corporal or carnal, but in a spiritual manner; yet truly and really,[3] while by faith they receive and apply unto themselves Christ crucified, and all the benefits of his death.[4]

Q. 171. How are they that receive the sacrament of the Lord's Supper to prepare themselves before they come unto it?

A. They that receive the sacrament of the Lord's Supper are, before they come, to prepare themselves thereunto; by examining themselves,[1] of their being in Christ,[2] of their sins and wants;[3] of the truth and measure of their knowledge,[4] faith,[5] repentance,[6] love to God and the brethren,[7] charity to all men,[8] forgiving those that have done them wrong;[9] of their desires after Christ,[10] and of their new obedience;[11] and by renewing the exercise of these graces,[12] by serious meditation,[13] and fervent prayer.[14]

Q. 172. May one who doubteth of his being in Christ, or of his due preparation, come to the Lord's Supper?

A. One who doubteth of his being in Christ, or of his due preparation to the sacrament of the Lord's Supper, may have true interest in Christ, though he be not yet assured thereof;[1] and in God's account hath it, if he be duly affected with the apprehension of the want of it,[2] and unfeignedly desirous to be found in Christ,[3] and to depart from iniquity;[4] in which case (because promises are made, and this sacrament is appointed, for the relief even of weak and doubting Christians)[5] he is to bewail his unbelief,[6] and labor to have his doubts resolved;[7] and so doing, he may and ought to come to the Lord's Supper, that he may be further strengthened.[8]

Q. 173. May any who profess the faith, and desire to come to the Lord's Supper, be kept from it?

A. Such as are found to be ignorant or scandalous, notwithstanding their profession of the faith, and desire to come to the Lord's Supper, may and ought to be kept from that sacrament by the power which Christ hath left in his church,[1] until they receive instruction, and manifest their reformation.[2]

Q. 174. What is required of them that receive the sacrament of the Lord's Supper in the time of the administration of it?

A. It is required of them that receive the sacrament of the Lord's Supper that, during the time of the administration of it, with all holy reverence and attention, they wait upon God in that ordinance; diligently observe the sacramental elements and actions;[1] heedfully discern the Lord's body,[2] and affectionately meditate upon his death and sufferings,[3] and thereby stir up themselves to a vigorous exercise of their graces; in judging themselves,[4] and sorrowing for sin;[5] in earnest hungering and thirsting after Christ,[6] feeding on him by faith,[7] receiving of his fullness,[8] trusting in his merits,[9] rejoicing in his love,[10] giving thanks for his grace;[11] in renewing of their covenant with God,[12] and love to all the saints.[13]

Q. 175. What is the duty of Christians after they have received the sacrament of the Lord's Supper?

A. The duty of Christians after they have received the sacrament of the Lord's Supper, is seriously to consider how they have behaved themselves therein, and with what success;[1] if they find quickening and comfort, to bless God for it,[2] beg the continuance of it, watch against relapse,[3] fulfill their vows,[4] and encourage themselves to a frequent attendance on that ordinance:[5] but if they find no present benefit, more exactly to review their preparation to, and carriage at, the sacrament;[6] in both which if they can approve themselves to God and their own consciences, they are to wait for the fruit of it in due time;[7] but if they see that they have failed in either, they are to be humbled,[8] and to attend upon it afterward with more care and diligence.[9]

Q. 176. Wherein do the sacraments of Baptism and the Lord's Supper agree?

A. The sacraments of Baptism and the Lord's Supper agree, in that the author of both is God;[1] the spiritual part of both is Christ and his benefits;[2] both are seals of the same covenant,[3] are to be dispensed by ministers of the gospel and by none other,[4] and to be continued in the church of Christ until his second coming.[5]

Q. 177. Wherein do the sacraments of Baptism and the Lord's Supper differ?

A. The sacraments of Baptism and the Lord's Supper differ, in that Baptism is to be administered but once, with water, to be a sign and seal of our regeneration and ingrafting into Christ,[1] and that even to infants;[2] whereas the Lord's Supper is to be administered often, in the elements of bread and wine, to represent and exhibit Christ as spiritual nourishment to the soul,[3] and to confirm our continuance and growth in him,[4] and that only to such as are of years and ability to examine themselves.[5]

Q. 178. What is prayer?

A.Prayer is an offering up of our desires unto God,[1] in the name of Christ,[2] by the help of his Spirit,[3] with confession of our sins,[4] and thankful acknowledgment of his mercies.[5]

Q. 179. Are we to pray unto God only?

A.God only being able to search the heart,[1] hear the requests,[2] pardon the sins,[3] and fulfill the desires of all,[4] and only to be believed in,[5] and worshiped with religious worship;[6] prayer, which is a special part thereof,[7] is to be made by all to him alone, and to none other.[8]

Q. 180. What is it to pray in the name of Christ?

A. To pray in the name of Christ is, in obedience to his command, and in confidence on his promises, to ask mercy for his sake:[1] not by bare mentioning of his name;[2] but by drawing our encouragement to pray, and our boldness, strength, and hope of acceptance in prayer, from Christ and his mediation.[3]

Q. 181. Why are we to pray in the name of Christ?

A. The sinfulness of man, and his distance from God by reason thereof, being so great, as that we can have no access into his presence without a mediator, and there being none in heaven or earth appointed to, or fit for, that glorious work but Christ alone, we are to pray in no other name but his only.[1]

Q. 182. How doth the Spirit help us to pray?

A. We not knowing what to pray for as we ought, the Spirit helpeth our infirmities, by enabling us to understand both for whom, and what, and how prayer is to be made; and by working and quickening in our hearts (although not in all persons, nor at all times in the same measure) those apprehensions, affections, and graces, which are requisite for the right performance of that duty.[1]

Q. 183. For whom are we to pray?

A. We are to pray for the whole church of Christ upon earth,[1] for magistrates,[2] and ministers,[3] for ourselves,[4] our brethren,[5] yea, our enemies,[6] and for all sorts of men living,[7] or that shall live hereafter;[8] but not for the dead.[9]

Q. 184. For what things are we to pray?

A. We are to pray for all things tending to the glory of God,[1] the welfare of the church,[2] our own[3] or others' good;[4] but not for anything that is unlawful.[5]

Q. 185. How are we to pray?

A. We are to pray with an awful apprehension of the majesty of God,[1] and deep sense of our own unworthiness,[2] necessities,[3] and sins;[4] with penitent,[5] thankful,[6] and enlarged hearts;[7] with understanding,[8] faith,[9] sincerity,[10] fervency,[11] love,[12] and perseverance,[13] waiting upon him[14] with humble submission to his will.[15]

Q. 186. What rule hath God given for our direction in the duty of prayer?

A. The whole Word of God is of use to direct us in the duty of praying;[1] but the special rule of direction is that form of prayer which our Saviour Christ taught his disciples, commonly called, "the Lord's Prayer."[2]

Q. 187. How is the Lord's Prayer to be used?

A.The Lord's Prayer is not only for direction, as a pattern according to which we are to make other prayers; but may be also used as a prayer so that it be done with understanding, faith, reverence, and other graces necessary to the right performance of the duty of prayer.[1]

Q. 188. Of how many parts doth the Lord's Prayer consist?

A. The Lord's Prayer consists of three parts: a preface, petitions, and a conclusion.

Q. 189. What doth the preface of the Lord's Prayer teach us?

A. The preface of the Lord's Prayer (contained in these words, "Our Father which art in heaven")[1] teacheth us, when we pray, to draw near to God with confidence of his fatherly goodness, and our interest therein;[2] with reverence, and all other childlike dispositions,[3] heavenly affections,[4] and due apprehensions of his sovereign power, majesty, and gracious condescension:[5] as also to pray with and for others.[6]

Q. 190. What do we pray for in the first petition?

A. In the first petition (which is, "Hallowed be thy name"),[1] acknowledging the utter inability and indisposition that is in ourselves and all men to honor God aright,[2] we pray: that God would by his grace enable and incline us and others to know, to acknowledge, and highly esteem him,[3] his titles,[4] attributes,[5] ordinances, word,[6] works, and whatsoever he is pleased to make himself known by;[7] and to glorify him in thought, word,[8] and deed;[9] that he would prevent and remove atheism,[10] ignorance,[11] idolatry,[12] profaneness,[13] and whatsoever is dishonorable to him;[14] and by his overruling providence, direct and dispose of all things to his own glory.[15]

Q. 191. What do we pray for in the second petition?

A. In the second petition (which is, "Thy Kingdom come"),[1] acknowledging ourselves and all mankind to be by nature under the dominion of sin and Satan,[2] we pray: that the kingdom of sin and Satan may be destroyed,[3] the gospel propagated throughout the world,[4] the Jews called,[5] the fullness of the Gentiles brought in;[6] that the church may be furnished with all gospel-officers and ordinances,[7] purged from corruption,[8] countenanced and maintained by the civil magistrate; that the ordinances of Christ may be purely dispensed, and made effectual to the converting of those that are yet in their sins, and the confirming, comforting, and building up of those that are already converted;[9] that Christ would rule in our hearts here,[10] and hasten the time of his second coming, and our reigning with him forever;[11] and that he would be pleased so to exercise the Kingdom of his power in all the world, as may best conduce to these ends.[12]

Q. 192. What do we pray for in the third petition?

A. In the third petition (which is, "Thy will be done on earth as it is in heaven"),[1] acknowledging that by nature we and all men are not only utterly unable and unwilling to know and do the will of God,[2] but prone to rebel against his Word,[3] to repine and murmur against his providence,[4] and wholly inclined to do the will of the flesh, and of the devil:[5] we pray that God would by his Spirit take away

from ourselves and others all blindness,[6] weakness,[7] indisposedness,[8] and perverseness of heart,[9] and by his grace make us able and willing to know, do, and
submit to his will in all things,[10] with the like humility,[11] cheerfulness,[12] faithfulness,[13] diligence,[14] zeal,[15] sincerity,[16] and constancy,[17] as the angels do in heaven.[18]

Q. 193. What do we pray for in the fourth petition?

A. In the fourth petition (which is, "Give us this day our daily bread"),[1] acknowledging that in Adam, and by our own sin, we have forfeited our right to all the
outward blessings of this life, and deserve to be wholly deprived of them by God,
and to have them cursed to us in the use of them;[2] and that neither they of themselves are able to sustain us,[3] nor we to merit,[4] or by our own industry to procure
them,[5] but prone to desire,[6] get,[7] and use them unlawfully:[8] we pray for ourselves
and others, that both they and we, waiting upon the providence of God from day
to day in the use of lawful means may, of his free gift, and as to his fatherly wisdom shall seem best, enjoy a competent portion of them,[9] and have the same continued and blessed unto us in our holy and comfortable use of them,[10] and
contentment in them;[11] and be kept from all things that are contrary to our temporal support and comfort.[12]

Q. 194. What do we pray for in the fifth petition?

A. In the fifth petition (which is, "Forgive us our debts, as we forgive our
debtors"),[1] acknowledging that we and all others are guilty both of original and
actual sin, and thereby become debtors to the justice of God, and neither we nor
any other creature can make the least satisfaction for that debt:[2] we pray for ourselves and others, that God of his free grace would, through the obedience and
satisfaction of Christ apprehended and applied by faith, acquit us both from the
guilt and punishment of sin,[3] accept us in his Beloved,[4] continue his favor and
grace to us,[5] pardon our daily failings,[6] and fill us with peace and joy, in giving
us daily more and more assurance of forgiveness;[7] which we are the rather
emboldened to ask, and encouraged to expect, when we have this testimony in
ourselves, that we from the heart forgive others their offenses.[8]

Q. 195. What do we pray for in the sixth petition?

A. In the sixth petition (which is, "And lead us not into temptation, but deliver us
from evil"),[1] acknowledging that the most wise, righteous, and gracious God, for
divers holy and just ends, may so order things that we may be assaulted, foiled,
and for a time led captive by temptations;[2] that Satan,[3] the world,[4] and the flesh,
are ready powerfully to draw us aside and ensnare us;[5] and that we, even after the
pardon of our sins, by reason of our corruption,[6] weakness, and want of watchfulness,[7] are not only subject to be tempted, and forward to expose ourselves unto
temptations,[8] but also of ouselves unable and unwilling to resist them, to recover
out of them, and to improve them;[9] and worthy to be left under the power of
them;[10] we pray: that God would so overrule the world and all in it,[11] subdue the
flesh,[12] and restrain Satan,[13] order all things,[14] bestow and bless all means of
grace,[15] and quicken us to watchfulness in the use of them, that we and all his
people may by his providence be kept from being tempted to sin;[16] or, if tempted,
that by his Spirit we may be powerfully supported and enabled to stand in the
hour of temptation;[17] or, when fallen, raised again and recovered out of it,[18] and

have a sanctified use and improvement thereof;[19] that our sanctification and salvation may be perfected,[20] Satan trodden under our feet,[21] and we fully freed from sin, temptation, and all evil forever.[22]

Q. 196. What doth the conclusion of the Lord's Prayer teach us?

A. The conclusion of the Lord's Prayer (which is, "For thine is the Kingdom, and the power, and the glory, for ever. Amen,"),[1] teacheth us to enforce our petitions with arguments,[2] which are to be taken, not from any worthiness in ourselves, or in any other creature, but from God,[3] and with our prayers to join praises,[4] ascribing to God alone eternal sovereignty, omnipotency, and glorious excellency;[5] in regard whereof, as he is able and willing to help us,[6] so we by faith are emboldened to plead with him that he would,[7] and quietly to rely upon him that he will, fullfill our requests.[8] And to testify our desires and assurance, we say, "Amen."[9]

Q. 1. General Note.—At several points the Larger Catechism is more specific in its statements than in Scriptures. These statements are inferences from the Scriptures, or from statements based on the Scriptures, or from the experience and observation of the church. In such cases no texts are cited; but reference is made to this general note.

   1. Rom. 11:36; I Cor. 10:31.

   2. Ps. 73:24–26; John 17:22, 24.

Q. 2.

   1. Rom. 1:19, 20; Ps. 19:1–4.

   2. I Cor. 1:21; I Cor. 2:9, 10.

Q. 3.

   1. Gal. 1:8, 9; Isa. 8:20; Luke 16:29, 31; II Tim. 3:15–17.

Q. 4.

   1. See General Note.

   2. John 16:13, 14; I Cor. 2:69.

Q. 5.

   1. See General Note.

Q. 6.

   1. John 4:24; Exod. 34:6, 7.

   2. Matt. 28:19; II Cor. 13:14.

   3. Eph. 1:11. See the context.

   4. Acts 4:27, 28; Isa. 42:9.

Q. 7.

   1. John 4:24.

   2. I Kings 8:27; Isa. 40:20.

   3. See General Note.

   4. Acts 17:24, 25.

   5. Ps. 90:2.

   6. Mal. 3:6; James 1:17.

   7. Rom. 11:33.

   8. Jer. 23:24; Ps. 139.

   9. Rev. 4:8.

  10. Heb. 4:13; Ps. 147:5.

  11. Rom. 16:27.

  12. Isa. 6:3; Rev. 15:4.

  13. Deut. 32:4.

  14. Exod. 34:6.

Q. 8.

   1. Deut. 6:4; I Cor. 8:4, 6; Jer. 10:10.

Q. 9.

   1. Matt. 3:16, 17; Matt. 28:19; II Cor. 13:14.

Q.10.

   1. Heb. 1:5.

   2. John 1:14.

   3. Gal. 4:6; John 15:26.

Q.11.

   1. Jer. 23:6; I John 5:20; Ps. 45:6; Acts 5:3, 4.

   2. John 1:1; Isa. 9:6; John 2:24, 25; I Cor. 2:10, 11; Heb. 9:14.

   3. Col. 1:16; Gen. 1:2; Ps. 104:30; John 1:3.

   4. Matt. 28:19; II Cor. 13:14.

Q.12.

   1. Eph. 1:4, 11; Acts 4:27, 28; Ps. 33:11.

Q.13.
1. I Tim. 5:21.
2. Eph. 1:4–6; II Thess. 2:13, 14; I Peter 1:2.
3. Rom. 9:17, 18, 21, 22; Jude 4; Matt. 11:25, 26; II Tim. 2:20.
Q.14.
1. Eph. 1:11; I Peter 1:1, 2.
Q.15.
1. Heb. 11:3; Rev. 4:11; Gen. 1.
Q.16.
1. Ps. 104:4; Col. 1:16.
2. Luke 20:36.
3. Gen. 1:31.
4. Matt. 24:36.
5. II Thess. 1:7.
6. Ps. 103:20, 21.
7. II Peter 2:4.
Q.17.
1. Gen. 1:27.
2. Gen. 2:7.
3. Gen. 2:22.
4. Gen. 2:7; Matt. 10:28; Luke 23:43.
5. Gen. 1:27.
6. Col. 3:10; Gen. 2:19, 20.
7. Eph. 4:24.
8. Rom. 2:14, 15.
9. Rom. 1:28.
10. Gen. 2:16, 17; Gen. 3:6.
Q.18.
1. Ps. 145:17.
2. Ps. 104:24; Isa. 28:29.
3. Heb. 1:3.
4. Ps. 103:19; Job, Chapters 38–41.
5. Matt. 10:29, 30; Gen. 45:7; Ps. 135:6.
6. Rom. 11:36; Isa. 63:14.
Q.19.
1. Jude 6; II Peter 2:4.
2. Job 1:12; Luke 10:17; Matt. 8:31.
3. I Tim. 5:21; Mark 8:38; Heb. 12:22.
4. Ps. 104:4; Heb. 1:14.
Q.20.
1. Gen. 2:8; Gen. 2:15, 16.
2. Gen. 1:28.
3. Gen. 2:18.
4. Gen. 1:27, 28.
5. Gen. 2:3.
6. Compare Gen. 2:16, 17, with Rom. 5:12–14; 10:5; Luke 10:25–28, and with the covenants made with Noah and Abraham.
7. Gen. 2:17.
Q.21.
1. Gen. 3:6–8, 13; II Cor. 11:3.
Q.22.
1. Acts 17:16. See under figure 6 above.

2. Gen. 2:17. Compare with Rom: 5:12–20, and with I Cor. 15:21, 22.

Q.23.

    1. Rom. 5:12; Gal. 3:10.

Q.24.

    1. Rom. 3:23; I John 3:4; James 4:17.

Q.25.

    1. Rom. 5:12, 19; I Cor. 15:22.

    2. Rom. 5:6; Eph. 2:1–3; Rom. 8:7, 8; Gen. 6:5; Rom. 3:10–20; Ps. 51:5; 58:3.

    3. James 1:14, 15; Matt. 15:19.

Q.26.

    1. Ps. 51:5; John 3:6.

Q.27.

    1. Gen. 3:8, 24.

    2. Eph. 2:2, 3.

    3. II Tim. 2:26; Luke 11:21, 22; Heb. 2:14.

    4. Rom. 6:23; Rom. 5:14.

Q.28.

    1. Eph. 4:18.

    2. Rom. 1:28.

    3. II Thess. 2:11.

    4. Rom. 2:5.

    5. Isa. 33:14; Gen. 4:13; Matt. 27:4; Heb. 10:27.

    6. Rom. 1:26.

    7. Gen. 3:17.

    8. Deut. 28:15–68.

    9. Rom. 6:21, 23.

Q.29.

    1. II Thess. 1:9; Mark 9:43, 44; Luke 16:24, 26; Matt. 25:41, 46; Rev. 14:11; John 3:36.

Q.30.

    1. I Thess. 5:9.

    2. Titus 3:4–7; Titus 1:2; Gal. 3:21; Rom. 3:20–22.

Q.31.

    1. I Cor. 15:22, 45; Eph. 1:4; II Tim. 1:9; Isa. 53:10, 11; Heb. 2:10, 11, 14.

Q.32.

    1. I Tim. 2:5.

    2. I John 5:11, 12.

    3. John 3:16; John 1:12; John 3:36.

    4. John 1:12, 13; John 3:5, 6, 8; Gal. 5:22, 28.

    5. Ezek. 36:27.

    6. James 2:18, 22.

    7. II Cor. 5:14, 15.

    8. Eph. 2:10, Titus 2:24; 3:8.

Q.33.

    1. II Cor. 3:6; Heb. 1:1, 2; 8:7, 8 ff.

Q.34.

    1. Rom. 15:8; Acts 3:20.

    2. Acts 3:20, 24.

    3. Heb. 10:1.

    4. Rom. 4:11.

    5. I Cor. 5:7; Exod. 12:14, 17, 24.

    6. Heb. 11:13.

7. Gal. 3:7–9; Heb. 11.

Q.35.
1. Matt. 28:19, 20.
2. Matt. 28:19.
3. I Cor. 11:23–26.
4. Heb. 8:6, 7.

Q.36.
1. I Tim. 2:5.
2. John 1:1; John 10:30; Phil. 2:6; Gal. 4:4; Col. 2:9; Phil. 2:5–11.

Q.37.
1. John 1:14; Matt. 26:38.
2. Luke 1:31, 35, 42; Gal. 4:4.
3. Heb. 4:15.

Q.38.
1. See General Note.

Q.39.
1. Rom. 5:19; Gal. 4:4, 5.
2. Heb. 2:14; Heb. 7:24, 25.
3. Heb. 4:15.
4. Gal. 4:5.
5. Heb. 4:14–16.

Q.40.
1. See General Note.

Q.41.
1. Matt. 1:21.

Q.42.
1. John 3:34; Luke 4:18–21.
2. Luke 4:14; Heb. 9:14; Matt. 28:18–20.
3. Acts 3:22; Luke 4:18, 21.
4. Heb. 5:5, 6; Heb. 4:14, 15.
5. Rev. 19:16; Isa. 9:6, 7; Ps. 2:6.

Q.43.
1. John 1:1, 4.
2. II Peter 1:21; II Cor. 2:9, 10.
3. Eph. 4:11–13; John 20:31.

Q.44.
1. Heb. 9:14, 28.
2. Heb. 2:17.
3. Heb. 7:25.

Q.45.
1. John 10:16, 27; Isa. 55:5.
2. I Cor. 12:28; Eph. 4:11, 12.
3. Matt. 28:19, 20.
4. Matt. 18:17, 18; I Cor. 5:4, 5; I Tim. 5:20; Titus 3:10.
5. Acts 5:31.
6. Rev. 22:12; Matt. 25:34–36; Rom. 2:7.
7. Rev. 3:19; Heb. 12:6, 7.
8. II Cor. 12:9, 10; Rom. 8:35–39.
9. I Cor. 15:25; Acts 12:17; Acts 18:9, 10.
10. Rom. 14:11; Col. 1:18; Matt. 28:19, 20.
11. Rom. 8:28.
12. II Thess. 1:8; Ps. 2:9.

Q.46.
   1. Phil. 2:6–8; II Cor. 8:9; Gal. 4:4.
Q.47.
   1. John 1:18. See citations under Q. 46 above.
Q.48.
   1. Gal. 4:4.
   2. Matt. 3:15; John 19:30; Rom. 5:19.
   3. Heb. 12:2, 3; Isa. 53:2, 3; Ps. 22:6.
   4. Matt. 4:1. See verses 2:12; Luke 4:1–14.
   5. Heb. 2:17, 18; Heb. 4:15; Isa. 52:13, 14.
Q.49.
   1. Matt. 27:4.
   2. Matt. 26:56.
   3. Luke 18:32, 33; Isa. 53:3.
   4. Matt. 27:26; John 19:34; Luke 22:63, 64.
   5. Luke 22:44; Matt. 27:46; Rom. 8:32.
   6. Rom. 4:25; I Cor. 15:3, 4; Isa. 53:10.
   7. Phil. 2:8; Heb. 12:2; Gal. 3:13.
Q.50.
   1. I Cor. 15:3, 4.
   2. Matt. 12:40; Luke 18:33.
Q.51.
   1. I Cor. 15:4.
   2. Luke 24:51; Acts 1:9–11.
   3. Eph. 1:20.
   4. Acts 1:11; Acts 17:31.
Q.52.
   1. Acts 2:24; Ps. 16:10.
   2. Luke 24:39.
   3. Rev. 1:18.
   4. John 10:18.
   5. Rom. 1:4.
   6. Rom. 4:25; I Cor. 15:17.
   7. Heb. 2:14; Rev. 1:18.
   8. Rom. 14:9.
   9. I Cor. 15:21, 22.
   10. Eph. 1:22, 23; Col. 1:18.
   11. Rom. 4:25.
   12. Eph. 2:5, 6; Col. 2:12.
   13. I Cor. 15:25, 26; Acts 12:17; Acts 18:9, 10.
   14. I Cor. 15:20; I Thess. 4:13–18.
Q.53.
   1. Acts 1:2, 3.
   2. Matt. 28:19, 20; Acts 1:8.
   3. Heb. 6:20; Eph. 4:8; Acts 1:9.
   4. Ps. 68:18.
   5. Col. 3:1, 2.
   6. John 14:2.
   7. Acts 3:21.
Q.54.
   1. Phil. 2:9.
   2. Acts 2:28. Compare Ps. 16:11.

3. John 17:5.
4. Eph. 1:22; I Peter 3:22.
5. Eph. 4:11, 12. See citations under Q. 45.
6. Rom. 8:34. See citations under Q. 44.

Q.55.
1. Heb. 9:24.
2. Heb. 1:3.
3. John 17:9, 20, 24.
4. Rom. 8:33, 34.
5. Rom. 5:1, 2.
6. Heb. 4:16.
7. Eph. 1:6.
8. I Peter 2:5; Rev. 8:3, 4.

Q.56.
1. Matt. 24:30; Luke 9:26; I Thess. 4:16; Acts 17:31; Matt. 25:31.

Q.57.
1. Heb. 9:12; I Cor. 1:30; Rom. 8:32; II Cor. 1:20.

Q.58.
1. John 1:12, 13; John 3:5, 6; Titus 3:5, 6.

Q.59.
1. John 6:37, 39; John 10:15, 16; Rom. 8:29, 30.
2. I Peter 1:2; II Thess. 2:13.

Q.60.
1. Rom. 10:14; II Thess. 1:8, 9; Acts 4:12; Rom. 1:18–32.
2. I Cor. 1:21; Rom. 1:18–32; Rom. 3:9–19.
3. John 4:22; Phil. 3:4–10.
4. Acts 4:12.
5. John 6:39, 44; John 17:9.

Q.61.
1. Rom. 9:6; Matt. 7:21; Matt. 13:41, 42.

Q.62.
1. I Cor. 1:2; I Cor. 12:12, 13; Rom. 15:1–12.
2. Gen. 17:7. (See the context.) Compare Gal. 3:7, 9, 14; Rom. 4; Acts 2:39; I Cor. 7:14; Mark 10:13–16.

Q.63.
1. I Cor. 12:28; Eph. 4:11, 12; Acts 13:1, 2; Isa. 49:14–16.
2. Matt. 16:18; Isa. 31:4, 5; Ps. 115:9–18.
3. Acts 2:42; Rom. 3:1, 2.
4. Ps. 147:19, 20; Rom. 9:4; Acts 16:31; Rev. 22:17.
5. John 6:37.

Q.64.
1. John 11:52; John 10:16; Eph. 1:10, 22, 23.

Q.65.
1. John 17:21; Eph. 2:5, 6; I John 1:3; John 17:24.

Q.66.
1. Eph. 2:8. (See context.)
2. I Cor. 6:17; John 10:28; Eph. 5:23, 30; John 15:1–5.
3. I Cor. 1:9; I Peter 5:10.

Q.67.
1. Eph. 1:18–20; II Tim. 1:9.
2. Titus 3:4, 5; Rom. 9–11; Eph. 2:4–10.
3. II Cor. 5:20; John 6:44; II Thess. 2:13, 14.

4. Acts 26:18.
5. Ezek. 11:19; Ezek. 36:26, 27.
6. John 6:45; Phil. 2:13; Deut. 30:6; Eph. 2:5.

Q.68.
1. Acts 13:48; John 6:39, 44; John 17:9.
2. Matt. 22:14.
3. Matt. 13:20, 21; Heb. 6:4–6.
4. Ps. 81:11, 12; John 12:38–40; Acts 28:25–27; John 6:64, 65; Prov. 1:24–32; Ps. 95:9–11.

Q.69.
1. Rom. 8:30.
2. Eph. 1:5.
3. I Cor. 1:30.

Q.70.
1. II Cor. 5:19, 21; Rom. 3:22, 24, 25; Rom. 4:5.
2. Eph. 1:6, 7; Rom. 3:28.
3. Rom. 3:24, 25; Rom. 5:17–19; Rom. 4:6–8.
4. Rom. 5:1; Acts 10:43; Gal. 2:16; Phil. 3:9; Rom. 3:25, 26.

Q.71.
1. See citations under Question 70.

Q.72.
1. Heb. 10:39.
2. Rom. 10:14, 17; II Thess. 2:13.
3. John 16:8, 9; Acts 16:30; Acts 2:37; Eph. 2:1; Acts 4:12; Rom. 7:9.
4. Rom. 10:8–10.
5. Acts 10:43; Gal. 2:15, 16; Acts 16:31.
6. Phil. 3:9; Acts 15:11.

Q.73.
1. Gal. 3:11; Rom. 3:28.
2. Titus 3:5–7; Rom. 4:5–8.
3. Phil. 3:9.

Q.74.
1. I John 3:1.
2. Eph. 1:5; Gal. 4:4, 5.
3. John 1:12
4. Rev. 3:12; II Cor. 6:18.
5. Gal. 4:6.
6. Ps. 103:13; Prov. 14:26; Matt. 6:32.
7. Rom. 8:17; Heb. 6:12.

Q.75.
1. Eph. 1:4; I Cor. 6:11; II Thess. 2:13.
2. Rom. 6:4–6; Eph. 4:23, 24; Phil. 3:10.
3. Acts 11:18; I John 3:9.
4. Jude 20; Eph. 3:16–18; Col. 1:10, 11; Rom. 6:4, 6, 14.

Q.76.
1. II Tim. 2:25; Luke 24:47.
2. Acts 11:18, 20, 21; Zech. 12:10; Acts 2:37.
3. Ezek. 18:30, 32; Luke 15:17, 18; Hos. 2:6, 7.
4. Ezek. 36:31; Ezek. 16:61, 63; Isa. 30:22.
5. Luke 22:61, 62; Zech. 12:10.
6. II Cor. 7:11; Acts 2:37.
7. Acts 26:18; Ezek. 14:6; I Kings 8:47, 48; I Sam. 7:3.

    8. Ps. 119:59, 128.

Q.77.

    1. I Cor. 6:11; I Cor. 1:30; Rom. 8:30.

    2. Rom. 4:6, 8; Phil. 3:8, 9; II Cor. 5:21.

    3. Ezek. 36:27.

    4. Rom. 3:24, 25.

    5. Rom. 6:6, 14.

    6. Rom. 8:1, 33, 34.

    7. I Cor. 3:1, 2; Mark 4:8, 28.

    8. I John 1:8, 10.

    9. II Cor. 7:1; Phil. 3:12–14; Eph. 4.11–15.

Q.78.

    1. Rom. 7:18, 23.

    2. Gal. 5:17; Heb. 12:1.

    3. Exod. 28:38; Rom. 7:18, 23.

Q.79.

    1. Jer. 31:3; John 13:1.

    2. I Cor. 1:8; Heb. 6:17; Heb. 13:20, 21; Isa. 54:10.

    3. I Cor. 12:27. Compare with Rom. 8:35–39.

    4. Heb. 7:25; Luke 22:32.

    5. I John 3:9; I John 2:27.

    6. Jer. 32:40; John 10:28; I Peter 1:5; Phil. 1:6.

Q.80.

    1. I John 2:3; I Cor. 2:12; I John 4:13, 16; I John 3:14, 18, 19, 21, 24; Rom. 8:16; I John 5:13.

Q.81.

    1. Isa. 50:10; Ps. 88.

    2. Ps. 31:22; Ps. 77:1–12; Ps. 30:6, 7; Ps. 51:8, 12.

    3. Job 13:15; Ps. 73:13–15, 23; I John 3:9; Isa. 54:7–11.

Q.82.

    1. II Cor. 3:18.

    2. Luke 23:43.

    3. I John 3:2; I Thess. 4:17; Rev. 22:3–5.

Q.83.

    1. Eph. 2:4–6.

    2. Rom. 5:5; II Cor. 1:22.

    3. Rom. 5:1, 2; Rom. 14:17.

    4. Gen. 4:13; Matt. 27:3–5; Heb. 10:27; Mark 9:44; Rom. 2:9.

Q.84.

    1. Rom. 6:23.

    2. Heb. 9:27.

    3. Rom. 5:12.

Q.85.

    1. Cor. 15:26, 55–57; Heb. 2:15.

    2. Isa. 57:1, 2; II Kings 22:20.

    3. Luke 16:25; II Cor. 5:1–8.

    4. Luke 23:43; Phil. 1:23.

Q.86.

    1. Luke 16:23; Luke 23:43; Phil. 1:23; II Cor. 5:6–8.

    2. Rom. 8:23; Ps. 16:9.

    3. I Thess. 4:14.

    4. Rom. 8:23.

5. Luke 16:23, 24; Acts 1:25; Jude 6.

Q.87.
1. Acts 24:15.
2. I Cor. 15:51–53; I Thess. 4:15–17; John 5:28, 29.
3. I Cor. 15:21–23, 42–44 [It is evidently the scope of the apostle's argument in this passage, to prove, that as all the natural seed of Adam, their covenant-head, were subjected to death by his offence; so all the spiritual seed of Christ, their new covenant-head, shall be raised from death, to an immortal life of glory and blessedness, by virtue of his resurrection. It is therefore a perversion of the Scripture, to adduce this text as a proof of universal redemption.] Phil. 3:21.
4. John 5:28, 29; Dan. 12:2; Matt. 25:33.

Q.88.
1. II Peter 2:4; Rev. 20:11–13.
2. Matt. 24:36, 42, 44; Luke 21:35, 36.

Q.89.
1. Matt. 25:33.
2. Rom. 2:15, 16. (See the context.)
3. Matt. 25:41, 42.
4. Matt. 25:46; II Thess. 1:8, 9; Luke 16:26; Mark 9:43, 44; Mark 14:21.

Q.90.
1. I Thess. 4:17.
2. Matt. 25:33; Matt. 10:32.
3. I Cor. 6:2, 3.
4. Matt. 25:34, 46.
5. Eph. 5:27; Rev. 7:17.
6. Ps. 16:11, I Cor. 2:9.
7. Heb. 12:22, 2
8. I John 3:2; I Cor. 13:12; I Thess. 4:17, 18; Rev. 22:3–5.

Q.91.
1. Deut. 29:29; Micah 6:8; I Sam. 15:22.

Q.92.
1. Rom. 10:5; Rom. 2:14, 15; Gen. 2:17.

Q.93.
1. James 2:10; Deut. 5:1, 31, 33; Luke 10:26, 27; I Thess. 5:23.
2. Rom. 10:5; Gal. 3:10.

Q.94.
1. Rom. 8:3; Gal. 2:16.
2. I Tim. 1:8; Gal. 3:19, 24.

Q.95.
1. Rom. 7:12.
2. Micah 6:8, Luke 10:26, 28, 37.
3. Ps. 19:11, 12; Rom. 3:20; Rom. 7:7.
4. Rom. 3:9, 23; Rom. 7:9, 13.
5. Gal. 3:21, 22.

Q.96.
1. Rom. 7:9; I Tim. 1:9, 10.
2. Gal. 3:24.
3. Rom. 1:20. (Compare Rom. 2:15.)
4. Gal. 3:10.

Q.97.
1. Rom. 7:4, 6; Rom. 6:14; Rom. 3:20; Rom. 8:1, 34; Gal. 3:13, 14; Rom. 8:3, 4; II Cor. 5:21.

2. Col. 1:12–14; Rom. 7:22; Titus 2:11–14.

Q.98.

    1. Matt. 19:17–19.

    2. Deut. 10:4; Exod. 34:1–4.

Q.99

    Rule 1.

    1. Ps. 19:7; James 2:10; Matt. 5:22, 28, 37, 44.

    Rule 2.

    1. Rom. 7:14; Deut. 6:5; Matt. 22:37–39; Matt. 12:36, 37. See citations under Rule 1 above.

    Rule 3.

    1. Col. 3:5; I Tim. 6:10; Exod. 20:3–5; Amos 8:5.

    Rule 4.

    1. Isa. 58:13; Matt. 15:4–6; Deut. 6:12. Compare with Matt. 4:9, 10.

    2. Eph. 4:18.

    3. Exod. 20:12. Compare with Prov. 30:17.

    4. Jer. 18:7, 8; Exod. 20:7. Compare with Ps. 15:1, 4, 5; Ps. 24:4, 5.

    Rule 5.

    1. Rom. 3:8; Heb. 11:25.

    2. Deut. 4:9.

    3. Matt. 12:7; Mark 14:7.

    Rule 6.

    1. I Thess. 5:22; Gal. 5:26; Heb. 10:24; Col. 3:21.

    Rule 7.

    1. Exod. 20:10; Deut. 6:6, 7; Josh. 24:15.

    Rule 8.

    1. Heb. 10:24.

    2. I Tim. 5:22; Eph. 5:11.

Q.101.

    1. Exod. 20:2.

Q.102.

    1. Luke 10:27.

Q.103.

    1. Exod. 20:3.

Q.104.

    1. The exposition of the Ten Commandments contained in the answers to Questions 104 to 148 are deduced from the Commandments themselves, and from the "Rules" set forth in Question 99. Texts under the specifications are given in order to show that the specifications are in accord with the general teaching of the Scriptures.

    2. I Chron. 28:9; Deut. 26:17; Isa. 43:10; Jer. 14:22.

    3. Ps. 95:6, 7; Matt. 4:10; Ps. 29:2.

    4. Mal. 3:16.

    5. Ps. 63:6.

    6. Eccl. 12:1.

    7. Ps. 18:1, 2.

    8. Mal. 1:6.

    9. Isa. 45:23; Ps. 96.

    10. Josh. 24:22.

    11. Deut. 6:5.

    12. Ps. 73:25.

    13. Isa. 8:13.

14. Exod. 14:31; Rom. 10:11; Acts 10:43.
15. Isa. 26:4; Ps. 40:4.
16. Ps. 130:7.
17. Ps. 37:4.
18. Ps. 32:11.
19. Rom. 12:11; Rev. 3:19; Num. 25:11.
20. Phil. 4:6.
21. Jer. 7:23; James 4:7; Rom. 12:1.
22. I John 3:22.
23. Neh. 13:8; Ps. 73:21; Ps. 119:136; Jer. 31:18, 19.
24. Micah 6:8.

Q.105.

1. Ps. 14:1.
2. Jer. 2:27, 28. Compare I Thess. 1:9.
3. Ps. 81:11.
4. Isa. 43:22, 23.
5. Jer. 4:22; Hos. 4:1, 6.
6. Jer. 2:32; Ps. 50:22.
7. Acts 17:23, 29.
8. Ps. 50:21.
9. Deut. 29:29.
10. Titus 1:16; Heb. 12:16.
11. Rom. 1:30.
12. II Tim. 3:2.
13. Phil. 2:21.
14. I John 2:15; I Sam. 2:29; Col. 3:2, 5.
15. I John 4:1.
16. Heb. 3:12.
17. Gal. 5:20; Titus 3:10.
18. Acts 26:9.
19. Ps. 78:22.
20. Ezek. 37:11.
21. Jer. 5:3.
22. Rom. 2:5.
23. Jer. 13:15.
24. Ps. 19:13.
25. Zeph. 1:12.
26. Matt. 4:7.
27. Rom. 3:8.
28. Jer. 17:5.
29. II Tim. 3:4.
30. Gal. 4:17; Rom. 10:2; John 16:2; Luke 9:54, 55.
31. Rev. 3:16.
32. Rev. 3:1.
33. Ezek. 14:5; Isa. 1:4, 5.
34. Hos. 4:12; Rev. 19:10; Col. 2:18; Rom. 1:25.
35. Lev. 20:6; I Sam. 28:7–11. Compare I Chron. 10:13, 14.
36. Acts 5:3.
37. Matt. 23:9.
38. Deut. 32:15; Prov. 13:13; II Sam. 12:9.
39. Acts 7:51; Eph. 4:30.
40. Ps. 73:2, 3. See verses 13–15, 22.

41. Dan. 5:23.

42. Deut. 8:17; Dan. 4:30.

43. Hab. 1:16.

Q.106.

    1. Ps. 44:20, 21; Ezek. 8:15–18.

    2. I Chron. 28:9.

Q.107.

    1. Exod. 20:4–6.

Q.108.

    1. Deut. 32:46; Matt. 28:20; I Tim. 6:13, 14; Acts 2:42.

    2. Phil. 4:6; Eph. 5:20.

    3. Deut. 17:18, 19; Acts 15:21; II Tim. 4:2; James 1:21; Acts 10:33.

    4. Matt. 28:19; I Cor. 11:23–30.

    5. Matt. 16:19; Matt. 18:17; I Cor. 5; I Cor. 12:28; John 20:23.

    6. Eph. 4:11, 12; I Tim. 5:17, 18; I Cor. 9:1–15.

    7. Joel 2:12; I Cor. 7:5.

    8. Deut. 6:13.

    9. Ps. 76:11; Isa. 19:21; Ps. 116:14, 18.

    10. Acts 17:16, 17; Ps. 16:4.

    11. Deut. 7:5; Isa. 30:22.

Q.109.

    1. Num. 15:39.

    2. Deut. 13:6, 8.

    3. Hos. 5:11; Micah 6:16.

    4. I Kings 11:33; I Kings 12:33.

    5. Deut. 12:30, 32.

    6. Deut. 4:15, 16; Acts 17:29; Rom. 1:21–25.

    7. Gal. 4:8; Dan. 3:18.

    8. Exod. 32:5.

    9. Exod. 32:8.

    10. I Kings 18:26, 28; Isa. 65:11.

    11. Acts 19:19.

    12. Mal. 1:7, 8, 14.

    13. Deut. 4:2.

    14. Ps. 106:39.

    15. Matt. 15:9.

    16. I Peter 1:18.

    17. Jer. 44:17.

    18. Isa. 65:3–5; Gal. 1:13, 14.

    19. I Sam. 13:12; I Sam. 15:21.

    20. Acts 8:18.

    21. Rom. 2:22; Mal. 3:8.

    22. Exod. 4:24–26.

    23. Matt. 22:25; Mal. 1:7, 12, 13.

    24. Matt. 23:13.

    25. Acts 13:45; I Thess. 2:15, 16.

Q.110.

    1. Exod. 20:5, 6.

    2. Exod. 34:13, 14.

    3. I Cor. 10:20–22; Deut. 32:16–19; Jer. 7:18–20; Ezek. 16:26, 27.

    4. Hos. 2:2–4.

    5. Deut. 5:29.

Q.111.
   1. Exod. 20:7.
Q.112.
   1. Matt. 6:9; Deut. 28:58; Ps. 68:4; Ps. 29:2; Rev. 15:3, 4.
   2. Mal. 1:14.
   3. Ps. 138:2.
   4. I Cor. 11:28, 29. See context.
   5. I Tim. 2:8.
   6. Jer. 4:2.
   7. Ps. 76:11.
   8. Acts 1:24, 26.
   9. Ps. 107:21, 22.
   10. Mal. 3:16.
   11. Ps. 8.
   12. Ps. 105:2, 5; Col. 3:17.
   13. Ps. 102:18.
   14. I Peter 3:15; Micah 4:5.
   15. Phil. 1:27.
   16. I Cor. 10:31.
   17. Jer. 32:39.
   18. I Peter 2:12.
Q.113.
   1. Mal. 2:2.
   2. Acts 17:23.
   3. Prov. 30:9.
   4. Mal. 1:6, 7, 12; Mal. 3:14.
   5. Jer. 7:4. See context. Col. 2:20 22.
   6. Exod. 5:2; Ps. 139:20.
   7. Ps. 50:16, 17.
   8. Isa. 5:12.
   9. II Kings 19:22; Lev. 24:11.
   10. Zech. 5:4.
   11. Rom. 12:14; I Sam. 17:43; II Sam. 16:5.
   12. Jer. 5:7; Jer. 23:10.
   13. Deut. 23:18; Acts 23:12.
   14. Esth. 3:7; Esth. 9:24.
   15. Ps. 24:4; Ezek. 17:19. See context.
   16. Mark 6:26; I Sam. 25:22, 32–34.
   17. Rom. 9:14, 19, 20.
   18. Deut. 29:29.
   19. Rom. 3:5, 7. See context.
   20. Ps. 73:12, 13.
   21. Matt. 5:21–48.
   22. Ezek. 13:22.
   23. II Peter 3:16; Matt. 22:29. See context, verses 23–32.
   24. Eph. 5:4.
   25. I Tim. 6:4, 5, 20; II Tim. 2:14; Titus 3:9.
   26. Deut. 18:10, 11. See context. Acts 19:13.
   27. II Tim. 4:3, 4; Jude 4; Rom. 13:13, 14; I Kings 21:9, 10.
   28. Acts 13:45.
   29. II Peter 3:3; Ps. 1:1.
   30. I Peter 4:4.

31. Acts 13:50. See verses 45, 46; Acts 4:18; Acts 19:9; I Thess. 2:16, Heb. 10:29.
32. II Tim. 3:5; Matt. 23:14; Matt. 6:1–3, 5, 16.
33. Mark 8:38.
34. Ps. 73:14, 15.
35. Eph. 5:15, 17; I Cor. 6:5, 6.
36. Isa. 5:4; II Peter 1:8, 9.
37. Rom. 2:23, 24.
38. Gal. 3:1, 3; Heb. 6:6.

Q.114
1. Exod. 20:7.
2. Lev. 19:12.
3. Deut. 28:58, Zech. 5:2–4; Ezek. 36:21–23.
4. I Sam. 2:12, 17, 22.

Q.115.
1. Exod. 20:8–11.

Q.116.
1. Isa. 56:2, 4, 6, 7.
2. Gen. 2:3; Luke 23:56.
3. I Cor. 16:2; Acts 20:7; John 20:19–27.

Q.117.
1. Exod. 20:8, 10.
2. Jer. 17:21, 22; Exod. 16:25–29; Neh. 13:15–22.
3. Matt. 12:1–14.
4. Lev. 23:3; Isa. 58:13; Luke 4:16; Acts 20:7.
5. Exod. 20:8; Luke 23:54, 56; Neh. 13:19.

Q.118.
1. These statements are necessary inferences from the relations which exist between governors and the governed.

Q.119.
1. Ezek. 22:26.
2. Ezek. 33:31, 32; Mal. 1:13; Amos 8:5.
3. Ezek. 23:38.
4. Jer. 17:27. See context. Isa. 58:13, 14.

Q.120.
1. Exod. 20:9.
2. Exod. 20:10.
3. Exod. 20:11.

Q.121.
1. Exod. 20:8.
2. Exod. 16:23; Luke 23:54. Compare Mark 15:42; Neh. 13:19.
3. Ezek. 20:12, 20.
4. Gen. 2:2, 3; Ps. 118:22, 24; Heb. 4.9.
5. Num. 15:37, 38, 40. See context.
6. Exod. 34:21.
7. See citation under figure 5 above.
8. Lam. 1:7; Neh. 13:15–23; Jer. 17:21–23.

Q.122.
1. Matt. 22:39.
2. Matt. 7:12.

Q.123
1. Exod. 20:12.

Q.124.
1. I Tim. 5:1, 2.

2. Gen. 4:20, 21; Gen. 45:8.
3. II Kings 5:13.
4. Gal. 4:19; II Kings 2:12; II Kings 13:14.
5. Isa. 49:23.
Q.125.
    1. Eph. 6:4; I Thess. 2:7, 8, 11; Num. 11:11, 12, 16.
    2. I Cor. 4:14–16.
Q.126.
    1. Eph. 5:21; I Peter 2:17; Rom. 12:10.
Q.127.
    1. Mal. 1:6; Lev. 19:3.
    2. Prov. 31:28; I Peter 3:6.
    3. Lev. 19:32; I Kings 2:19.
    4. I Tim. 2:1, 2.
    5. Heb. 13:7; Phil. 3:17.
    6. Eph. 6:1, 5–7; I Peter 2:13, 14; Rom. 13:1–6; Heb. 13:17; Prov. 4:3, 4; Prov. 23:22.
    7. Heb. 12:9; I Peter 2:18–20.
    8. Titus 2:9, 10.
    9. Matt. 22:21; Rom. 13:6, 7; I Tim. 5:17, 18; Gal. 6:6; Gen. 45:11; Gen. 47:12.
    10. Gen. 9:23; I Peter 2:18; Prov. 23:22.
    11. Ps. 127:3, 5; Prov. 31:23.
Q.128.
    1. Matt. 15:5, 6.
    2. Ps. 106:16.
    3. I Sam. 8:7; Isa. 3:5.
    4. II Sam. 15:1–12.
    5. Exod. 21:15.
    6. I Sam. 10:27.
    7. I Sam. 2:25.
    8. Deut. 21:18, 20, 21.
    9. Prov. 30:11, 17.
    10. Prov. 19:26.
Q.129.
    1. Col. 3:19; Titus 2:4.
    2. I Sam. 12:23; Job. 1:5.
    3. I Kings 8:55, 56; Gen. 49:28.
    4. Deut. 6:6, 7.
    5. Eph. 6:4.
    6. I Peter 3:7.
    7. Rom. 13:3; I Peter 2:14.
    8. Rom. 13:4.
    9. Prov. 29:15; Rom. 13:4.
    10. I Tim. 5:8; Isa. 1:10, 17; Eph. 6:4.
    11. I Tim. 4:12; Titus 2:2–14.
    12. I Kings 3:28.
    13. Titus 2:15.
Q.130.
    1. Ezek. 34:2, 4.
    2. Phil. 2:21.
    3. John 5:44, John 7:18.
    4. Isa. 56:10, 11; Deut. 17:17.
    5. Acts 4:18; Dan. 3:4–6.
    6. Exod. 5:10–19; Matt. 23:2, 4.

7. Matt. 14:8. Compare with Mark 6:24.

8. Jer. 5:30, 32; II Sam. 13:28.

9. Jer. 6:13, 14; Ezek. 13:9, 10.

10. John 7:46–49; John 9:28.

11. I Peter 2:19, 20; Heb. 12:10; Deut. 25:3.

12. Lev. 19:29; Isa. 58:7; Gen. 38:11, 26.

13. Eph. 6:4.

14. Gen. 9:21; I Kings 12:13, 14; I Kings 1:6; I Sam. 3:13.

Q.131.

1. I Peter 2:17.

2. Rom. 12:10; Phil. 2:3.

3. Rom. 12:15, 16; Phil. 2:4.

Q.132.

1. Rom. 13:8.

2. Prov. 14:21; Isa. 65:5; II Tim. 3.3.

3. Acts 7:9; Gal. 5:26.

4. I John 3:12; Matt. 20:15; Num. 12:2; Luke 15:28, 29.

5. Matt. 20:25–27; III John 9; Luke 2:24–26.

Q.133.

1. Exod. 20:12.

2. Eph. 6:2, 3; Deut. 5:16; I Kings 8.25.

Q.134.

1. Exod. 20:13.

Q.135.

1. Eph. 5:29; Matt. 10:23.

2. Ps. 82:4; Deut. 22:8.

3. Matt. 5:22; Jer. 26:15, 16.

4. Eph. 4:26.

5. Prov. 22:24, 25; I Sam. 25:32, 33; Deut. 22:8.

6. Prov. 1:10, 11, 15; Matt. 4:6, 7.

7. I Kings 21:9, 10, 19; Gen. 37:21, 22; I Sam. 24:12 and 26:9–11.

8. Prov. 24:11, 12; I Sam. 14:45.

9. Luke 21:19; James 5:8; Heb. 12:5.

10. Ps. 37:8, 11; I Peter 3:3, 4.

11. Prov. 17:22; I Thess. 5:16.

12. Prov. 23:20; Prov. 25:16.

13. Prov. 23:29, 30; I Tim. 5:23.

14. Matt. 9:12; Isa. 38:21.

15. Ps. 127:2.

16. II Thess. 3:10, 12.

17. Mark 6:31; I Tim. 4:8.

18. I Cor. 13:4, 5; I Sam. 19:4, 5.

19. Rom. 13:10; Prov. 10:12.

20. Zech. 7:9; Luke 10:33, 34.

21. Col. 3:12.

22. Rom. 12:18.

23. I Peter 3:8, 9; I Cor. 4:12, 13.

24. Col. 3:13; James 3:17; I Peter 2:20; Rom. 12:20, 21; Matt. 5:24.

25. I Thess. 5:14; Matt. 25:35, 36; Prov. 31:8, 9; Isa. 58:7.

Q.136.

1. Acts 16:28; Prov. 1:18.

2. Gen. 9:6.

3. Exod. 21:14; Num. 35:31, 33.

4. Deut. 20:1; Heb. 11:32–34; Jer. 48:10.
5. Exod. 22:2.
6. Matt. 25:42, 43; James 2:15, 16.
7. Matt. 5:22.
8. I John 3:15; Prov. 10:12; Lev. 19:17.
9. Prov. 14:30.
10. Rom. 12:19.
11. James 4:1; Eph. 4:31.
12. Matt. 6:34.
13. Luke 21:34.
14. Exod. 20:9, 10.
15. I Peter 4:3, 4.
16. Prov. 15:1; Prov. 12:18.
17. Isa. 3:15; Exod. 1:14.
18. Gal. 5:15.
19. Num. 35:16.
20. Prov. 28:17; Exod. 21:18–36.
Q.137.
1. Exod. 20:14.
Q.138.
1. I Thess. 4:4, 5.
2. Eph. 4:29; Col. 4:6.
3. I Peter 3:2.
4. I Cor. 7:2; Titus 2:4, 5.
5. Matt. 5:28.
6. Prov. 23:31, 33; Jer. 5:7.
7. Prov. 2:16, 20; I Cor. 5:9.
8. I Tim. 2:9.
9. I Cor. 7:9.
10. Prov. 5:18, 19.
11. I Peter 3:7; I Cor. 7:5.
12. I Tim. 5:13, 14; Prov. 31:27.
13. Prov. 5:8.
Q.139.
1. Prov. 5:7; Prov. 4:23, 27.
2. Heb. 13:4; Eph. 5:5; Gal. 5:19.
3. II Sam. 13:14; Mark 6:18; I Cor. 5:1, 13.
4. Rom. 1:26, 27; Lev. 20:15, 16.
5. Matt. 15:19; Col. 3:5; Matt. 5:28.
6. Eph. 5:3, 4; Prov. 7:5, 21; Prov. 19:27.
7. Isa. 3:16; II Peter 2:14.
8. Prov. 7:10, 13.
9. I Tim. 4:3.
10. Lev. 18:1–21.
11. II Kings 23:7; Lev. 19:29; Jer. 5:7.
12. Matt. 19:10–12.
13. I Tim. 5:14, 15; Gen. 38:26.
14. Matt. 19:5; I Cor. 7:2.
15. Matt. 5:32; Mal. 2:16.
16. See citations under Question 138. I Cor. 7:12, 13.
17. Ezek. 16:49; Jer. 5:7.
18. Eph. 5:11; Prov. 5:8.
19. Rom. 13:13; I Peter 4:3; Mark 6:22.

20. Rom. 13:14; II Peter 2:17, 18.

Q.140.

    1. Exod. 20:15.

Q.141.

    1. Ps. 15:2, 4; Micah 6:8; Zech. 8:16.

    2. Rom. 13:7.

    3. Lev. 6:4, 5; Luke 19:8.

    4. Deut. 15:7, 8, 10; Gal. 6:10; Luke 6:30, 38.

    5. I Tim. 6:8, 9.

    6. I Tim. 5:8.

    7. Prov. 27:23, 24; I Tim. 6:17, 18.

    8. Eph. 4:28; Rom. 12:5–8.

    9. Prov. 10:4; Rom. 12:11.

    10. Prov. 12:27; Prov. 21:20; John 6:12.

    11. I Cor. 6:7.

    12. Prov. 11:15; Prov. 6:1–5.

    13. Lev. 25:35; Phil. 2:4; Deut. 22:1–4; Exod. 23:4, 5.

Q.142.

    1. Prov. 23:21; I John 3:17; James 2:15, 16.

    2. Eph. 4:28.

    3. Ps. 62:10.

    4. I Tim. 1:10; Exod. 21:16.

    5. Prov. 29:24; Ps. 50:18.

    6. I Thess. 4:6.

    7. Prov. 11:1; Prov. 20:10.

    8. Deut. 19:14; Prov. 23:10.

    9. Amos 8:5; Ps. 37:21.

    10. Luke 16:11.

    11. Ezek. 22:29; Lev. 25:17.

    12. Matt. 23:25; Ezek. 22:12.

    13. Isa. 33:15.

    14. Prov. 3:30; I Cor. 6:7.

    15. Isa. 5:8; Micah 2:2.

    16. Prov. 11:26.

    17. Acts 19:19. See context.

    18. James 5:4; Prov. 21:6.

    19. Luke 12:15; Prov. 1:19.

    20. I John 2:15, 16; Prov. 23:5; Ps. 62:10.

    21. Matt. 6:25, 34.

    22. Ps. 73:3; James 5:9.

    23. II Thess. 3:11; Prov. 18:9.

    24. Prov. 21:17; Prov. 23:20, 21; Prov. 28:19.

    25. Deut. 12:7; Deut. 16:14.

Q.143.

    1. Exod. 20:16.

Q.144.

    1. Eph. 4:25.

    2. III John 12.

    3. Prov. 31:9.

    4. Ps. 15:2.

    5. Jer. 9:3.

    6. Jer. 42:4; Acts 20:20.

    7. Acts 20:27.

8. Lev. 19:15; Prov. 14:15.
9. Isa. 63:8; Col. 3:9; II Cor. 1:17.
10. Heb. 6:9; I Cor. 13:4, 5.
11. III John 4; Rom. 1:8.
12. II Cor. 12:21; Ps. 119:158.
13. Prov. 17:9; I Peter 4:8.
14. I Cor. 1:4, 5; II Tim. 1:4, 5.
15. Ps. 82:3.
16. I Cor. 13:4, 6, 7.
17. Ps. 15:3.
18. Prov. 25:23.
19. Prov. 26:24, 25.
20. Ps. 101:5.
21. II Cor. 11:18, 23; Prov. 22:1; John 8:49.
22. Ps. 15:4.
23. Phil. 4:8.

Q.145.
1. Luke 3:14.
2. Lev. 19:15; Hab. 1:4.
3. Prov. 19:5; Prov. 6:16, 19.
4. Acts 6:13.
5. Jer. 9:3; Ps. 12:3, 4; Ps. 52:1–4.
6. Prov. 17:15.
7. Isa. 5:23.
8. I Kings 21:8.
9. Lev. 5:1; Acts 5:3.
10. Lev. 19:17; Isa. 58:1.
11. Isa. 59:4.
12. Prov. 29:11.
13. I Sam. 22:9, 10; Ps. 52:1.
14. Ps. 56:5; Matt. 26:60, 61. Compare John 2:19.
15. Gen. 3:5; Gen. 26:7, 9.
16. Isa. 59:13.
17. Col. 3:9; Lev. 19:11.
18. Ps. 50:20.
19. Ps. 15:3; Rom. 1:30.
20. James 4:11; Titus 3:2.
21. Lev. 19:16.
22. Rom. 1:29; Prov. 16:28.
23. Isa. 28:22; Gen. 21:9; Gal. 4:29.
24. I Cor. 6:10.
25. Matt. 7:1.
26. James 2:13.
27. John 7:24; Rom. 2:1.
28. Rom. 3:8; Ps. 69:10.
29. Ps. 12:2, 3.
30. II Tim. 3:2.
31. Luke 18:11; Gal. 5:26; Exod. 4:10, 14; Acts 12:22.
32. Isa. 29:20, 21; Matt. 7:3.
33. Gen. 3:12, 13; Prov. 28:13; Gen. 4:9.
34. Prov. 25:9; Gen. 9:22.
35. Exod. 23:1.
36. Jer. 20:10; Prov. 29:12.

37. Acts 7:57.
38. I Cor. 13:4, 5; I Tim. 6:4.
39. Matt. 21:15; Num. 11:29.
40. Dan. 6:3, 4; Ezra 4:12, 13.
41. Jer. 48:27.
42. Matt. 27:28, 29; Ps. 35:15, 16.
43. I Cor. 3:21; Jude 16; Acts 12:22.
44. Rom. 1:31; II Tim. 3:3.
45. II Sam. 12:14; I Sam. 2:24.
46. Phil. 3:18, 19; II Peter 2:2; II Sam. 12:13, 14.

Q.146.
1. Exod. 20:17.

Q.147.
1. Heb. 13:5; I Tim. 6:6.
2. Rom. 12:15; Phil. 2:4; I Tim. 1:5.

Q.148.
1. I Cor. 10:10.
2. Gal. 5:26; James 3:14, 16.
3. Ps. 112:9, 10; Neh. 2:10.
4. Rom. 7:7; Deut. 5:21; Col. 3:5; Rom. 13:9.

Q.149.
1. James 3:2; John 15:5.
2. I Kings 8:46; Ps. 17:15; I John 1:8–2:6.
3. Gen. 8:21; James 1:14; Gen. 6:5. See citations under figure 2 above.
4. Ps. 19:12; James 3:2, 8.

Q.150.
1. Heb. 2:2, 3; Ezra 9:14; Ps. 78:17, 32, 56.

Q.151.
1. Jer. 2:8.
2. I Kings 11:9.
3. II Sam. 12:14; I Cor. 5:1.
4. James 4:17; Luke 12:47.
5. John 3:10; Jer. 5:4, 5; II Sam. 12:7–9; Ezek. 8:11, 12.
6. Rom. 2:21, 23, 24.
7. Gal. 2:14; II Peter 2:2.
8. I John 5:10; Matt. 21:38, 39.
9. I Sam. 2:25; Acts 5:4.
10. Rom. 2:4.
11. Mal. 1:14; I Cor. 10:21, 22.
12. John 3:18, 36; Heb. 12:25.
13. Heb. 6:4–6; Heb. 10:29; Matt. 12:31, 32; Eph. 4:30.
14. Num. 12:8; Jude 8.
15. Prov. 30:17; Ps. 41:9; Ps. 55:12–14.
16. Zech. 2:8.
17. I Cor. 8:11, 12; Rom. 14:13, 15, 21.
18. I Thess. 2:15, 16; Matt. 23:34–38.
19. Isa. 3:9.
20. Ezek. 20:12, 13.
21. Col. 3:5; I Tim. 6:10.
22. Micah 2:1, 2.
23. Rom. 2:23, 24; Matt. 18:7.
24. Prov. 6:32–35; Matt. 16:26.

25. Matt. 11:21–24; John 15:22.
26. Deut. 32:6; Isa. 1:2, 3; Ezra 9:13, 14.
27. Jer. 5:3; Amos 4:8–11.
28. Rom. 1:20, 21.
29. Rom. 1:32; Dan. 5:22.
30. Prov. 29:1.
31. Matt. 18:17; Titus 3:10.
32. Rom. 13:1–5.
33. Ps. 78:34, 36, 37; Jer. 42:5, 6, 20–22; Prov. 20:25; Lev. 26:25; Jer. 31:32; Prov. 2:17; Ezek. 17:18.
34. Ps. 36:4; Jer. 6:16.
35. Num. 15:30; Jer. 6:15; Ps. 52:1.
36. Ezek. 35:5, 6; III John 10.
37. Num. 14:22.
38. Zech. 7:11, 12.
39. Prov. 2:14.
40. Jer. 9:3, 5; Isa. 57:17.
41. II Peter 2:20, 21; Heb. 6:4, 6.
42. Isa. 22:12–14; II Kings 5:26.
43. Jer. 7:10, 11.
44. Ezek. 23:38.
45. Isa. 58:3, 4.
46. I Cor. 11:20, 21; Jer. 7:9, 10.
47. Prov. 7:14, 15.
48. Neh. 9:13–16; II Chron. 36:15, 16.
49. Isa. 3:9; I Sam. 2:22–24.

Q.152.
1. James 2:10, 11.
2. Mal. 1:14.
3. Deut. 32:6.
4. Hab. 1:13; I Peter 1:15, 16; Lev. 11:45.
5. I John 3:4; Rom. 7:12.
6. Gal. 3:10; Eph. 5:6.
7. Deut. 28:15; Prov. 13:21.
8. Matt. 25:41; Rom. 6:21, 23.
9. Heb. 9:22; I John 1:7; I Peter 1:18, 19.

Q.153.
1. Acts 20:21; Mark 1:15; John 3:18.
2. See texts cited under Q. 154.

Q.154.
1. Matt. 28:19, 20; Acts 2:42, 46; I Tim. 4:16; I Cor. 1:21; Eph. 5:19, 20; Eph. 6:17, 18.

Q.155.
1. Jer. 23:28, 29; Heb. 4:12; Acts 17:11, 12; Acts 26:18.
2. Acts 2:37, 41; Acts 8:27–38.
3. II Cor. 3:18; Col. 1:27.
4. II Cor. 10:4, 5; Rom. 6:17.
5. Ps. 19:11; Col. 1:28; Eph. 6:16, 17; Matt. 4:7, 10.
6. Eph. 4:11, 12; Acts 20:32; II Tim. 3:15, 16; I Cor. 3:9–11.
7. Rom. 16:25; I Thess. 3:2, 13; Rom. 10:14–17.

Q.156.
1. Deut. 17:18, 19; Isa. 34:16; John 5:39; Rev. 1:3.
2. Deut. 6:6, 7; Ps. 78:5, 6.

3. I Cor. 14:18, 19. See context.
Q.157.
    1. Ps. 119:97; Neh. 8:5; Isa. 66:2.
    2. I Thess. 2:13; II Peter 1:16–21.
    3. Ps. 119:18; Luke 24:44–48.
    4. James 1:21, 22; I Peter 2:2; Mark 4:20.
    5. Acts 17:11; Deut. 11:13.
    6. Acts 8:30, 34; Matt. 13:23.
    7. Ps. 1:2; Ps. 119:97.
    8. Acts 2:38, 39; II Sam. 12:7; II Chron. 34:21.
    9. Gal. 1:15, 16; Prov. 3:5.
    10. Ps. 119:18; Luke 24:45.
Q.158.
    1. I Tim. 3:2, 6; II Tim. 2:2; Mal. 2:7.
    2. Rom. 10:15; I Tim. 4:14.
Q.159.
    1. Titus 2:1, 8.
    2. Acts 18:25; II Tim. 4:2.
    3. I Cor. 14:9.
    4. I Cor. 2:4.
    5. Jer. 23:28; I Cor. 4:1, 2; Matt. 24:45–47.
    6. Acts 20:27.
    7. Col. 1:28; II Tim. 2:15.
    8. I Cor. 3:2; Heb. 5:12–14; I Thess. 2:7; Luke 12:42.
    9. Acts 18:25; II Tim. 4:5.
    10. II Cor. 5:13, 14; Phil. 1:15–17.
    11. II Cor. 12:15; I Thess. 3:12.
    12. II Cor. 4:2; II Cor. 2:17.
    13. John 7:18; I Thess. 2:4–6.
    14. I Cor. 9:19–22.
    15. II Cor. 12:19; Eph. 4:12.
    16. I Tim. 4:16; II Tim. 2:10; Acts 26:16–18.
Q.160.
    1. Ps. 84:1, 2, 4; Ps. 27:4; Prov. 8:34.
    2. Luke 8:18; I Peter 2:1, 2; James 1:21.
    3. Ps. 119:18; Eph. 6:18, 19.
    4. Acts 17:11.
    5. Heb. 4:2.
    6. II Thess. 2:10.
    7. James 1:21; Ps. 25:9.
    8. Acts 17:11; Acts 2:41.
    9. I Thess. 2:13.
    10. Heb. 2:1.
    11. Deut. 6:6, 7.
    12. Ps. 119:11; Prov. 2:1–5.
    13. Luke 8:15; James 1:25.
Q.161.
    1. I Peter 3:21; Acts 8:13, 23; I Cor. 3:7; I Cor. 6:11.
Q.162.
    1. Matt. 28:19; Matt. 26:26, 27.
    2. Rom. 4:11; I Cor. 11:24, 25.
    3. Rom. 9:8; Gal. 3:27, 29; Gal. 5:6; Gal. 6:15.

4. Acts 2:38; I Cor. 10:16; Acts 22:16.
5. I Cor. 11:24–26.
6. Rom. 6:4; I Cor. 10:21.
7. I Cor. 12:13; I Cor. 10:17; Eph. 4:3–5.
8. I Cor. 10:21.

Q.163.
1. See Confession of Faith, Chapter XXIX, Section 2, and passages there cited.

Q.164.
1. Matt. 28:19; Matt. 26:26, 27; I Cor. 11:23–26.

Q.165.
1. Matt. 28:19.
2. Gal. 3:27; Rom. 6:3.
3. Acts 22:16; Mark 1:4; Rev. 1:5.
4. John 3:5; Titus 3:5.
5. Gal. 3:26, 27.
6. I Cor. 15:29.
7. Acts 2:41.
8. Rom. 6:4.

Q.166.
1. Acts 2:41.
2. Acts 2:38, 39; I Cor. 7:14; Luke 18:16; Rom. 11:16; Gen. 17:7–9, compare with Col. 2:11, 12; Gal. 3:17, 18, 29.

Q.167.
1. Ps. 22:10, 11.
2. Rom. 6:3–5.
3. Rom. 6:2, 3; I Cor. 1:11–13.
4. I Peter 3:21; Rom. 4:11, 12.
5. Rom. 6:2–4.
6. Gal. 3:26, 27.
7. Rom. 6:22.
8. I Cor. 12:13, 25, 26. See context.

Q.168.
1. I Cor. 11:26.
2. Matt. 26:26, 27; I Cor. 11:23–27.
3. I Cor. 10:16, 21:4. I Cor. 10:17.

Q.169.
1. See General Note.

Q.170.
1. The specifications enumerated in answers to Questions 170–175 are deduced from the nature of the Lord's Supper as set forth in the New Testament. The texts are given to show that these specifications are in accord with the general tenor of the Scriptures. Acts 3:21.
2. Gal. 3:1; Heb. 11:1.
3. John 6:51, 53. See context.
4. I Cor. 10:16.

Q.171.
1. I Cor. 11:28.
2. II Cor. 13:5.
3. I Cor. 5:7. Compare Exod. 12:15.
4. I Cor. 11:29.
5. II Cor. 13:5. See citation under figure 2 above.
6. I Cor. 11:31.

7. I Cor. 10:17.

8. I Cor. 5:8; I Cor. 11:18, 20.

9. Matt. 5:23, 24.

10. John 7:37; Luke 1:53; Isa. 55:1.

11. I Cor. 5:8.

12. Heb. 10:21, 22, 24; Ps. 26:6.

13. I Cor. 11:24.

14. Matt. 26:26; II Chron. 30:18, 19.

Q.172.

    1. Isa. 50:10.

    2. Isa. 54:7, 8, 10; Matt. 5:3, 4; Ps. 31:22.

    3. Ps. 42:11.

    4. II Tim. 2:19; Rom. 7:24, 25.

    5. Matt. 26:28; Matt. 11:28; Isa. 4:11, 29, 31.

    6. Mark 9:24.

    7. Acts 16:30; Acts 9:6.

    8. I Cor. 11:28; Matt. 11:28.

Q.173.

    1. I Cor. 11:29; I Cor. 5:11; Matt. 7:6.

    2. I Cor. 5:4, 5; II Cor. 2:5–8.

Q.174

    1. Gal. 3:1.

    2. I Cor. 11:29.

    3. Luke 22:19.

    4. I Cor. 11:31.

    5. Zech. 12:10.

    6. Ps. 63:1, 2.

    7. Gal. 2:20; John 6:35.

    8. John 1:16; Col. 1:19.

    9. Phil. 3:9.

    10. I Peter 1:8; I Chron. 30:21.

    11. Ps. 22:26.

    12. Jer. 50:5; Ps. 50:5.

    13. I Cor. 10:17; Acts 2:42.

Q.175.

    1. I Cor. 11:17, 30, 31.

    2. II Cor. 2:14; Acts 2:42, 46, 47.

    3. I Cor. 10:12; Rom. 11:20.

    4. Ps. 50:14.

    5. I Cor. 11:25, 26; Ps. 27:4; Acts 2:42.

    6. Ps. 77:6; Ps. 139:23, 24.

    7. Ps. 123:1, 2; Isa. 8:17.

    8. Hos. 14:2; Hos. 6:1, 2.

    9. II Cor. 7:11; I Chron. 15:12–14.

Q.176.

    1. Matt. 28:19; I Cor. 11:23.

    2. Rom. 6:3, 4; I Cor. 10:16.

    3. Col. 2:11, 12. Compare with Rom. 4:11; Matt. 26:27, 28.

    4. See General Note.

    5. Matt. 28:20; I Cor. 11:26.

Q.177.

    1. Matt. 3:11; Gal. 3:27; Titus 3:5.

2. Acts 2:38, 39; I Cor. 7:14. See citations under Q. 166, figure 2.

3. I Cor. 11:26; Col. 2:19.

4. I Cor. 10:16; John 6:51–53.

5. I Cor. 11:28.

Q.178.

1. Ps. 62:8.

2. John 16:23, 24.

3. Rom. 8:26.

4. Dan. 9:4; Ps. 32:5, 6.

5. Phil. 4:6.

Q.179.

1. I Kings 8:39; Acts 1:24; Rom. 8.27.

2. Ps. 65:2.

3. Micah 7:18.

4. Ps. 145:16, 19.

5. II Sam. 22:32; John 14:1.

6. Matt. 4:10.

7. I Cor. 1:2.

8. Luke 4:8; Isa. 42:8; Jer. 3:23.

Q.180.

1. John 14:13, 14; Dan. 9:17.

2. Luke 6:46; Matt. 7:21.

3. Heb. 4:14–16; I John 5:13–15.

Q.181.

1. John 14:6; Eph. 3:12; I Tim. 2:5; John 6:27; Col. 3:17; Heb. 7:25–27; 13:15.

Q.182.

1. Rom. 8:26; Ps. 80:18; Ps. 10:17; Zech. 12:10.

Q.183.

1. Eph. 6:18; Ps. 28:9.

2. I Tim. 2:1, 2.

3. II Thess. 3:1; Col. 4:3.

4. Gen. 32:11.

5. James 5:16; II Thess. 1:11.

6. Matt. 5:44.

7. I Tim. 2:1, 2. See under figure 2. above.

8. John 17:20; II Sam. 7:29.

9. This statement is based on the absence of any command to pray for the dead, and of any example in the Scriptures of such prayer.

Q.184.

1. Matt. 6:9.

2. Ps. 51:18; Ps. 122:6.

3. Matt. 7:11.

4. Ps. 125:4; I Thess. 5:23; II Thess. 3:16.

5. I John 5:14; James 4:3.

Q.185.

1. Ps. 33:8; Ps. 95:6.

2. Gen. 18:27; Ps. 144:3.

3. Ps. 86:1; Luke 15:17–19.

4. Ps. 130:3; Luke 18:13.

5. Ps. 51:17; Zech. 12:10–14.

6. Phil. 4:6; I Thess. 5:18.

7. Ps. 81:10; Eph. 3:20, 21.

8. I Cor. 14:15.
9. Heb. 10:22; James 1:6.
10. Heb. 10:22; Ps. 145:18; Ps. 17:1; John 4:24.
11. James 5:16.
12. I Tim. 2:8; Matt. 5:23, 24.
13. Eph. 6:18.
14. Micah 7:7.
15. Matt. 26:39.

Q.186.
1. II Tim. 3:16, 17; I John 5:14.
2. Matt. 6:9–13; Luke 11:2–4.

Q.187.
1. Matt. 6:9; Luke 11:2.

Q.189.
1. Matt. 6:9.
2. Luke 11:13; Rom. 8:15.
3. Ps. 95:6, 7; Isa. 64:9.
4. Ps. 123:1; Lam. 3:41.
5. Ps. 104:1; Isa. 63:15; Ps. 113:4–6.
6. Acts 12:5; Zech. 8:21.

Q.190.
1. Matt. 6:9.
2. II Cor. 3:5; Ps. 51:15.
3. Ps. 67:2, 3; Ps. 72:19; Eph. 3:20, 21.
4. Ps. 83:18.
5. Ps. 145:6–8; Ps. 86:10–15.
6. II Thess. 3:1; Ps. 107:32; II Cor. 2:14.
7. Ps. 8 and 145, throughout.
8. Ps. 19:14.
9. Phil. 1:11.
10. Ps. 79:10; Ps. 67:1–4.
11. Eph. 1:17, 18.
12. Ps. 97:7.
13. Ps. 74:18, 22.
14. Jer. 14:21; II Kings 19:16.
15. Isa. 64:1, 2; II Chron. 20:6, 10–12.

Q.191.
1. Matt. 6:10.
2. Eph. 2:2, 3.
3. Ps. 68:1; Rev. 12:9.
4. II Thess. 3:1.
5. Rom. 10:1; Ps. 67:2.
6. Rom. 11:25; Ps. 67:1–7.
7. Matt. 9:38.
8. Eph. 5:26, 27; Mal. 1:11.
9. II Cor. 4:2; Acts 26:18; II Thess. 2:16, 17.
10. Eph. 3:14, 17.
11. Rev. 22:20.
12. Isa. 64:1, 2; II Chron. 20:6, 10–12.

Q.192.
1. Matt. 6:10.
2. I Cor. 2:14; Rom. 8:5, 8.

3. Rom. 8:7.
4. Matt. 20:11, 12; Ps. 73:3.
5. Titus 3:3; Eph. 2:2, 3. See Q. 191 under figure 2.
6. Eph. 1:17, 18.
7. Eph. 3:16.
8. Matt. 26:40, 41; Rom. 7:24, 25.
9. Ezek. 11:19; Jer. 31:18.
10. Ps. 119:35; Acts 21:14; I Sam. 3:18.
11. Ps. 123:2; Ps. 131:2; Micah 6:8.
12. Ps. 100:2.
13. Isa. 38:3; Eph. 6:6.
14. Ps. 119:4.
15. Rom. 12:11.
16. II Cor. 1:12.
17. Ps. 119:112; Rom. 2:7.
18. Ps. 103:20–22; Dan. 7:10.

Q.193.
1. Matt. 6:11.
2. Gen. 3:17; Lam. 3:22; Deut. 28: 15–68.
3. Deut. 8:3.
4. Gen. 32:10.
5. Deut. 8:18; Prov. 10:22.
6. Luke 12:15; Jer. 6:13.
7. Hos. 12:7.
8. James 4:3.
9. Gen. 28:20, 21; James 4:13, 15; Ps. 90:17; Ps. 144:12–15.
10. I Tim. 4:4, 5; Prov. 10:22.
11. I Tim. 6:6, 8.
12. Prov. 30:8, 9.

Q.194.
1. Matt. 6:12.
2. Matt. 18:24; Rom. 5:19; Rom. 3:9, 19. See context. Ps. 130:3; Micah 6:6, 7.
3. Rom. 5:19; Rom. 3:24, 25; Acts 13:39.
4. Eph. 1:6.
5. II Peter 1:2.
6. Hos. 14:2; Ps. 143:2; Ps. 130:3.
7. Rom. 15:13; Rom. 5:1, 2; Ps. 51:7–12.
8. Luke 11:4; Matt. 18:35; Matt. 6:14, 15.

Q.195.
1. Matt. 6:13.
2. II Chron. 32:31; Job 2:6.
3. I Peter 5:8; Job 2:2.
4. Luke 21:34; Mark 4:19.
5. James 1:14.
6. Gal. 5:17; Rom. 7:18.
7. Matt. 26:41.
8. I Tim. 6:9; Prov. 7:22.
9. Rom. 7:18, 19.
10. Ps. 81:11, 12.
11. John 17:15; Rom. 8:28.
12. Ps. 51:10; Ps. 119:133.
13. Heb. 2:18; I Cor. 10:13; II Cor. 12:8.

14. Rom. 8:28.
15. Heb. 13:20, 21; Eph. 4:11, 12.
16. Matt. 26:41; Ps. 19:13.
17. I Cor. 10:13; Eph. 3:14–16.
18. Ps. 51:12.
19. I Peter 5:10; I Peter 1:6, 7.
20. I Thess. 3:13.
21. Rom. 16:20.
22. I Thess. 5:23.

Q.196.
1. Matt. 6:13.
2. Job. 23:3, 4; Jer. 14:20, 21.
3. Dan. 9:4, 7–9, 16, 19.
4. Phil. 4:6.
5. I Chron. 29:10–13.
6. Eph. 3:20, 21; Luke 11:13; Ps. 84:11.
7. Eph. 3:12; Heb. 10:19–22.
8. I John 5:14; Rom. 8:32.
9. I Cor. 14:16; Rev. 22:20, 21.

PARALLEL
INDEX

How to Use this Index

Teachers frequently ask students to "compare and contrast" various things such as novels, concepts, theories, or events. There is good reason for such an exercise. As one puts things side by side in order to see how they are alike and how they differ, one then asks questions that lead to learning. "Why does A omit what B includes?" "These were written in different times, so why are they so similar?" Students of the Bible are also familiar with this side-by-side method, which is demonstrated in parallel Bibles and in various editions of the parallel Gospels.

Here, three catechisms have been printed in parallel so the reader may compare and contrast these expressions of faith. The Westminster Larger Catechism and (to a greater extent) the Study Catechism and the Heidelberg Catechism are organized using the traditional "catechetical trilogy," consisting of the Apostles' Creed, the Ten Commandments, and the Lord's Prayer. Traditionally, it was thought that if one learned all that was contained in those three texts, one would know everything necessary to be grounded and to grow in faith.

As you study these catechisms you will see that, while they deal with doctrines that unfold from creed, commandments, and prayer, they deal with these doctrines in different ways. Some catechisms devote much space to discussing certain themes, while others devote less space (or, in some cases, none at all). Sometimes a theme will not appear in its expected place but will show up elsewhere. For example, the Westminster Larger Catechism deals with the work of the Holy Spirit in its treatment of Scripture rather than in the creedal affirmations concerning the Holy Spirit. Or the catechisms may touch on the same themes but access them with quite different questions. As you study, you will notice that each catechism has its own internal logic. What historical circumstances or theological assumptions account for the similarities and differences? It is our hope that you will ask these and many other questions.

THE LARGER CATECHISM

Q. 1. What is the chief and highest end of man?
A. Man's chief and highest end is to glorify God, and fully to enjoy him forever.

Q. 2. How doth it appear that there is a God?
A. The very light of nature in man, and the works of God, declare plainly that there is a God; but his Word and Spirit only, do sufficiently and effectually reveal him unto men for their salvation.

Q. 3. What is the Word of God?
A. The holy Scriptures of the Old and New Testaments are the Word of God, the only rule of faith and obedience.

Q. 4. How doth it appear that the Scriptures are the Word of God?
A. The Scriptures manifest themselves to be the Word of God, by their majesty and purity; by the consent of all the parts, and the scope of the whole, which is to give all glory to God; by their light and power to convince and convert sinners, to comfort and build up believers unto salvation. But the Spirit of God, bearing witness by and with the Scriptures in the heart of man, is alone able fully to persuade it that they are the very word of God.

Q. 5. What do the Scriptures principally teach?
A. The Scriptures principally teach, what man is to believe concerning God, and what duty God requires of man.

THE STUDY CATECHISM

HEIDELBERG CATECHISM

Question 1. What is God's purpose for your life?

God wills that I should live by the grace of the Lord Jesus Christ, for the love of God, and in the communion of the Holy Spirit.

Q. 1. What is your only comfort, in life and in death?

A. That I belong—body and soul, in life and in death—not to myself but to my faithful Savior, Jesus Christ, who at the cost of his own blood has fully paid for all my sins and has completely freed me from the dominion of the devil; that he protects me so well that without the will of my Father in heaven not a hair can fall from my head; indeed, that everything must fit his purpose for my salvation. Therefore, by his Holy Spirit, he also assures me of eternal life, and makes me wholeheartedly willing and ready from now on to live for him.

Question 2. How do you live by the grace of the Lord Jesus Christ?

I am not my own. I have been bought with a price. The Lord Jesus Christ loved me and gave himself for me. I entrust myself completely to his care, giving thanks each day for his wonderful goodness.

Q. 2. How many things must you know that you may live and die in the blessedness of this comfort?

A. Three. First, the greatness of my sin and wretchedness. Second, how I am freed from all my sins and their wretched consequences. Third, what gratitude I owe to God for such redemption.

Question 3. How do you live for the love of God?

I love because God first loved me. God loves me in Christ with a love that never ends. Amazed by grace, I no longer live for myself. I live for the Lord who died and rose again, triumphant over death, for my sake. Therefore, I take those around me to heart, especially those in particular need, knowing that Christ died for them no less than for me.

PART I
Of Man's Misery

Q. 3. Where do you learn of your sin and its wretched consequences?

A. From the Law of God.

Question 4. How do you live in the communion of the Holy Spirit?

By the Holy Spirit, I am made one with the Lord Jesus Christ. I am baptized into Christ's body, the church, along with all others who confess him by faith. As a member of this community, I trust in God's Word, share in the Lord's Supper, and turn to God constantly in prayer. As I grow in grace and knowledge, I am led to do the good works that God intends for my life.

Q. 4. What does the Law of God require of us?

A. Jesus Christ teaches this in a summary in Matthew 22:37–40: "You shall love the Lord your God with all your heart, and with all your soul, and with all your mind. This is the great and first commandment. And a second is like it, you shall love your neighbor

THE LARGER CATECHISM

as yourself. On these two commandments depend all the law and the
prophets." (Cf. Luke 10:27.)

Q. 5. Can you keep all this perfectly?
A. No, for by nature I am prone to hate
God and my neighbor.

LORD'S DAY 3

**Q. 6. Did God create man evil and
perverse like this?**
A. No. On the contrary, God created
man good and in his image, that is, in
true righteousness and holiness, so
that he might rightly know God his
Creator, love him with his whole heart,
and live with him in eternal blessedness, praising and glorifying him.

**Q. 7. Where, then, does this corrup-
tion of human nature come from?**
A. From the fall and disobedience of
our first parents, Adam and Eve, in the
Garden of Eden; whereby our human
life is so poisoned that we are all conceived and born in the state of sin.

**Q. 8. But are we so perverted that
we are altogether unable to do good
and prone to do evil?**
A. Yes, unless we are born again
through the Spirit of God.

LORD'S DAY 4

**Q. 9. Is not God unjust in requiring
of man in his Law what he cannot do?**
A. No, for God so created man that he
could do it. But man, upon the instigation of the devil, by deliberate disobedience, has cheated himself and all his
descendants out of these gifts.

**Q. 10. Will God let man get by with
such disobedience and defection?**
A. Certainly not, for the wrath of God
is revealed from heaven, both against

THE LARGER CATECHISM

our inborn sinfulness and our actual sins, and he will punish them according to his righteous judgment in time and in eternity, as he has declared: "Cursed be everyone who does not abide by all things written in the book of the Law, and do them."

Q. 11. But is not God also merciful?
A. God is indeed merciful and gracious, but he is also righteous. It is his righteousness which requires that sin committed against the supreme majesty of God be punished with extreme, that is, with eternal punishment of body and soul.

PART II
Of Man's Redemption

LORD'S DAY 5
Q. 12. Since, then, by the righteous judgment of God we have deserved temporal and eternal punishment, how may we escape this punishment, come again to grace, and be reconciled to God?
A. God wills that his righteousness be satisfied; therefore, payment in full must be made to his righteousness, either by ourselves or by another.

Q. 13. Can we make this payment ourselves?
A. By no means. On the contrary, we increase our debt each day.

Q. 14. Can any mere creature make the payment for us?
A. No one. First of all, God does not want to punish any other creature for man's debt. Moreover, no mere creature can bear the burden of God's eternal wrath against sin and redeem others from it.

THE LARGER CATECHISM

Q. 15. Then what kind of mediator and redeemer must we seek?
A. One who is a true and righteous man and yet more powerful than all creatures, that is, one who is at the same time true God.

LORD'S DAY 6
Q. 16. Why must he be a true and righteous man?
A. Because God's righteousness requires that man who has sinned should make reparation for sin, but the man who is himself a sinner cannot pay for others.

Q. 17. Why must he at the same time be true God?
A. So that by the power of his divinity he might bear as a man the burden of God's wrath, and recover for us and restore to us righteousness and life.

Q. 18. Who is this mediator who is at the same time true God and a true and perfectly righteous man?
A. Our Lord Jesus Christ, who is freely given to us for complete redemption and righteousness.

Q. 19. Whence do you know this?
A. From the holy gospel, which God himself revealed in the beginning in the Garden of Eden, afterward proclaimed through the holy patriarchs and prophets and foreshadowed through the sacrifices and other rites of the Old Covenant, and finally fulfilled through his own well-beloved Son.

LORD'S DAY 7
Q. 20. Will all men, then, be saved through Christ as they became lost through Adam?
A. No. Only those who, by true faith,

What Man Ought to Believe
Concerning God

Q. 6. What do the Scriptures make known of God?
A. The Scriptures make known what God is, the persons in the Godhead, his decrees, and the execution of his decrees.

Q. 7. What is God?
A. God is a Spirit, in and of himself infinite in being, glory, blessedness, and perfection; all-sufficient, eternal, unchangeable, incomprehensible, everywhere present, almighty; knowing all things, most wise, most holy, most just, most merciful and gracious, long- suffering, and abundant in goodness and truth.

Q. 8. Are there more Gods than one?
A. There is but one only, the living and true God.

Q. 9. How many persons are there in the Godhead?
A. There be three persons in the Godhead: the Father, the Son, and the Holy Ghost; and these three are one true, eternal God, the same in substance, equal in power and glory; although distinguished by their personal properties.

Q. 10. What are the personal properties of the three persons in the Godhead?
A. It is proper to the Father to beget his Son, and to the Son to be begotten of the Father, and to the Holy Ghost to proceed from the Father and the Son, from all eternity.

are incorporated into him and accept all his benefits.

Q. 21. What is true faith?
A. It is not only a certain knowledge by which I accept as true all that God has revealed to us in his Word, but also a wholehearted trust which the Holy Spirit creates in me through the gospel, that, not only to others, but to me also God has given the forgiveness of sins, everlasting righteousness and salvation, out of sheer grace solely for the sake of Christ's saving work.

I. The Apostles' Creed

Question 5. What does a Christian believe?

All that is promised in the gospel. A summary is found in the Apostles' Creed, which affirms the main content of the Christian faith.

[Apostles' Creed]

Q. 22. What, then, must a Christian believe?
A. All that is promised us in the gospel, a summary of which is taught us in the articles of the Apostles' Creed, our universally acknowledged confession of faith.

Q. 23. What are these articles?
A. I believe in God the Father Almighty, Maker of Heaven and earth; And in Jesus Christ, his only-begotten Son, our Lord; who was conceived by the Holy Spirit, born of the Virgin Mary; suffered under Pontius Pilate, was crucified, dead, and buried; he descended into hell; the third day he rose again from the dead; he ascended into heaven, and sits at the right hand of God the Father Almighty; from thence he shall come to judge the living and the dead. I believe in the Holy Spirit; the holy catholic Church; the communion of saints; the forgiveness of sins; the resurrection of the body; and the life everlasting.

LORD'S DAY 8
Q. 24. How are these articles divided?
A. Into three parts: The first concerns

Q. 11. How doth it appear that the Son and the Holy Ghost are equal with the Father?
A. The Scriptures manifest that the Son and the Holy Ghost are God equal with the Father, ascribing unto them such names, attributes, works, and worship, as are proper to God only.

Q. 12. What are the decrees of God?
A. God's decrees are the wise, free, and holy acts of the counsel of his will, whereby, from all eternity, he hath, for his own glory, unchangeably foreordained whatsoever comes to pass in time, especially concerning angels and men.

Q. 13. What hath God especially decreed concerning angels and men?
A. God, by an eternal and immutable decree, out of his mere love, for the praise of his glorious grace, to be manifested in due time, hath elected some angels to glory; and, in Christ, hath chosen some men to eternal life, and the means thereof; and also, according to his sovereign power, and the unsearchable counsel of his own will (whereby he extendeth or withholdeth favor as he pleaseth) hath passed by, and foreordained the rest to dishonor and wrath, to be for their sin inflicted, to the praise of the glory of his justice.

Q. 14. How doth God execute his decrees?
A. God executeth his decrees in the works of creation and providence, according to his infallible foreknowledge, and the free and immutable counsel of his own will.

Q. 15. What is the work of creation?
A. The work of creation is that wherein God did in the begin-

THE STUDY CATECHISM	HEIDELBERG CATECHISM

<table>
<tr><td></td><td>God the Father and our creation; the second, God the Son and our redemption; and the third, God the Holy Spirit and our sanctification.</td></tr>
<tr><td></td><td>Q. 25. Since there is only one Divine Being, why do you speak of three, Father, Son, and Holy Spirit?
A. Because God has thus revealed himself in his Word, that these three distinct persons are the one, true, eternal God.</td></tr>
<tr><td></td><td style="text-align:center">Of God the Father</td></tr>
</table>

Question 6. What is the first article of the Apostles' Creed?
"I believe in God the Father Almighty, Maker of heaven and earth."

Question 7. What do you believe when you confess your faith in "God the Father Almighty"?
That God is a God of love, and that God's love is powerful beyond measure.

Question 8. How do you understand the love and power of God?
Through Jesus Christ. In his life of compassion, his death on the cross, and his resurrection from the dead, I see how vast is God's love for the world—a love that is ready to suffer for our sakes, yet so strong that nothing will prevail against it.

Question 9. What comfort do you receive from this truth?
This powerful and loving God is the one whose promises I may trust in all the circumstances of my life, and to whom I belong in life and in death.

Question 10. Do you make this confession only as an individual?

Q. 26. What do you believe when you say: "I believe in God the Father Almighty, Maker of heaven and earth"?
A. That the eternal Father of our Lord Jesus Christ, who out of nothing created heaven and earth with all that is in them, who also upholds and governs them by his eternal counsel and providence, is for the sake of Christ his Son my God and my Father. I trust in him so completely that I have no doubt that he will provide me with all things necessary for body and soul. Moreover, whatever evil he sends upon me in this troubled life he will turn to my good, for he is able to do it, being almighty God, and is determined to do it, being a faithful Father.

Q. 27. What do you understand by the providence of God?
A. The almighty and ever-present power of God whereby he still upholds, as it were by his own hand, heaven and earth together with all creatures, and rules in such a way that leaves and grass, rain and drought, fruitful and unfruitful years, food and

ning, by the word of his power, make of nothing, the world and all things therein for himself, within the space of six days, and all very good.

Q. 16. How did God create angels?
A. God created all the angels, spirits, immortal, holy, excelling in knowledge, mighty in power, to execute his commandments, and to praise his name, yet subject to change.

Q. 17. How did God create man?
A. After God had made all other creatures, he created man, male and female; formed the body of the man of the dust of the ground, and the woman of the rib of man; endued them with living, reasonable, and immortal souls; made them after his own image, in knowledge, righteousness and holiness, having the law of God written in their hearts, and power to fulfill it, with dominion over the creatures; yet subject to fall.

Q. 18. What are God's works of providence?
A. God's works of providence are his most holy, wise, and powerful preserving, and governing all his creatures; ordering them, and all their actions, to his own glory.

Q. 19. What is God's providence toward the angels?
A. God by his providence permitted some of the angels, willfully and irrecoverably, to fall into sin and damnation, limiting and ordering that, and all their sins, to his own glory; and established the rest in holiness and happiness; employing them all, at his pleasure, in the administrations of his power, mercy, and justice.

Q. 20. What was the providence of God toward man in the estate in which he was created?
A. The providence of God toward man in the estate in which he was created was, the placing him in paradise, appointing him to dress it, giving him liberty to eat of the fruit of the earth, putting the creatures under his dominion, ordaining marriage for his help, affording him communion with himself, and instituting the Sabbath; entering into a covenant of life with him, upon condition of personal, perfect, and perpetual obedience, of which the tree of life was a pledge; and forbidding to eat of the tree of the knowledge of good and evil, upon the pain of death.

Q. 21. Did man continue in that estate wherein God at first created him?
A. Our first parents, being left to the freedom of their own will, through the temptation of Satan, transgressed the command-

No. With the apostles, prophets, and martyrs, with all those through the ages who have loved the Lord Jesus Christ, and with all who strive to serve him on earth here and now, I confess my faith in the God of loving power and powerful love.

Question 11. When the creed speaks of "God the Father," does it mean that God is male?
No. Only creatures having bodies can be either male or female. But God has no body, since by nature God is Spirit. Holy Scripture reveals God as a living God beyond all sexual distinctions. Scripture uses diverse images for God, female as well as male. We read, for example, that God will no more forget us than a woman can forget her nursing child (Isa. 49:15). " 'As a mother comforts her child, so will I comfort you,' says the Lord" (Isa. 66:13).

Question 12. Why then does the creed speak of God the Father?
First, because God is identified in the New Testament as the Father of our Lord Jesus Christ. Second, because Jesus Christ is the eternal Son of this Father. Third, because when we are joined to Christ through faith, we are adopted as sons and daughters into the relationship he enjoys with his Father.

Question 13. When you confess the God and Father of our Lord Jesus Christ, are you elevating men over women and endorsing male domination?
No. Human power and authority are trustworthy only as they reflect God's mercy and kindness, not abusive patterns of domination. As Jesus taught his disciples, "The greatest among you

drink, health and sickness, riches and poverty, and everything else, come to us not by chance but by his fatherly hand.

Q. 28. What advantage comes from acknowledging God's creation and providence?
A. We learn that we are to be patient in adversity, grateful in the midst of blessing, and to trust our faithful God and Father for the future, assured that no creature shall separate us from his love, since all creatures are so completely in his hand that without his will they cannot even move.

227

ment of God, in eating the forbidden fruit, and thereby fell from the estate of innocency wherein they were created.

Q. 22. Did all mankind fall in that first transgression?
A. The covenant being made with Adam, as a public person, not for himself only, but for his posterity, all mankind, descending from him by ordinary generation, sinned in him, and fell with him in that first transgression.

Q. 23. Into what estate did the Fall bring mankind?
A. The Fall brought mankind into an estate of sin and misery.

Q. 24. What is sin?
A. Sin is any want of conformity unto, or transgression of, any law of God, given as a rule to the reasonable creature.

Q. 25. Wherein consists the sinfulness of that estate whereinto man fell?
A. The sinfulness of that estate whereinto man fell, consisteth in the guilt of Adam's first sin, the want of that righteousness wherein he was created, and the corruption of his nature, whereby he is utterly indisposed, disabled, and made opposite unto all that is spiritually good, and wholly inclined to all evil, and that continually; which is commonly called original sin, and from which do proceed all actual transgressions.

Q. 26. How is original sin conveyed from our first parents unto their posterity?
A. Original sin is conveyed from our first parents unto their posterity by natural generation, so as all that proceed from them in that way, are conceived and born in sin.

Q. 27. What misery did the Fall bring upon mankind?
A. The Fall brought upon mankind the loss of communion with God, his displeasure and curse; so as we are by nature children of wrath, bondslaves to Satan, and justly liable to all punishments in this world and that which is to come.

Q. 28. What are the punishments of sin in this world?
A. The punishments of sin in this world, are either inward, as blindness of mind, a reprobate sense, strong delusions, hardness of heart, horror of conscience, and vile affections; or outward, as the curse of God upon the creatures for our sake, and all other evils that befall us in our bodies, names, estates, relations, and employments; together with death itself.

will be your servant" (Matt. 23:11). God the Father sets the standard by which all misuses of power are exposed and condemned. "Call no one your father on earth," said Jesus, "for you have one Father—the one in heaven" (Matt. 23:9). In fact God calls women and men to all ministries of the church.

Question 14. If God's love is powerful beyond measure, why is there so much evil in the world?
No one can say why, for evil is a terrible abyss beyond all rational explanation. Its ultimate origin is obscure. Its enormity perplexes us. Nevertheless, we boldly affirm that God's triumph over evil is certain. In Jesus Christ God suffers with us, knowing all our sorrows. In raising him from the dead, God gives new hope to the world. Our Lord Jesus Christ, crucified and risen, is himself God's promise that suffering will come to an end, that death shall be no more, and that all things will be made new.

Question 15. What do you believe when you say that God is "Maker of heaven and earth"?
First, that God called heaven and earth, with all that is in them, into being out of nothing simply by the power of God's Word. Second, that by that same power all things are upheld and governed in perfect wisdom, according to God's eternal purpose.

Question 16. What does it mean to say that we human beings are created in the image of God?
That God created us to live together in love and freedom—with God, with one another, and with the world. Our distinctive capacities—reason, imagi-

Q. 29. What are the punishments of sin in the world to come?

A. The punishments of sin in the world to come are everlasting separation from the comfortable presence of God, and most grievous torments in soul and body, without intermission, in hell fire forever.

Q. 30. Doth God leave all mankind to perish in the estate of sin and misery?

A. God doth not leave all men to perish in the estate of sin and misery, into which they fell by the breach of the first covenant, commonly called the covenant of works; but of his mere love and mercy delivereth his elect out of it, and bringeth them into an estate of salvation by the second covenant, commonly called the covenant of grace.

Q. 31. With whom was the covenant of grace made?

A. The covenant of grace was made with Christ as the second Adam, and in him with all the elect as his seed.

Q. 32. How is the grace of God manifested in the second covenant?

A. The grace of God is manifested in the second covenant, in that he freely provideth and offereth to sinners a mediator, and life and salvation by him; and requiring faith as the condition to interest them in him, promiseth and giveth his Holy Spirit to all his elect, to work in them that faith, with all other saving graces; and to enable them unto all holy obedience as the evidence of the truth of their faith and of their thankfulness to God, and as the way which he hath appointed them to salvation.

Q. 33. Was the covenant of grace always administered after one and the same manner?

A. The covenant of grace was not always administered after the same manner, but the administrations of it under the Old Testament were different from those under the New.

Q. 34. How was the covenant of grace administered under the Old Testament?

A. The covenant of grace was administered under the Old Testament, by promises, prophecies, sacrifices, circumcision, the passover, and other types and ordinances; which did all foresignify Christ then to come, and were for that time sufficient to build up the elect in faith in promised Messiah, by whom they then had full remission of sin and eternal salvation.

nation, volition, and so on—are given primarily for this purpose. We are created to be loving companions of others so that something of God's goodness may be reflected in our lives.

Question 17. What does our creation in God's image reflect about God's reality?

Our being created in and for relationship is a reflection of the Holy Trinity. In the mystery of the one God, the three divine persons—Father, Son and Holy Spirit—live in, with, and for one another eternally in perfect love and freedom.

Question 18. What does our creation in God's image reflect about God's love for us?

We are created to live wholeheartedly for God. When we honor our Creator as the source of all good things, we are like mirrors reflecting back the great beam of love that God shines on us. We are also created to honor God by showing love toward other human beings.

Question 19. As creatures made in God's image, what responsibility do we have for the earth?

God commands us to care for the earth in ways that reflect God's loving care for us. We are responsible for ensuring that the earth's gifts be used fairly and wisely, that no creature suffers from the abuse of what we are given, and that future generations may continue to enjoy the abundance and goodness of the earth in praise to God.

Question 20. Was the image of God lost when we turned from God by falling into sin?

Q. 35. How is the covenant of grace administered under the New Testament?
A. Under the New Testament, when Christ the substance was exhibited, the same covenant of grace was, and still is to be, administered in the preaching of the Word, and the administration of the sacraments of Baptism, and the Lord's Supper; in which grace and salvation are held forth in more fullness, evidence, and efficacy to all nations.

Yes and no. Sin means that all our relations with others have become distorted and confused. Although we did not cease to be *with* God, our fellow human beings, and other creatures, we did cease to be *for* them; and although we did not lose our distinctive human capacities *completely,* we did lose the ability to use them *rightly,* especially in relation to God. Having ruined our connection with God by disobeying God's will, we are persons with hearts curved in upon ourselves. We have become slaves to the sin of which we are guilty, helpless to save ourselves, and are free, so far as freedom remains, only within the bounds of sin.

Question 21. What does it mean to say that Jesus Christ is the image of God?
Despite our turning from God, God did not turn from us, but instead sent Jesus Christ in the fullness of time to restore our broken humanity. Jesus lived completely for God, by giving himself completely for us, even to the point of dying for us. By living so completely for others, he manifested what he was—the perfect image of God. When by grace we are conformed to him through faith, our humanity is renewed according to the divine image that we lost.

Question 22. What do you understand by God's providence?
That God not only preserves the world, but also continually attends to it, ruling and sustaining it with wise and benevolent care. God is concerned for every creature: "The eyes of all look to you, and you give them their food in due season. You open your hand, you satisfy the desire of every

THE LARGER CATECHISM

living thing" (Ps. 145:15). In particular, God provides for the world by bringing good out of evil, so that nothing evil is permitted to occur that God does not bend finally to the good. Scripture tells us, for example, how Joseph said to his brothers: "As for you, you meant evil against me; but God meant it for good, to bring it about that many people should be kept alive, as they are today" (Gen. 50:20).

Question 23. What comfort do you receive by trusting in God's providence?

The eternal Father of our Lord Jesus Christ watches over me each day of my life, blessing and guiding me wherever I may be. God strengthens me when I am faithful, comforts me when discouraged or sorrowful, raises me up if I fall, and brings me at last to eternal life. Entrusting myself wholly to God's care, I receive the grace to be patient in adversity, thankful in the midst of blessing, courageous against injustice, and confident that no evil afflicts me that God will not turn to my good.

Question 24. What difference does your faith in God's providence make when you struggle against bitterness and despair?

When I suffer harm or adversity, my faith in God's providence upholds me against bitterness and despair. It reminds me when hope disappears that my heartache and pain are contained by a larger purpose and a higher power than I can presently discern. Even in grief, shame, and loss, I can still cry out to God in lament, waiting on God to supply my needs, and to bring me healing and comfort.

THE LARGER CATECHISM

Question 25. Did God need the world in order to be God?

No. God would still be God, eternally perfect and inexhaustibly rich, even if no creatures had ever been made. Yet without God, all created beings would simply fail to exist. Creatures can neither come into existence, nor continue, nor find fulfillment apart from God. God, however, is self-existent and self-sufficient.

Question 26. Why then did God create the world?

God's decision to create the world was an act of grace. In this decision God chose to grant existence to the world simply in order to bless it. God created the world to reveal God's glory, to share the love and freedom at the heart of God's triune being, and to give us eternal life in fellowship with God.

Question 27. Does your confession of God as Creator contradict the findings of modern science?

No. My confession of God as Creator answers three questions: Who?, How?, and Why? It affirms that (a) the triune God, who is self-sufficient, (b) called the world into being out of nothing by the creative power of God's Word (c) for the sake of sharing love and freedom. Natural science has much to teach us about the particular mechanisms and processes of nature, but it is not in a position to answer these questions about ultimate reality, which point to mysteries that science as such is not equipped to explore. Nothing basic to the Christian faith contradicts the findings of modern science, nor does anything essential to modern science contradict the Christian faith.

Q. 36. Who is the Mediator of the covenant of grace?
A. The only Mediator of the covenant of grace is the Lord Jesus Christ, who being the eternal Son of God, of one substance and equal with the Father, in the fullness of time became man, and so was, and continues to be, God and man, in two entire distinct natures, and one person, forever.

Q. 37. How did Christ, being the Son of God, become man?
A. Christ, the Son of God, became man by taking to himself a true body, and a reasonable soul, being conceived by the power of the Holy Ghost, in the womb of the Virgin Mary, of her substance, and born of her, yet without sin.

Q. 38. Why was it requisite that the Mediator should be God?
A. It was requisite that the Mediator should be God; that he might sustain and keep the human nature from sinking under the infinite wrath of God, and the power of death; give worth and efficacy to his sufferings, obedience, and intercession; and to satisfy God's justice, procure his favor, purchase a peculiar people, give his Spirit to them, conquer all their enemies, and bring them to everlasting salvation.

Q. 39. Why was it requisite that the Mediator should be man?
A. It was requisite that the Mediator should be man; that he might advance our nature, perform obedience to the law, suffer and make intercession for us in our nature, have a fellow feeling of our infirmities; that we might receive the adoption of sons, and have comfort and access with boldness unto the throne of grace.

Q. 40. Why was it requisite that the Mediator should be God and man in one person?
A. It was requisite that the Mediator who was to reconcile God and man, should himself be both God and man, and this in one person; that the proper works of each nature might be accepted of God for us, and relied on by us, as the works of the whole person.

Q. 41. Why was our Mediator called Jesus?
A. Our Mediator was called Jesus, because he saveth his people from their sins.

Of God the Son

Question 28. What is the second article of the Apostles' Creed?

"And I believe in Jesus Christ, his only Son, our Lord. He was conceived by the Holy Spirit, born of the Virgin Mary, suffered under Pontius Pilate, was crucified, dead and buried. He descended into hell. On the third day he rose again from the dead. He ascended into heaven and is seated at the right hand of the Father. He will come again to judge the living and the dead."

Question 29. What do you believe when you confess your faith in Jesus Christ as "God's only Son"?

That Jesus Christ is a unique person who was sent to do a unique work.

Question 30. How do you understand the uniqueness of Jesus Christ?

No one else will ever be God incarnate. No one else will ever die for the sins of the world. Only Jesus Christ is such a person, only he could do such a work, and he in fact has done it.

Question 31. What do you affirm when you confess your faith in Jesus Christ as "our Lord"?

That having been raised from the dead he reigns with compassion and justice over all things in heaven and on earth, especially over those who confess him by faith; and that by loving and serving him above all else, I give glory and honor to God.

Question 32. What do you affirm when you say he was "conceived by

Q. 29. Why is the Son of God called JESUS, which means SAVIOR?

A. Because he saves us from our sins, and because salvation is to be sought or found in no other.

Q. 30. Do those who seek their salvation and well-being from saints, by their own efforts, or by other means really believe in the only Savior Jesus?

A. No. Rather, by such actions they deny Jesus, the only Savior and Redeemer, even though they boast of belonging to him. It therefore follows that either Jesus is not a perfect Savior, or those who receive this Savior with true faith must possess in him all that is necessary for their salvation.

Q. 31. Why is he called CHRIST, that is, the ANOINTED ONE?

A. Because he is ordained by God the Father and anointed with the Holy Spirit to be *our chief Prophet* and *Teacher,* fully revealing to us the secret purpose and will of God concerning our redemption; to be *our only High Priest,* having redeemed us by the one sacrifice of his body and ever interceding for us with the Father; and to be *our eternal King,* governing us by his Word and Spirit, and defending and sustaining us in the redemption he has won for us.

Q. 32. But why are you called a Christian?

A. Because through faith I share in Christ and thus in his anointing, so that I may confess his name, offer myself a

Q. 42. Why was our Mediator called Christ?

A. Our Mediator was called Christ, because he was anointed with the Holy Ghost above measure; and so set apart, and fully furnished with all authority and ability, to execute the office of prophet, priest, and king of his church, in the estate both of his humiliation and exaltation.

Q. 43. How doth Christ execute the office of a prophet?

A. Christ executeth the office of a prophet, in his revealing to the church in all ages, by his Spirit and Word, in divers ways of administration, the whole will of God, in all things concerning their edification and salvation.

Q. 44. How doth Christ execute the office of a priest?

A. Christ executeth the office of a priest, in his once offering himself a sacrifice without spot to God, to be a reconciliation for the sins of his people; and in making continual intercession for them.

Q. 45. How doth Christ execute the office of a king?

A. Christ executeth the office of a king, in calling out of the world a people to himself; and giving them officers, laws, and censures, by which he visibly governs them; in bestowing saving grace upon his elect, rewarding their obedience, and correcting them for their sins, preserving and supporting them under all their temptations and sufferings; restraining and overcoming all their enemies, and powerfully ordering all things for his own glory, and their good; and also in taking vengeance on the rest, who know not God, and obey not the gospel.

Q. 46. What was the estate of Christ's humiliation?

A. The estate of Christ's humiliation was that low condition, wherein he, for our sakes, emptying himself of his glory, took upon him the form of a servant, in his conception and birth, life, death, and after his death until his resurrection.

Q. 47. How did Christ humble himself in his conception and birth?

A. Christ humbled himself in his conception and birth, in that, being from all eternity the Son of God in the bosom of the Father, he was pleased in the fullness of time to become the Son of man, made of a woman of low estate, and to be born to her, with divers circumstances of more than ordinary abasement.

Q. 48. How did Christ humble himself in his life?

the Holy Spirit and born of the Virgin Mary"?

First, that being born of a woman, Jesus was truly a human being. Second, that our Lord's incarnation was a holy and mysterious event, brought about solely by free divine grace surpassing any human possibilities. Third, that from the very beginning of his life on earth, he was set apart by his unique origin for the sake of accomplishing our salvation.

Question 33. What is the significance of affirming that Jesus is truly God?

Only God can properly deserve worship. Only God can reveal to us who God is. And only God can save us from our sins. Being truly God, Jesus meets these conditions. He is the proper object of our worship, the self-revelation of God, and the Savior of the world.

Question 34. What is the significance of affirming that Jesus is also truly a human being?

Being truly human, Jesus entered fully into our fallen situation and overcame it from within. By his pure obedience, he lived a life of unbroken unity with God, even to the point of accepting a violent death. As sinners at war with grace, this is precisely the kind of life we fail to live. When we accept him by faith, he removes our disobedience and clothes us with his perfect righteousness.

Question 35. How can Jesus be truly God and yet also truly human at the same time?

The mystery of Jesus Christ's divine-human unity passes our understanding; only faith given by the Holy Spirit

living sacrifice of gratitude to him, and fight against sin and the devil with a free and good conscience throughout this life and hereafter rule with him in eternity over all creatures.

LORD'S DAY 13

Q. 33. Why is he called GOD'S ONLY-BEGOTTEN SON, since we also are God's children?

A. Because Christ alone is God's own eternal Son, whereas we are accepted for his sake as children of God by grace.

Q. 34. Why do you call him OUR LORD?

A. Because, not with gold or silver but at the cost of his blood, he has redeemed us body and soul from sin and all the dominion of the devil, and has bought us for his very own.

LORD'S DAY 14

Q. 35. What is the meaning of: "Conceived by the Holy Spirit, born of the Virgin Mary"?

A. That the eternal Son of God, who is and remains true and eternal God, took upon himself our true manhood from the flesh and blood of the Virgin Mary through the action of the Holy Spirit, so that he might also be the true seed of David, like his fellow men in all things, except for sin.

Q. 36. What benefit do you receive from the holy conception and birth of Christ?

A. That he is our Mediator, and that, in God's sight, he covers over with his innocence and perfect holiness the sinfulness in which I have been conceived.

LORD'S DAY 15

Q. 37. What do you understand by the word "suffered"?

A. Christ humbled himself in his life, by subjecting himself to the law, which he perfectly fulfilled, and by conflicting with the indignities of the world, temptations of Satan, and infirmities in his flesh; whether common to the nature of man, or particularly accompanying that his low condition.

Q. 49. How did Christ humble himself in his death?
A. Christ humbled himself in his death, in that having been betrayed by Judas, forsaken by his disciples, scorned and rejected by the world, condemned by Pilate, and tormented by his persecutors; having also conflicted with the terrors of death and the powers of darkness, felt and borne the weight of God's wrath, he laid down his life an offering for sin, enduring the painful, shameful, and cursed death of the cross.

Q. 50. Wherein consisted Christ's humiliation after his death?
A. Christ's humiliation after his death consisted in his being buried, and continuing in the state of the dead, and under the power of death till the third day, which hath been otherwise expressed in these words: "He descended into hell."

Q. 51. What was the estate of Christ's exaltation?
A. The estate of Christ's exaltation comprehendeth his resurrection, ascension, sitting at the right hand of the Father, and his coming again to judge the world.

Q. 52. How was Christ exalted in his resurrection?
A. Christ was exalted in his resurrection, in that, not having seen corruption in death (of which it was not possible for him to be held), and having the very same body in which he suffered, with the essential properties thereof (but without mortality and other common infirmities belonging to this life), really united to his soul, he rose again from the dead the third day by his own power; whereby he declared himself to be the Son of God, to have satisfied divine justice, to have vanquished death and him that had the power of it, and to be Lord of quick and dead. All which he did as a public person the head of his church, for their justification, quickening in grace, support against enemies, and to assure them of their resurrection from the dead at the last day.

Q. 53. How was Christ exalted in his ascension?
A. Christ was exalted in his ascension, in that having, after his resurrection, often appeared unto, and conversed with his apos-

enables us to affirm it. When Holy Scripture depicts Jesus as someone with divine power, status, and authority, it presupposes his humanity. And when it depicts him as someone with human weakness, neediness and mortality, it presupposes his deity. We cannot understand how this should be, but we can trust that the God who made heaven and earth is free to become God incarnate and thus to be God with us in this wonderful and awe-inspiring way.

Question 36. How did God use the people of Israel to prepare the way for the coming of Jesus?
God made a covenant with Israel, promising that God would be their light and their salvation, that they would be God's people, and that through them all the peoples of the earth would be blessed. Therefore, no matter how often Israel turned away from God, God still cared for them and acted on their behalf. In particular, God sent them prophets, priests, and kings. Each of these was "anointed" by God's Spirit—prophets, to declare God's word; priests, to make sacrifice for the people's sins; and kings, to rule justly in the fear of God, upholding the poor and needy, and defending the people from their enemies.

Question 37. Was the covenant with Israel an everlasting covenant?
Yes. With the coming of Jesus the covenant with Israel was expanded and confirmed. By faith in him Gentiles were welcomed into the covenant. This throwing open of the gates confirmed the promise that through Israel God's blessing would come to all peoples. Although for the

A. That throughout his life on earth, but especially at the end of it, he bore in body and soul the wrath of God against the sin of the whole human race, so that by his suffering, as the only expiatory sacrifice, he might redeem our body and soul from everlasting damnation, and might obtain for us God's grace, righteousness, and eternal life.

Q. 38. Why did he suffer "under Pontius Pilate" as his judge?
A. That he, being innocent, might be condemned by an earthly judge, and thereby set us free from the judgment of God which, in all its severity, ought to fall upon us.

Q. 39. Is there something more in his having been crucified than if he had died some other death?
A. Yes, for by this I am assured that he took upon himself the curse which lay upon me, because the death of the cross was cursed by God.

LORD'S DAY 16
Q. 40. Why did Christ have to suffer "death"?
A. Because the righteousness and truth of God are such that nothing else could make reparation for our sins except the death of the Son of God.

Q. 41. Why was he "buried"?
A. To confirm the fact that he was really dead.

Q. 42. Since, then, Christ died for us, why must we also die?
A. Our death is not a reparation for our sins, but only a dying to sin and an entering into eternal life.

tles, speaking to them of the things pertaining to the Kingdom of God, and giving them commission to preach the gospel to all nations; forty days after his resurrection, he, in our nature, and as our head, triumphing over enemies, visibly went up into the highest heavens, there to receive gifts for men, to raise up our affections thither, and to prepare a place for us, where himself is, and shall continue till his second coming at the end of the world.

Q. 54. How is Christ exalted in his sitting at the right hand of God?

A. Christ is exalted in his sitting at the right hand of God, in that as God-man he is advanced to the highest favor with God the Father, with all fullness of joy, glory, and power over all things in heaven and earth; and doth gather and defend his church, and subdue their enemies; furnisheth his ministers and people with gifts and graces, and maketh intercession for them.

Q. 55. How doth Christ make intercession?

A. Christ maketh intercession, by his appearing in our nature continually before the Father in heaven, in the merit of his obedience and sacrifice on earth; declaring his will to have it applied to all believers; answering all accusations against them; and procuring for them quiet of conscience, notwithstanding daily failings, access with boldness to the throne of grace, and acceptance of their persons and services.

Q. 56. How is Christ to be exalted in his coming again to judge the world?

A. Christ is to be exalted in his coming again to judge the world, in that he, who was unjustly judged and condemned by wicked men, shall come again at the last day in great power, and in the full manifestation of his own glory, and of his Father's, with all his holy angels, with a shout, with the voice of the archangel, and with the trumpet of God, to judge the world in righteousness.

Q. 57. What benefits hath Christ procured by his mediation?

A. Christ by his mediation hath procured redemption, with all other benefits of the covenant of grace.

Q. 58. How do we come to be made partakers of the benefits which Christ hath procured?

A. We are made partakers of the benefits which Christ hath procured, by the application of them unto us, which is the work especially of God the Holy Ghost.

244

most part Israel has not accepted Jesus as the Messiah, God has not rejected Israel. God still loves Israel, and God is their hope, "for the gifts and the calling of God are irrevocable" (Rom. 11:29). The God who has reached out to unbelieving Gentiles will not fail to show mercy to Israel as the people of the everlasting covenant.

Question 38. Why was the title "Christ," which means "anointed one," applied to Jesus?
Jesus Christ was the definitive prophet, priest, and king. All of the Lord's anointed in Israel anticipated and led finally to him. In assuming these offices Jesus not only transformed them, but also realized the purpose of Israel's election for the sake of the world.

Question 39. How did Jesus Christ fulfill the office of prophet?
He was God's Word to a dying and sinful world; he embodied the love he proclaimed. His life, death, and resurrection became the great Yes that continues to be spoken despite how often we have said No. When we receive this Word by faith, Christ himself enters our hearts, that he may dwell in us forever, and we in him.

Question 40. How did Jesus Christ fulfill the office of priest?
He was the Lamb of God that took away the sin of the world; he became our priest and sacrifice in one. Confronted by our hopelessness in sin and death, Christ interceded by offering himself—his entire person and work—in order to reconcile us to God.

Question 41. How did Jesus Christ fulfill the office of king?

Q. 43. What further benefit do we receive from the sacrifice and death of Christ on the cross?
A. That by his power our old self is crucified, put to death, and buried with him, so that the evil passions of our mortal bodies may reign in us no more, but that we may offer ourselves to him as a sacrifice of thanksgiving.

Q. 44. Why is there added: "He descended into hell"?
A. That in my severest tribulations I may be assured that Christ my Lord has redeemed me from hellish anxieties and torment by the unspeakable anguish, pains, and terrors which he suffered in his soul both on the cross and before.

LORD'S DAY 17
Q. 45. What benefit do we receive from "the resurrection" of Christ?
A. First, by his resurrection he has overcome death that he might make us share in the righteousness which he has obtained for us through his death. Second, we too are now raised by his power to a new life. Third, the resurrection of Christ is a sure pledge to us of our blessed resurrection.

LORD'S DAY 18
Q. 46. How do you understand the words: "He ascended into heaven"?
A. That Christ was taken up from the earth into heaven before the eyes of his disciples and remains there on our behalf until he comes again to judge the living and the dead.

Q. 47. Then, is not Christ with us unto the end of the world, as he has promised us?
A. Christ is true man and true God. As a man he is no longer on earth, but in

Q. 59. Who are made partakers of redemption through Christ?

A. Redemption is certainly applied, and effectually communicated, to all those for whom Christ hath purchased it; who are in time by the Holy Ghost enabled to believe in Christ, according to the gospel.

Q. 60. Can they who have never heard the gospel, and so know not Jesus Christ nor believe in him, be saved by their living according to the light of nature?

A. They who having never heard the gospel, know not Jesus Christ, and believe not in him, cannot be saved, be they never so diligent to frame their lives according to the light of nature, or the laws of that religion which they profess; neither is there salvation in any other, but in Christ alone, who is the Saviour only of his body the church.

Q. 61. Are all they saved who hear the gospel, and live in the church?

A. All that hear the gospel, and live in the visible church, are not saved; but only they who are true members of the church invisible.

He was the Lord who took the form of a servant; he perfected royal power in weakness. With no sword but the sword of righteousness, and no power but the power of love, Christ defeated sin, evil, and death by reigning from the cross.

Question 42. What do you affirm when you say that he "suffered under Pontius Pilate"?
First, that our Lord was humiliated, rejected, and abused by the temporal authorities of his day, both religious and political. Christ thus aligned himself with all human beings who are oppressed, tortured, or otherwise shamefully treated by those with worldly power. Second, and even more importantly, that our Lord, though innocent, submitted himself to condemnation by an earthly judge so that through him we ourselves, though guilty, might be acquitted before our heavenly Judge.

Question 43. What do you affirm when you say that he was "crucified, dead, and buried"?
That when our Lord passed through the door of real human death, he showed us that there is no sorrow he has not known, no grief he has not borne, and no price he was unwilling to pay in order to reconcile us to God.

Question 44. What do you affirm when you say that he "descended into hell"?
That our Lord took upon himself the full consequences of our sinfulness, even the agony of abandonment by God, in order that we might be spared.

his divinity, majesty, grace, and Spirit, he is never absent from us.

Q. 48. But are not the two natures in Christ separated from each other in this way, if the humanity is not wherever the divinity is?
A. Not at all; for since divinity is incomprehensible and everywhere present, it must follow that the divinity is indeed beyond the bounds of the humanity which it has assumed, and is nonetheless ever in that humanity as well, and remains personally united to it.

Q. 49. What benefit do we receive from Christ's ascension into heaven?
A. First, that he is our Advocate in the presence of his Father in heaven. Second, that we have our flesh in heaven as a sure pledge that he, as the Head, will also take us, his members, up to himself. Third, that he sends us his Spirit as a counterpledge by whose power we seek what is above, where Christ is, sitting at the right hand of God, and not things that are on earth.

LORD'S DAY 19
Q. 50. Why is there added: "And sits at the right hand of God"?
A. Because Christ ascended into heaven so that he might manifest himself there as the Head of his church, through whom the Father governs all things.

Q. 51. What benefit do we receive from this glory of Christ, our Head?
A. First, that through his Holy Spirit he pours out heavenly gifts upon us, his members. Second, that by his power he defends and supports us against all our enemies.

THE LARGER CATECHISM

Question 45. Why did Jesus have to suffer as he did?

Because grace is more abundant—and sin more serious—than we suppose. However cruelly we may treat one another, all sin is primarily against God. God condemns sin, yet never judges apart from grace. In giving Jesus Christ to die for us, God took the burden of our sin into God's own self to remove it once and for all. The cross in all its severity reveals an abyss of sin swallowed up by the suffering of divine love.

Question 46. What do you affirm when you say that "on the third day he rose again from the dead"?

That our Lord could not be held by the power of death. Having died on the cross, he appeared to his followers, triumphant from the grave, in a new, exalted kind of life. In showing them his hands and his feet, the one who was crucified revealed himself to them as the Lord and Savior of the world.

Question 47. What do you affirm when you say that "he ascended into heaven and is seated at the right hand of the Father"?

First, that Christ has gone to be with the Father, hidden except to the eyes of faith. Second, however, that Christ is not cut off from us in the remote past, or in some place from which he cannot reach us, but is present to us here and now by grace. He reigns with divine authority, protecting us, guiding us, and interceding for us until he returns in glory.

Question 48. How do you understand the words that "he will come again to judge the living and the dead"?

Q. 52. What comfort does the return of Christ "to judge the living and the dead" give you?

A. That in all affliction and persecution I may await with head held high the very Judge from heaven who has already submitted himself to the judgment of God for me and has removed all the curse from me; that he will cast all his enemies and mine into everlasting condemnation, but he shall take me, together with all his elect, to himself into heavenly joy and glory.

THE LARGER CATECHISM

Like everyone else, I too must stand in fear and trembling before the judgment seat of Christ. But the Judge is the one who submitted to judgment for my sake. Nothing will be able to separate me from the love of God in Christ Jesus my Lord. All the sinful failures that cause me shame will perish as through fire, while any good I may have done will be received with gladness by God.

Question 49. Will all human beings be saved?

No one will be lost who can be saved. The limits to salvation, whatever they may be, are known only to God. Three truths above all are certain. God is a holy God who is not to be trifled with. No one will be saved except by grace alone. And no judge could possibly be more gracious than our Lord and Savior, Jesus Christ.

Question 50. Is Christianity the only true religion?

Religion is a complex matter. When used as a means to promote self-justification, war-mongering, or prejudice, it is a form of sin. Too often all religions—and not least Christianity—have been twisted in this way. Nevertheless, by grace, despite all disobedience, Christianity offers the truth of the gospel. Although other religions may enshrine various truths, no other can or does affirm the name of Jesus Christ as the hope of the world.

Question 51. How will God deal with the followers of other religions?

God has made salvation available to all human beings through Jesus Christ, crucified and risen. How God will deal with those who do not know or follow

THE LARGER CATECHISM

Christ, but who follow another tradition, we cannot finally say. We can say, however, that God is gracious and merciful, and that God will not deal with people in any other way than we see in Jesus Christ, who came as the Savior of the world.

Question 52. How should I treat non-Christians and people of other religions?

As much as I can, I should meet friendship with friendship, hostility with kindness, generosity with gratitude, persecution with forbearance, truth with agreement, and error with truth. I should express my faith with humility and devotion as the occasion requires, whether silently or openly, boldly or meekly, by word or by deed. I should avoid compromising the truth on the one hand and being narrow-minded on the other. In short, I should always welcome and accept these others in a way that honors and reflects the Lord's welcome and acceptance of me.

Question 53. What is the third article of the Apostles' Creed?

"I believe in the Holy Spirit, the holy catholic church, the communion of saints, the forgiveness of sins, the resurrection of the body, and the life everlasting. Amen."

Question 54. What do you believe when you confess your faith in the Holy Spirit?

Apart from the Holy Spirit, our Lord can neither be loved, nor known, nor served. The Holy Spirit is the personal bond by which Jesus Christ unites us to himself, the teacher who opens our hearts to Christ, and the comforter who leads us to repentance, empower-

The Holy Spirit

LORD'S DAY 20

Q. 53. What do you believe concerning "the Holy Spirit"?

A. First, that, with the Father and the Son, he is equally eternal God; second, that God's Spirit is also given to me, preparing me through a true faith to share in Christ and all his benefits, that he comforts me and will abide with me forever.

THE LARGER CATECHISM

ing us to live in Christ's service. As the work of the one Holy Spirit, our love, knowledge, and service of Christ are all inseparably related.

Question 55. How do we receive the Holy Spirit?

By receiving the Word of God. As the midwife of the new creation, the Spirit arrives with the Word, brings us to rebirth, and assures us of eternal life. The Spirit nurtures, corrects, and strengthens us with the pure spiritual milk of the Word (1 Pet. 2:2).

Question 56. What do you mean when you speak of "the Word of God"?

"Jesus Christ, as he is attested for us in Holy Scripture, is the one Word of God which we have to hear, and which we have to trust and obey in life and in death" (Barmen Declaration, Article I).

Question 57. Isn't Holy Scripture also the Word of God?

Yes. Holy Scripture is also God's Word because of its content, its function, and its origin. Its central content is Jesus Christ, the living Word. Its basic function is to deepen our love, knowledge, and service of him as our Savior and Lord. And its ultimate origin is in the Holy Spirit, who spoke through the prophets and apostles, and who inspires us with eager desire for the truths that Scripture contains.

Question 58. Isn't preaching also the Word of God?

Yes. Preaching and other forms of Christian witness are also God's Word when they are faithful to the witness of Holy Scripture. By the power of the Spirit, preaching actually gives to us

THE LARGER CATECHISM

what it proclaims—the real presence
of our Lord Jesus Christ. Faith comes
by hearing God's Word in the form of
faithful proclamation.

**Question 59. Does the Holy Spirit
ever speak apart from God's Word
in its written and proclaimed forms?**
Since the Spirit is not given to the
church without the Word, true proclamation depends on Scripture. Since
the Word cannot be grasped without
the Spirit, true interpretation depends
on prayer. However, as the wind blows
where it will, so may the Spirit speak
or work in people's lives in unexpected or indirect ways, yet always
according to the Word, never contradicting or diluting it.

**Question 60. Aren't people without
faith sometimes wiser than those
who have faith?**
Yes. The important question for the
church is not so much where an insight
may come from as the norm by which
to test it. Truth is where one finds it,
whether inside or outside the church,
and whether supporting or contradicting one's own most cherished opinions. Our faithful discernment of what
is true, however, depends finally on
God's Word as conveyed in Holy
Scripture. The church is therefore
reformed and always being reformed
according to the Word of God.

**Question 61. Doesn't modern criti-
cal scholarship undermine your
belief that Holy Scripture is a form
of God's Word?**
No. The methods of modern scholarship are a good servant but a bad master. They are neither to be accepted nor
rejected uncritically. Properly used they

Q. 62. What is the visible church?
A. The visible church is a society made up of all such as in all ages and places of the world do profess the true religion, and of their children.

Q. 63. What are the special privileges of the visible church?
A. The visible church hath the privilege of being under God's special care and government; of being protected and preserved in all ages, notwithstanding the opposition of all enemies; and of enjoying the communion of saints, the ordinary means of salvation, and offers of grace by Christ, to all members of it, in the ministry of the gospel, testifying that whosoever believes in him shall be saved, and excluding none that will come unto him.

Q. 64. What is the invisible church?
A. The invisible church is the whole number of the elect, that have been, are, or shall be gathered into one under Christ the head.

Q. 65. What special benefits do the members of the invisible church enjoy by Christ?
A. The members of the invisible church, by Christ, enjoy union and communion with him in grace and glory.

Q. 66. What is that union which the elect have with Christ?
A. The union which the elect have with Christ is the work of God's grace, whereby they are spiritually and mystically, yet really and inseparably, joined to Christ as their head and husband; which is done in their effectual calling.

Q. 67. What is effectual calling?
A. Effectual calling is the work of God's almighty power and grace, whereby (out of his free and especial love to his elect, and from nothing in them moving him thereunto) he doth in his

help us rightly and richly interpret Scripture; improperly used they can usurp the place of faith (or establish an alternative faith). Wise interpreters use these methods in the service of faithful witness and understanding. The methods of modern scholarship remain a useful tool, while Holy Scripture remains reliable in all essential matters of faith and practice.

Question 62. What do you affirm when you speak of "the holy catholic church"?

The church is the company of all faithful people who have given their lives to Jesus Christ, as he has given and gives himself to them. Since Christ cannot be separated from his people, the church is holy because he is holy, and universal (or "catholic") in significance because he is universal in significance. Despite all its remaining imperfections here and now, the church is called to become ever more holy and catholic, for that is what it already is in Christ.

Question 63. What is the mission of the church?

The mission of the church is to bear witness to God's love for the world in Jesus Christ.

Question 64. What forms does this mission take?

The forms are as various as the forms of God's love, yet the center is always Jesus Christ. The church is faithful to its mission when it extends mercy and forgiveness to the needy in ways that point finally to him. For in the end it is always by Christ's mercy that the needs of the needy are met.

LORD'S DAY 21

Q. 54. What do you believe concerning "the Holy Catholic Church"?

A. I believe that, from the beginning to the end of the world, and from among the whole human race, the Son of God, by his Spirit and his Word, gathers, protects, and preserves for himself, in the unity of the true faith, a congregation chosen for eternal life. Moreover, I believe that I am and forever will remain a living member of it.

accepted time invite and draw them to Jesus Christ, by his Word and Spirit; savingly enlightening their minds, renewing and powerfully determining their wills, so as they (although in themselves dead in sin) are hereby made willing and able, freely to answer his call, and to accept and embrace the grace offered and conveyed therein.

Q. 68. Are the elect only effectually called?
A. All the elect, and they only, are effectually called; although others may be, and often are, outwardly called by the ministry of the Word, and have some common operations of the Spirit, who, for their willful neglect and contempt of the grace offered to them, being justly left in their unbelief, do never truly come to Jesus Christ.

Q. 69. What is the communion in grace, which the members of the invisible church have with Christ?
A. The communion in grace, which the members of the invisible church have with Christ, is their partaking of the virtue of his mediation, in their justification, adoption, sanctification, and whatever else in this life manifests their union with him.

Q. 70. What is justification?
A. Justification is an act of God's free grace unto sinners, in which he pardoneth all their sin, accepteth and accounteth their persons righteous in his sight; not for anything wrought in them, or done by them, but only for the perfect obedience and full satisfaction of Christ, by God imputed to them and received by faith alone.

Q. 71. How is justification an act of God's free grace?
A. Although Christ by his obedience and death, did make a proper, real, and full satisfaction to God's justice in the behalf of them that are justified: yet inasmuch as God accepteth the satisfaction from a surety, which he might have demanded of them; and did provide this surety, his only Son, imputing his righteousness to them, and requiring nothing of them for their justification, but faith, which also is his gift, their justification is to them of free grace.

Q. 72. What is justifying faith?
A. Justifying faith is a saving grace, wrought in the heart of a sinner, by the Spirit and the Word of God; whereby he, being convinced of his sin and misery, and of the disability in himself and all other creatures to recover him out of his lost condition,

Question 65. Who are the needy?
The hungry need bread, the homeless need a roof, the oppressed need justice, and the lonely need fellowship. At the same time—on another and deeper level—the hopeless need hope, sinners need forgiveness, and the world needs the gospel. On this level no one is excluded, and all the needy are one. Our mission as the church is to bring hope to a desperate world by declaring God's undying love—as one beggar tells another where to find bread.

Question 66. What do you affirm when you speak of "the communion of saints"?
All those who live in union with Christ, whether on earth or with God in heaven, are "saints." Our communion with Christ makes us members one of another. As by his death he removed our separation from God, so by his Spirit he removes all that divides us from each other. Breaking down every wall of hostility, he makes us, who are many, one body in himself. The ties that bind us in Christ are deeper than any other human relationship.

Question 67. How do you enter into communion with Christ and so with one another?
By the power of the Holy Spirit as it works through Word and sacrament. Because the Spirit uses them for our salvation, Word and sacrament are called "means of grace." The Scriptures acknowledge two sacraments as instituted by our Lord Jesus Christ—baptism and the Lord's Supper.

Question 68. What is a sacrament?
A sacrament is a special act of Chris-

Q. 55. What do you understand by "the communion of saints"?
A. First, that believers one and all, as partakers of the Lord Christ, and all his treasures and gifts, shall share in one fellowship. Second, that each one ought to know that he is obliged to use his gifts freely and with joy for the benefit and welfare of other members.

Q. 56. What do you believe concerning "the forgiveness of sins"?
A. That, for the sake of Christ's reconciling work, God will no more remember my sins or the sinfulness with which I have to struggle all my life long; but that he graciously imparts to me the righteousness of Christ so that I may never come into condemnation.

LORD'S DAY 22
Q. 57. What comfort does "the resurrection of the body" give you?
A. That after this life my soul shall be immediately taken up to Christ, its Head, and that this flesh of mine, raised by the power of Christ, shall be reunited with my soul, and be conformed to the glorious body of Christ.

not only assenteth to the truth of the promise of the gospel, but receiveth and resteth upon Christ and his righteousness therein held forth, for pardon of sin, and for the accepting and accounting of his person righteous in the sight of God for salvation.

Q. 73. How doth faith justify a sinner in the sight of God?
A. Faith justifies a sinner in the sight of God, not because of those other graces which do always accompany it, or of good works that are the fruits of it; nor as if the grace of faith, or any act thereof, were imputed to him for justification; but only as it is an instrument, by which he receiveth and applieth Christ and his righteousness.

Q. 74. What is adoption?
A. Adoption is an act of the free grace of God, in and for his only Son Jesus Christ, whereby all those that are justified are received into the number of his children, have his name put upon them, the Spirit of his Son given to them, are under his Fatherly care and dispensations, admitted to all the liberties and privileges of the sons of God, made heirs of all the promises, and fellow heirs with Christ in glory.

Q. 75. What is sanctification?
A. Sanctification is a work of God's grace, whereby they, whom God hath, before the foundation of the world, chosen to be holy, are, in time, through the powerful operation of his Spirit, applying the death and resurrection of Christ unto them, renewed in their whole man after the image of God; having the seeds of repentance unto life, and all other saving graces, put into their hearts, and those graces so stirred up, increased and strengthened, as that they more and more die unto sin, and rise into newness of life.

Q. 76. What is repentance unto life?
A. Repentance unto life is a saving grace, wrought in the heart of a sinner by the Spirit and Word of God, whereby out of the sight and sense, not only of the danger, but also of the filthiness and odiousness of his sins, and upon the apprehension of God's mercy in Christ to such as are penitent, he so grieves for, and hates his sins, as that he turns from them all to God, purposing and endeavoring constantly to walk with him in all the ways of new obedience.

Q. 77. Wherein do justification and sanctification differ?
A. Although sanctification be inseparably joined with justifica-

tian worship, instituted by Christ, which uses a visible sign to proclaim the promise of the gospel for the forgiveness of sins and eternal life. The sacramental sign seals this promise to believers by grace and brings to them what is promised. In baptism the sign is that of water; in the Lord's Supper, that of bread and wine.

Question 69. How do you understand the relationship between the word of promise and the sacramental sign?

Take away the word of promise, and the water is merely water, or the bread and wine, merely bread and wine. But add water, or bread and wine, to the word of promise, and it becomes a visible word. In this form it does what by grace the word always does: it brings the salvation it promises, and conveys to faith the real presence of our Lord Jesus Christ. The sacraments are visible words which uniquely assure and confirm that no matter how greatly I may have sinned, Christ died also for me, and comes to live in me and with me.

Question 70. What is the main difference between baptism and the Lord's Supper?

While I receive baptism only once, I receive the Lord's Supper again and again. Being unrepeatable, baptism indicates not only that Christ died for our sins once and for all, but that by grace we are also united with him once and for all through faith. Being repeatable, the Lord's Supper indicates that as we turn unfilled to him again and again, our Lord continually meets us in the power of the Holy Spirit to renew and deepen our faith.

Question 71. What is baptism?

Q. 58. What comfort does the article concerning "the life everlasting" give you?

A. That, since I now feel in my heart the beginning of eternal joy, I shall possess, after this life, perfect blessedness, which no eye has seen, nor ear heard, nor the heart of man conceived, and thereby praise God forever.

LORD'S DAY 23

Q. 59. But how does it help you now that you believe all this?

A. That I am righteous in Christ before God, and an heir of eternal life.

Q. 60. How are you righteous before God?

A. Only by true faith in Jesus Christ. In spite of the fact that my conscience accuses me that I have grievously sinned against all the commandments of God, and have not kept any one of them, and that I am still ever prone to all that is evil, nevertheless, God, without any merit of my own, out of pure grace, grants me the benefits of the perfect expiation of Christ, imputing to me his righteousness and holiness as if I had never committed a single sin or had ever been sinful, having fulfilled myself all the obedience which Christ has carried out for me, if only I accept such favor with a trusting heart.

Q. 61. Why do you say that you are righteous by faith alone?

A. Not because I please God by virtue of the worthiness of my faith, but because the satisfaction, righteousness, and holiness of Christ alone are my righteousness before God, and because I can accept it and make it mine in no other way than by faith alone.

tion, yet they differ in that God, in justification, imputeth the righteousness of Christ; in sanctification, his Spirit infuseth grace, and enableth to the exercise thereof; in the former, sin is pardoned; in the other, it is subdued; the one doth equally free all believers from the revenging wrath of God, and that perfectly in this life, that they never fall into condemnation; the other is neither equal in all, nor in this life perfect in any, but growing up to perfection.

Q. 78. Whence ariseth the imperfection of sanctification in believers?

A. The imperfection of sanctification in believers ariseth from the remnants of sin abiding in every part of them, and the perpetual lusting of the flesh against the Spirit; whereby they are often foiled with temptations, and fall into many sins, are hindered in all their spiritual service, and their best works are imperfect and defiled in the sight of God.

Q. 79. May not true believers, by reason of their imperfections, and the many temptations and sins they are overtaken with, fall away from the state of grace?

A. True believers, by reason of the unchangeable love of God, and his decree and covenant to give them perseverance, their inseparable union with Christ, his continual intercession for them, and the Spirit and seed of God abiding in them, can neither totally nor finally fall away from the state of grace, but are kept by the power of God through faith unto salvation.

Q. 80. Can true believers be infallibly assured that they are in the estate of grace, and that they shall persevere therein unto salvation?

A. Such as truly believe in Christ, and endeavor to walk in all good conscience before him, may, without extraordinary revelation, by faith grounded upon the truth of God's promises, and by the Spirit enabling them to discern in themselves those graces to which the promises of life are made, and bearing witness with their spirits that they are the children of God, be infallibly assured that they are in the estate of grace, and shall persevere therein unto salvation.

Q. 81. Are all true believers at all times assured of their present being in the estate of grace, and that they shall be saved?

A. Assurance of grace and salvation not being of the essence of faith, true believers may wait long before they obtain it; and, after the enjoyment thereof, may have it weakened and inter-

Baptism is the sign and seal through which we are joined to Christ.

Question 72. What does it mean to be baptized?

My baptism means that I am joined to Jesus Christ forever. I am baptized into his death and resurrection, along with all who have received him by faith. As I am baptized with water, he baptizes me with his Spirit, washing away all my sins and freeing me from their control. My baptism is a sign that one day I will rise with him in glory, and may walk with him even now in newness of life.

Question 73. Are infants also to be baptized?

Yes. Along with their believing parents, they are included in the great hope of the gospel and belong to the people of God. Forgiveness and faith are both promised to them as gifts through Christ's covenant with his people. These children are therefore to be received into the community by baptism, nurtured in the Word of God, and confirmed at an appropriate time by their own profession of faith.

Question 74. Should infants be baptized if their parents or guardians have no relation to the church?

No. It would be irresponsible to baptize an infant without at least one Christian parent or guardian who promises to nurture the infant in the life of the community and to instruct it in the Christian faith.

Question 75. In what name are you baptized?

In the name of the Trinity. After he was raised from the dead, our Lord appeared to his disciples and said to

LORD'S DAY 24

Q. 62. But why cannot our good works be our righteousness before God, or at least a part of it?
A. Because the righteousness which can stand before the judgment of God must be absolutely perfect and wholly in conformity with the divine Law. But even our best works in this life are all imperfect and defiled with sin.

Q. 63. Will our good works merit nothing, even when it is God's purpose to reward them in this life, and in the future life as well?
A. This reward is not given because of merit, but out of grace.

Q. 64. But does not this teaching make people careless and sinful?
A. No, for it is impossible for those who are ingrafted into Christ by true faith not to bring forth the fruit of gratitude.

The Holy Sacraments

LORD'S DAY 25

Q. 65. Since, then, faith alone makes us share in Christ and all his benefits, where does such faith originate?
A. The Holy Spirit creates it in our hearts by the preaching of the holy gospel, and confirms it by the use of the holy Sacraments.

Q. 66. What are the Sacraments?
A. They are visible, holy signs and seals instituted by God in order that by their use he may the more fully disclose and seal to us the promise of the gospel, namely, that because of the one sacrifice of Christ accomplished on the cross he graciously grants us the forgiveness of sins and eternal life.

Q. 67. Are both the Word and the Sacraments designed to direct our

mitted, through manifold distempers, sins, temptations, and desertions; yet are they never left without such a presence and support of the Spirit of God, as keeps them from sinking into utter despair.

Q. 82. What is the communion in glory which the members of the invisible church have with Christ?

A. The communion in glory which the members of the invisible church have with Christ, is in this life, immediately after death, and at last perfected at the resurrection and day of judgment.

Q. 83. What is the communion in glory with Christ, which the members of the invisible church enjoy in this life?

A. The members of the invisible church have communicated to them, in this life, the first fruits of glory with Christ, as they are members of him their head, and so in him are interested in that glory which he is fully possessed of; and as an earnest thereof, enjoy the sense of God's love, peace of conscience, joy in the Holy Ghost, and hope of glory. As, on the contrary, the sense of God's revenging wrath, horror of conscience, and a fearful expectation of judgment, are to the wicked the beginning of the torment which they shall endure after death.

Q. 84. Shall all men die?

A. Death being threatened as the wages of sin, it is appointed unto all men once to die; for that all have sinned.

Q. 85. Death being the wages of sin, why are not the righteous delivered from death, seeing all their sins are forgiven in Christ?

A. The righteous shall be delivered from death itself at the last day, and even in death are delivered from the sting and curse of it; so that although they die, yet it is out of God's love, to free them perfectly from sin and misery, and to make them capable of further communion with Christ in glory, which they then enter upon.

Q. 86. What is the communion in glory with Christ, which the members of the invisible church enjoy immediately after death?

A. The communion in glory with Christ, which the members of the invisible church enjoy immediately after death, is in that their souls are then made perfect in holiness,and received into the highest heavens, where they behold the face of God in light

266

them, "Go and make disciples of all nations, baptizing them in the name of the Father and of the Son and of the Holy Spirit" (Matt. 28:19).

Question 76. What is the meaning of this name?

It is the name of the Holy Trinity. The Father is God, the Son is God, and the Holy Spirit is God. And yet they are not three gods, but one God in three persons. We worship God in this mystery.

Question 77. What is the Lord's Supper?

The Lord's Supper is the sign and seal by which our communion with Christ is renewed.

Question 78. What does it mean to share in the Lord's Supper?

When we celebrate the Lord's Supper, the Lord Jesus Christ is truly present, pouring out his Spirit upon us. By his Spirit, the bread that we break and the cup that we bless share in our Lord's own body and blood. Through them he once offered our life to God; through them he now offers his life to us. As I receive the bread and the cup, remembering that Christ died even for me, I feed on him in my heart by faith with thanksgiving, and enter his risen life, so that his life becomes mine, and my life becomes his, to all eternity.

Question 79. Who may receive the Lord's Supper?

All baptized Christians who rejoice in so great a gift, who confess their sins, and who draw near with faith intending to lead a new life, may receive the Lord's Supper. This includes baptized children who have expressed a desire to participate, and who have been

faith to the one sacrifice of Jesus Christ on the cross as the only ground of our salvation?
A. Yes, indeed, for the Holy Spirit teaches in the gospel and confirms by the holy Sacraments that our whole salvation is rooted in the one sacrifice of Christ offered for us on the cross.

Q. 68. How many Sacraments has Christ instituted in the New Testament?
A. Two, holy Baptism and the holy Supper.

Holy Baptism

LORD'S DAY 26
Q. 69. How does holy Baptism remind and assure you that the one sacrifice of Christ on the cross avails for you?
A. In this way: Christ has instituted this external washing with water and by it has promised that I am as certainly washed with his blood and Spirit from the uncleanness of my soul and from all my sins, as I am washed externally with water which is used to remove the dirt from my body.

Q. 70. What does it mean to be washed with the blood and Spirit of Christ?
A. It means to have the forgiveness of sins from God, through grace, for the sake of Christ's blood which he shed for us in his sacrifice on the cross, and also to be renewed by the Holy Spirit and sanctified as members of Christ, so that we may more and more die unto sin and live in a consecrated and blameless way.

Q. 71. Where has Christ promised that we are as certainly washed with

and glory; waiting for the full redemption of their bodies, which even in death continue united to Christ, and rest in their graves as in their beds, till at the last day they be again united to their souls. Whereas the souls of the wicked are at their death cast into hell, where they remain in torments and utter darkness; and their bodies kept in their graves, as in their prisons, until the resurrection and judgment of the great day.

Q. 87. What are we to believe concerning the resurrection?
A. We are to believe that, at the last day, there shall be a general resurrection of the dead, both of the just and unjust; when they that are then found alive shall in a moment be changed; and the selfsame bodies of the dead which are laid in the grave, being then again united to their souls forever, shall be raised up by the power of Christ. The bodies of the just, by the Spirit of Christ, and by virtue of his resurrection as their head, shall be raised in power, spiritual, and incorruptible, and made like to his glorious body: and the bodies of the wicked shall be raised up in dishonor by him as an offended judge.

Q. 88. What shall immediately follow after the resurrection?
A. Immediately after the resurrection shall follow the general and final judgment of angels and men, the day and hour whereof no man knoweth, that all may watch and pray, and be ever ready for the coming of the Lord.

Q. 89. What shall be done to the wicked at the day of judgment?
A. At the day of judgment, the wicked shall be set on Christ's left hand, and upon clear evidence, and full conviction of their own consciences, shall have the fearful but just sentence of condemnation pronounced against them; and thereupon shall be cast out from the favorable presence of God, and the glorious fellowship with Christ, his saints, and all his holy angels, into hell, to be punished with unspeakable torments both of body and soul, with the devil and his angels forever.

Q. 90. What shall be done to the righteous at the day of judgment?
A. At the day of judgment, the righteous, being caught up to Christ in the clouds, shall be set on his right hand, and, there openly acknowledged and acquitted, shall join with him in the judging of reprobate angels and men; and shall be received into heaven, where they shall be fully and forever freed from all sin

instructed in the meaning of the sacrament in a way they can understand.

Question 80. What do you mean when you speak of "the forgiveness of sins"?

That because of Jesus Christ, God no longer holds my sins against me. Christ alone is my righteousness and my life; Christ is my only hope. Grace alone, not my merits, is the basis on which God has forgiven me in him. Faith alone, not my works, is the means by which I receive Christ into my heart, and with him the forgiveness that makes me whole. Christ alone, grace alone, and faith alone bring the forgiveness I receive through the gospel.

Question 81. Does forgiveness mean that God condones sin?

No. God does not cease to be God. Although God is merciful, God does not condone what God forgives. In the death and resurrection of Christ, God judges what God abhors everything hostile to love—by abolishing it at the very roots. In this judgment the unexpected occurs: good is brought out of evil, hope out of hopelessness, and life out of death. God spares sinners, and turns them from enemies into friends. The uncompromising judgment of God is revealed in the suffering love of the cross.

Question 82. Does your forgiveness of those who have harmed you depend on their repentance?

No. I am to forgive as I have been forgiven. The gospel is the astonishing good news that while we were yet sinners Christ died for us. Just as God's forgiveness of me is unconditional, and so precedes my confession of sin

his blood and Spirit as with the water of baptism?

A. In the institution of Baptism which runs thus: "Go therefore and make disciples of all nations, baptizing them in the name of the Father and of the Son and of the Holy Spirit." "He who believes and is baptized will be saved: but he who does not believe will be condemned." This promise is also repeated where the Scriptures call baptism "the water of rebirth" and the washing away of sins.

LORD'S DAY 27

Q. 72. Does merely the outward washing with water itself wash away sins?

A. No; for only the blood of Jesus Christ and the Holy Spirit cleanse us from all sins.

Q. 73. Then why does the Holy Spirit call baptism the water of rebirth and the washing away of sins?

A. God does not speak in this way except for a strong reason. Not only does he teach us by Baptism that just as the dirt of the body is taken away by water, so our sins are removed by the blood and Spirit of Christ; but more important still, by the divine pledge and sign he wishes to assure us that we are just as truly washed from our sins spiritually as our bodies are washed with water.

Q. 74. Are infants also to be baptized?

A. Yes, because they, as well as their parents, are included in the covenant and belong to the people of God. Since both redemption from sin through the blood of Christ and the gift of faith from the Holy Spirit are promised to

and misery; filled with inconceivable joy; made perfectly holy and happy both in body and soul, in the company of innumerable saints and angels, but especially in the immediate vision and fruition of God the Father, of our Lord Jesus Christ, and of the Holy Spirit, to all eternity. And this is the perfect and full communion, which the members of the invisible church shall enjoy with Christ in glory, at the resurrection and day of judgment.

and repentance, so my forgiveness of those who have harmed me does not depend on their confessing and repenting of their sin. However, when I forgive the person who has done me harm, giving up any resentment or desire to retaliate, I do not condone the harm that was done or excuse the evil of the sin.

Question 83. How can you forgive those who have really hurt you?

I cannot love my enemies, I cannot pray for those who persecute me, I cannot even be ready to forgive those who have really hurt me, without the grace that comes from above. I cannot be conformed to the image of God's Son, apart from the power of God's Word and Spirit. Yet I am promised that I can do all things through Christ who strengthens me.

Question 84. What do you mean when you speak of "the resurrection of the body"?

Because Christ lives, we will live also. The resurrection of the body celebrates our eternal value to God as living persons, each one with a unique and distinctive identity. Indeed, the living Savior who goes before us was once heard, seen, and touched in person, after the discovery of his empty tomb. The resurrection of the body means hope for the whole person, because it is in the unity of body and soul, not in soul alone, that I belong in life and in death to my faithful Savior Jesus Christ.

Question 85. What is the nature of resurrection hope?

Resurrection hope is a hope for the transformation of this world, not a hope for escape from it. It is the hope

these children no less than to their parents, infants are also by baptism, as a sign of the covenant, to be incorporated into the Christian church and distinguished from the children of unbelievers. This was done in the Old Covenant by circumcision. In the New Covenant baptism has been instituted to take its place.

The Holy Supper

LORD'S DAY 28

Q. 75. How are you reminded and assured in the Holy Supper that you participate in the one sacrifice of Christ on the cross and in all his benefits?

A. In this way: Christ has commanded me and all believers to eat of this broken bread, and to drink of this cup in remembrance of him. He has thereby promised that his body was offered and broken on the cross for me, and his blood was shed for me, as surely as I see with my eyes that the bread of the Lord is broken for me, and that the cup is shared with me. Also, he has promised that he himself as certainly feeds and nourishes my soul to everlasting life with his crucified body and shed blood as I receive from the hand of the minister and actually taste the bread and the cup of the Lord which are given to me as sure signs of the body and blood of Christ.

Q. 76. What does it mean to eat the crucified body of Christ and to drink his shed blood?

A. It is not only to embrace with a trusting heart the whole passion and death of Christ, and by it to receive the forgiveness of sins and eternal life. In addition, it is to be so united more and

THE LARGER CATECHISM

that evil in all its forms will be utterly eradicated, that past history will be redeemed, and that all the things that ever were will be made new. It is the hope of a new creation, a new heaven and a new earth, in which God is really honored as God, human beings are truly loving, and peace and justice reign on earth.

Question 86. Does resurrection hope mean that we don't have to take action to relieve the suffering of this world?

No. When the great hope is truly alive, small hopes arise even now for alleviating the sufferings of the present time. Reconciliation—with God, with one another, and with oneself—is the great hope God has given to the world. While we commit to God the needs of the whole world in our prayers, we also know that we are commissioned to be instruments of God's peace. When hostility, injustice and suffering are overcome here and now, we anticipate the end of all things—the life that God brings out of death, which is the meaning of resurrection hope.

Question 87. What do you affirm when you speak of "the life everlasting"?

That God does not will to be God without us, but instead grants to us creatures—fallen and mortal as we are—eternal life. Communion with Jesus Christ is eternal life itself. In him we were chosen before the foundation of the world. By him the eternal covenant with Israel was taken up, embodied, and fulfilled. To him we are joined by the Holy Spirit through faith, and adopted as children, the sons and daughters of God. Through him

more to his blessed body by the Holy Spirit dwelling both in Christ and in us that, although he is in heaven and we are on earth, we are nevertheless flesh of his flesh and bone of his bone, always living and being governed by one Spirit, as the members of our bodies are governed by one soul.

Q. 77. Where has Christ promised that he will feed and nourish believers with his body and blood just as surely as they eat of this broken bread and drink of this cup?

A. In the institution of the holy Supper which reads: The Lord Jesus on the night when he was betrayed took bread, and when he had given thanks, he broke it, and said, "this is my body which is for you. Do this in remembrance of me." In the same way also the cup, after supper, saying, "this cup is the new covenant in my blood. Do this, as often as you drink it, in remembrance of me." For as often as you eat this bread and drink the cup, you proclaim the Lord's death until he comes.

This promise is also repeated by the apostle Paul: When we bless "the cup of blessing," is it not a means of sharing in the blood of Christ? When we break the bread, is it not a means of sharing the body of Christ? Because there is one loaf, we, many as we are, are one body; for it is one loaf of which we all partake.

LORD'S DAY 29

Q. 78. Do the bread and wine become the very body and blood of Christ?

A. No, for as the water in baptism is not changed into the blood of Christ, nor becomes the washing away of sins

THE LARGER CATECHISM

we are raised from death to new life. For him we shall live to all eternity.

Question 88. Won't heaven be a boring place?

No. Heaven is our true home, a world of love. There the Spirit shall be poured out into every heart in perfect love. There the Father and the Son are united in the loving bond of the Spirit. There we shall be united with them and one another. There we shall at last see face to face what we now only glimpse as through a distant mirror. Our deepest, truest delights in this life are only a dim foreshadowing of the delights that await us in heaven. "You show me the path of life. In your presence there is fullness of joy; in your right hand are pleasures forevermore" (Ps. 16:11).

by itself, but is only a divine sign and confirmation of it, so also in the Lord's Supper the sacred bread does not become the body of Christ itself, although, in accordance with the nature and usage of sacraments, it is called the body of Christ.

Q. 79. Then why does Christ call the bread his body, and the cup his blood, or the New Covenant in his blood, and why does the apostle Paul call the Supper "a means of sharing" in the body and blood of Christ?

A. Christ does not speak in this way except for a strong reason. He wishes to teach us by it that as bread and wine sustain this temporal life so his crucified body and shed blood are the true food and drink of our souls for eternal life. Even more, he wishes to assure us by this visible sign and pledge that we come to share in his true body and blood through the working of the Holy Spirit as surely as we receive with our mouth these holy tokens in remembrance of him, and that all his sufferings and his death are our own as certainly as if we had ourselves suffered and rendered satisfaction in our own persons.

LORD'S DAY 30
Q. 80. What difference is there between the Lord's Supper and the papal Mass?

A. The Lord's Supper testifies to us that we have complete forgiveness of all our sins through the one sacrifice of Jesus Christ which he himself has accomplished on the cross once for all; (and that through the Holy Spirit we are incorporated into Christ, who is now in heaven with his true body at the right hand of the Father and is there to be worshiped). But the Mass

THE LARGER CATECHISM

teaches that the living and the dead do not have forgiveness of sins through the sufferings of Christ unless Christ is again offered for them daily by the priest (and that Christ is bodily under the form of bread and wine and is therefore to be worshiped in them). Therefore the Mass is fundamentally a complete denial of the once for all sacrifice and passion of Jesus Christ (and as such an idolatry to be condemned).

Q. 81. Who ought to come to the table of the Lord?
A. Those who are displeased with themselves for their sins, and who nevertheless trust that these sins have been forgiven them and that their remaining weakness is covered by the passion and death of Christ, and who also desire more and more to strengthen their faith and improve their life. The impenitent and hypocrites, however, eat and drink judgment to themselves.

Q. 82. Should those who show themselves to be unbelievers and enemies of God by their confession and life be admitted to this Supper?
A. No, for then the covenant of God would be profaned and his wrath provoked against the whole congregation. According to the ordinance of Christ and his apostles, therefore, the Christian church is under obligation, by the office of the keys, to exclude such persons until they amend their lives.

LORD'S DAY 31
Q. 83. What is the office of the keys?
A. The preaching of the holy gospel and Christian discipline. By these two means the kingdom of heaven is opened to believers and shut against unbelievers.

THE LARGER CATECHISM

Q. 84. How is the kingdom of heaven opened and shut by the preaching of the holy gospel?

A. In this way: The kingdom of heaven is opened when it is proclaimed and openly testified to believers, one and all, according to the command of Christ, that as often as they accept the promise of the gospel with true faith all their sins are truly forgiven them by God for the sake of Christ's gracious work. On the contrary, the wrath of God and eternal condemnation fall upon all unbelievers and hypocrites as long as they do not repent. It is according to this witness of the gospel that God will judge the one and the other in this life and in the life to come.

Q. 85. How is the kingdom of heaven shut and opened by Christian discipline?

A. In this way: Christ commanded that those who bear the Christian name in an unchristian way either in doctrine or in life should be given brotherly admonition. If they do not give up their errors or evil ways, notification is given to the church or to those ordained for this by the church. Then, if they do not change after this warning, they are forbidden to partake of the holy Sacraments and are thus excluded from the communion of the church and by God himself from the kingdom of Christ. However, if they promise and show real amendment, they are received again as members of Christ and of the church.

PART III
Thankfulness

LORD'S DAY 32
Q. 86. Since we are redeemed from our sin and its wretched consequences

THE LARGER CATECHISM

by grace through Christ without any merit of our own, why must we do good works?
A. Because just as Christ has redeemed us with his blood he also renews us through his Holy Spirit according to his own image, so that with our whole life we may show ourselves grateful to God for his goodness and that he may be glorified through us; and further, so that we ourselves may be assured of our faith by its fruits and by our reverent behavior may win our neighbors to Christ.

Q. 87. Can those who do not turn to God from their ungrateful, impenitent life be saved?
A. Certainly not! Scripture says, "Surely you know that the unjust will never come into possession of the kingdom of God. Make no mistake: no fornicator or idolater, none who are guilty either of adultery or of homosexual perversion, no thieves or grabbers or drunkards or slanderers or swindlers, will possess the kingdom of God."

LORD'S DAY 33
Q. 88. How many parts are there to the true repentance or conversion of man?
A. Two: the dying of the old self and the birth of the new.

Q. 89. What is the dying of the old self?
A. Sincere sorrow over our sins and more and more to hate them and to flee from them.

Q. 90. What is the birth of the new self?
A. Complete joy in God through Christ and a strong desire to live according to the will of God in all good works.

Having Seen What the Scriptures Principally Teach Us
to Believe Concerning God, It Follows to Consider
What They Require as the Duty of Man

[Ten Commandments]

Q. 91. What is the duty which God requireth of man?

A. The Duty which God requireth of man is obedience to his
revealed will.

Q. 92. What did God at first reveal unto man as the rule of his obedience?

A. The rule of obedience revealed to Adam in the estate of
innocence, and to all mankind in him, besides a special command, not to eat of the fruit of the tree of knowledge of good
and evil, was the moral law.

Q. 93. What is the moral law?

A. The moral law is the declaration of the will of God to
mankind, directing and binding everyone to personal, perfect,
and perpetual conformity and obedience thereunto, in the frame
and disposition of the whole man, soul and body, and in performance of all those duties of holiness and righteousness
which he oweth to God and man: promising life upon the fulfilling, and threatening death upon the breach of it.

Q. 94. Is there any use of the moral law to man since the Fall?

A. Although no man since the Fall can attain to righteousness
and life by the moral law, yet there is great use thereof, as well
common to all men, as peculiar either to the unregenerate, or
the regenerate.

Q. 95. Of what use is the moral law to all men?

A. The moral law is of use to all men, to inform them of the
holy nature and will of God, and of their duty binding them to
walk accordingly; to convince them of their disability to keep
it, and of the sinful pollution of their nature, hearts, and lives,
to humble them in the sense of their sin and misery, and thereby
help them to a clearer sight of the need they have of Christ, and
of the perfection of his obedience.

Q. 91. But what are good works?
A. Only those which are done out of true faith, in accordance with the Law of God, and for his glory, and not those based on our own opinion or on the traditions of men.

[Ten Commandments]

II. The Ten Commandments

LORD'S DAY 34

Question 89. What are the Ten Commandments?
The Ten Commandments give a summary of God's law for our lives. They teach us how to live rightly with God and one another.

Q. 92. What is the law of God?
A. God spoke all these words saying:

FIRST COMMANDMENT
"I am the Lord your God, who brought you out of the land of Egypt, out of the house of bondage. You shall have no other gods before Me."

Question 90. Why did God give this law?
After rescuing the people of Israel from their slavery in Egypt, God led them to Mount Sinai, where they received the law through Moses. It was the great charter of liberty for Israel, a people chosen to live in covenant with God and to serve as a light to the nations. It remains the charter of liberty for all who would love, know, and serve the Lord today.

SECOND COMMANDMENT
"You shall not make yourself a graven image, or any likeness of anything that is in heaven above, or that is in the earth beneath, or that is in the water under the earth; you shall not bow down to them or serve them; for I the Lord your God am a jealous God, visiting the iniquity of the fathers upon the children to the third and fourth generation of those who hate Me, but showing steadfast love to thousands of those who love Me and keep My commandments."

Question 91. Why should you obey this law?
Not to win God's love, for God already loves me. Not to earn my salvation, for Christ has earned it for me. Not to avoid being punished, for then I would obey out of fear. With gladness in my heart I should obey God's law out of gratitude, for God has blessed me by it and given it for my well-being.

THIRD COMMANDMENT
"You shall not take the name of the Lord your God in vain; for the Lord will not hold him guiltless who takes His name in vain."

Question 92. What are the uses of God's law?
God's law has three uses. First, it shows me how grievously I fail to live

FOURTH COMMANDMENT
"Remember the sabbath day, to keep it holy. Six days you shall labor, and do all your work; but the seventh day is a sabbath to the Lord your God; in it you

Q. 96. What particular use is there of the moral law to unregenerate men?
A. The moral law is of use to unregenerate men, to awaken their consciences to flee from the wrath to come, and to drive them to Christ; or, upon their continuance in the estate and way of sin, to leave them inexcusable, and under the curse thereof.

Q. 97. What special use is there of the moral law to the regenerate?
A. Although they that are regenerate and believe in Christ be delivered from the moral law as a covenant of works, so as thereby they are neither justified nor condemned: yet, besides the general uses thereof common to them with all men, it is of special use to show them how much they are bound to Christ for his fulfilling it, and enduring the curse thereof, in their stead and for their good; and thereby to provoke them to more thankfulness, and to express the same in their greater care to conform themselves thereunto as the rule of their obedience.

Q. 98. Wherein is the moral law summarily comprehended?
A. The moral law is summarily comprehended in the Ten Commandments, which were delivered by the voice of God upon Mount Sinai, and written by him on two tables of stone; and are recorded in the twentieth chapter of Exodus; the first four commandments containing our duty to God, and the other six our duty to man.

Q. 99. What rules are to be observed for the right understanding of the Ten Commandments?
A. For the right understanding of the Ten Commandments, these rules are to be observed:
1. That the law is perfect, and bindeth everyone to full conformity in the whole man unto the righteousness thereof, and unto entire obedience forever; so as to require the utmost perfection of every duty, and to forbid the least degree of every sin.
2. That it is spiritual, and so reacheth the understanding, will, affections, and all other powers of the soul; as well as words, works, and gestures.
3. That one and the same thing, in divers respects, is required or forbidden in several commandments.
4. That as, where a duty is commanded, the contrary sin is forbidden; and where a sin is forbidden, the contrary duty is commanded; so, where a promise is annexed, the contrary threatening is included; and where a threatening is annexed, the contrary promise is included.

according to God's will, driving me to pray for God's mercy. Second, it functions to restrain even the worst of sinners through the fear of punishment. Finally, it teaches me how to live a life which bears witness to the gospel, and spurs me on to do so.

shall not do any work, you, or your son, or your daughter, your manservant, or your maidservant, or your cattle, or the sojourner who is within your gates; for in six days the Lord made heaven and earth, the sea, and all that is in them, and rested the seventh day; therefore the Lord blessed the sabbath day and hallowed it."

FIFTH COMMANDMENT
"Honor your father and your mother, that your days may be long in the land which the Lord your God gives you."

SIXTH COMMANDMENT
"You shall not kill."

SEVENTH COMMANDMENT
"You shall not commit adultery."

EIGHTH COMMANDMENT
"You shall not steal."

NINTH COMMANDMENT
"You shall not bear false witness against your neighbor."

TENTH COMMANDMENT
"You shall not covet your neighbor's house; you shall not covet your neighbor's wife, or his manservant, or his maidservant, or his ox, or his ass, or anything that is your neighbor's."

Q. 93. How are these commandments divided?
A. Into two tables, the first of which teaches us in four commandments how we ought to live in relation to God; the other, in six commandments, what we owe to our neighbor.

5. That what God forbids, is at no time to be done; what he commands is always our duty; and yet every particular duty is not to be done at all times.

6. That, under one sin or duty, all of the same kind are forbidden or commanded; together with all the causes, means, occasions, and appearances thereof, and provocations thereunto.

7. That what is forbidden or commanded to ourselves, we are bound, according to our places, to endeavor that it may be avoided or performed by others, according to the duty of their places.

8. That in what is commanded to others, we are bound, according to our places and callings, to be helpful to them: and to take heed of partaking with others in what is forbidden them.

Q. 100. What special things are we to consider in the Ten Commandments?

A. We are to consider in the Ten Commandments: the preface, the substances of the commandments themselves, and the several reasons annexed to some of them the more to enforce them.

Q. 101. What is the preface to the Ten Commandments?

A. The preface to the Ten Commandments is contained in these words: "I am the Lord thy God, which have brought thee out of the land of Egypt, out of the house of bondage." Wherein God manifesteth his sovereignty, as being Jehovah, the eternal, immutable, and almighty God; having his being in and of himself, and giving being to all his words and works; and that he is a God in covenant, as with Israel of old, so with all his people; who as he brought them out of their bondage in Egypt, so he delivered us from our spiritual thralldom; and that therefore we are bound to take him for our God alone, and to keep all his commandments.

Q. 102. What is the sum of the four Commandments which contain our duty to God?

A. The sum of the four Commandments containing our duty to God is, to love the Lord our God with all our heart, and with all our soul, and with all our strength, and with all our mind.

Q. 103. Which is the First Commandment?

A. The First Commandment is, "Thou shalt have no other gods before me."

Q. 104. What are the duties required in the First Commandment?

A. The duties required in the First Commandment are: the

THE STUDY CATECHISM   HEIDELBERG CATECHISM

Question 93. What is the first com-mandment?
"You shall have no other gods before me" (Ex. 20:3; Deut. 5:7).

Question 94. What do you learn from this commandment?

Q. 94. What does the Lord require in the first commandment?
A. That I must avoid and flee all idol-atry, sorcery, enchantments, invoca-tion of saints or other creatures because of the risk of losing my salva-tion. Indeed, I ought properly to

knowing and acknowledging of God to be the only true God, and our God; and to worship and glorify him accordingly; by thinking, meditating, remembering, highly esteeming, honoring, adoring, choosing, loving, desiring, fearing of him; believing him; trusting, hoping, delighting, rejoicing in him; being zealous for him; calling upon him, giving all praise and thanks, and yielding all obedience and submission to him with the whole man; being careful in all things to please him, and sorrowful when in anything he is offended; and walking humbly with him.

Q. 105. What are the sins forbidden in the First Commandment?

A. The sins forbidden in the First Commandment are: atheism, in denying or not having a God; idolatry, in having or worshipping more gods than one, or any with, or instead of the true God; the not having and vouching him for God, and our God; the omission or neglect of anything due to him, required in this commandment; ignorance, forgetfulness, misapprehensions, false opinions, unworthy and wicked thoughts of him; bold and curious searchings into his secrets; all profaneness, hatred of God, self- love, self-seeking, and all other inordinate and immoderate setting of our mind, will, or affections upon other things, and taking them off from him in whole or in part; vain credulity, unbelief, heresy, misbelief, distrust, despair, incorrigibleness, and insensibleness under judgments, hardness of hear, pride, presumption, carnal security, tempting of God; using unlawful means, and trusting in lawful means; carnal delights and joys, corrupt, blind, and indiscreet zeal; lukewarmness, and deadness in the things of God; estranging ourselves, and apostatizing from God; praying or giving any religious worship to saints, angels, or any other creatures; all compacts and consulting with the devil, and hearkening to his suggestions; making men the lords of our faith and conscience; slighting and despising God, and his commands; resisting and grieving of his Spirit, discontent and impatience at his dispensations, charging him foolishly for the evils he inflicts on us; and ascribing the praise of any good, we either are, have, or can do, to fortune, idols, ourselves, or any other creature.

Q. 106. What are we especially taught by these words "before me," in the First Commandment?

A. These words "before me," or "before my face," in the First Commandment, teach us, that God, who seeth all things, taketh special notice of, and is much displeased with, the sin of hav-

No loyalty comes before my loyalty to God. I should worship and serve only God, expect all good from God alone, and love, fear, and honor God with all my heart.

acknowledge the only true God, trust in him alone, in humility and patience expect all good from him only, and love, fear and honor him with my whole heart. In short, I should rather turn my back on all creatures than do the least thing against his will.

Q. 95. What is idolatry?
A. It is to imagine or possess something in which to put one's trust in place of or beside the one true God who has revealed himself in his Word.

ing any other God; that so it may be an argument to dissuade from it, and to aggravate it as a most impudent provocation; as also to persuade us to do as in his sight, whatever we do in his service.

Q. 107. Which is the Second Commandment?

A. The Second Commandment is, "Thou shalt not make unto thee any graven image, or any likeness of any thing that is in heaven above, or that is in the earth beneath, or that is in the water under the earth: thou shalt not bow down thyself to them, nor serve them: for I the Lord thy God am a jealous God, visiting the iniquity of the fathers upon the children unto the third and fourth generation of them that hate me; and shewing mercy unto thousands of them that love me, and keep my commandments."

Q. 108. What are the duties required in the Second Commandment?

A. The duties required in the Second Commandment are: the receiving, observing, and keeping pure and entire, all such religious worship and ordinances as God hath instituted in his Word; particularly prayer and thanksgiving in the name of Christ; the reading, preaching, and hearing of the Word; the administration and receiving of the sacraments; church government and discipline; the ministry and maintenance thereof; religious fasting; swearing by the name of God; and vowing unto him: as also the disapproving, detesting, opposing all false worship; and, according to each one's place and calling, removing it, and all monuments of idolatry.

Q. 109. What are the sins forbidden in the Second Commandment?

A. The sins forbidden in the Second Commandment are: all devising, counseling, commanding, using, and any wise approving any religious worship not instituted by God himself; the making any representation of God, of all, or of any of the three Persons, either inwardly in our mind, or outwardly in any kind of image or likeness of any creature whatsoever; all worshiping of it, or God in it or by it; the making of any representation of feigned deities, and all worship of them, or service belonging to them; all superstitious devices, corrupting the worship of God, adding to it, or taking from it, whether invented and taken up of ourselves, or received by tradition from others, though under the title of antiquity, custom, devotion, good intent, or any other pretense whatsoever; simony,

Question 95. What is the second commandment?

"You shall not make for yourself an idol" (Ex. 20:4; Deut. 5:8).

Q. 96. What does God require in the second commandment?

A. That we should not represent him or worship him in any other manner than he has commanded in his word.

Question 96. What do you learn from this commandment?

First, when I treat anything other than God as though it were God, I practice idolatry. Second, when I assume that my own interests are more important than anything else, I make them into idols, and in effect make an idol of myself.

Q. 97. Should we, then, not make any images at all?

A. God cannot and should not be pictured in any way. As for creatures, although they may indeed be portrayed, God forbids making or having any likeness of them in order to worship them, or to use them to serve him.

Q. 98. But may not pictures be tolerated in churches in place of books for unlearned people?

A. No, for we must not try to be wiser than God who does not want his people to be taught by means of lifeless idols, but through the living preaching of his Word.

sacrilege; all neglect, contempt, hindering, and opposing the worship and ordinances which God hath appointed.

Q. 110. What are the reasons annexed to the Second Commandment, the more to enforce it?

A. The reasons annexed to the Second Commandment, the more to enforce it, contained in these words, "For I the Lord thy God am a jealous God, visiting the iniquity of the fathers upon the children unto the third and fourth generation of them that hate me; and shewing mercy unto thousands of them that love me, and keep my commandments;" are, besides God's sovereignty over us, and propriety in us, his revengeful indignation against all false worship, as being a spiritual whoredom; accounting the breakers of this Commandment such as hate him, and threatening to punish them unto divers generations, and esteeming the observers of it such as love him and keep his commandments, and promising mercy to them unto many generations.

Q. 111. What is the Third Commandment?

A. The Third Commandment is, "Thou shalt not take the name of the Lord thy God in vain; for the Lord will not hold him guiltless that taketh his name in vain."

Q. 112. What is required in the Third Commandment?

A. The Third Commandment requires, that the name of God, his titles, attributes, ordinances, the word, sacraments, prayer, oaths, vows, lots, his works, and whatsoever else there is whereby he makes himself known, be holily and reverently used in thought, meditation, word, and writing; by an holy profession, and answerable conversation, to the glory of God, and the good of ourselves and others.

Q. 113. What are the sins forbidden in the Third Commandment?

A. The sins forbidden in the Third Commandment are: the not using of God's name as is required; and the abuse of it in an ignorant, vain, irreverent, profane, superstitious, or wicked mentioning or otherwise using the titles, attributes, ordinances, or works; by blasphemy; perjury; all sinful cursing, oaths, vows, and lots; violating our oaths and vows, if lawful; and fulfilling them, if of things unlawful; murmuring and quarreling at, curious prying into and misapplying of God's decrees and providence; misinterpreting, misapplying, or any way perverting the Word, or any part of it, to profane jests, curious and unprofitable questions, vain janglings, or the maintaining of false doctrines; abusing it, the creatures, or anything contained

Question 97. What is the third commandment?

"You shall not make wrongful use of the name of the Lord your God" (Ex. 20:7; Deut. 5:11).

Question 98. What do you learn from this commandment?

I should use God's name with reverence and awe. God's name is taken in vain when used to support wrong. It is insulted when used carelessly, as in a curse or a pious cliché.

Q. 99. What is required in the third commandment?

A. That we must not profane or abuse the name of God by cursing, by perjury, or by unnecessary oaths. Nor are we to participate in such horrible sins by keeping quiet and thus giving silent consent. In a word, we must not use the holy name of God except with fear and reverence so that he may be rightly confessed and addressed by us, and be glorified in all our words and works.

Q. 100. Is it, therefore, so great a sin to blaspheme God's name by cursing and swearing that God is also angry with those who do not try to prevent and forbid it as much as they can?

A. Yes, indeed; for no sin is greater or provokes his wrath more than the profaning of his name. That is why he commanded it to be punished with death.

Q. 101. But may we not swear oaths by the name of God in a devout manner?

under the name of God, to charms, or sinful lusts and practices; the maligning, scorning, reviling, or any way opposing of God's truth, grace, and ways; making profession of religion in hypocrisy, or for sinister ends; being ashamed of it, or a shame to it, by uncomfortable, unwise, unfruitful, and offensive walking or backsliding from it.

Q. 114. What reasons are annexed to the Third Commandment?
A. The reasons annexed to the Third Commandment, in these words, "the Lord thy God," and, "for the Lord will not hold him guiltless that taketh his name in vain," are because he is the Lord and our God, therefore his name is not to be profaned, or any way abused by us; especially because he will be so far from acquitting and sparing the transgressors of this Commandment, as that he will not suffer them to escape his righteous judgment, albeit many such escape the censures and punishments of men.

Q. 115. Which is the Fourth Commandment?
A. The Fourth Commandment is, "Remember the sabbath day, to keep it holy. Six days shalt thou labour, and do all thy work: but the seventh day is the sabbath of the Lord thy God: in it thou shalt not do any work, thou, nor thy son, nor thy daughter, thy manservant, nor thy maidservant, nor thy cattle, nor thy stranger that is within thy gates; for in six days the Lord made heaven and earth, the sea, and all that in them is, and rested the seventh day: wherefore the Lord blessed the sabbath day, and hallowed it."

Q. 116. What is required in the Fourth Commandment?
A. The Fourth Commandment requireth of all men the sanctifying or keeping holy to God such set times as he hath appointed in his Word, expressly one whole day in seven; which was the seventh from the beginning of the world to the resurrection of Christ, and the first day of the week ever since, and so to continue to the end of the world; which is the Christian Sabbath, and in the New Testament called "the Lord's Day."

Q. 117. How is the Sabbath or Lord's Day to be sanctified?
A. The Sabbath, or Lord's Day, is to be sanctified by an holy resting all that day, not only from such works as are at all times sinful, but even from such worldly employments and recreations as are on other days lawful; and making it our delight to spend the whole time (except so much of it as is to be taken up

THE STUDY CATECHISM	HEIDELBERG CATECHISM

A. Yes, when the civil authorities require it of their subjects, or when it is otherwise needed to maintain and promote fidelity and truth, to the glory of God and the welfare of our neighbor. Such oath- taking is grounded in God's Word and has therefore been rightly used by God's people under the Old and New Covenants.

Q. 102. May we also swear by the saints or other creatures?
A. No; for a lawful oath is a calling upon God, as the only searcher of hearts, to bear witness to the truth, and to punish me if I swear falsely. No creature deserves such honor

LORD'S DAY 38

Question 99. What is the fourth commandment?
"Remember the Sabbath Day, and keep it holy" (Ex. 20:8; Deut. 5:12).

Q. 103. What does God require in the fourth commandment?
A. First, that the ministry of the gospel and Christian education be maintained, and that I diligently attend church, especially on the Lord's day, to hear the Word of God, to participate in the holy Sacraments, to call publicly upon the Lord, and to give Christian service to those in need. Second, that I cease from my evil works all the days of my life, allow the Lord to work in me through his Spirit, and thus begin in this life the eternal Sabbath.

Question 100. What do you learn from this commandment?
God requires a special day to be set apart so that worship can be at the center of my life. It is right to honor God with thanks
and praise, and to hear and receive God's Word, so that I may have it in my heart, and on my lips, and put it into practice in my life.

Question 101. Why set aside one day a week as a day of rest?
First, working people should not be taken advantage of by their employers (Deut. 5:14). My job should not be my tyrant, for my life is more than my work. Second, God requires me to put time aside for the regular study of Holy Scripture and for prayer, not only by myself but also with others, not least those in my own household.

in works of necessity and mercy) in the public and private exercise of God's worship. And, to that end, we are to prepare our hearts, and with such foresight, diligence, and moderation, to dispose, and seasonably to dispatch our worldly business, that we may be the more free and fit for the duties of the day.

Q. 118. Why is the charge of keeping the Sabbath more specially directed to governors of families and other superiors?
A. The charge of keeping the Sabbath is more specially directed to governors of families and other superiors, because they are bound not only to keep it themselves, but to see that it be observed by all those that are under their charge; and because they are prone ofttimes to hinder them by employments of their own.

Q. 119. What are the sins forbidden in the Fourth Commandment?
A. The sins in the Fourth Commandment are: all omissions of the duties required, all careless, negligent, and unprofitable performing of them, and being weary of them; all profaning the day by idleness, and doing that which is in itself sinful; and by all needless works, words, and thoughts about our worldly employments and recreations.

Q. 120. What are the reasons annexed to the Fourth Commandment, the more to enforce it?
A. The reasons annexed to the Fourth Commandment, the more to enforce it, are taken from the equity of it, God allowing us six days of seven for our own affairs, and reserving but one for himself, in these words, "Six days shalt thou labour, and do all thy work;" from God's challenging a special propriety in that day. "The seventh day is the sabbath of the Lord thy God;" from the example of God who "in six days . . . made heaven and earth, the sea, and all that in them is, and rested the seventh day;" and from that blessing which God put upon that day, not only in sanctifying it to be a holy day for his service, but in ordaining it to be a means of blessing to us in our sanctifying it, "wherefore the Lord blessed the sabbath day, and hallowed it."

Q. 121. Why is the word "remember" set in the beginning of the Fourth Commandment?
A. The word "remember" is set in the beginning of the Fourth Commandment, partly because of the great benefit of remembering it, we being thereby helped in our preparation to keep it; and, in keeping it, better to keep all the rest of the Command-

Question 102. Why do we Christians usually gather on the first day of the week?
In worshiping together on the first day of the week, we celebrate our Lord's resurrection, so that the new life Christ brought us might begin to fill our whole lives.

Question 103. What is the best summary of the first four commandments?
These teach me how to live rightly with God. Jesus summed them up with the commandment he called the first and greatest: "You shall love the Lord your God with all your heart, and with all your soul, and with all your mind" (Matt. 22:37; Deut. 6:5).

ments and to continue a thankful remembrance of the two great benefits of creation and redemption, which contain a short abridgement of religion: and partly because we are ready to forget it, for that there is less light of nature for it, and yet it restraineth our natural liberty in things at other times lawful; that it cometh but once in seven days, and many worldly businesses come between, and too often take off our minds from thinking of it, either to prepare for it, or to sanctify it; and that Satan with his instruments much labor to blot out the glory, and even the memory of it, and to bring in all irreligion and impiety.

Q. 122. What is the sum of the six Commandments which contain our duty to man?
A. The sum of the six Commandments which contain our duty to man is, to love our neighbor as ourselves, and to do to others what we would have them to do to us.

Q. 123. Which is the Fifth Commandment?
A. The Fifth Commandment is, "Honour thy father and thy mother: that thy days may be long upon the land which the Lord thy God giveth thee."

Q. 124. Who are meant by "father" and "mother," in the Fifth Commandment?
A. By "father" and "mother" in the Fifth Commandment, are meant not only natural parents, but all superiors in age and gifts; and especially such as by God's ordinance are over us in place of authority, whether in family, church, or commonwealth.

Q. 125. Why are superiors styled "father" and "mother"?
A. Superiors are styled "father" and "mother" both to teach them in all duties towards their inferiors, like natural parents, to express love and tenderness to them, according to their several relations, and to work inferiors to a greater willingness and cheerfulness in performing their duties to their superiors, as to their parents.

Q. 126. What is the general scope of the Fifth Commandment?
A. The general scope of the Fifth Commandment is, the performance of those duties which we mutually owe in our several relations, as inferiors, superiors, or equals.

Q. 127. What is the honor which inferiors owe to superiors?
A. The honor which inferiors owe to their superiors is: all due

Question 104. What is the fifth commandment?

"Honor your father and your mother" (Ex. 20:12; Deut. 5:16).

Q. 104. What does God require in the fifth commandment?

A. That I show honor, love, and faithfulness to my father and mother and to all who are set in authority over me; that I submit myself with respectful obedience to all their careful instruction and discipline; and that I also bear patiently their failures, since it is God's will to govern us by their hand.

Question 105. What do you learn from this commandment?

Though I owe reverence to God alone, I owe genuine respect to my parents, both my mother and father. God wills me to listen to them, be thankful for the benefits I receive from them, and be considerate of their needs, especially in old age.

Question 106. Are there limits to your obligation to obey them?

Yes. No mere human being is God. Blind obedience is not required, for everything should be tested by loyalty and obedience to God. When it seems as though I should not obey, I should always be alert to possible self-deception on my part and should pray that we may all walk in the truth of God's will.

reverence in heart, word, and behavior; prayer and thanksgiving for them; imitation of their virtues and graces; willing obedience to their lawful commands and counsels, due submission to their corrections; fidelity to, defense and maintenance of their persons and authority, according to their several ranks, and the nature of their places; bearing with their infirmities, and covering them in love, that so they may be an honor to them and to their government.

Q. 128. What are the sins of inferiors against their superiors?
A. The sins of inferiors against their superiors are: all neglect of the duties required toward them; envying at, contempt of, and rebellion against their persons and places, in their lawful counsels, commands, and corrections; cursing, mocking, and all such refractory and scandalous carriage, as proves a shame and dishonor to them and their government.

Q. 129. What is required of superiors towards their inferiors?
A. It is required of superiors, according to that power they receive from God, and that relation wherein they stand, to love, pray for, and bless their inferiors; to instruct, counsel, and admonish them; countenancing, commending, and rewarding such as do well; and discountenancing, reproving, and chastising such as do ill; protecting, and providing for them all things necessary for soul and body; and, by grave, wise, holy, and exemplary carriage, to procure glory to God, honor to themselves, and so to preserve that authority which God hath put upon them.

Q. 130. What are the sins of superiors?
A. The sins of superiors are, besides the neglect of the duties required of them an inordinate seeking of themselves, their own glory, ease, profit or pleasure; commanding things unlawful, or not in the power of inferiors to perform; counseling, encouraging, or favoring them in that which is evil; dissuading, discouraging, or discountenancing them in that which is good; correcting them unduly; careless exposing or leaving them to wrong, temptation, and danger; provoking them to wrath; or any way dishonoring themselves, or lessening their authority, by an unjust, indiscreet, rigorous, or remiss behavior.

Q. 131. What are the duties of equals?
A. The duties of equals are: to regard the dignity and worth of each other, in giving honor to go one before another, and to rejoice in each other's gifts and advancement as their own.

THE STUDY CATECHISM   **HEIDELBERG CATECHISM**

Q. 132. What are the sins of equals?

A. The sins of equals are, besides the neglect of the duties required, the undervaluing of the worth, envying the gifts, grieving at the advancement or prosperity one of another, and usurping pre-eminence one over another.

Q. 133. What is the reason annexed to the Fifth Commandment the more to enforce it?

A. The reason annexed to the Fifth Commandment in these words, "that thy days may be long upon the land which the Lord thy God giveth thee," is an express promise of long life and prosperity, as far as it shall serve for God's glory and their own good, to all such as keep this Commandment.

Q. 134. Which is the Sixth Commandment?

A. The Sixth Commandment is, "Thou shalt not kill."

Q. 135. What are the duties required in the Sixth Commandment?

A. The duties required in the Sixth Commandment are: all careful studies and lawful endeavors, to preserve the life of ourselves and others, by resisting all thoughts and purposes, subduing all passions, and avoiding all occasions, temptations, and practices, which tend to the unjust taking away the life of any; by just defense thereof against violence; patient bearing of the hand of God, quietness of mind, cheerfulness of spirit, a sober use of meat, drink, physic, sleep, labor, and recreation; by charitable thoughts, love, compassion, meekness, gentleness, kindness; peaceable, mild, and courteous speeches and behavior, forbearance, readiness to be reconciled, patient bearing and forgiving of injuries, and requiting good for evil; comforting and succoring the distressed, and protecting and defending the innocent.

Q. 136. What are the sins forbidden in the Sixth Commandment?

A. The sins forbidden in the Sixth Commandment are: all taking away the life of ourselves, or of others, except in case of public justice, lawful war, or necessary defense; the neglecting or withdrawing the lawful or necessary means of preservation of life; sinful anger, hatred, envy, desire of revenge; all excessive passions; distracting cares; immoderate use of meat, drink, labor, and recreation; provoking words; oppression, quarreling, striking, wounding, and whatsoever else tends to the destruction of the life of any.

Question 107. What is the sixth commandment?

"You shall not murder" (Ex. 20:13; Deut. 5:17).

Question 108. What do you learn from this commandment?

God forbids anything that harms my neighbor unfairly. Murder or injury can be done not only by direct violence but also by an angry word or a clever plan, and not only by an individual but also by unjust social institutions. I should honor every human being, including my enemy, as a person made in God's image.

LORD'S DAY 40

Q. 105. What does God require in the sixth commandment?

A. That I am not to abuse, hate, injure, or kill my neighbor, either with thought, or by word or gesture, much less by deed, whether by myself or through another, but to lay aside all desire for revenge; and that I do not harm myself or willfully expose myself to danger. This is why the authorities are armed with the means to prevent murder.

Q. 106. But does this commandment speak only of killing?

A. In forbidding murder God means to teach us that he abhors the root of murder, which is envy, hatred, anger, and desire for revenge, and that he regards all these as hidden murder.

Q. 107. Is it enough, then, if we do not kill our neighbor in any of these ways?

A. No; for when God condemns envy, hatred, and anger, he requires us to love our neighbor as ourselves, to show patience, peace, gentleness, mercy, and friendliness toward him, to prevent injury to him as much as we can, also to do good to our enemies.

Q. 137. Which is the Seventh Commandment?

A. The Seventh Commandment is, "Thou shalt not commit adultery."

Q. 138. What are the duties required in the Seventh Commandment?

A. The duties required in the Seventh Commandment are: chastity in body, mind, affections, words, and behavior, and the preservation of it in ourselves and others; watchfulness over the eyes and all the senses; temperance, keeping of chaste company, modesty in apparel, marriage by those that have not the gift of continency, conjugal love, and cohabitation; diligent labor in our callings; shunning of all occasions of uncleanness, and resisting temptations thereunto.

Q. 139. What are the sins forbidden in the Seventh Commandment?

A. The sins forbidden in the Seventh Commandment, besides the neglect of the duties required, are: adultery, fornication, rape, incest, sodomy, and all unnatural lusts; all unclean imaginations, thoughts, purposes, and affections; all corrupt or filthy communications, or listening thereunto; wanton looks, impudent or light behavior, immodest apparel, prohibiting of lawful, and dispensing with unlawful marriages; allowing, tolerating, keeping of stews, and resorting to them; entangling vows of single life, undue delay of marriage; having more wives or husbands than one at the same time; unjust divorce or desertion; idleness, gluttony, drunkenness, unchaste company; lascivious songs, books, pictures, dancings, stageplays, and all other provocations to, or acts of, uncleanness either in ourselves or others.

Q. 140. Which is the Eighth Commandment?

A. The Eighth Commandment is, "Thou shalt not steal."

Q. 141. What are the duties required in the Eighth Commandment?

A. The duties required in the Eighth Commandment are: truth, faithfulness, and justice in contracts and commerce between man and man; rendering to everyone his due; restitution of goods unlawfully detained from the right owners thereof; giving and lending freely, according to our abilities, and the necessities of others; moderation of our judgments, wills, and affections, concerning worldly goods; a provident care and

THE STUDY CATECHISM

Question 109. What is the seventh commandment?

"You shall not commit adultery" (Ex. 20:14; Deut. 5:18).

Question 110. What do you learn from this commandment?

God requires fidelity and purity in sexual relations. Since love is God's great gift, God expects me not to corrupt it, or confuse it with momentary desire or the selfish fulfillment of my own pleasures. God forbids all sexual immorality, whether in married or in single life.

Question 111. What is the eighth commandment?

"You shall not steal" (Ex. 20:15; Deut. 5:19).

Question 112. What do you learn from this commandment?

God forbids all theft and robbery, including schemes, tricks, or systems that unjustly take what belongs to someone else. God requires me not to be driven by greed, not to misuse or

HEIDELBERG CATECHISM

Q. 108. What does the seventh commandment teach us?

A. That all unchastity is condemned by God, and that we should therefore detest it from the heart, and live chaste and disciplined lives, whether in holy wedlock or in single life.

Q. 109. Does God forbid nothing more than adultery and such gross sins in this commandment?

A. Since both our body and soul are a temple of the Holy Spirit, it is his will that we keep both pure and holy. Therefore he forbids all unchaste actions, gestures, words, thoughts, desires and whatever may excite another person to them.

Q. 110. What does God forbid in the eighth commandment?

A. He forbids not only the theft and robbery which civil authorities punish, but God also labels as theft all wicked tricks and schemes by which we seek to get for ourselves our neighbor's goods, whether by force or under the pretext of right, such as false weights and measures, deceptive advertising or merchandising, counterfeit money, exorbitant interest, or any other means

study to get, keep, use, and dispose of those things which are necessary and convenient for the sustentation of our nature, and suitable to our condition; a lawful calling, and a diligence in it; frugality; avoiding unnecessary lawsuits, and suretyship, or other like engagements; and an endeavor by all just and lawful means to procure, preserve, and further the wealth and outward estate of others, as well as our own.

Q. 142. What are the sins forbidden in the Eighth Commandment?

A. The sins forbidden in the Eighth Commandment besides the neglect of duties required, are: theft, robbery, man stealing, and receiving anything that is stolen; fraudulent dealing, false weights and measures, removing landmarks, injustice and unfaithfulness in contracts between man and man, or in matters of trust; oppression, extortion, usury, bribery, vexatious lawsuits, unjust enclosures and depopulations; engrossing commodities to enhance the price, unlawful callings, and all other unjust or sinful ways of taking or withholding from our neighbor what belongs to him, or of enriching ourselves; covetousness, inordinate prizing and affecting worldly goods; distrustful and distracting cares and studies in getting, keeping, and using them; envying at the prosperity of others; as likewise idleness, prodigality, wasteful gaming, and all other ways whereby we do unduly prejudice our own outward estate; and defrauding ourselves of the due use and comfort of that estate which God hath given us.

Q. 143. Which is the Ninth Commandment?

A. The Ninth Commandment is, "Thou shalt not bear false witness against thy neighbour."

Q. 144. What are the duties required in the Ninth Commandment?

A. The duties required in the Ninth Commandment are: the preserving and promoting of truth between man and man, and the good name of our neighbor, as well as our own; appearing and standing for the truth; and from the heart, sincerely, freely, clearly, and fully, speaking the truth, and only the truth, in matters of judgment and justice, and in all other things whatsoever; a charitable esteem of our neighbors, loving, desiring, and rejoicing in their good name; sorrowing for, and covering of their infirmities; freely acknowledging of their gifts and graces, defending their innocency; a ready receiving of good report, and unwillingness to admit of an evil report concerning them; discouraging talebearers, flatterers, and slanderers; love and

waste the gifts I have been given, and not to distrust the promise that God will supply my needs.

forbidden by God. He so forbids all greed and misuse and waste of his gifts.

Q. 111. But what does God require of you in this commandment?
A. That I work for the good of my neighbor wherever I can and may, deal with him as I would have others deal with me, and do my work well so that I may be able to help the poor in their need.

LORD'S DAY 43

Question 113. What is the ninth commandment?

"You shall not bear false witness against your neighbor" (Ex. 20:16; Deut. 5:20).

Question 114. What do you learn from this commandment?

God forbids me to damage the honor or reputation of my neighbor. I should not say false things against anyone for the sake of money, favor, or friendship, for the sake of revenge, or for any other reason. God requires me to speak the truth, to speak well of my neighbor when I can, and to view the faults of my neighbor with tolerance when I cannot.

Q. 112. What is required in the ninth commandment?
A. That I do not bear false witness against anyone, twist anyone's words, be a gossip or a slanderer, or condemn anyone lightly without a hearing. Rather I am required to avoid, under penalty of God's wrath, all lying and deceit as the works of the devil himself. In judicial and all other matters I am to love the truth, and to speak and confess it honestly. Indeed, insofar as I am able, I am to defend and promote my neighbor's good name.

care of our own good name, and defending it when need requireth; keeping of lawful promises; studying and practicing of whatsoever things are true, honest, lovely, and of good report.

Q. 145. What are the sins forbidden in the Ninth Commandment?

A. The sins forbidden in the Ninth Commandment are: all prejudicing of the truth, and the good name of our neighbors as well as our own, especially in public judicature; giving false evidence, suborning false witnesses, wittingly appearing and pleading for an evil cause, outfacing and overbearing the truth; passing unjust sentence, calling evil good, and good evil; rewarding the wicked according to the work of the righteous, and the righteous according to the work of the wicked; forgery, concealing the truth, undue silence in a just cause, and holding our peace when iniquity calleth for either a reproof from ourselves, or complaint to others; speaking the truth unseasonably, or maliciously to a wrong end, or perverting it to a wrong meaning, or in doubtful and equivocal expression, to the prejudice of truth or justice; speaking untruth, lying, slandering, backbiting, detracting, talebearing, whispering, scoffing, reviling; rash, harsh, and partial censuring; misconstruing intentions, words, and actions; flattering, vainglorious boasting, thinking or speaking too highly or too meanly of ourselves or others; denying the gifts and graces of God; aggravating smaller faults; hiding, excusing, or extenuating of sins, when called to a free confession; unnecessarily discovering of infirmities; raising false rumors; receiving and countenancing evil reports, and stopping our ears against just defense; evil suspicion; envying or grieving at the deserved credit of any; endeavoring or desiring to impair it, rejoicing in their disgrace and infamy; scornful contempt, fond admiration, breach of lawful promises; neglecting such things as are of good report; and practicing or not avoiding ourselves, or not hindering what we can in others, such things as procure an ill name.

Q. 146. Which is the Tenth Commandment?

A. The Tenth Commandment is, "Thou shalt not covet thy neighbour's house, thou shalt not covet thy neighbour's wife, nor his manservant, nor his maidservant, nor his ox, nor his ass, nor any thing that is thy neighbour's."

Q. 147. What are the duties required in the Tenth Commandment?

Question 115. Does this commandment forbid racism and other forms of negative stereotyping?
Yes. In forbidding false witness against my neighbor, God forbids me to be prejudiced against people who belong to any vulnerable, different, or disfavored social group. Jews, women, homosexuals, racial and ethnic minorities, and national enemies are among those who have suffered terribly from being subjected to the slurs of social prejudice. Negative stereotyping is a form of falsehood that invites actions of humiliation, abuse, and violence as forbidden by the commandment against murder.

Question 116. What is the tenth commandment?
"You shall not covet what is your neighbor's" (Ex. 20:17; Deut. 5:21).

Q. 113. What is required in the tenth commandment?
A. That there should never enter our heart even the least inclination or thought contrary to any commandment of God, but that we should always hate sin with our whole heart and find satisfaction and joy in all righteousness.

Question 117. What do you learn from this commandment?
My whole heart should belong to God

A. The duties required in the Tenth Commandment are: such a full contentment with our own condition, and such a charitable frame of the whole soul towards our neighbor, as that all our inward motions and affections touching him, tend unto and further all that good which is his.

Q. 148. What are the sins forbidden in the Tenth Commandment?
A. The sins forbidden in the Tenth Commandment are: discontentment with our own estate; envying, and grieving at the good of our neighbor, together with all inordinate motions and affections to anything that is his.

Q. 149. Is any man able perfectly to keep the Commandments of God?
A. No man is able, either of himself, or by any grace received in this life, perfectly to keep the Commandments of God; but doth daily break them in thought, word, and deed.

Q. 150. Are all transgressions of the law of God equally heinous in themselves, and in the sight of God?
A. All transgressions of the law of God are not equally heinous; but some sins in themselves, and by reason of several aggravations, are more heinous in the sight of God than others.

Q. 151. What are those aggravations that make some sins more heinous than others?
A. Sins receive their aggravations,
1. From the persons offending: if they be of riper age, greater experience, or grace; eminent for profession, gifts, place, office, guides to others, and whose example is likely to be followed by others.
2. From the parties offended: if immediately against God, his attributes, and worship; against Christ, and his grace: the Holy Spirit, his witness, and workings; against superiors, men of eminency, and such as we stand especially related and engaged unto; against any of the saints, particularly weak brethren, the souls of them or any other; and the common good of all or many.
3. From the nature and quality of the offense: if it be against the express letter of the law, break many commandments, contain in it many sins: if not only conceived in the heart, but break forth in words and actions, scandalize others, and admit no reparation: if against means, mercies, judgments, light of nature, conviction of conscience, public or private admonition,

alone, not to money or the things of this world. "Coveting" means desiring something wrongfully. I should not resent the good fortune or success of my neighbor or allow envy to corrupt my heart.

Question 118. What is the best summary of the last six commandments?

These teach me how to live rightly with my neighbor. Jesus summed them up with the commandment which is like the greatest one about loving God: "You shall love your neighbor as yourself" (Matt. 22:39; Lev. 19:18).

Question 119. Can you obey these commandments perfectly?

No. I am at once a forgiven sinner and a forgiven sinner. As a sinner without excuse, I fail to obey these commandments as God requires. "For whoever keeps the whole law but fails in one point has become accountable for all of it" (James 2:10). I should not adjust the law to my failures, nor reduce my failures before God. Yet there is more grace in God than sin in me. While I should not cease to pray to God for mercy, I can be confident that God is forgiving and that I will be set free from all my sins. By grace I can confess my sins, repent of them, and grow in love and knowledge day by day.

Q. 114. But can those who are converted to God keep these commandments perfectly?

A. No, for even the holiest of them make only a small beginning in obedience in this life. Nevertheless, they begin with serious purpose to conform not only to some, but to all the commandments of God.

Q. 115. Why, then, does God have the ten commandments preached so strictly since no one can keep them in this life?

A. First, that all our life long we may become increasingly aware of our sinfulness, and therefore more eagerly seek forgiveness of sins and righteousness in Christ. Second, that we may constantly and diligently pray to God for the grace of the Holy Spirit, so that more and more we may be renewed in the image of God, until we attain the goal of full perfection after this life.

censures of the church, civil punishments; and our prayers, purposes, promises, vows, covenants, and engagements to God or men: if done deliberately, willfully, presumptuously, impudently, boastingly, maliciously, frequently, obstinately, with light, continuance, or relapsing after repentance. 4. From circumstances of time, and place: if on the Lord's Day, or other times of divine worship; or immediately before, or after these, or other helps to prevent or remedy such miscarriages; if in public, or in the presence of others, who are thereby likely to be provoked or defiled.

Q. 152. What doth every sin deserve at the hands of God?
A. Every sin, even the least, being against the sovereignty, goodness, and holiness of God,and against his righteous law, deserveth his wrath and curse, both in this life, and that which is to come; and cannot be expiated but by the blood of Christ.

Q. 153. What doth God require of us, that we may escape his wrath and curse due to us by reason of the transgression of the law?
A. That we may escape the wrath and curse of God due to us by reason of the transgression of the law, he requireth of us repentance towards God, and faith towards our Lord Jesus Christ, and the diligent use of the outward means whereby Christ communicates to us the benefits of his mediation.

Q. 154. What are the outward means whereby Christ communicates to us the benefits of his mediation?
A. The outward and ordinary means, whereby Christ communicates to his church the benefits of his mediation, are all his ordinances, especially the Word, sacraments, and prayer, all which are made effectual to the elect for their salvation.

Q. 155. How is the Word made effectual to salvation?
A. The Spirit of God maketh the reading, but especially the preaching of the Word, an effectual means of enlightening, convincing, and humbling sinners, of driving them out of themselves, and drawing them unto Christ, of conforming them to his image, and subduing them to his will; of strengthening them against temptations and corruptions; of building them up in grace, and establishing their hearts in holiness and comfort through faith unto salvation.

Q. 156. Is the Word of God to be read by all?
A. Although all are not permitted to read the Word publicly to

THE STUDY CATECHISM   HEIDELBERG CATECHISM

the congregation, yet all sorts of people are bound to read it apart by themselves, and with their families; to which end, the Holy Scriptures are to be translated out of the original into the language of every people unto whom they come.

Q. 157. How is the Word of God to be read?

A. The Holy Scriptures are to be read with an high and reverent esteem of them; with a firm persuasion that they are the very Word of God, and that he only can enable us to understand them; with desire to know, believe, and obey, the will of God revealed in them; with diligence, and attention to the matter and scope of them; with meditation, application, self-denial, and prayer.

Q. 158. By whom is the Word of God to be preached?

A. The Word of God is to be preached only by such as are sufficiently gifted, and also duly approved and called to that office.

Q. 159. How is the Word of God to be preached by those that are called thereunto?

A. They that are called to labor in the ministry of the Word are to preach sound doctrine, diligently, in season, and out of season, plainly, not in the enticing word of man's wisdom, but in demonstration of the Spirit, and of power; faithfully, making known the whole counsel of God; wisely, applying themselves to the necessities and capacities of the hearers; zealously, with fervent love to God, and the souls of his people; sincerely, aiming at his glory, and their conversion, edification, and salvation.

Q. 160. What is required of those that hear the Word preached?

A. It is required of those that hear the Word preached, that they attend upon it with diligence, preparation, and prayer; examine what they hear by the Scriptures; receive the truth with faith, love, meekness, and readiness of mind, as the Word of God; meditate, and confer of it; hide it in their hearts, and bring forth the fruit of it in their lives.

Q. 161. How do the sacraments become effectual means of salvation?

A. The sacraments become effectual means of salvation, not by any power in themselves or any virtue derived from the piety or intention of him by whom they are administered; but only by the working of the Holy Ghost, and the blessing of Christ by whom they are instituted.

THE STUDY CATECHISM   HEIDELBERG CATECHISM

Q. 162. What is a sacrament?

A. A sacrament is an holy ordinance instituted by Christ in his church, to signify, seal and exhibit unto those that are within the covenant of grace, the benefits of his mediation; to strengthen and increase their faith and all other graces; to oblige them to obedience; to testify and cherish their love and communion one with another, and to distinguish them from those that are without.

Q. 163. What are the parts of a sacrament?

A. The parts of a sacrament are two: the one, an outward and sensible sign used according to Christ's own appointment; the other, an inward and spiritual grace thereby signified.

Q. 164. How many sacraments hath Christ instituted under the New Testament?

A. Under the New Testament Christ hath instituted in his church only two sacraments, baptism, and the Lord's Supper.

Q. 165. What is Baptism?

A. Baptism is a sacrament of the New Testament, wherein Christ hath ordained the washing with water in the name of the Father, and of the Son, and of the Holy Ghost, to be a sign and seal of ingrafting into himself, of remission of sins by his blood, and regeneration by his Spirit; of adoption, and resurrection unto everlasting life: and whereby the parties baptized are solemnly admitted into the visible church, and enter into an open and professed engagement to be wholly and only the Lord's.

Q. 166. Unto whom is Baptism to be administered?

A. Baptism is not to be administered to any that are out of the visible church, and so strangers from the covenant of promise, till they profess their faith in Christ, and obedience to him; but infants descending from parents, either both or but one of them, professing faith in Christ, and obedience to him, are, in that respect, within the covenant, and are to be baptized.

Q. 167. How is our Baptism to be improved by us?

A. The needful but much neglected duty of improving our Baptism, is to be performed by us all our life long, especially in the time of temptation, and when we are present at the administration of it to others, by serious and thankful consideration of the nature of it and of the ends for which Christ instituted it, the privileges and benefits conferred and sealed thereby, and our solemn vow made therein; by being humbled

THE STUDY CATECHISM   HEIDELBERG CATECHISM

for our sinful defilement, our falling short of, and walking contrary to, the grace of Baptism and our engagements; by growing up to assurance of pardon of sin, and of all other blessings sealed to us in that sacrament; by drawing strength from the death and resurrection of Christ, into whom we are baptized, for the mortifying of sin, and quickening of grace; and by endeavoring to live by faith, to have our conversation in holiness and righteousness, as those that have therein given up their names to Christ, and to walk in brotherly love, as being baptized by the same Spirit into one body.

Q. 168. What is the Lord's Supper?

A. The Lord's Supper is a sacrament of the New Testament, wherein by giving and receiving bread and wine according to the appointment of Jesus Christ, his death is showed forth; and they that worthily communicate, feed upon his body and blood to their spiritual nourishment and growth in grace; have their union and communion with him confirmed; testify and renew their thankfulness and engagement to God, and their mutual love and fellowship each with other, as members of the same mystical body.

Q. 169. How hath Christ appointed bread and wine to be given and received in the sacrament of the Lord's Supper?

A. Christ hath appointed the ministers of his Word in the administration of this sacrament of the Lord's Supper, to set apart the bread and wine from common use by the word of institution, thanksgiving, and prayer; to take and break the bread, and to give both the bread and the wine to the communicants; who are by the same appointment to take and eat the bread, and to drink the wine; in thankful remembrance that the body of Christ was broken and given, and his blood shed for them.

Q. 170. How do they that worthily communicate in the Lord's Supper feed upon the body and blood of Christ therein?

A. As the body and the blood of Christ are not corporally or carnally present in, with, or under the bread and wine in the Lord's Supper; and yet are spiritually present to the faith of the receiver, no less truly and really than the elements themselves are to their outward senses; so they that worthily communicate in the sacrament of the Lord's Supper, do therein feed upon the body and blood of Christ, not after a corporal or carnal, but in a spiritual manner; yet truly and really, while by faith they

receive and apply unto themselves Christ crucified, and all the benefits of his death.

Q. 171. How are they that receive the sacrament of the Lord's Supper to prepare themselves before they come unto it?

A. They that receive the sacrament of the Lord's Supper are, before they come, to prepare themselves thereunto; by examining themselves, of their being in Christ, of their sins and wants; of the truth and measure of their knowledge, faith, repentance, love to God and the brethren, charity to all men, forgiving those that have done them wrong; of their desires after Christ, and of their new obedience; and by renewing the exercise of these graces, by serious meditation, and fervent prayer.

Q. 172. May one who doubteth of his being in Christ, or of his due preparation, come to the Lord's Supper?

A. One who doubteth of his being in Christ, or of his due preparation to the sacrament of the Lord's Supper, may have true interest in Christ, though he be not yet assured thereof; and in God's account hath it, if he be duly affected with the apprehension of the want of it, and unfeignedly desirous to be found in Christ, and to depart from iniquity; in which case (because promises are made, and this sacrament is appointed, for the relief even of weak and doubting Christians) he is to bewail his unbelief, and labor to have his doubts resolved; and so doing, he may and ought to come to the Lord's Supper, that he may be further strengthened.

Q. 173. May any who profess the faith, and desire to come to the Lord's Supper, be kept from it?

A. Such as are found to be ignorant or scandalous, notwithstanding their profession of the faith, and desire to come to the Lord's Supper, may and ought to be kept from that sacrament by the power which Christ hath left in his church, until they receive instruction, and manifest their reformation.

Q. 174. What is required of them that receive the sacrament of the Lord's Supper in the time of the administration of it?

A. It is required of them that receive the sacrament of the Lord's Supper that, during the time of the administration of it, with all holy reverence and attention, they wait upon God in that ordinance; diligently observe the sacramental elements and actions; heedfully discern the Lord's body, and affectionately meditate upon his death and sufferings, and thereby stir up

THE STUDY CATECHISM   HEIDELBERG CATECHISM

themselves to a vigorous exercise of their graces; in judging themselves, and sorrowing for sin; in earnest hungering and thirsting after Christ, feeding on him by faith, receiving of his fullness, trusting in his merits, rejoicing in his love, giving thanks for his grace; in renewing of their covenant with God, and love to all the saints.

Q. 175. What is the duty of Christians after they have received the sacrament of the Lord's Supper?

A. The duty of Christians after they have received the sacrament of the Lord's Supper, is seriously to consider how they have behaved themselves therein, and with what success; if they find quickening and comfort, to bless God for it, beg the continuance of it, watch against relapse, fulfill their vows, and encourage themselves to a frequent attendance on that ordinance: but if they find no present benefit, more exactly to review their preparation to, and carriage at, the sacrament; in both which if they can approve themselves to God and their own consciences, they are to wait for the fruit of it in due time; but if they see that they have failed in either, they are to be humbled, and to attend upon it afterward with more care and diligence.

Q. 176. Wherein do the sacraments of Baptism and the Lord's Supper agree?

A. The sacraments of Baptism and the Lord's Supper agree, in that the author of both is God; the spiritual part of both is Christ and his benefits; both are seals of the same covenant, are to be dispensed by ministers of the gospel and by none other, and to be continued in the church of Christ until his second coming.

Q. 177. Wherein do the sacraments of Baptism and the Lord's Supper differ?

A. The sacraments of Baptism and the Lord's Supper differ, in that Baptism is to be administered but once, with water, to be a sign and seal of our regeneration and ingrafting into Christ, and that even to infants; whereas the Lord's Supper is to be administered often, in the elements of bread and wine, to represent and exhibit Christ as spiritual nourishment to the soul, and to confirm our continuance and growth in him, and that only to such as are of years and ability to examine themselves.

Q. 178. What is prayer?

A. Prayer is an offering up of our desires unto God, in the name of Christ, by the help of his Spirit, with confession of our sins, and thankful acknowledgment of his mercies.

Prayer

III. The Lord's Prayer

Question 120. What is prayer?
Prayer means calling upon God whose Spirit is always present with us. In prayer we approach God with rever-

Q. 116. Why is prayer necessary for Christians?
A. Because it is the chief part of the gratitude which God requires of us, and

Q. 179. Are we to pray unto God only?
A. God only being able to search the heart, hear the requests, pardon the sins, and fulfill the desires of all, and only to be believed in, and worshiped with religious worship; prayer, which is a special part thereof, is to be made by all to him alone, and to none other.

Q. 180. What is it to pray in the name of Christ?
A. To pray in the name of Christ is, in obedience to his command, and in confidence on his promises, to ask mercy for his sake; not by bare mentioning of his name; but by drawing our encouragement to pray, and our boldness, strength, and hope of acceptance in prayer, from Christ and his mediation.

Q. 181. Why are we to pray in the name of Christ?
A. The sinfulness of man, and his distance from God by reason thereof, being so great, as that we can have no access into his presence without a mediator, and there being none in heaven or earth appointed to, or fit for, that glorious work but Christ alone, we are to pray in no other name but his only.

Q. 182. How doth the Spirit help us to pray?
A. We not knowing what to pray for as we ought, the Spirit helpeth our infirmities, by enabling us to understand both for whom, and what, and how prayer is to be made; and by working and quickening in our hearts (although not in all persons, nor at all times in the same measure) those apprehensions, affections, and graces, which are requisite for the right performance of that duty.

Q. 183. For whom are we to pray?
A. We are to pray for the whole church of Christ upon earth, for magistrates, and ministers, for ourselves, our brethren, yea, our enemies, and for all sorts of men living, or that shall live hereafter; but not for the dead.

Q. 184. For what things are we to pray?
A. We are to pray for all things tending to the glory of God, the welfare of the church, our own or others' good; but not for anything that is unlawful.

Q. 185. How are we to pray?
A. We are to pray with an awful apprehension of the majesty of God, and deep sense of our own unworthiness, necessities, and sins; with penitent, thankful, and enlarged hearts; with under-

ence, confidence, and humility. Prayer involves both addressing God in praise, confession, thanksgiving, and supplication, and listening for God's word within our hearts. When we adore God, we are filled with wonder, love, and praise before God's heavenly glory, not least when we find it hidden in the cross of Golgotha. When confessing our guilt to God, we ask for forgiveness with humble and sorry hearts, remembering that God is gracious as well as holy. When giving thanks to God, we acknowledge God's great goodness, rejoicing in God for all that is so wonderfully provided for us. Finally, when calling upon God to hear our requests, we affirm that God draws near in every need and sorrow of life, and ask God to do so again.

Question 121. What is the purpose of prayer?

Prayer brings us into communion with God. The more our lives are rooted in prayer, the more we sense how wonderful God is in grace, purity, majesty, and love. Prayer means offering our lives completely to God, submitting ourselves to God's will, and waiting faithfully for God's grace. Through prayer God frees us from anxiety, equips us for service, and deepens our faith.

Question 122. How does God respond to our prayers?

God takes all our prayers into account, weighing them with divine wisdom, and responding to them by a perfect will. Although for the time being God's answers may seem beyond our understanding, or sometimes even bitter, we know nonetheless that they are always determined by the grace of our

because God will give his grace and Holy Spirit only to those who sincerely beseech him in prayer without ceasing, and who thank him for these gifts.

Q. 117. What is contained in a prayer which pleases God and is heard by him?

A. First, that we sincerely call upon the one true God, who has revealed himself to us in his Word, for all that he has commanded us to ask of him. Then, that we thoroughly acknowledge our need and evil condition so that we may humble ourselves in the presence of his majesty. Third, that we rest assured that, in spite of our unworthiness, he will certainly hear our prayer for the sake of Christ our Lord, as he has promised us in his Word.

Q. 118. What has God commanded us to ask of him?

A. All things necessary for soul and body which Christ the Lord has included in the prayer which he himself taught us.

Q. 119. What is the Lord's Prayer?

A. "Our Father who art in heaven, hallowed be thy name. Thy kingdom come, thy will be done, on earth as it is in heaven. Give us this day our daily bread; and forgive us our debts, as we also have forgiven our debtors; and lead us not into temptation, but deliver us from evil, for thine is the kingdom and the power and the glory, forever. Amen."

Our Lord's Prayer

LORD'S DAY 46
Q. 120. Why has Christ commanded us to address God: "Our Father"?

standing, faith, sincerity, fervency, love, and perseverance, waiting upon him with humble submission to his will.

Q. 186. What rule hath God given for our direction in the duty of prayer?

A. The whole Word of God is of use to direct us in the duty of praying; but the special rule of direction is that form of prayer which our Saviour Christ taught his disciples, commonly called, "the Lord's Prayer."

Q. 187. How is the Lord's Prayer to be used?

A. The Lord's Prayer is not only for direction, as a pattern according to which we are to make other prayers; but may be also used as a prayer so that it be done with understanding, faith, reverence, and other graces necessary to the right performance of the duty of prayer.

Q. 188. Of how many parts doth the Lord's Prayer consist?

A. The Lord's Prayer consists of three parts; a preface, petitions, and a conclusion.

Q. 189. What doth the preface of the Lord's Prayer teach us?

A. The preface of the Lord's Prayer (contained in these words, "Our Father which art in heaven") teacheth us, when we pray, to draw near to God with confidence of his fatherly goodness, and our interest therein; with reverence, and all other childlike dispositions, heavenly affections, and due apprehensions of his sovereign power, majesty, and gracious condescension: as also to pray with and for others.

Lord Jesus Christ. God answers our prayers, particularly for temporal blessings, only in ways that are compatible with the larger purposes of God's glory and our salvation. Communion with God is finally the answer within the answers to all our prayers.

Question 123. What encourages us to pray each day?

The God who has adopted us as children is the God who encourages and commands us to pray. When we pray, we respond with love to that greater love which meets us from above. Before we enter into prayer, God is ready to grant all that we need. We may turn to God with confidence each day, not because we are worthy, but simply because of God's grace. By praying we acknowledge that we depend on grace for all that is good, beautiful, life-giving and true.

Question 124. What prayer serves as our rule or pattern?

Our rule or pattern is found in the Lord's Prayer, which Jesus taught to his disciples:

> Our Father in heaven,
>   hallowed be your name,
>   your kingdom come,
>   your will be done,
>   on earth as in heaven.
> Give us today our daily bread.
> Forgive us our sins
>   as we forgive those who sin
>   against us.
> Save us from the time of trial
>   and deliver us from evil.
> For the kingdom, the power and the
>   glory are yours
>   now and for ever. Amen.

These words express everything that we may desire and expect from God.

A. That at the very beginning of our prayer he may awaken in us the childlike reverence and trust toward God which should be the motivation of our prayer, which is that God has become our Father through Christ and will much less deny us what we ask him in faith than our human fathers will refuse us earthly things.

Q. 121. Why is there added: "who art in heaven"?

A. That we may have no earthly conception of the heavenly majesty of God, but that we may expect from his almighty power all things that are needed for body and soul.

Q. 190. What do we pray for in the first petition?
A. In the first petition (which is, "Hallowed be thy name"), acknowledging the utter inability and indisposition that is in ourselves and all men to honor God aright, we pray: that God would by his grace enable and incline us and others to know, to acknowledge, and highly esteem him, his titles, attributes, ordinances, word, works, and whatsoever he is pleased to make himself known by; and to glorify him in thought, word, and deed; that he would prevent and remove atheism, ignorance,

Question 125. What is the design of the Lord's Prayer?

The Lord's Prayer falls into two parts, preceded by an opening address, and concluded by a "doxology" or word of praise. Each part consists of three petitions. The first part concerns God's glory; the second part, our salvation. The first part involves our love for God; the second part, God's love for us. The petitions in part one will not be fulfilled perfectly until the life to come; those in part two relate more directly to our present needs here and now.

Question 126. What is meant by addressing God as "Our Father in heaven"?

By addressing God as "our Father," we draw near with childlike reverence, and place ourselves securely in God's hands. Although God is certainly everywhere, God is said to exist and dwell "in heaven." For while God is free to enter into the closest relationship with the creature, God does not belong to the order of created beings. "Heaven" is the seat of divine authority, the place from which God reigns in glory and brings salvation to earth. Our opening address expresses our confidence that we rest securely in God's intimate care and that nothing on earth lies beyond the reach of God's grace.

Question 127. What is meant by the first petition, "Hallowed be your name"?

This petition is placed first, because it comprehends the goal and purpose of the whole prayer. The glory of God's name is the highest concern in all that we pray and do. God's "name" stands for God's being as well as for God's

LORD'S DAY 47

Q. 122. What is the first petition?

A. "Hallowed be thy name." That is: help us first of all to know thee rightly, and to hallow, glorify, and praise thee in all thy works through which there shine thine almighty power, wisdom, goodness, righteousness, mercy, and truth. And so order our whole life in thought, word, and deed that thy name

idolatry, profaneness, and whatsoever is dishonorable to him; and by his overruling providence, direct and dispose of all things to his own glory.

Q. 191. What do we pray for in the second petition?

A. In the second petition (which is, "Thy Kingdom come"), acknowledging ourselves and all mankind to be by nature under the dominion of sin and Satan, we pray: that the kingdom of sin and Satan may be destroyed, the gospel propagated throughout the world, the Jews called, the fullness of the Gentiles brought in; that the church may be furnished with all gospel-officers and ordinances, purged from corruption, countenanced and maintained by the civil magistrate; that the ordinances of Christ may be purely dispensed, and made effectual to the converting of those that are yet in their sins, and the confirming, comforting, and building up of those that are already converted; that Christ would rule in our hearts here, and hasten the time of his second coming, and our reigning with him forever; and that he would be pleased so to exercise the Kingdom of his power in all the world, as may best conduce to these ends.

Q. 192. What do we pray for in the third petition?

A. In the third petition (which is, "Thy will be done on earth as it is in heaven"), acknowledging that by nature we and all men are not only utterly unable and unwilling to know and do the will of God, but prone to rebel against his Word, to repine and murmur against his providence, and wholly inclined to do the will of the flesh, and of the devil: we pray that God would by his Spirit take away from ourselves and others all blindness, weakness, indisposedness, and perverseness of heart, and by his grace make us able and willing to know, do, and submit to his will in all things, with the like humility, cheerfulness, faithfulness, diligence, zeal, sincerity, and constancy, as the angels do in heaven.

attributes and works. When we pray for this name to be "hallowed," we ask that we and all others will know and glorify God as God really is, and that all things will be so ordered that they serve God truly for God's sake.

Question 128. What is meant by the second petition, "Your kingdom come"?
We are asking God to come and rule among us through faith, love and justice—and not through any one of them without the others. We pray for both the church and the world, that God will rule in our hearts through faith, in our personal relationships through love, and in our institutional affairs through justice. We ask especially that the gospel will not be withheld from us, but rightly preached and received. We pray that the church will be upheld and increase, particularly when in distress; and that all the world will more and more submit to God's reign, until that day when crying and pain are no more, and we live forever with God in perfect peace.

Question 129. What is meant by the third petition, "Your will be done, on earth as in heaven"?
Of course, God's will is always done, and will surely come to pass, whether we desire it or not. But the phrase "on earth as in heaven" means that we ask for the grace to do God's will on earth in the way that it is done in heaven—gladly and from the heart. We thus ask that all opposition to God's will might be removed from the earth, and especially from our own hearts. We ask for the freedom to conform our desires and deeds more fully to God's, so that we might be completely delivered

may never be blasphemed on our account, but may always be honored and praised.

LORD'S DAY 48
Q. 123. What is the second petition?
A. "Thy kingdom come." That is: so govern us by thy Word and Spirit that we may more and more submit ourselves unto thee. Uphold and increase thy church. Destroy the works of the devil, every power that raises itself against thee, and all wicked schemes thought up against thy holy Word, until the full coming of thy kingdom in which thou shalt be all in all.

LORD'S DAY 49
Q. 124. What is the third petition?
A. "Thy will be done, on earth, as it is in heaven." That is: grant that we and all men may renounce our own will and obey thy will, which alone is good, without grumbling, so that everyone may carry out his office and calling as willingly and faithfully as the angels in heaven.

Q. 193. What do we pray for in the fourth petition?
A. In the fourth petition (which is, "Give us this day our daily bread"), acknowledging that in Adam, and by our own sin, we have forfeited our right to all the outward blessings of this life, and deserve to be wholly deprived of them by God, and to have them cursed to us in the use of them; and that neither they of themselves are able to sustain us, nor we to merit, or by our own industry to procure them, but prone to desire, get, and use them unlawfully: we pray for ourselves and others, that both they and we, waiting upon the providence of God from day to day in the use of lawful means may, of his free gift, and as to his fatherly wisdom shall seem best, enjoy a competent portion of them, and have the same continued and blessed unto us in our holy and comfortable use of them, and contentment in them and be kept from all things that are contrary to our temporal support and comfort.

Q. 194. What do we pray for in the fifth petition?
A. In the fifth petition (which is, "Forgive us our debts, as we forgive our debtors"), acknowledging that we and all others are guilty both of original and actual sin, and thereby become debtors to the justice of God, and neither we nor any other creature can make the least satisfaction for that debt: we pray for ourselves and others, that God of his free grace would, through the obedience and satisfaction of Christ apprehended and applied by faith, acquit us both from the guilt and punishment of sin, accept us in his Beloved, continue his favor and grace to us, pardon our daily failings, and fill us with peace and joy, in giving us daily more and more assurance of forgiveness; which we are the rather emboldened to ask, and encouraged to expect, when we have this testimony in ourselves, that we from the heart forgive others their offenses.

Q. 195. What do we pray for in the sixth petition?
A. In the sixth petition (which is, "And lead us not into temptation, but deliver us from evil"), acknowledging that the most

from our sin. We yield ourselves, in life and in death, to God's will.

Question 130. What is meant by the fourth petition, "Give us today our daily bread"?
We ask God to provide for all our needs, for we know that God, who cares for us in every area of our life, has promised us temporal as well as spiritual blessings. God commands us to pray each day for all that we need and no more, so that we will learn to rely completely on God. We pray that we will use what we are given wisely, remembering especially the poor and the needy. Along with every living creature we look to God, the source of all generosity, to bless us and nourish us, according to the divine good pleasure.

Question 131. What is meant by the fifth petition, "Forgive us our sins as we forgive those who sin against us"?
We pray that a new and right spirit will be put within us. We ask for the grace to treat others, especially those who harm us, with the same mercy that we have received from God. We remember that not one day goes by when we do not need to turn humbly to God for our own forgiveness. We know that our reception of this forgiveness can be blocked by our unwillingness to forgive others. We ask that we will not delight in doing evil, nor in avenging any wrong, but that we will survive all cruelty without bitterness and overcome evil with good, so that our hearts will be knit together with the mercy and forgiveness of God.

Question 132. What is meant by the final petition, "Save us from the time of trial and deliver us from evil"?

LORD'S DAY 50
Q. 125. What is the fourth petition?
A. "Give us this day our daily bread." That is: be pleased to provide for all our bodily needs so that thereby we may acknowledge that thou art the only source of all that is good, and that without thy blessing neither our care and labor nor thy gifts can do us any good. Therefore, may we withdraw our trust from all creatures and place it in thee alone.

LORD'S DAY 51
Q. 126. What is the fifth petition?
A. "And forgive us our debts, as we also have forgiven our debtors." That is: be pleased, for the sake of Christ's blood, not to charge to us, miserable sinners, our many transgressions, nor the evil which still clings to us. We also find this witness of thy grace in us, that it is our sincere intention heartily to forgive our neighbor.

LORD'S DAY 52
Q. 127. What is the sixth petition?
A. "And lead us not into temptation, but deliver us from evil." That is: since

wise, righteous, and gracious God, for divers holy and just ends, may so order things that we may be assaulted, foiled, and for a time led captive by temptations; that Satan, the world, and the flesh, are ready powerfully to draw us aside and ensnare us; and that we, even after the pardon of our sins, by reason of our corruption, weakness, and want of watchfulness, are not only subject to be tempted, and forward to expose ourselves unto temptations, but also of ourselves unable and unwilling to resist them, to recover out of them, and to improve them; and worthy to be left under the power of them; we pray: that God would so overrule the world and all in it, subdue the flesh, and restrain Satan, order all things, bestow and bless all means of grace, and quicken us to watchfulness in the use of them, that we and all his people may by his providence be kept from being tempted to sin; or, if tempted, that by his Spirit we may be powerfully supported and enabled to stand in the hour of temptation; or, when fallen, raised again and recovered out of it, and have a sanctified use and improvement thereof; that our sanctification and salvation may be perfected, Satan trodden under our feet, and we fully freed from sin, temptation, and all evil forever.

Q. 196. What doth the conclusion of the Lord's Prayer teach us?
A. The conclusion of the Lord's Prayer (which is, "For thine is the Kingdom, and the power, and the glory, for ever. Amen."), teacheth us to enforce our petitions with arguments, which are to be taken, not from any worthiness in ourselves, or in any other creature, but from God; and with our prayers to join praises, ascribing to God alone eternal sovereignty, omnipotency, and glorious excellency; in regard whereof, as he is able and willing to help us, so we by faith are emboldened to plead with him that he would, and quietly to rely upon him that he will, fulfill our requests. And to testify our desires and assurance, we say, "Amen."

We ask God to protect us from our own worst impulses and from all external powers of destruction in the world. We ask that we might not yield to despair in the face of seemingly hopeless circumstances. We pray for the grace to remember and believe, despite our unbelief, that no matter how bleak the world may sometimes seem, there is nonetheless a depth of love which is deeper than our despair, and that this love—which delivered Israel from slavery in Egypt and raised our Lord Jesus from the dead—will finally swallow up forever all that would now seem to defeat it.

we are so weak that we cannot stand by ourselves for one moment, and besides, since our sworn enemies, the devil, the world, and our own sin, ceaselessly assail us, be pleased to preserve and strengthen us through the power of thy Holy Spirit so that we may stand firm against them, and not be defeated in this spiritual warfare, until at last we obtain complete victory.

Question 133. What is meant by the closing doxology, "For the kingdom, the power and the glory are yours now and for ever"?
We give God thanks and praise for the kingdom more powerful than all enemies, for the power perfected in the weakness of love, and for the glory that includes our well-being and that of the whole creation, both now and to all eternity. We give thanks and praise to God as made known through Christ our Lord.

Q. 128. How do you close this prayer?
A. "For thine is the kingdom and the power and the glory, forever." That is: we ask all this of thee because, as our King, thou art willing and able to give us all that is good since thou hast power over all things, and that by this not we ourselves but thy holy name may be glorified forever.

Question 134. What is meant by the word "Amen"?
"Amen" means "so be it" or "let it be so." It expresses our complete confidence in the triune God, the God of the covenant with Israel as fulfilled through our Lord Jesus Christ, who makes no promise that will not be kept, and whose steadfast love and mercy endures forever.

Q. 129. What is the meaning of the little word "Amen"?
A. Amen means: this shall truly and certainly be. For my prayer is much more certainly heard by God than I am persuaded in my heart that I desire such things from him.